T3-BNV-484

THE GIFT OF
THOMAS JOSEPH WHITE
M.D., L.H.D., F.A.C.P.
TO THE LIBRARY OF
CABRINI COLLEGE
1981

Land *of* Liberty

Land of Liberty

*Being an informal
history of the common people
and their heroes*

by

FRED HAMLIN

Thomas Y. Crowell Company
NEW YORK

Grateful acknowledgment and thanks are extended to the following publishers, for the privilege of reprinting the following selections:
From *Listen to the People*, copyright 1941 by Stephen Vincent Benét (Rinehart & Co., Inc.). From *Western Star*, by Stephen Vincent Benét, copyright 1943 by Rosemary Carr Benét (Rinehart & Co., Inc.). From *A Social History of the American Family*, by Arthur W. Calhoun, reprinted by permission of the publishers, The Arthur H. Clark Company. From *Paul Revere and the World He Lived In*, by Esther Forbes, reprinted by permission of Houghton Mifflin Company, publishers. From *General William Booth Enters into Heaven*, by Vachel Lindsay, by permission of The Macmillan Company, publishers. From *The Diary of Cotton Mather*, reprinted by permission of the Massachusetts Historical Society, publishers.

From *Will Rogers*, by P. J. O'Brien, reprinted by permission of the John C. Winston Company, publishers. From *Jefferson*, by Saul K. Padover, reprinted by permission of Harcourt, Brace and Company, publishers. From *Phantom Fame*, by Harry Reichenbach, reprinted by permission of Simon and Schuster, Inc., copyright 1931 by Lucinda Reichenbach and David Freedman. From *The Letters of Sacco and Vanzetti*, edited by Marion Denman Frankfurter and Gardner Jackson, by permission of The Viking Press, publishers. From *The People Yes*, by Carl Sandburg, reprinted by permission of Harcourt, Brace and Company, publishers. From *Huckleberry Finn*, by Mark Twain, by permission of Harper and Brothers.

To

MARGARET

Author's Note

The pages which follow are an attempt at telling, from the viewpoint of the common man and his heroes and his enemies, the epic saga of democracy's progress in the United States of America.

Attempted also is to show that whatever democratic progress we have had has come the very hard way. Advocating democracy, as George Bancroft once pointed out, "is no holiday pastime." When, along that way, some of our number indicated that democracy could be a happy society in which everybody worked and nobody pushed anybody around, solemn voices were raised to damn it by some other name. For the essence of democracy is human progress. Progress means change; and change is met by opposition from those in power, who meantime loudly profess allegiance to one or another of our great leaders, long dead, or give lip service to our great ideals.

Another thing: whatever happened in American history, this generality would seem to prevail—no American wants to do anything by halves. For better or worse, his individual goal is to be superlative. Failing, his heroes are a Rockefeller—or a Lincoln. He has only scorn for Mr. Inbetween.

If these pages succeed in enlightening any reader as to his rightful role in the continuing drama or if they encourage him to defend himself and to push back by a full and intelligent use of the powers which it is his responsibility to wield forcefully under his voting franchise, then this book will have served its purpose. History is most valuable when it is applied personally and in the contemporary scene; and historical enlightenment, however superficial, makes for a better democracy.

Nor can we gaze upon the far horizons of the Republic without sheer delight in the knowledge that its people, whatever their faults, have raised up for the world's amaze more colorful personalities, good, and bad, and more truly great human beings, than any other one group in the history of mankind.

FRED HAMLIN

Acknowledgments

I am grateful to a great many persons for helping me prepare and write this book; especially to Dean R. Brimhall, for introducing me to Priddy Meeks, and for keeping me off the wrong trails in the West; to George F. Willison for guiding me toward source material of early American history and for criticizing parts of the manuscript; to Anthony Wayne Smith III for reading and auditing the passages concerning American labor; and to Mrs. Marguerita Dobert and Mrs. Talbot Hamlin for general research.

Three persons worked with me from beginning to end, encouraging, advising, and inspiring far beyond the call of duty. These were Arthur B. Tourtellot, editor of this series; Miss Virginia Bass, who supervised much of the research, criticized the early drafts and typed the entire book; and Margaret Meriwether Bartlett Hamlin, who not only worked with me on the manuscript but generaled me, one collie dog and two exuberant boys, thereby avoiding a complete route of both author and family, a task which would in turn unquestionably have routed an Eisenhower.

FRED HAMLIN

CONTENTS

MAN'S VOICE

> . . . All through my life, whenever the skies were dark,
> There came to me many fine and solid citizens,
> Wringing their hands, despairing of the Republic,
> Because we couldn't do this and shouldn't do that.
> And yet, each time, I saw the Republic grow
> Like a great elm tree, through each fault and failure,
> And spreading its branches over all the people.
> Look at the morning sun. There is the Republic.
> Not yesterday, but there, the breaking day.

—STEPHEN VINCENT BENÉT, *Listen to the People*

As soon as histories are properly told, there is no more need of romances. The gaggery and gilt of a million years will not prevail. . . .

Cheer up slaves and horrify despots and re-examine all you have been told at school or church or in any book, dismissing whatever insults your own soul.

—WALT WHITMAN

I painfully reflect that in almost every political controversy . . . the leisured classes, the educated classes, the wealthy classes, the titled classes, have been in the wrong. The common people—the toilers, the men of uncommon sense—these have been responsible for nearly all of the social reform measures which the world accepts today.

—W. E. GLADSTONE

[1]

The Wilderness (1620–1754)

How convenient it would be to many of our great men and great families of
doubtful origin, could they have the privilege of the heroes of yore, who,
whenever their origin was involved in obscurity, modestly announced themselves descended from a God.

—Washington Irving

The pride of ancestry increases in the ratio of distance.

—George William Curtis

Before the white man came, the land was lush and vastly lonely and
untamed.

Where the cities now are, with their harsh, hard pavements, their
skyscrapers, their tall apartment buildings, their sprawling, smoke-
belching factories—where now are the lawns, the corner drugstores,
the schoolhouses, the churches, the cast-iron statues and town
squares and libraries—everywhere, before the white man came, were
towering wildernesses, or prairies stretching beyond the horizon,
or high lonely hills and mountains, unscarred by ax or minehole or
highway.

The sky was darkened over the land by migratory birds, and the
nights were poignant with the cries of owl, and whippoorwill, and
the omnipresent quail. At the rivers' edges leaned massive willows
and bald cypress, tupelo, and black gum and sweet gum. The plains
were black with buffalo and the flatlands carpeted in places with
wild strawberry tall enough to stain a horse crimson to thigh and
belly. Underbrush was rich with bear, wildcat, deer, rabbit, coon,
and possum, and the streams swarmed with bass, speckled and rainbow trout, catfish and perch.

In this wilderness, where lived some half million Indians in the
area now occupied by the United States—hardly two persons to each

1

square mile—a man could spend most of his lifetime completely alone, calling himself hoarse *hallo-oo*. A lifetime on a continent, one man, a tiny, slow-moving speck in the illimitable vistas of plains and deserts or under the great trees, hacking his way through the sometimes almost impenetrable underbrush, pacing off history a small step at a time, calling *halloo hallo-oo*, but seldom indeed hearing an answering human voice where now are New York, Philadelphia, Charleston, Chicago, St. Louis, Omaha, Denver, Seattle, San Francisco. . . .

Because the land was untamed, it was cruel. Man's life was often cut short by beast or weather or disease or lack of wilderness lore.

But the land was gentle in contrast to those who came to rule it. These were, for the most part, common men; but it is one of the characteristics of the common man that if, by luck, ability, or unadulterated gall, he gets a cut ahead of his fellows, ninety-nine times out of a hundred he gets too big for his britches; he abuses his power, and particularly does he abuse his fellow man.

Everyone who came to America in the beginning—with a very few exceptions—was a common man. The passengers on the *Mayflower* were typical. Willison points out in his *Saints and Strangers* that they "had one bond in common. All were lower class. . . . There was not a drop of blue blood to be found anywhere among them. . . . They were of the common people and in conscious revolt against the aristocratic principle so-called, a fact which seems to have escaped some of their descendants with their proofs of 'blood' and pathetic interest in coats of arms."

But it was not left for the descendants to forget their humble origins; many of the resourceful commoners who rose above the masses during the early colonial days immediately attempted to outroyal the aristocrats from whom they had fled, and the common man thus found himself ruled by two groups—lay and church—unrivaled in arrogance in the history of the nation.

Within a decade after the first successful settlement at Jamestown, Virginia, in 1607, a caste system struck deep roots there and began to flower. To varying degrees this was the trend in all the colonies. A merchant and shipping class, abetted by the churchmen, rose and became prosperous in the North to match the southern planter.

Them as had, got, and the average citizen toiled out his days in poverty if not outright slavery.

Never was a land, dedicated ostensibly to freedom, less free. Never were men, lured by the promise of freedom, more bitterly betrayed. And women. And children.

Kidnaped children were among America's first slaves. In 1619, the London Company imported to Virginia one hundred children "save such as dyed on the waie." These were indentured—conditioned slavery generally limited to seven years. Colonists promptly asked for another hundred boys and girls. From fourteen to fifteen hundred were imported in one year, 1627—all kidnaped from the Continent. Thousands of others were shanghaied also from Britain as the trade grew. European relatives sold unwanted child dependents.

All the colonies joined in the practice. Even the more civilized and tolerant Dutch took an economic view. "Please to continue to send others (almshouse children) from time to time," wrote a New York official, "but . . . strong . . . as little profit is to be expected without labor."

Adults swelled the totals. Certain types of British criminals were exported if they chose indenture instead of imprisonment, which, the prisons being what they were, they usually did. These were not guilty of crime in the modern sense. They were charged with such offenses as debts of as little as two or three pounds, or poaching, or tearing down a fence. The penalty in that day for stealing a few vegetables was to be drawn apart by two horses. To steal and kill an animal left you subject to having your nose and ears cut off. Hanging could be decreed for theft and for debt. To be indentured was a welcome way out.

Before the Revolution, approximately half of the colonial population arrived on these shores as indentured slaves.

Free adults in the British Isles and Germany sold themselves to ship captains in exchange for passage to the New World, where the captain sold the passengers for servants. Families were broken up without mercy. If a husband, wife, or child died at sea, others in the family had their period of slavery extended to make up for the captain's loss.

3

The length of servitude to planters in the South was determined legally—by the planters. Masters interpreted the conditions of servitude in Massachusetts and New York. In Florida in the middle of the eighteenth century, families, including children, were put to work on land for ten years, at the end of which time the land reverted to the owner, who countered with another ten-year offer. The indentures were clothed in rags, fed hominy at a community mess, and housed in shacks. The death rate was as high as the conditions were poor, and often whole settlements of workers were wiped out by epidemic.

Punishment in the New World was patterned on that of the Old, where you could be hanged for stealing a loaf of bread, and half-hanged, revived, and whipped through the town for begging. In the colonies, even a free man was whipped at "the cart's end" in his own town and then in neighboring towns for immorality. One Robert Bartlett of Connecticut "for his gross misdemeanor in slandering a Mrs. Mary Finnicke" was pilloried for five hours and imprisoned for six months. A Captain Kemble of Boston, returning from three years at sea and kissing his wife on the steps of their home, got two hours in the stocks for this "lewed and unseemly behavior." A Connecticut couple, John Lewis and Sarah Chapman, were in 1670 tried for "sitting together on the Lord's Day under an apple tree in Goodman Chapman's orchard." A couple gathering peas on Sunday were fined, and even preachers felt the weight of the law for such offenses as amassing a fortune of eight hundred dollars, bowling, wearing multicolored stockings, and jumping over fences. One free man was fined heavily for saying "curse ye woodchuck" and another put in the stocks for shouting "damn ye cow."

Punishments for bonded servants were correspondingly severe. To jump an indenture—"stealth of oneself"—was punishable by death in Maryland. As late as 1750 a white runaway was hunted and punished in the same fashion as was his Negro counterpart. Caught and unclaimed, he was resold. Caught and returned, he was usually given seven more years of servitude if he survived the beating received on capture. Flogging was commonplace for small infractions. One of the most serious crimes in the eyes of the southern masters was for an indenture to attempt to make money for himself.

Puritan New England was equally callous. With the coming of

4

newspapers, advertisements describing runaways and offering rewards were numerous. When, in 1630, Massachusetts colony suffered a depression, prudent husbandmen turned their indentures out into the snow to shift for themselves, and held onto their cattle.

Some indentures broke under the pressures put upon them; and, when in due course they were freed, they became the ancestors of the nation's "poor whites." Some few fought their way to the top. A tale of the times concerns an indentured boy who was kidnaped by a sea captain and sold in America to a master whose daughter he married. Came the day when the former indenture bought the captain, now a convict. The captain was so frightened that he committed suicide.

But the large majority of the indentures either died in poverty or took the only other way out—westward into the wilderness.

Children throughout the colonies, even if not indentured, and excepting the few wealthy, were groomed from birth to share the heavy responsibilities of their elders; and if the elders had had their way, the colonial child would have been a completely obedient, angelic slavey from the day he walked. Wrote the Reverend Francis Higginson from Salem in 1629, "Little children here by setting of corne may earne much more than their owne maintenance."

Even had Higginson objected to child labor, the state would have overruled him unless he had had enough money to buy his way out. In seventeenth-century Massachusetts colony it was the law that children of the poor be put to work "which may bee profitable to the commonwealth." Reluctant parents were ordered to "dispose of their severall children . . . abroad for servants . . . by indentures according to their ages or capacities"; otherwise "the selectmen will take their said children from them and place them with such masters as they shall provide according as the law directs."

Eight years was considered a reasonable age for a youth to begin full-time adult labor, and in those times adults worked as much as eighteen hours daily. In Maryland, said a contemporary observer, "from antient custom . . . the sons work as well as the servants; so that before they eat their bread, they are commonly taught how to earn it." Boys managed their responsibilities with "a serious, grave and watching care, as if they had been masters of families,

5

trained in that domestick and governing power from their cradles."

Higher education was for only that handful of elite boys whose parents could afford tutors, travel, and tuition to universities, preferably Oxford or Cambridge. Playing the harpsichord or spinet, and needlework, were deemed sufficient intellectual activity for the well-to-do girl.

Although masters were supposed to teach their servants to read and write, education of the masses was cursory or nonexistent. Girls were limited to domestic arts only. Penn Charter School, founded in Philadelphia in 1698, was for fifty years the only public school in the province. The Dutch had flourishing common schools for the time in New York, and schools increased steadily in number in New England, but widespread education was a thing of the future.

Discipline was Spartan. Many a New England boy shared the fate of Josiah Quincy, who almost from babyhood started his day, winter and summer, by being dipped in icy pump water. This was thought health insurance, as were thin-soled shoes which let in the wet freely.

New England children were disciplined with horrendous tales of the hell in store for the disobedient. One of the Mathers wrote a book for kiddies entitled "Some Examples of Children in Whom the Fear of God was Remarkably Budding before They Died." Another contemporary juvenile: "A Token for Children. Being the exact account of the Conversation and Holy and Exemplary Lives of Several Young Children."

Bible reading by the head of the house, long prayers, church attendance and memorizing Scriptures were almost universally required. Church balconies were especially designed as pious prisons for boys, who were locked up for the duration of the services. Children were encouraged to be formal and meek, and far more emphasis was put on manners in the early years at school than on the ABC's. If a child was impudent, he was told that he was delirious or bewitched, and the penalty for an incorrigible child under the law —used as a threat, not practiced—was death. Death was prescribed for the New Jersey child who struck or cursed his parents.

Thus the adult rules, expressing the adult hopes. The childish responses were, as in all ages, not up to expectations. A Connecticut parent complained of youth who were constantly "smiling and larfing and intiseing others to the same evil." The Dutch levied a two-guilder fine on parents whose children were "caught in the streets playing, racing and shouting previous to the termination of the last preaching." Children's hats or "upper garments" were taken by enforcement officers to assure payment of fines. Coasting was frowned upon by the burghers of Albany, who authorized anybody to "take any slee or slees from all and every such boys and girls rydeing or offering to ryde . . . and break any slee or slees into pieces." "Sing not, hum not, wriggle not," ruled a child's book of etiquette, adding revealingly: "When anyone speaks to thee, stand up. Say not I have heard it before. Never endeavor to help him out if he tells it not right. Snigger not; never question the truth of it."

Of the boys of Boston, Esther Forbes records in *Paul Revere and the World He Lived In*: "They worked hours that would supposedly kill a modern boy and had often too much energy left over. They lied, seduced their masters' daughters, fell through the ice and drowned. They left careless fires and burned down bakeshops or overheated tar in the caboose of a ship and burned up the ship. They stole great wigs and silver spoons. They ran away and were whipped publicly and privately. A man close to the period says it seems to have been the ambition of every apprentice 'to harass their masters as much as possible without getting flogged for it.'"

Boys, even in Colonial America, would be boys.

Next to the children, the brunt of the double blow of the frontier and a greedy ruling class was taken by the women. Their lot was perhaps the more poignant because to them the New World was bright with promises.

This was owing to the most impelling demand of colonial society —for bigger and better families. Families were encouraged to migrate in groups from England by financial interests promoting settlement in the colonies. Virginia offered one hundred acres to a migrating man and wife, with fifty more for each child. Georgia gave land to a man with family, and money and land both went as bounties for children in South Carolina. Everywhere, families were the unit of society, and the larger they were, the more successful. Twenty to twenty-five children under one rooftree were common

7

enough to pass unnoticed, and there were men and women who died, leaving a hundred to a hundred and fifty progeny.

Women were therefore in great demand. "If any maid or single woman have a desire to go over," wrote one correspondent of the colonies in 1666, "(and) if they be but civil, and under fifty years of age, some honest man or other will purchase them for their wives" and "they will think themselves in the golden age." The initial boatload of servant girls sent to Jamestown, many of whom helped found the first families of Virginia, were nearly all married before sundown of the day the boat touched shore.

So great was the demand that girls frequently were able to assert themselves in matters matrimonial. The pressure to increase the population permitted marriages early and often. Occasionally brides were reported playing with dolls. A woman of twenty was considered a "stale maid"; one of twenty-five, "antient"; in New England unmarried women were called "thornbacks." Grandmothers of less than thirty were recorded. Mourning was brief, widows (with an estate) at a premium. The first marriage in Plymouth united Edward Winslow, a widower of seven weeks, to Susanna White, a widow of less than twelve weeks. In another case meat cooked for a funeral was served at the wedding table. For a woman to remarry as many as six times was not unusual.

Bachelors were correspondingly rare, and society all but outlawed them. A man had to pay taxes for celibacy, seldom was permitted to live anywhere except where a court ordered him, and was offered bounties by the state if he married. This often led to hasty unions. A story, matched in scores of colonial communities, concerned the Gravesend widower who saw a milkmaid for the first time in his life one afternoon, and made her his bride within a few hours. To win a wife, men advertised, listing their masculine charms.

Once united in holy wedlock, the colonial dame was quickly made to cope with the unholy circumstances of her unimaginably difficult environment.

With household facilities that were more primitive the nearer she lived to the wilderness or the lower her economic scale, in a society whose prevailing attitude was completely undemocratic if not medieval, and against the appallingly effective superstitions, diseases, and shortages of the era, she squared off to the major task set for her—raising a large family.

Her coming to grips with realities was blunt and to the point. "Let no man despise advice and counsel of his wife," said one colonial, putting it as diplomatically as possible, "tho she be a woman." Governor Winthrop believed that the young wife of a friend went insane "by occasion of giving herself wholly to reading and writing." Had she "not gone out of her way and calling to meddle in such things as are proper for men, whose minds are stronger, etc., she had kept her wits."

Divorce could be obtained in most places only by an act of the legislature.

Famine was always just around the corner. Living quarters, far from being the neat cottages and verandahed mansions pictured in the books, were originally crude wigwamlike structures plastered with mud and notable for one dubious convenience—a fireplace. Bradford, noting that hardy Spanish conquistadors had been praised for living four or five days on a few grains of corn, remarked drily that the Pilgrims in the early days "thought it as good as a feast," going two or three months with neither "bread nor any kind of corne."

Although most women were gradually emancipated from all but housework, in the beginning they worked in the fields. Ducking stools were provided for gossips, the scarlet letter (in New England), for unmarried mothers and harlots. While bastardy became frequent, the man never paid.

For the colonial housewife, whose major duty was childbearing and rearing, medicine had worse than nothing to offer. It consisted largely of superstitions dignified by time—fourteen or fifteen hundred years of time reaching back into the Dark Ages and beyond, back to the second century, when lived the Greek, Claudius Galen, who believed that the body was composed of certain "humors" which made a man ill if they got out of balance, and which could be brought back into balance by bleeding.

Galen's theories had been elaborated upon down through the years, but seldom questioned. Directions for bloodletting, reports Castiglione, "were extremely minute, determined almost always by astrological considerations . . . whether one should bleed from one

9

vein rather than another . . . the age and temperament of the patient, the season of the year and the locality." Bloodletting "doses" ran all the way from a pint to cure a hangover to Hippocrates' Heroic Treatment for Hectic Fever—bleeding the patient upright till he fainted, laying him down till he came to, and then seating him upright and bleeding him till he fainted again.

Fantastic powers were attributed to bloodsucking vampires, and evil spirits were known to cause spasms, convulsions, and epilepsy. Treatment by the stylish family practitioner customarily was an oration to the patient in double talk larded with Latin. "The darker, more mysterious, and lethal" doctors' apothecary shops looked, notes Esther Forbes, "the more faith the populace had in their efficiency. The days of witchcraft were not long over." Vultures' bones strung around the neck were considered by some experts as a cure for headaches, wolf dung helped colic, a fat beaver tail increased a man's sexual potency. Medical doctors looked down upon surgery and bloodletting, which were in the process of being taken over from barbers. Obstetrics was considered by most medics as fit only for that busiest of colonial dames, the midwife.

Hospitals (New York Bellevue 1735, New Orleans 1737, Pennsylvania 1751) rivaled sickrooms as incubators of disease. Fresh air was permitted in neither. Doctors and attendants customarily carried a sponge soaked in vinegar or a cresset of smoking sulphur to allay the stench. Ward adult patients were kept three or four to the bed, children six to eight, all grouped head to heels on the theory that they would convey diseases one to another if face to face. A poor patient who ran out of money was sent either to the poorhouse or dumped into the street to die. Lice were everywhere, and baths were considered harmful.

Surgery was worse than primitive, the only anaesthetic being liquor—if the patient could afford it. Amputations for broken arms and legs were standard. An infected, feverish post-operation wound was considered a good sign—the body was throwing off poison. Decayed teeth were burned out with a hot wire and the cavity filled with molten lead or gold. A hot iron or boiling tar was used for cauterization. A few bold men bootlegged bodies from cemeteries for dissection, but first-hand study of the inner man was considered sacrilegious. The human body was divided into two parts, the Similar (Skin, Flesh, Nerves) and the Dissimilar (Fingers, Toes). After an operation sawdust was sprinkled over the bloodstained floor and walls. . . .

The connection of filth with infection being unknown, puerperal fever was as common as the death of child or mother or both. John Knyveton, an English interne in 1751-1752, reveals the naïveté of the times when, after the death of a young mother who had been his patient, he describes himself "pondering on the Cause of this Malignant Fever that does so Fiercely gripe women just delivered, and [I] can only assume that it results from the State of Flux into which a Females Body is thrown at her effort to rid herself of Child. I cannot," he adds, "bring myself to believe as is held by the Clergy, that it is a Natural Punishment laid upon Woman by God for tempting Adam in the garden."

"Here lies —— —— with twenty small children," reads a Plymouth tombstone. "Indeed," says President Clap of Yale (1740-1766), crediting his wife with a masterpiece of understatement: "Indeed, she would sometimes say to me that bearing, tending and burying children was hard work, and that she had done a great deal of it for one of her age (she had six children, whereof she buried four, and died in the twenty-fourth year of her age)."

A mother who succeeded in getting an offspring through babyhood faced epidemic threats beyond the imaginings of a modern mind. Smallpox, yellow fever, and cholera led a procession of other contagions, not the least of which were measles, whooping cough, and scarlet fever. Inoculation (but not vaccination) for smallpox was used with moderate success in the Boston epidemic of 1721, but everywhere pockmarks were commonplace. Quarantine for the masses consisted in being sent to a pesthouse.

The farther you got from the seaboard, the more rudimentary was the medical lore. Many a man or a woman became an emergency midwife; many a woman, a make-shift surgeon. Frontier superstitions rivaled the imaginary cures of the medics: For snake bite, kill the snake, cut it open, and apply the warm flesh to the wound. Sweep under an invalid's bed and he'll die. Childish fits can be cured by putting the child's feet in the open body of a fresh-killed chicken. Gunpowder will keep away the plague. Take buckshot for boils—one per boil. Cut a baby's hair before he's a year old and he'll never walk. And the way to remove warts . . .

Everything considered, it is one of the miracles of all time that the colonial mother was so eminently successful. Despite a high death rate, the birth rate quickly took a commanding lead. "If in Europe they have but four births to a marriage," said Benjamin Franklin in 1751, "we may here reckon eight." Foreigners were constantly amazed, as well they might have been. "No human consideration," reported Felix de Beaujour, "operates as a hindrance to reproduction, and the inhabitants swarm on the rich land in the same manner as do the insects." Even the Frenchman's own notoriously reproductive pioneer countrymen were outdone. From the earliest colonial times until the census of 1840, says John R. Commons, "the people of the United States multiplied more rapidly than the people of any other modern nation, not excepting the prolific French Canadians."

The era of champion motherhood reached its apex in Kentucky, where from 1820-1860 a white population estimated at nearly a million was exported to other frontier areas. "If this figure is correct," says Calhoun, who finds no reason for doubting it, "the fecundity of the Kentucky population in its first eighty years must have been unsurpassed."

The national box-score (including immigrants):

1620	1650	1700	1750	1800	1850
200*	5,000*	400,000*	2,000,000*	5,308,483	23,191,876

* Generous estimates.

At least the colonial mother usually ended her days with more to show for her labors than her mate, the common man. If unindentured, he was in competition with the dirt-cheap indentured labor, followed, toward the end of the era, by out-and-out Negro slaves. In the South, most middle- and all labor-class freemen were denied the vote. They were not even permitted gentlemen's pleasures, as witness the Williamsburg tailor who was fined a hundred pounds for betting on his mare, "it being contrary to law for a laborer to make a race." Connecticut, typical of the northern town-meeting country, granted

12

franchise to "freemen"—those possessing an estate worth forty pounds. This eliminated 75 per cent of the eligible males.

Taxes were high, wages low, depressions frequent, and life on land or sea a bitter struggle against death by disaster, disease, or starvation. A free man who succeeded in living out his allotted years and earning enough to keep himself and his dependents alive was fortunate indeed. If he did not conform to the rules laid down by his masters, he was soon caught up with and disciplined, for even though he lived in a heavily populated area, America was a nation of villages-growing-to-small-cities, where gossip was standard entertainment. About 1690, Boston, with a population of some 7,000, was the largest community in the country. Philadelphia had approximately 4,000 citizens, New York some 3,900, and Charleston 1,100.

Each community was isolated from the others, shut off from the rest of the world by often impassable roads, wilderness trails, endless miles of ocean. Until almost the end of the period, man's only reliable means of transporting himself by land were horseback or shank's mare. Wagons or any wheeled vehicles were rare: as late as 1697, Philadelphia had no more than thirty. Regular colonial postal service was nonexistent until Benjamin Franklin organized it, beginning in 1753. From three to six months, depending on the weather, was required to get messages to and from England and the Continent.

Early America, by circumstances if not by choice, was almost simon-pure isolationist, and it was the rare man who dared challenge the discipline and surveillance which was standard in its small, watchful, ingrown settlements, schooled in amusing themselves with chatter concerning their neighbors' doings.

Indeed, gossip might be considered the chief amusement of the common folk in colonial times. Not infrequently harmful, the talk sometimes got so far out of hand that it led to disaster. In Salem, Massachusetts, in the summer of 1692, nineteen persons were condemned to die for witchcraft. Typical of the victims was the wife of an innocent old man who attended the trials for amusement and gossiped his spouse into the hangman's noose.

A more admirable mate of gossip was yarning. At many a fireside, at wilderness campfires, in taverns over steaming pots of hot buttered rum, in tossing fo'castles and dirt-floored shanties, the common men

13

and women of the colonies spun tales epitomizing their hardships and their hopes, folk-imaginings which, polished by a multitude of tongues, have come down to us as one of our richest heritages—the lustiest folk-tales of world history. In this field of art we find our first true sign of democracy, here first the creative genius of a people expressing themselves without regard to race, color, or previous condition of servitude. A fireside teller of tales, a nameless ghost on a trackless continent, was our first and among our greatest literary figures. Sandburg expresses it most aptly in *The People, Yes:*

"Who made Paul Bunyan, who gave him birth as a myth, who joked him into life as the Master Lumberjack, who fashioned him forth as an apparition easing the hours of men amid axes and trees, saws and lumber? The people, the bookless people, they made Paul and had him alive long before he got into the books for those who read. He grew up in shanties, around the hot stoves of winter, among socks and mittens drying, in the smell of tobacco smoke and the roar of laughter mocking the outside weather. And some of Paul came overseas in wooden bunks below decks in sailing vessels. And some of Paul is as old as the hills, young as the alphabet."

While Paul Bunyan was aborning in the minds of the whites, another embryo was forming slowly in the minds of the Negroes—a giant of a black man named John Henry, who was full grown the day he was born, to whom toil was a game, whose every gesture was a feat of strength and whose feats of eating were so colossal that one time after he'd had a snack, a button busted loose from his shirt and killed a rabbit a hundred yards away.

Then there were the beginnings of the Uncle Remus stories about the shrewd and resourceful rabbit who outwitted his oppressor the fox, legends of the land and of its names, plaintive songs of love and death and peace everlasting for those who mourned, and gay tunes for those who would be gay. Old Stormalong sailed the seven seas, defying the elements; sailor chanties condemned the cruel skipper to a watery grave. And as the years went by, the voice of the people gained in strength and tone and created a language that was boastful and colorful and downright and unsophisticated.

There were other colonial amusements. Dolls dressed in the latest fashions from England were displayed for a few pence for the delectation of girls and women. Boys and men hunted and fished. Everybody went to church and enjoyed its social aspects, and (ah, somber folk) everybody went to funerals. Quoth the colonial Joseph Eliot in all seriousness: "The days wherein I buried my wife and son were the best I ever had in the world."

Love-making, especially in the early days, was free and easy. "Chaperonage," says Calhoun in his *A Social History of the American Family*, "seems to have been unknown in colonial life. Men took long rides with the damsel on the pillion behind them. . . . Even in New England, maidens enjoyed large liberty. . . . It was impossible in the wild, rough, new land where every hand was needed for urgent labor, to think of secluding girls." Lack of lights and, especially in the South, of screens, made an early bedtime customary— winter at about seven, summer at about eight; but youth overcame the deadlines by beginning dates as early as three. The Dutch and others permitted bundling until it was outlawed by their critics.

Esther Forbes, in *Paul Revere and the World He Lived In*, describes Revere's Boston courtship of Sara Orne in the 1750's:

"He may have taken his girl rowing on the harbor, and, after a picnic on one of the islands, lain for hours, silent, with his head in her lap, as did other young courting men of the period. . . . A neighbor's chaise might be hired and a lovely day spent as far out as the Blue Hills of Milton. If the young couple spent the night with friends, no questions would be asked. Strict chaperonage was unheard of, and young people of much more pretentious households than the Reveres and the Ornes were allowed a freedom not to be known again in this country until the rise of the automobile.

"There were plenty of frolics during which an old English roughness of manner and courting customs came to the top. . . . About the time Paul went courting, another man described the fun he was having 'when kisses and drams set the virgins aflame,' and the party seems to have ended up in a catch-as-catch-can.

> " 'The chairs in wild order flew quite round the room,
> Some threatened with firebrands, some with a broom,
> While others, resolved to increase the uproar,
> Lay tussling the girls in wild heaps on the floor.'

"But Jacob Bailey, the young school-master poet, did not like such 'scenes of vile lewdness.'

15

    " 'Quite sick of confusion, dear Dolly and I
      Retired from the hubbub new pleasures to try.' "

Everywhere, weddings called for a celebration, often prolonged.
In some places guests scrambled for the bride's garter to win luck and
an early marriage; in others, bridesmaids and groomsmen put the
newlyweds to bed. Liquor flowed freely following the ceremony
and, especially in the middle colonies, for a week afterward. Friends
visited the bride and groom, or the couple toured the countryside,
stopping a night at the house of each friend. Often the fun lasted until the following Sunday, when the bride chose the sermon text at
her church and she and her man took a front-row seat in the balcony
and rose in the midst of the services to rotate slowly several times for
all to see.

And everybody went to blazes. From the first important American
fire in November, 1613, when the Dutch ship *Tiger* burned to the
waterline in New York harbor while its forlorn crew watched from
where they had fled ashore, conflagrations were frequent and well
attended.

The 1613 Dutch victims made history that winter by being the
first white men to build habitations on Manhattan Island and in the
spring salvaged the hull of the *Tiger*, rebuilt it, and sailed home.

But with the coming of other settlers, fires continued to thrive.
They were so prevalent on Manhattan by 1657 that taxes were levied
for 250 "leathern fire buckets, and also to have made some fire ladders and fire hooks." Similar taxes were levied in communities
throughout the colonies. Defective chimneys caused most fires. Penalty for being a firebug was death at the stake. Citizens were required
to have fire buckets on the premises, and "every person who shall
suffer his house to be on fire" was fined.

When George Washington, as an old man riding home to Mount
Vernon in the night, saw a lurid light against the sky and galloped
off toward it "hell for leather," he was as much in the historical
traditions of his people as were the fire laddies who followed gallop-
ing horses and blazing engine in the nineteenth century and are the
volunteer groups of today. Blazes throughout the colonies were
fought by everybody except the extremely aged, the extremely
young, and the bedridden. Every bell in town clamored alarm. Men
ran through the streets shouting, "Throw out your buckets! Throw

out your buckets!" and the good husbandman and his wife and servants, his slaves and children, having obeyed, scrambled into their clothes and rushed forth to help pass water to the blaze and return the empty buckets to the source of supply.

Fires were notable for striking in the night, for the amount of shouting on the part of the men, the screams of the women, the fact that anyone crossing the bucket line was doused and then led off by the constable, the additional fact that very little water reached the blaze, and the penultimate fact that the burning building was usually reduced to ashes. The rest of the night was spent in caring for the homeless—and drinks all round.

Wind fanned a blaze into a community disaster. In 1711, after a particularly pestilential blaze in Boston, Increase Mather wrote a pamphlet on the theme that if citizenry would cease sinning, so would fires. Fires continued to multiply.

Many a common man, alone or with his family, trudged stubbornly westward, and despite the incredible difficulties that confronted him, occupying the fullness of his energies, cherished in his soul the dream of a society in which all would be born with an approximation of equal opportunity. He fled a society in which nothing existed to nourish that promise. He visioned it ahead of him in the sunset. But there were times when, glancing backward, the sunrise looked equally bright.

As early as 1620, on the very threshold of colonial history, there was mutiny aboard the *Mayflower*, servants forcing their masters to draw up a bill of particulars, ostensibly outlining the rights of the common man. Says George F. Willison in *Saints and Strangers:*

". . . the Mayflower Compact has been hailed as a great charter of freedom, which it was. It did not apply to all, to be sure, and its promise of 'just & equall lawes' was often more honored in the breach than the observance. But for its day it was an extraordinary document, a remarkable statement of revolutionary new principles, an important milestone in our long, hard, and often bloody ascent from feudalism, from that degrading 'aristocratic' system of power and privilege for the few which had held Europe in irons for centuries, vestiges of which still remain to plague us. It is also the fashion, as every school child knows, to hail the compact in the most extravagant terms as the very cornerstone of American democracy, which it most certainly was not. As the circumstances of its birth reveal, it was conceived as an instrument to maintain the status quo on the *Mayflower*, to show inferiors in general and servants in particular their place and keep them where they belonged—i.e., under the thumbs of their masters. As is evident from the merest glance at the history of Plymouth, the Pilgrim leaders did not believe in equalitarian democracy though they were moving in that direction. They favored a change in the hierarchical structure above them, but not below."

Other straws were in the wind. When Sir Edmund Andros, first governor of the consolidated New England colonies, destroyed civil liberties just before the end of the seventeenth century, he was overthrown. Captain Jacob Leisler, hanged for leading a rebellion from Long Island to New York against the oligarchy of large landowners and wealthy merchants, challenged all the oppressed. "Weep not for us," he said to the crowd of common folk watching as he approached the gallows in a driving rain, "but for yourselves, that remain behind in misery and vexation."

Some three thousand German indentures, settled as an investment by their masters along the Hudson River and in Pennsylvania, staged the nation's first slow-down strike by pacing their work to an unprofitable speed until liberated, when they settled in the valley of the Schoharie and became prosperous farmers.

Even freedom of the press came in for a brief role upon the colonial stage. John Peter Zenger, an immigrant from Germany who published the *New York Weekly Journal* in 1734, criticized the powers that were and found himself in jail. He was defended by Andrew Hamilton, a Philadelphia lawyer then eighty—and won the verdict!

And there was the Albany convention of 1754. Called for the ostensible purpose of making peace between the colonies and the Indians of the Six Nations, who were being courted by the French, it was recognized by Benjamin Franklin and others as an opportunity for the colonies, for the first time, to act in unison. Up to that point they had dealt separately—and ineffectively—with Mother England. Franklin, using the Indians and the French as an excuse, went so far as to publish in his *Philadelphia Gazette* on May 9, 1754 (he probably drew it), what was probably America's first cartoon, picturing a snake cut into pieces, each marked with the name of a colony. The caption read, "Join or Die."

Some colonies, including Virginia and New Jersey, did not heed the warning. When the delegates arrived in Albany, they were given the chore of writing a speech for Governor De Lancey of New York. But while De Lancey was going over their handiwork, the delegates resolved that some kind of colonial union was necessary, and assigned a committee which brought in what it called "short hints" for a plan. Franklin succeeded in getting the resultant document approved at Albany, but nothing came of it. When the delegates took it home, they found no acceptance; if they had, the crown would undoubtedly have thrown it out.

While the governor was speaking at Albany, Washington was surrendering to the French at Fort Necessity; the French-English struggle for a continent had begun. The Mohawk sachem Hendrick (Tiyanoga) stung the delegates with a bitter speech, saying, among other things, "Look at the French; they are men. . . . you are all like women, bare and open, without any fortifications." As Franklin pointed out later, ". . . history is full of the errors of states and princes. . . . The best public measures are therefore seldom adopted from previous wisdom, but are forced by the occasion."

The occasion for throwing off the English yoke—and the yoke of their colonial masters—had not come; and even those who preached revolt offered no true democracy in exchange, but a change to more tolerant rulers. Men like Roger Williams and Nathaniel Bacon, radical as they were considered in their time, would have regarded with horror rule by the will of the people. They advocated, rather, a rule by the will of *their* people.

They also found it difficult to win and hold a following, for if the common man has proved nothing else in his three-hundred-odd years of progress in America, he has proved himself as slow to anger against a minority that harms him as he is slow to gratitude toward one he deems helpful. But his anger once roused is devastating; his gratitude, once expressed, sticks in his memory as long as time. And the people prevail—the will of the people prevails.

[2]

The Colonials

Roger Williams and the Puritan Dynasty

Christian morality and piety . . . are the last hope of the American Republic, and the only adequate means of bridling and holding in salutary check that rampant freedom . . . so characteristic of the American people.

—CALVIN COLTON

JEHOVAH: Did I ever mention publicly how Hell got started? . . . It was this way: I thought I'd do something nice for a lot of theologians who had, after all, been doing the best they could, according to their lights; so I gave them an enormous tract of Heaven to do what they pleased with—set it apart for them to inhabit and administer. I didn't pay any attention to it for a few thousand years, and when I looked at it again, they'd made it into Hell.

—DON MARQUIS, *Chapters for the Orthodox*

I believe we are descended from the Puritans, who nobly fled from a land of despotism to a land of freedom, where they could not only enjoy their own religion, but prevent everybody else from enjoying *his.*

—ARTEMUS WARD

An Indian promise is no more than to have a pig by the tail.

—PARSON MOXON OF CONNECTICUT

Athwart the progenitive and potentially democratic progress of New England's colonial common man stood, for nearly a century, a small Puritan theocracy sired by the belief that they alone knew how to govern to God's satisfaction. Mothered by medieval Christian intolerance, they stood ready to strike down any who dare dissent.

These Puritans saw blacks and whites only; there were no grays, no colors. In the soul of the Puritan burned a fierce flame, for better or for worse.

"Under the extreme rule of orthodoxy," says Worthington Chaun-

20

cey Ford, "the result was not only benumbing and provincial, but produced a morbid general condition . . . the great importance attached to theology made real progress impossible. The period was sterile—glacial."

The dynasty was begun in 1630 by John Winthrop, founder of the Massachusetts Bay Company. In Winthrop's hierarchy were such men as John Cotton and Richard Mather, whose youngest son (by John Cotton's widow) was Increase Mather. Increase became a second-generation king of the theocracy. The third and last generation was ruled by the son of Increase, Cotton Mather (1663-1728), child of the dynasty's fondest dreams and teachings, embodiment of what they represented and of how tragically they failed.

Winthrop and the first generation devoted their major efforts to fighting off religious competition, their hatred being most bitter against those contemporaries who represented Christianity at its best, notably the Quakers. Puritan policy as stated by Thomas Prence, who for years stood at Winthrop's right hand, was that all Quakers deserved death, "both they, their wives and their children, without pity or mercy." Quakers who had the temerity to enter the Puritan domain were hanged, whipped, branded, or beaten senseless. "I would carry fire in one hand, and fagots in the other, to burn all the Quakers in the world!" cried John Wilson, one of the Puritan zealots. They justified Quaker hangings, Willison notes, "with bland sophistry . . . by saying that . . . having been warned to stay away, [the Quakers] knew what their punishment would be if they came into the colony, and were therefore . . . suicides."

The second generation, typified by Increase Mather, was notable for its fight against the lay government being imposed upon it from England.

The third generation, led by Cotton Mather, at one time or another fought everyone, for his became a lost cause.

From beginning to end, all opposed the weakest and most numerous elements in their society, the Indians and the common people. The Indians were deluged with pious promises and then double crossed and done to death to the accompaniment of equally pious platitudes.

As for the common people, "democracy," Winthrop said, "is amongst civil nations accounted the meanest and worst of all forms of government" and "a manifest breach of the Fifth Commandment" —Honor thy father and thy mother. "The best part (of a society) is always the least, and of that best part, the wiser part is always the lesser." God did not ordain democratic government as fit "either for church or commonwealth," John Cotton concurred. "If the people be governors, who shall be governed?" That no such political disease should lay the colony by the heels, the Puritans first limited the vote to well-to-do freemen, later to members of the church only. A dissenter within the church promptly lost both his membership and his vote.

Because he was born and reared at the height of the New England theocracy, because he was precocious, and because he carried their tenets to the ultimate extreme, becoming the "compleat" Puritan, Cotton Mather was the best—and the worst—of them.

Introspective to the verge of perversion and insanity, he could do no wrong except before God.

In the Presence, he groveled, wheedled, bargained, and worked himself into ecstasies of self-abasement. "I humbled and loathed myself before God for my former iniquities and my present infirmities," he notes in his voluminous diary. "Being prostrate in the dust of my study floor," he says again, "after many fears of a sad, heavy, woeful heart . . . the Lord made an inexpressible descent upon me" and "a stream of tears gushed out of my eyes." Again: "Horrible agonies and amazements took hold of my soul this day, when I was . . . entertaining myself with the manifold instances of my sinfulness and wretchedness." He wrote the "true picture of Cotton Mather, wherein I have, with black, but yet with true characters, described my own vileness at such a rate that it cannot be looked upon without horror of soul; but I resolve often to look upon it."

No extreme was too far for him to crawl. "There are with me," he said, "the usual evacuations of nature, to be daily attended. I would not only improve the time which these call for, to form some thoughts of piety . . . but . . . would . . . more particularly study, that the thoughts I form on these occasions may be of some abasing tendency. The actions themselves carry humiliation in them, and a Christian ought always to think humbly of himself, and be full of self-abasement and self-abhorring reflections. By loathing of himself continually, and being very sensible of what are his own loathsome circumstances, a Christian does what is very pleasing to heaven. My life . . . ought to be filled with such things; and now I contrive certain spots of time, in which I shall be by nature itself invited unto them."

"I have certainly," he once summed up, "been one of the filthiest creatures upon earth."

But wrestling before the Lord had its rewards: with God's help and to Mather's own knowledge, Cotton, despite his self-loathing, was always unquestionably in the right. Daily he thanked God for an "unblemished reputation." In 1717, looking back on more than fifty years of life, he portrayed himself as a man who abstained from "all appearances of evil," a Christian full of "continual projections to do good, . . . meekness under provocation, . . . watchful against all ungoverned anger, . . . full of patience under calamities," and with "a spirit sweetly reconciled unto humiliations"—withal, godly and glorifying God.

Often and again, God so ordered the affairs of men as to honor his brilliant agent. Cotton prayed once before a "vast congregation," telling them that "wonderful reliefs would be sent unto us against the famine that was . . . distressing us." Sure enough, the "night following there arrived a little fleet [from England] of corn and flour."

In 1692, he says that he anticipated the Salem witch trials, which, it turned out, far from being tragic death knells for nineteen of the village's citizens, were actually only another device of the devil to torment Cotton. "In the spring of this year," he records, "I preached . . . a sermon upon temptations; and now, behold, my poor country entered quickly into temptation." After the trials he wrote: ". . . this assault of the evil angels upon the country was intended by hell as a particular defiance unto my poor endeavors to bring the souls of men unto heaven."

God was unusually circumspect in guiding him through the difficult days of the trials, leaving Cotton at the end in the position to deny the charges of an enraged citizenry that he had been chiefly responsible for the hangings, at the same time making it possible for him to keep the friendship of the judges.

He told the judges—he recorded afterward—that he was "afraid of proceding to convict and condemn a person as a confederate with afflicted demons upon so feeble an evidence as a spectral representation." He also "offered" [again he speaks in retrospect] "that if the possessed people might be scattered far asunder I would singly provide for six of them; and we would see whether without more bitter methods prayer and fasting would not put an end unto these heavy trials. But my offer (which none of my revilers would have been so courageous or so charitable as to have made) was not accepted."

Perhaps the misunderstanding came from Cotton's lack of courage to bring his offer forcibly to public attention at the time, certainly getting it none of the publicity that accompanied his attendance at the hanging of five of the "bewitched," at which he remarked that they all died by "a righteous sentence." Even after the spectacle was ended he took pains to note that he "saw in most of the judges . . . exemplary piety" and "could not but speak honorably of their persons on all occasions and my compassion upon the sight of their difficulties."

Nor was his approval of the hangings out of character with his lifelong attitude in such matters. At nineteen, a boy wonder, he had favored equally summary treatment of those other enemies of God's Puritans, the Quakers. He wrote in his youthful enthusiasm to the governor of Massachusetts to inform him that "there be now at sea a ship called the *Welcome*, which has on board one hundred or more of the heretics and malignants called Quakers, with W. Penn, who is the chief scamp, at the head of them. The General Court has accordingly given sacred orders . . . to waylay the said *Welcome* . . . and make captive said Penn and his ungodly crew . . . selling the whole lot to Barbadoes, where slaves fetch good prices in rum and sugar, and we shall not only do the Lord great good by punishing the wicked but we shall make great good for his minister and people. Yours in the bowels of Christ. . . ."

Tightly as they ruled and horrible as were the visitations of their wrath, the Puritans had few dissenters rise to plague them; only one was outstandingly successful. The name of this most courageous American, a man of such charm that even his enemies cherished his friendship, but of such controversial propensities that most of his life was embroiled—this first American defender of freedom's rights was Roger Williams.

24

After a two-months winter voyage, he arrived with a new wife at Boston early in 1631 just as John Winthrop and his followers were consolidating their dictatorship. Winthrop, who had organized the Massachusetts Bay Company and come over in 1630, was a man of wealth for his time and place, and one who, though personally so tolerant that he was able to hold Williams' friendship throughout his lifetime, nevertheless knew a good thing when he saw it and nurtured his own particular brand of absolutism with the unwavering ruthlessness of a born dictator. He so arranged Massachusetts affairs, indeed, as to become king in pretentions and powers, if not in name. Once established, he was attended by halberdiers in full dress, including great axes and plush, skirted coats. Yet he was broad enough in his judgments to regard Roger Williams without the neurotic asperity that later characterized Cotton Mather. Indeed, Winthrop said to the tempestuous challenger at one point, "Sir, we have often tried your patience but could never conquer it." His balanced though autocratic mind won from Williams the tribute, "though he was carried with the stream for my banishment, yet he personally and tenderly loved me to his last breath." Of the numerous letters Williams wrote in his lifetime, most were to Winthrop.

On his arrival in the New World, Williams was ostensibly one of the ruling class, having become a Puritan as a boy. The son of a London tailor, and less than thirty when he set foot in Boston, nevertheless he had had a notable career in England. The protégé of Sir Edward Coke, champion of common law against the king, Williams devised his own shorthand to take notes of Star Chamber proceedings, and saw at first hand Coke brilliantly perform before the bar.

His protégé learned so quickly and so well that Sir Edward sponsored him as a student at Cambridge, from which Williams was graduated in 1627. He became an ardent Separatist and, after a disappointing love affair with a girl of rank, was wed to Mary Barnard and a year later sailed for Boston.

His original plan had been to study Indian languages and become a missionary, but from this he was temporarily diverted by the Boston Puritans, who invited him to serve their church. Williams declined, charging that the Massachusetts congregation had not entirely separated from the Church of England. He also favored separation of church and state, which Boston leaders decidedly did not. They were horrified when, further, he plumped for absolute freedom of worship. He added insult to injury by accepting a call from what he then considered the more acceptable congregation at Salem.

Painfully conscious that their every move must be meticulously correct lest Williams shoot it full of holes or enlist support from his influential political-legal friends in England, the theocracy moved cautiously toward absolutism.

They first ruled that "for time to come, no man shall be admitted to the freedom of this body politic but such as are members of some church within the limits of the same," to which Williams promptly replied, "I affirm it . . . against the testimony of Christ Jesus for the civil state to impose upon the . . . people a religion, a worship, a ministry. . . ." Instead, the state should permit "free and absolute . . . conscience to all men in what is merely spiritual." Anything less than absolute religious freedom was "body-killing, soul-killing and state-killing" and would "pluck up the roots and foundations of all common society . . . blow out the candle and . . . make a noise in the dark with a sound and cry of a guilty land, a guilty state, soul-murderers, soul-killers, soul-seducers, rebels against the Lord. . . ."

In Cotton Mather's words, soon the colony was "like to be set on fire by the rapid motion of a windmill in the head of one particular man"—and the windmill had only just begun to spin.

The theocracy hounded Williams until he left Salem for the more tolerant climate of the Pilgrims at Plymouth. Here he was not unwelcome despite a controversy he soon stirred among the Pilgrim fathers. He had the temerity to contend in all seriousness that the land should be given back to the Indians, its legal owners.

His stand was the more authentic and disconcerting because he had begun missionary work, leaving the Pilgrim settlement for weeks at a time to visit the natives, sustaining himself with "a painful patient spirit . . . in their filthy smoky holes, and . . . to gain their tongue."

The opinion concerning land ownership was circulated privately among the Plymouth high command and was so unequivocal that they welcomed Williams' announcement that he would like to accept a call back to Salem. Here the battle with the Puritan theocracy was immediately renewed when they attacked his defense of the natives, which struck at the most sensitive nerve in the Puritan body politic.

To keep the peace—for once—Williams pointed out that he had not voiced his views publicly, and apologized, one of his opponents later testified, "very submissively."

But the truce was shortlived, if for no other reason than that the Puritan fathers were pressing toward unqualified theocracy and it was inevitable that Williams' democratic Christianity would explode in their faces each time the theocrats advanced. When they demanded for their General Court two oaths, first of submission then of allegiance, oaths which in essence renounced obedience to king and parliament should a governor be sent over whom the theocracy did not like, Williams refused on the grounds that a civil oath was impossible for a Christian and that the oaths in question were untenable.

Citizens refusing to take either oath were subject to banishment. Williams, undaunted, formulated his reasons for declining in a sermon accusing the colony of seven sins, among them the sins of taking land not belonging to them, usurping the franchise of the common man, and bigotry.

The charges hit the Puritan pocketbook as well as the Puritan conscience, committed as they were both to Christian ideals and to conquest of the people and the Indians. The Puritan response, as is always the response of those in power when so assailed, was to throw logic and justice out the window and welcome inflammatory denunciation at the door. Roger Williams was a cancer in the body politic, an anti-Christ. The fathers gave him a year to recant or leave the colony.

Worst of the dilemmas that Williams posed, and one with which he haunted the theocracy as long as he lived, had to do with that most tragic American minority, the Indian.

Concerning this problem more than any other did Puritan policy clash with Puritan piety, and it was the more vexing in light of Williams' peaceful and lifelong friendship with the natives. Protesting their good intentions at every step, the Puritans pursued a program of predatory piety that pointed the way toward the ultimate white-man attitude, summed up some two centuries later by Phillip Henry Sheridan—"The only good Indians I ever saw were dead." Cotton Mather listed as adversaries of the Lord "the devil, Quakers, and

Indians." Led by the clergy, the people were encouraged to regard the natives as "children of Satan." The sooner they could be exterminated, the better. "How oft," noted Roger Williams in 1645, "have I heard both the English and Dutch (not only the civil, but the most debauched and profane) say, 'These heathen dogs, better kill a thousand of them than that we Christians should be endangered or troubled with them; better they were all cut off, and then we shall be no more troubled with them: they have spilt our Christian blood, the best way to make riddance of them, cut them all off, and so make way for Christians.' "

The Indians had land rights—Winthrop was the first to recognize it. "If we leave them sufficient for their use," he ruled, "we may lawfully take the rest." Ignored was the Indian communal belief that he was merely sharing his hunting grounds, not selling them for all time, when he accepted trinkets from the white man.

Tribal Indian wars feature the histories of the early days; seldom is it emphasized that during the 1630's these bloodthirsty savages saw the Puritans drive the Dutch from Connecticut; saw two Indian chiefs murdered in cold blood by the whites; and saw many of their number sold into slavery to the West Indies and many others thrown overboard to drown from a white man's ship in Long Island Sound. When the Indians retaliated by murdering nine persons, including three women, at Wethersfield, Connecticut, in 1637, it was called by the white men a massacre, while the burning and shooting of some seven hundred Indians to avenge the nine deaths was called a mighty victory. "Thus the Lord was pleased to smite our enemies in the hinder parts," declared Major John Mason, adding revealingly: "and to give us their land for our inheritance."

As the Christian attitude toward the savage red men crystallized, bounties were offered for Indian scalps. They became more valuable than any other prize of the hunt, reaching a high after Braddock's defeat in 1755, when some $150 was offered for the scalp of every male Indian over the age of ten, and $50 for the scalp of an Indian woman. So callous had become the white attitude by the time of the Revolution that one diarist warrior in the north recorded he "sent out a party . . . for Indians . . . and skinned two of them from their hips down for bootlegs; one pair for the Major and one for myself."

Thus was the way paved for taking other lands by preëmption, which reached a climax between 1795 and 1809 along the eastern seaboard, forcing the native to give up some 48,000,000 acres. Thus were excuses found for paying off a year's fur catch with a few bottles of liquor and, when an Indian leader arose in the Middle West preaching abstinence, further excuses to annihilate him. This was the great "victory" of Tippecanoe, based on Tecumseh's claim, denied by the whites, that they were trespassing on his hunting grounds— a victory that from another viewpoint might have been regarded as a massacre.

But the other viewpoint was never to be heard. In 1835, flinging pious hypocrisy to the winds, Andrew Jackson virtually ordered all red men to settle west of the Mississippi, and by 1850 the land sacred to the Indian from Texas to Canada and from coast to coast was being staked off by the empire builders and by land-hungry movers. The conquest begun in all piety some two hundred years before by the Puritans had been completed in all realism by those who followed.

Roger Williams stood trial for his opposition to the theocracy at Cambridge, Massachusetts, in the fall of 1635. There was no indictment, no jury. The fifty persons taking an official part in the trial represented less than five hundred "freemen" out of the 12,000 settlers in New England. For two days, singlehanded, he defended himself with all the skill he had learned from Sir Edward Coke. It threw the Puritan fathers into confusion, but did not deter them from their purpose. He was sentenced to "depart from this jurisdiction within six weeks next ensuing," but the verdict was softened by the General Court, postponing his departure to the following spring, after he pled the approach of winter, his ill health, and the pregnancy of his wife. He could postpone his departure, the General Court ruled, if he would "not go about to draw others to his opinions." John Cotton led the prosecution, deserting in the crisis for what Williams later said was "public credit and favor" and "swimming with the stream of outward credit and profit."

But the trial was in restrospect perhaps the most salutary event in the tempestuous Williams' life, forcing him to flee to the Narragansett Bay area (he had to flee in the dead of winter after all to avoid deportation to England), to found what became Rhode Island, to crystallize his ideas and to broaden them to include the rights of the downtrodden white man as well as of the downtrodden Indian. Sturdy, unyielding, and outspoken, he carved the first distinct bench-mark for the democracy which was to be born a century and a half later.

His philosophy became more bold, even his writing more succinct. His two masterpieces, *Christenings Make Not Christians* (1645), and *The Bloudy Tenant of Persecution* (1644), boldly delineated his be-liefs, all of which refuted and shamed the Puritan precepts.

In the former he accused the Massachusetts fathers of "having no more of Christ than the name . . . unconverted and un-Christian Christians." As for the Indians, "If we respect their sins, they are far short of European sinners. They neither abuse such corporal mercies for they have them not; nor sin they against the gospel light . . . as the men of Europe do." Even if they did out-sin the European, "they are not the further from the great ocean of mercy." And "they are intelligent, many very ingenuous, plain-hearted, inquisitive and . . . prepared with many convictions"—not, in sum, to be beaten into submission. For conversion to true Christianity cannot be ac-complished "by force of arms and swords of steel"—Christ "with earthly weapons . . . never did compel."

"The will in worship," said Roger Williams, "is like a free vote." He added a warning: "The not discerning of this truth has let out the blood of thousands in civil combustions in all ages . . . and it is yet like to be the dissolution of that which is called the Christian world."

As with religion, so with the franchise: freedom of both were essential to a sound social order. Despite his wife chose to cling to the religion of the Puritans and despite some of those who settled with him in Providence became his political opponents, he stuck staunchly to both precepts. In outlining his political beliefs he also laid the cornerstone for American political philosophy devised in the Revolution more than a century later. In *The Bloudy Tenant of Per-secution* he wrote:

"The . . . foundation of civil power lies in the people . . . and . . . a people may erect and establish what form of government seems to them most meet for their civil condition: it is evident that such governments as are by them erected and established have no more power, nor for no longer time, than . . . the people consenting and agreeing shall betrust them with."

It was inevitable that *The Bloudy Tenant* should draw fire from the Puritans. John Cotton, in 1647, was their spokesman with *The Bloudy Tenant Washed and Made White in the Blood of the Lamb*, so flimsy a response that Williams dismissed it as "Mr. Cotton's fig-leaf evasions and distinctions" in his reply *The Bloudy Tenant Made Yet More Bloudy through Mr. Cotton's Attempt to Wash It White* (1653).

From that point for almost twenty years the controversial Mr. Williams indulged himself in only minor quarrels, devoting his time to developing freedom of worship and franchise in Providence, establishing his title to the colony, working among the Indians, prospering in trade, preaching, and carrying on a voluminous correspondence with John Winthrop, with England, and with diverse enemies. But it is characteristic of his vigor that after the twenty years had passed, he was stout enough to engage in one of the most wearing debates of his career. Paradoxically, it was with the Quakers, whose right to freedom of worship he had once so staunchly defended.

Williams had read George Fox's *The Great Mystery of the Great Whore Unfolded; and Anti-Christ's Kingdom Revealed unto Destruction* (London, 1659). When Fox came to this country in 1671, Williams promptly challenged him to debate upon fourteen points (all insulting to the Quakers), charging among other things that the Friends were unchristian and "more obstructive and destructive to the conversion of salvation of the souls of the people than most of the religions this day extant in the world."

Fox (Williams said later) "slyly" left for England without acknowledging the challenge, but three Quakers accepted it in his name. Williams had stipulated that seven of the points be argued in Newport, seven in Providence. The old man—he was in his seventies —journeyed the thirty miles to the Quaker town alone. "God graciously assisted me in rowing all day with my old bones," he wrote, "so that I got to Newport toward the midnight before the morning appointed."

The debating was so acrimonious on Williams' part that even his brother protested. One of the three opponents, W. Edmundson, particularly roused the Williams ire and "would often vapor and preach long and when I had patiently waited till the gust was over and began to speak, then would he stop my mouth with a very wholesome clout of a grievous interruption."

But he had enough energy after the debates were over—a day per point, beginning at nine in the morning and ending at four in the afternoon—to write them up in a long-winded book. Edmund Burrows, a co-promoter with Fox of Quakerism, aided the patriarch's failing wit in devising a title for the volume, *George Fox Digged out of His Burrowes*.

The remaining years of his life were comparatively peaceful, and he died honored by friend and foe alike, but not before he had paid off the Puritans in perhaps the most revealing and succinct analysis ever made of any or all of them. John Cotton's son wrote, damning Williams for his controversies with the elder Cotton.

"Sir," the old liberal replied, "I pray (you) forget not that your father was not God."

Cotton Mather was only twenty-one when Roger Williams died; for forty-four years he lived on, the most unhappy of all his contemporaries, surrounded by fears, bedeviled by infirmities, tragically alone—and dogged by tragedy.

He buried two wives and all but two of his fifteen children. His favorite son, Increase, became, in the view of his exacting father, a wastrel and a slave of the devil. "The evil that I greatly feared is come upon me," he wrote in 1717. "An harlot big with a bastard accuses my poor son Cressy."

At times, Cotton's fears almost overwhelmed him. He was constantly begging the Lord to "bid me to believe that I shall be saved," and from the outset of his career feared he might be left "without necessary supplies of speech for my ministry." His fear-wracked mind rivaled his nerve-wracked body in poising on the verge of collapse: "I found my soul under strong distempers; and especially an idle frame of soul was a plague upon me. . . . I fell into an exceeding bitterness of spirit and I was filled with fears that the Spirit of God was going to take a sad farewell of me." Incessantly he was haunted by the "bodings of a dark cloud hanging over my family," a fear of personal disaster too often realized to be entirely imagined. He even distrusted members of his family. "I write this in Latin," he notes in one passage, "lest my dear wife . . . should understand it."

Always he was plagued by fears of his enemies—"the cursed reproaches" of an "unworthy, ungodly, ungrateful people." He quotes a theory that ministers "who meet abuses from sorry and scoundrel people" are suffering, as it were, from "the Egyptian plague of lice," and adds, "I am very lousy, it seems." Seldom did those opposed to him leave him in peace and often they resorted to violence, as when, during his smallpox campaign, someone hurled a bomb through a window in his house. It failed to explode.

This was one of the rare occasions when public opposition to him was undeserved—he fought stubbornly for inoculation to stop the Boston smallpox epidemic of 1721. Again, after he had helped found and finance a Negro church and school, a wag named a slave "Cotton Mather." Whatever the circumstances, he was thoroughly disliked most of his life, and returned the emotion with an unholy hate teamed with neurotic fears.

He was also forever in fear of "invading devils" who stole his sermon notes, killed off his children, played hob in Salem to his everlasting discomfort, and dogged members of his congregations. Always, in the end, he came out winner; but some of the contests were extremely taxing to his habitually frayed mind and body.

When one of his children died shortly after birth from an intestinal obstruction, Cotton "had great reason to suspect a witchcraft . . . because my wife . . . was affrighted with an horrible spectre in our porch, which fright caused her bowels to turn within her." The specter had gone around the neighborhood boasting of its foul deed. "And besides all this, the child was no sooner born, but a suspected (bewitched) woman sent unto my father a letter full of railing against myself, wherein she told him, he little knew what might quickly befall some of his posterity."

Going to Salem to preach a year after the trials, Cotton was still pursued by Salem's particular devils. His sermon notes were stolen "with such circumstances that I am somewhat satisfied the spectres, or agents in the invisible world, were the robbers." Cotton remembered enough of the notes to deliver his sermons, "so that the devil got nothing," and on going back to Boston learned from a neighborhood lass who was devil-ridden that specters had bragged to her of the theft. But the devils confessed that they could not always keep the notes from Cotton, and months later the lost pages turned up, "eighteen separate quarter sheets" that had been "dropped here and there about the streets of Lyn."

From youth until death he was haunted by physical ailments. At eighteen he recorded, "My diseases are so complicated that I am not able so much as distinctly to mention them . . . much less . . . remedy them." "I live in pains, and want your prayers," he wrote John Cotton. "Now illness and vapor, with an aguish indisposition, grows upon me," he noted when he was only thirty-three. "I live in exceeding misery and I can see nothing but a speedy death approaching." And so it went through a fear-torn life that, miraculously, did not end until he was sixty-five.

It ended as it had begun, steeped in fear and earmarked for defeat. New elements had risen to wreck the old theocracy. He alone of all the great Puritan leaders was left to breast the whelming tide of change, and he knew that he was not enough.

But had he been privileged to see into the future, perhaps he would have died not without consolation. He and the men he exemplified have been so idealized with time that today they are ranged with such men as Roger Williams as the religious forefathers of the nation. More puzzling still, a coterie of their blood and spiritual descendants, as bigoted as they, carry on their tradition of intolerance, tainting our modern democracy despite the fact that it grew, not with their aid, but despite their smug hatred and baneful opposition.

The Rebel

Nearly all the extensive Virginia estates were obtained by corrupt means.
—ARTHUR W. CALHOUN, *A Social History of the American Family*

Liberty is poorly served by men whose good intent is quelled from one failure or two failures or any number of failures, or from the casual indifference or ingratitude of the people, or from the sharp show of the tushes of power, or the bringing to bear soldiers and cannon.

—WALT WHITMAN

While Roger Williams opposed the church and the king's henchmen, with Nathaniel Bacon, the Rebel, it was the other way around.

He was tall, dark, handsome, and theatrical, this Nat Bacon, and not unaware that history was on his side. He had been less than two years old when Charles I was executed by order of Parliament, and was six in 1653 when red-faced, raucous-voiced, drably dressed Puritanical Oliver Cromwell, scion of a once-wealthy and profligate family, became Protector of Great Britain. Nat Bacon, like Cromwell, was of privileged people and, also like Oliver, loved war and horses as much as he hated oppression. Indeed, Cromwell's death in 1658, and the restoration of Charles II to the throne in 1660, may have helped decide Bacon, as he grew to manhood, to emigrate to Virginia.

Prior to his departure, he was graduated from Cambridge and had a year of travel on the Continent. In 1674, over the violent protests of her father, Sir Edward, who cut her off without dowry, the young man wooed and won Elizabeth Duke, and brought her with him when he came to Jamestown, then capital of Virginia.

With him also he must have brought considerable funds despite his father-in-law, for Bacon quickly acquired two plantations— Bacon's Quarters, within the present city limits of Richmond, and Curles Neck on the James, forty miles above Jamestown. Here he settled with his bride, but his charm and a talent for spell-binding oratory soon led to such popularity that the young couple found themselves in frequent demand at the colonial capital.

Although only twenty-seven, the Rebel began his meteoric political and military career as a member of the Governor's Council, whose president was his cousin, Nat Bacon, Sr.

The governor of Virginia was Sir William Berkeley, an old hand in the New World. The son of Sir Maurice Berkeley, Sir William's brother was John, first Lord Berkeley of Stratton, one of the proprietors of the Carolinas.

William, after finishing at Oxford in 1629, went to Canada in his mid-twenties as one of the royal commissioners. On his return, Charles I appointed him a gentleman of the privy chamber.

He did all the right things for a man of his time and position, and did most of them well, even to writing a play, *The Lost Lady—A Tragy Comedy*, published in London by Jo. Okes in 1639 and sold "at the Signe of the Holy Lambe on Ludgate-hill."

This drama, in the Shakespearean tradition, complete with resounding iambic, philosophy, classical names, and even a grave-digger's scene, gives a hint of the man if not the times.

News of the death of the Lost Lady comes to her fiancé, a king, as the play opens. She has been murdered by her uncle when he discovers from a soothsayer her marriage plans. At first overcome with grief, the king finds consolation and a prospective wife in one Hermione, but she in turn loves another. A soothsayer, a Moorish woman, advises Hermione to temporize; and the king is persuaded to visit the Lost Lady's grave. Here the girl's ghost stoutly upbraids him for his short memory and for not avenging her death, which she blames on the tattle-tale soothsayer—none other than the Moorish lady. The king straightway poisons the Moor, who faints. When her face is bathed to revive her, she fades white—it's none other than the Lost Lady herself! Horror-struck, the king begs a friend to kill him, but an antidote restores his betrothed. "A notable wooing this!" remarks a bystander. "And as notably finish'd," the king concludes.

Among the author's philosophical asides:

> "The Gods give us permission to be false
> When they exclude us from all other ways
> Which may preserve our faith."

In 1642, still in his early thirties, Sir William became governor of Virginia and reigned except during the Reformation with a despotism which increased notably after he was restored to his post at its close. By the time of Bacon's arrival, despite Virginia's boast of having, in its House of Burgesses, the first representative assembly in North America, Berkeley's was an absolute monarchy with Sir William—not Charles II—the king. "The sole author of the most substantial part of the government," intoned one Thomas Ludwell, a Berkeley favorite," . . . is the governor."

The policies of his rule he had outlined during a visit to England in the 'sixties, and in a few succinct and pertinent aphorisms which have kept memory of him verdant to this day. Early though he came in Virginia history, he saw the economic peril of tobacco raising to the exclusion of all other crops, putting planters in the position where "they can neither handsomely subsist with it, nor without it." Yet the

36

contemporary economic value of the "vicious, ruinous plant" did not escape his notice, bringing as it did "more money to the Crown, than all the Islands in America besides." He favored and did what he could to promote diversified crops, always, of course, within the limits of his own economic interests.

The difficulty was that crops did not interest him. One who had first come to America on the eve of its colonial expansion, he had early been impressed by the quick and easy profits in the fur trade. Through the years he had specialized in furs, regardless of competition or—toward the end—the violent protests of Virginia's frontier agriculturists. One of his chief points in his paper of 1663, "A Discourse and View of Virginia," which he published in London, was the value of this fur trade with the Indians and how the British had "suffered the Dutch to enrich themselves on our discoveries, who have on our precincts settled a Trade of Beaver with the Indians, amounting to 200,000 skins a year." The Dutch, he added with outrage, had in addition sold the savages firearms.

For the rest, Sir William was a Cavalier, scorning alike the church and the citizenry. "The ministers," he once said, "should pray oftener and preach less." Book learning for the masses was an even greater peril. He thanked God that there were neither schools nor printing presses in Virginia—"learning has brought disobedience into the world."

Virginia's representative government was plausible enough on paper. It consisted of a House of Burgesses, manned by planters whose duty was to assist the governor and his council, both appointed by the crown, and with veto power over the burgesses. The council could also originate bills and was a sort of supreme court over the local courts.

The House of Burgesses was hardly a democratic body at best, since it represented only voters of considerable means. But it was too democratic for Sir William, who scotched it with devices borrowed from home. When a set of burgesses were chosen suited to his regal tastes, he persuaded them to raise the taxes on every male over sixteen regardless of whether he had a vote, keeping the burgesses happy with handsome salaries, a manservant and two horses each,

37

opportunities to charge the citizenry fat fees, and free liquor rations for themselves and their staffs. He capped their delight by refusing to call another election.

"Men are more valuable in any calling," he explained solemnly, "in proportion to their experience."

This situation had prevailed for more than a decade when Bacon arrived.

Sir William's council members, called by the people "the grandees," were, of course, favorites. They shared the loot. The bulk of this, beyond taxes, came in fur trade with the Indians, reason enough for Sir William to deny hotly that he was meeting the Dutch gifts to the savages gun for gun, and fulsome reason for him to wink if a warlike tribe occasionally murdered a stray planter and his family on the outskirts of the colony.

The old man—he was nearing seventy—added domestic sunshine to this idyllic economic and political scene by taking unto himself a young wife and settling back to round out his days at "Green Spring," his plantation four miles from Jamestown. Sir William was king, and the king could do no wrong.

But by the fateful year 1676, in the opinion of the frontier planters, the king could do no right. He answered their plea for defenses against the Indians by building forts on the edges of the wilderness. The frontiersmen responded by reporting "their condition every bit as bad, if not worse, than before the forts were made." Help was again requested after a particularly sanguine Indian murder in 1675. Sir William organized an expedition against the savages and then, at the last minute, called it off. An estimated seventy-one of some eighty-two frontier plantations were abandoned, but when their owners petitioned for permission to defend themselves, Berkeley turned them down. To aggravate the unrest, tobacco crops were bad—and the fur trade prospered.

With Bacon's Quarters a vulnerable outpost of the plantation system, its young owner, that charming but outspoken twenty-nine-year-old Johnny-come-lately member of the king's council, became the mouthpiece of the opposition.

"If the redskins meddle with me, damn my blood," he said publicly, "I'll harry them, commission or no commission."

He was a leader in drawing a petition to London, a "Complaint From Heaven, with a Huy and Crye" to "Our great Gratious Kinge and Souveraigne Charles ye ii King of Engel'd etc. with his parliament" charging among other things that "old Governr. Barkly" had been "altered by marrying a young Wyff from his wonted publicq good to a covetous Fole-age."

Sir William's reply to this was to levy more taxes to pay the bill for a delegation of complainants to go to England. Open opposition between him and Bacon flamed when the overseer of Bacon's Quarters, a favorite with his master, was murdered by the Indians. The Rebel was true to his oath. Commission or no commission, he rounded up planters and signed up recruits, winning their confidence by listing them "upon a large paper, writing their names circularwise, that their ring-leaders might not be found out"—the first recorded Round Robin in the New World. Nat himself became "General Bacon, by consent of the people."

Overnight, at the court of Sir William, the new general and his men became "rebels and mutineers." An expedition was sent out to arrest them. The Rebel was dismissed from the council and Sir William gallantly assured Elizabeth Bacon that her young husband would hang when captured. The Jamestown janissariat transformed Bacon, the charming courtier, to a black-haired villain "of an ominous, pensive, melancholy aspect; of a pestilent and prevalent logical discourse tending to atheism in most companies, not given to much talk, or to make sudden replies; of a most imperious and dangerous hidden pride of heart, despising the wisest of his neighbors for their ignorance and very ambitious and arrogant." Bacon's rebellion was not officially on, but the lines were drawn indelibly.

Berkeley's men sent to capture the Rebel soon gave up the chase, and Bacon had to go a far piece into Carolina before encountering Indians worthy of his mettle. All the local savages, wilderness-wise and forewarned, eluded him. He finally encountered two formidable tribes which would have wiped out his little expedition had he not divided the savages by propaganda and then conquered the stronger group in bloody battle.

He returned to Virginia to defy Berkeley with flowing prose, the style and content of which, condensed, was echoed during the Revolution a hundred years later. "If here be . . . treason," he said at one point, "Lord Almighty judge and let the guilty die!" Taking care to keep out of the old man's reach, he dispatched a letter to Jamestown, saying that he "abhorred rebellion or the opposing of laws or government," and expressing the hope that the rumors of Sir William's ire had been exaggerated. He ended: "I dare be as brave as I am innocent, who am, in spite of all your high resentment, unfeignedly, your Honor's humble and obedient servant."

Sir William, conceding nothing, waitful, made a concession. For the first time in fourteen years he called for election of a new House of Burgesses. But the royal luck was low. The representative returned from Henrico county was that "worst of men"—Bacon.

There followed a brief, two-act, seventeenth-century truce as difficult for a modern mind to comprehend as to imagine that today's sleeping, vinegrown ruins along the wide and peaceful James once were as spic as a chromium facade, with even the gravestones unweathered and clearly legible, and the streets and buildings teeming with lusty colonial life.

Bacon approached Jamestown by the river, aboard a sloop, accompanied by forty bodyguards. He sent word ashore to ask if he could land. Sir William responded with cannon fire. Moving the sloop out of range, Bacon waited till dark and went ashore for a conference with Richard Lawrence, an ally, married to a wealthy widow and keeper of a fashionable Jamestown inn—"atheistical and scandalous" in the eyes of the Berkeleyites. Neither man was picked up by the governor's soldiery, although their meeting must have taken place almost under the gubernatorial nose.

Subsequently, Sir William sent an expedition which captured the sloop and Bacon, who was taken to the State House to be upbraided by the governor as "the greatest rebel that ever was in Virginia." Yet Berkeley paroled the prisoner on his honor, and next day, while his truculent followers looked on, Bacon pled guilty to rebellion and disobedience and threw himself upon the mercy of the court. Sir William listened and then burst out:

"God forgive you, I forgive you!"

He went further, fining the captain who had captured the Rebel under orders from Sir William, permitting Bacon to take his seat in the House, and even restoring him to his post in the Council!

But if the old man had bowed publicly to the will of the people, inwardly he was obdurate. He must have felt that the gods, having excluded him from all other ways of preserving his faith, had given him permission to be false. Certainly, in Bacon he had found a Moor who refused to come white, for the young man promptly began a bloodless revolution of laws calling for frequent elections, widened suffrage, audit of public expenditures, no trade with the Indians, and an expedition against them commanded by himself. Sir William, in desperation, delayed signing the necessary papers and commissions and secretly plotted to have his rival either assassinated or imprisoned.

Bacon, getting wind of the danger and impatient at the governor's delays, fled upcountry, recruited a small army, and marched on Jamestown. The final scene of the first act took place before the State House, where burgesses and council watched from the windows as Berkeley, never a coward, stoutly denounced the Rebel from the steps and, so the legend is, bared his gray chest saying:

"Here, shoot me! 'Fore God, a fair mark, shoot!"

Bacon restrained his men, and Sir William drew his sword, challenging the Rebel to a duel. Bacon responded:

"Sir, I came not, nor intend, to hurt a hair of Your Honor's head, and as for your sword, your honor may please to put it up; it shall rust in the scabbard before ever I shall desire you to draw it. I come for a commission against the heathen . . . and . . . God damn my blood . . . a commission I will have before I go!"

The governor's reply was to turn and start toward his private quarters in the State House, at which point Nat Bacon's temper stopped His Honor short.

"I'll kill Governor, Council, Burgesses and all," he promised, adding, if we are to believe contemporary accounts of the incident: "And then I'll sheath my sword in its own heart's blood."

"We *will* have it! We *will* have it!" shouted the soldiers, meaning the commission to fight the Indians.

Bacon ordered them to prepare to fire.

A burgess broke the tension. Waving a handkerchief from a State House window, he answered the chant of the soldiers with another.

"You *shall* have it, you *shall* have it!" he promised.

After more wrangling, and with the greatest reluctance, Berkeley

41

next day signed commissions for Bacon and thirty officers, plus a letter to King Charles exonerating the Rebel from all that he had done. Came a rumor that the Indians were on the warpath not twenty-five miles from the capital, and Bacon marched off with colors flying.

Act one curtain, amid loud applause.

The first scene of the second act opened on the edge of the wilderness, with the Rebel making a dramatic speech of loyalty to his men, followed by their equally dramatic pledge of loyalty to him, huzzahs, fierce statements against the savage red man, sound of trumpets, the march—and then, a messenger. Sir William, said the messenger, had backslid again.

Undaunted, Bacon turned to his men.

"Gentlemen and Fellow Soldiers," he said, "the Governor is now in Gloucester County endeavoring to raise forces against us, having declared us rebels and traitors; if true, crimes too great for pardon. . . . . Now then, we must be forced to turn our swords to our own defense, or expose ourselves to their mercies. . . . Therefore . . . let us descend [to Jamestown] to know the reasons why such proceedings are used against us." So much for protocol. But Nat Bacon spiced his conclusion with his temper: "They are all damned cowards," he said, "and you shall see they will not dare meet us in the field to try the justness of our cause."

But it was not to be. The governor's forces, recruited on the ruse that they would fight Indians, deserted him when they discovered that the foe was Bacon. The "tragy comedy" was ended as Sir William fled by boat to the eastern shore of Virginia, and Bacon, realizing at last that he would be hanged for a sheep if not a goat, got down to the serious business of rebellion.

Bacon set up headquarters at the Middle Plantation, later to become Williamsburg, and broadcast an invitation to all colonists to come there for a meeting on the Indian war and future colonial peace.

The meeting took place in early August of 1676, debate centering around an oath Bacon wrote pledging loyalty to him and a fight against any of the king's troops who might appear, until the colonists' case could be presented to London. Many opposed this oath until the Rebel threatened to resign his leadership if they would not accept it.

Lest "while he went abroad to destroy the wolves, the foxes . . . should come and devour the sheep," Bacon sent an expedition of two hundred to capture Sir William and pack him off to England to stand trial for his "demerits toward His Majesty's subjects of Virginia." Other opponents were jailed. Bacon turned stubbornly toward the wilderness and the savage Indian.

A last glimmering of comedy flashed across the scene before the clouds of tragedy and defeat closed in. The Rebel could find no Indians. It was only after the most arduous search, through the notorious heat of a Tidewater August and the depths of the swamps, that he and his men succeeded in bashing in the head of a native woman who misled them as a guide, and chased the formerly friendly Queen of Pamunkey into the depths of the wilderness, capturing forty-five of her astonished and most unwarlike warriors to show to the folks back home.

While Bacon was on this expedition, the old fox had eluded his water-borne trap. Indeed, by fast talking, he had succeeded in capturing the ship that Bacon had sent after him. Sir William hanged the captain forthwith and, in early September, chased the Rebel's corporal guard out of Jamestown and re-established himself. Bacon and all his ilk were again proclaimed criminals-at-large.

The Rebel's returning army consisted of forty-five Indian prisoners and a hundred-and-thirty-odd flea-bitten whites. The others of a noble thousand had deserted or begged off during the abortive wilderness campaign. Sir William defended Jamestown with six hundred well-entrenched and well-paid hirelings whom he had brought with him from the eastern shore. But he underestimated the silver conviction of Bacon's tongue. Almost doubling his army with recruits picked up along the way, Nat assembled the men and delivered one of his orations. The army cheered assent—they would attack! By mid-September, after going through the formality of announcing his presence to Sir William by parading in full view of Jamestown before his troops to a trumpet blast, the Rebel built a barricade cutting the capital off from the mainland.

Sir William responded in character. It was all a mistake, he announced. He had ordered his men not to fire on the ragged army besieging the town. A conference seemed in order—how about a conference?

Bacon had learned his lesson. He refused.

On the third day, becoming convinced that the young man was going to be difficult, the governor's soldiers attacked under orders, but not with spirit, a contemporary recording that they "went out with heavy hearts, but returned with light heels."

Bacon captured some cannon and mounted them in full view of the Jamestown defenders by also capturing some of their wives and using them as a shield while the guns were installed. Berkeley, with his men deserting by the scores to the other side, did not wait for the finish. He saw Jamestown burned to the ground from the deck of a schooner, and reported to London that the Rebel set fire to the church with "his own sacrilegious hand." Climaxing his indignities, Bacon settled down in the solid comfort of Sir William's "Green Spring" to reorganize the colony.

And then his luck suddenly ran out. Soldiers, fearing the arrival of an army from England, began to desert. Others angered the neighborhood by their plundering. In October, hoarse with oratory to hold his little band together and full of plans for another expedition to capture Berkeley, Bacon came down with malaria and in a few days was dead.

The news was received joyfully by Sir William, who found time from the pressing problems of reassuming the governorship to write a medical analysis to England. Bacon had not died of fever, Sir William contended, but from the wrath of God. The Rebel swore his "usual oath—God damn my blood" at least "a thousand times a day" and God had obliged him by so infecting it that it bred vermin in "an incredible number," thus bringing him to his death.

As he moved back in, Sir William hanged rebels wholesale without trial. He would have "hanged half the country if they (the Assembly) had let him alone," said one observer. By the close of the year in which it had begun, the rebellion was at an end.

Bacon's body is said to rest in the James River in a coffin weighted with rocks. All who had been close to him, including Richard Lawrence, the tavernkeeper, were hanged. Bacon's young wife, true to the colonial traditions in matters matrimonial, married shortly after his death and, when her second husband died, married again.

Sir William's was a hollow victory. He died on returning to England to present his case to the king. The story is that death came of a broken heart because a royal audience was denied him, and that Charles II once remarked, "The old fool has hanged more men in that naked country than I have done for the murder of my father."

The Indians came no more; with a new governor and less dictatorial times, Bacon's laws were re-adopted and peace among the people was restored.

The legend of Bacon's courage inspired the revolutionaries who broke completely with England a century later.

He was no premature Jefferson of democracy, not yet a Jackson, this "prosperous rebel," this well-heeled Robin Hood. His goal was never even a republic. Repeatedly he protested loyalty to the king. He did not object to the royal system under which the colony lived, but rather to the king's henchmen as personified in Sir William; Nat Bacon thought that he could do the job more to the satisfaction of the king and of his colonial subjects. When he talked of the voice of the people, he referred to his following of landowners as opposed to Berkeley's. It never occurred to him to include the common man in his balloting. When he drew up the oath of rebellion at the Middle Plantation, taking it was limited to men "of what quality soever, excepting servants."

Yet he had courage; during his rebellion he touched the hem of freedom. And these things were tonic to Washington, Jefferson, Tom Paine, Patrick Henry, Franklin, and the others, beacons of hope in an historic background otherwise black with the unallayed successes of the monarchists.

[3]

The Frontiers (1754–1832)

From the people the countries get their armies.
By the people the armies are fed, clothed, armed.
Out of the smoke and ashes of the war
The people build again. . . .
    And after the strife of war begins the strife of peace.
                                    —CARL SANDBURG, *The People, Yes*

The people who least wanted the Revolutionary War were those who raised the issues leading up to it in the quarter-century before it came. The issues revolved around who was to get the profits from the meager prosperity of the colonies. The people who raised the issues were British financiers and traders, and colonial American businessmen. Both sides opposed war, many of their number speaking out against it even after it was declared.

Though the prosperity was indeed meager, considering that all America was still a frontier, it was spectacular. Steadily, commerce had increased. Villages became towns and cities. Real estate and trade along the coast boomed. By the eve of the Revolution, Philadelphia boasted a population of some forty thousand, New York thirty, Boston twenty.

Communications improved, as instanced by the opening of a regular stage service between New York and Philadelphia in 1759 and the less spectacular but steady expansion of Franklin's intercolony postal service. By the end of the era, as dramatic in its time as air transport in the twentieth century, there appeared the mighty six-horse, three-ton-cargo Conestoga wagon to speed trade both along the coast and into the hinterlands.

Other developments followed. From a poor start with Benjamin Harris' *Publick Occurrences* in 1690, the number of newspapers rose to seven by 1720 and to five times that figure before the Revolution.

46

Benjamin Franklin and a number of others encouraged organization of libraries and education for the masses.

British prohibitions against manufacturing encouraged artisans, making the era the most notable in American history for its craftsmanship. More than four hundred silversmiths worked in colonial America. Metalwork, glass, spinning and weaving, cabinet and furniture making—folk artists by the hundreds combined to enhance colonial good living and prosperity.

Observing these things, French and English financiers and empire builders, impatient after more than a century of small profits, closed in to claim all that they could of the new surpluses and cash so toilsomely acquired by the provincials.

The French were dismissed with comparative ease, meeting defeat from the colonies and the British in 1763. But the American businessman was not permitted thereafter to crawl back into his shell and answer the mail from London with small payments and tales of woe. His foreign masters were determined to collect handsomely.

Implementing this resolve were a set of British laws restricting ocean traffic to English (including colonial) ships, confining trade within limits designed to benefit London merchants, and prohibiting manufacturing and paper money in the colonies. Laws passed in America were subject to vetoes in London; upon particularly sensitive economic subjects, the colonials were ordered not to legislate.

To enforce these measures was the Board of Trade and Plantations, backed by merchants, Parliament, numberless other boards, commissions, trade associations and monopolists, and a formidable battery of London barristers.

There followed decades of jockeying notable for the originality of the taxes and regulations devised by the British and for the genius with which Americans avoided them.

Up to a point, it was largely a case of one group of businessmen trying to dominate or out-smart another and, although tempers sometimes flared, open conflict seemed remote if for no other reason than that all the men of property concerned usually wound up with a handsome profit. Besides, as many an American businessman believed so strongly that he sided with the British when war came, conflicts result in bad times and bad times mean bad business. Even further, there is no profit in declaring open war on your boss.

47

But it was a different matter when ordinary American citizens were dragged into the economic struggle—by the British in order to demonstrate their authority and to raise more taxes, by the American businessman in an effort to convince London that the taxes were exorbitant. The ordinary American cherished in his heart illusions about equality and freedom; democracy was a frontier he was eager to explore. Once these things seemed involved, he took the situation deeply to heart. Above the protests of conservative American businessmen, he began making trouble for which the business groups had not bargained and which embarrassed them exceedingly.

Newspapers got out of hand and began to speak bluntly. "A colonist," said the Boston *Gazette* as early as 1765, "cannot make a button, a horseshoe, nor a hobnail, but some sooty ironmonger or respectable buttonmaker of Britain shall bawl and squall that his honor's worship is most egregiously maltreated, injured, cheated, and robbed by the rascally American republicans." Lawyers like Patrick Henry shouted of liberty—or death. Artisans—workmen, no less—organized themselves into mobs under a variety of names, most notably the Sons of Liberty. These men, dignifying their actions with patriotic motives, soon developed Red-Coat-baiting into a pastime, tar-and-feathering into a fine art, and house-burning into a major sport.

Incident followed incident. In the spring of 1770, British soldiers at Boston were harassed by crowds of laborers until they finally fired on them, killing four. This was promptly publicized by patriots as "the Boston Massacre." Again, in December, 1773, a British cargo of tea was destroyed—the Boston Tea Party. All up and down the coast, British soldiers were bullied and beaten. Few dared go far from their garrison, and when General Gage had the temerity to move out of Boston in April, 1775, to secure some native gunpowder stored at Concord and to capture the patriots John Hancock and Samuel Adams, every American along the way who had a gun began to shoot.

War inevitably followed.

When the brunt of it fell upon the ordinary citizenry who had, in the end, started it, they responded by weaving into the homespun of the national personality bright threads of tradition which were to characterize it for generations to come.

48

Chief creation was the American soldier, that grumbling and hypercritical crusader for the freedom of man, who wins wars despite self-seeking politicians, profiteers, and incompetent generals and admirals, but, not once decelerating his growl or his criticisms, follows the good leader through hell and high water. Both—and more—were the soldier's lot during the Revolution.

It is easy to rationalize the facts in retrospect, but any logical, unemotional, cautious average citizen could have reached only one conclusion in the war-laden spring of 1775: play ball with the British.

If he became a soldier of the king, he joined a well-fed, well-armed, well-clothed professional army backed by one of the most powerful empires of the day, wealthy and willing to pay heavily in sound money to break up a rebellion.

If he pioneered the frontier of American·militarism, he became a bum rivaling the last straggler in a horde of beggars, one of an ever-changing mass of ragamuffins who wandered in and out of the camps almost at will.

Privates in the Continental army were paid—when and if—$6.66 a month in money that grew increasingly worthless. They were supposed to "find their own arms and clothes." By December, 1778, "a rat in the shape of a horse is not to be bought for less than £200," Washington wrote, and by the following spring a "wagon-load of money will not purchase a wagon-load of provisions." By May, 1779, butter in Philadelphia was $2 or $3 a pound, a hat $400, a suit of clothes $1,600, fishhooks 50 cents, handkerchiefs $100. Still the money poured from the presses, hitting bottom in 1781, when $100 in Continental specie was estimated to be worth $7,400 in inflated paper. A pair of boots cost $600, six yards of chintz $900. Tom Paine paid $300 for a pair of stockings and Jefferson more than $100 a quart for brandy.

Backed by the printing-press currency, a will-o'-the-wisp Congress, and big and little war profiteers, the soldier's future held for him financial and incredible physical hardships, death on the field or the gallows, eventual political and social ostracism.

His dependents shared disaster. If they lived near the wilderness, his departure enhanced their chances of murderous attack by Indians, immediately aware of the war between the whites. Profiteers drew no line between military and civilian victims. Often a soldier's family went into debt in the absent warrior's name, and he returned to face bankruptcy and a debtor's prison. If he died in service, Congress passed the buck to the states for taking care of his dependents. As it turned out, the national legislators, urged on by Alexander Hamilton and Washington himself, even crossed up the GI's in the postwar era, thimble-rigging national finances in such a way that money-minded speculators made some $40,000,000, and the soldiers, with few exceptions, got paid off at from ten to fifty cents on the dollar.

It is a tribute to the consistent and unyielding stupidity of the British colonial policy that nearly a quarter of a million Americans— 10 per cent of the total population—at one time or another during the war threw logic and caution to the winds and viewed the realities with such high emotion that they joined the mob at least for a time, faced the hardships, and risked the multitudinous disgraces of defeat.

The Revolutionary foot-soldier was lucky if he could boast a century-old, bell-barreled matchlock. Muskets were numerous, though many blew up because of profiteer workmanship or overuse, and flintlocks too often missed fire. The rifle was so new a weapon that Washington spelled it with two f's. Many men fought armed only with spears. Even these were so fashioned by the greedy war contractors that, as Washington complained to Congress, they could "answer no sort of purpose." Homemade or heirloom swords, cutlasses, pikes, halberds, axes, pitchforks, rapiers, bows and arrows, tomahawks, and even sticks and stones were at times pressed into the fight.

The original Revolutionary supply of gunpowder, most valued war material of the time, was left over from the French and Indian conflicts. Ninety per cent of new powder used until 1778 was imported a few precious pounds at a time. Enroute to Boston to take command of the Continental Army, Washington found "not more than four barrels of powder in the City of New York." "Our powder is wasting fast," he noted as the fighting got under way, "notwithstanding the strictest care, economy, and attention are paid to it. The long series of wet weather, which we have had, renders the greater part of what has been served out to our men of no use." Later from Boston he reported "only 184 barrels of powder in all . . . not sufficient to give 25 muskets cartridges to each man, and scarcely to serve the artillery in any brisk action one single day." British troops carried

50

more than double the amount, with plentiful reserves. Three years later it was the same story. "The commander-in-chief," Washington ruled in the spring of 1778, "calls on all officers to pay the strictest attention to the orders of the twenty-eighth of January last respecting their men's ammunition, and in addition to that order he directs that whenever a noncommissioned officer or soldier is detected in discharging his piece or otherwise wasting his ammunition, the first commanding officer he is brought before shall order him to be tied up immediately and receive thirty-nine lashes on his bare back."

Many a back did not have to be stripped of shirt or jacket to take the lashes, for the soldiery often lacked not only a uniform, but sufficient clothing whatsoever. Men wore the buckskin hunting shirt and tanned tow cloth breeches in which they joined up. They wore homespun. They wore the 1777 government issue of linen hunting shirt, overalls, and a sleeved leather or woolen jacket. Official blue army coats appeared on scattered troops in the same year. Campaigning reduced many of these to rags as the war went on.

During the winter of 1776-1777, Washington's troops suffered severely from lack of shoes, some refusing to march, others braving snow and ice in bare feet. A wool shortage led to the issue of linen clothes to the troops. "Their distresses," Washington informed Congress, "are extremely great, many of them being entirely naked."

From Ticonderoga in December, 1776, one observer reported: "For all this army . . . of twelve or thirteen thousand men . . . no more than nine hundred pair of shoes have been sent. One-third at least of the poor wretches is now barefoot, and in this condition obliged to do duty. . . . It cannot be viewed in any milder light than black murder." Blood stained the snow of all the winter bivouacs.

Shelter and food were in character. During the opening two—and worst—years of the war, tents were often fashioned of rags too flimsy to be worn as clothing. No funds were provided for shelter. If the men stopped long enough to make a permanent encampment, as at Valley Forge, they built huts of mud and logs, but on the march most were forced to sleep in the open. Base of the army diet was salt pork. Often the troops went without fresh vegetables for months on end, lacking funds to buy them. Profiteers were among the camp followers.

Every man had to look out for his own cooking early in the war; throughout the campaigning, food sanitation was practically nonexistent. Dysentery was an occupational disease, scurvy not infrequent. For the wounded there was the special hell of eighteenth-century surgery aggravated by some volunteer doctors who had never so much as seen an operation. A hospital building at Valley Forge with capacity for 250 wounded was jammed with nearly a thousand.

Wounded unfit for further duty were turned out to shift for themselves. Many begged in the streets of the cities.

Yet the Revolutionary GI saw to it, despite difficulties, that his became perhaps the most happy-go-lucky and certainly the most nonchalant fighting organization in all history.

To the despair of his high command, especially Washington, he took all the punishment devised to discipline him and continued to obey the commands of his own conscience, ably abetted by the will of a frontier mule. He elected—and demoted—his immediate superior officers as the spirit moved him. The troops "regarded their officers no more than broomsticks," wailed their commander-in-chief. Officers were knocked down, pulled off their horses and beaten, and threatened with death.

Most of the heavy campaigning was done in the summer, and in the summer, since childhood, the wilderness countryside had been the playground of the ordinary enlisted man. He took to it like a small boy to a swimming hole. Tough, durable, and unschooled in the continental formalities that were supposed to go with warfare, he took also with gusto to fighting the enemy. Within very slight limitations, he did otherwise as he pleased.

A man would desert to the British. A few days later he would be back on duty, well armed, and wearing an outfit of good fabric dyed an astonishing mottle that might once have been red. Sometimes he didn't bother to dye it, but fought against the "lobsters" in one of their own uniforms.

A farmer-soldier would desert in the fall in time for harvest and report unblushingly back for duty after the first spring planting. Desertions were so prevalent that Washington remarked wryly at one time, "We shall be obliged to detach one half the army to bring back the other." At one camp, when a neighboring dairyman tried to profiteer in milk and butter, farmers among the troops commandeered his cows until he came to terms. So proficient did the soldiery become at foraging that one reason given for wintering at Valley Forge was its remoteness from raid-tempting farms.

For morale purposes, the Revolutionary GI heartened himself by remembering the justness of his cause and his own resourcefulness as contrasted with the fatuous, formalized generalship of the British.

It further embarrassed his leaders when the Revolutionary GI substituted for formal declarations of freedom the blunt oratory of revolt as written by an unshaven, gin-bibbing renegade son of a pious Thetford, England, corset maker—a rebel trained in the slums of London—a Philadelphia rank-and-filer with a pen mightier than a sword—Tom Paine, common-man spokesman of the Revolution.

His words were oil on its dying flame when first he wrote a booklet in the darkling winter of 1775-1776, signing it "Common Sense." He was a prodigal prophet of freedom—*Common Sense* he gave, without asking a tuppence of royalties, to a Philadelphia printer on the sole condition that it would be widely circulated. By spring, counting numerous pirated editions, it had become America's first best-seller.

It and his other Revolutionary writings were extraordinary for another and more far-reaching reason—in them, for the first time, we hear, clear and unequivocally, the voice of democracy.

Those who had spoken before, spoke not for the democratic principle, but—like many another who followed, to this day—for a "democracy" under which they, a man or a handful of men, could rule without being stigmatized by the name of ruler. God was the star toward which the Puritans pointed the people, meantime picking their pockets of sovereignty. Liberty was the cry of the planter, the merchant, the landowner—for themselves. Freedom was the cry of most of the politicians—always with an eye on the logic of the times, the testy temper of Mother England, possible reduction of taxes, and their own advancement. The few exceptions spoke in the high-flown language of the eighteenth century.

Tom Paine spoke not for himself but for the people, and in their own straightforward tongue.

53

During a brief time the thunderclap of his uncompromising democratic idealism flashed through the clouds of oppression. Before his time, the clouds had seldom lifted; afterward they were to lower again, settling over the land for long years during which the people were deluged with pious platitudes, specious promises, and dominance of the many by the few.

Exaggeration that it is to say Tom Paine's words gave birth to democracy, it is undeniable that they heralded its birth.

And his readers, common men in or out of uniform, were heartened and fought on. . . .

But they were equally inspired in different ways, and were amused both before and during the Revolution by the writings and goings-on of Tom Paine's first American friend, Benjamin Franklin, the poor man's Socrates, who had given the colonies a postal service and encouraged the spread of education. Perhaps more than any other, he bridged the gap for the average American between post- and ante-Revolutionary days.

Franklin's prose was also homey, and he wrote shrewdly of practical things, seldom presenting the thoughts of his dazzling mind in such a way that it blinded his readers.

Most famous among his contemporaries for *Poor Richard*, his almanac which first appeared more than two-score years before the Revolution, he wrote not alone the copybook maxims that have been drummed into schoolboy heads ever since, but also many a salty quip that hinted at the real personality of the author, while winking sometimes bawdily at the peccadilloes of mankind.

Love and marriage were favorite subjects. "Neither a fortress nor a maiden will hold out long after they begin to parley," he observed, and "Keep your eyes wide open before marriage, half shut afterwards." "He that takes a wife takes care." Some wives are not saintly: "Why does the blind man's wife paint herself?" Nor should the husband tempt his nature too far: "Let thy maidservant be faithful, strong and homely." But even if he is faithful, the Puritan code is a threat to his moral standing:

> "You cannot pluck roses without fear of thorns,
> Nor enjoy a fair wife without danger of horns."

"Love and lordship hate companions," he said, and again, with gentle somberness: "There are no ugly loves nor handsome prisons."

Other pleasures did not miss his attention. "Never spare the parson's wine nor the baker's pudding," he advised. Drinking did not necessarily lead to an early grave: "There's more old drunkards than old doctors." And you might as well enjoy yourself, for if you "Fly pleasures . . . they'll follow you."

The professions as well as mankind generally came in for barbed comment. On lawyers: "A countryman between two lawyers is like a fish between two cats." Doctors: "He's a fool who makes his doctor his heir." Rulers: "The king's cheese is half wasted in parings; but no matter, 'tis made of the people's milk." "Kings and bears often worry their keepers." Traders: "Bargaining has neither friends nor relations."

On people generally, he was blandly cynical. "The family of fools is ancient," he said, later stating it: "He that has neither fools nor beggars among his kindred is the son of thundergust."

Poor Richard's mentor was not one to pass up the sweets of life, fruits of which included lovers in three nations, recurring cases of gout, and at least one bastard son. Franklin authored drinking songs to which he gave voice with cronies over rum and Madeira in Philadelphia taverns. He gave "Advice to a Young Man on the Choice of a Mistress," in which he recommended old women in preference to young ones on the grounds that they would handle the affair with more prudence and discretion and less danger—and "lastly, they are so grateful!"

His career helped make his mind the most sophisticated as well as the most brilliant of his time. For nearly twenty years before the Revolution he represented the colonies in London in one capacity or another, and during the war he was America's ambassador to France. Gossip seethed around him, not only concerning his shrewd diplomatic maneuvers and his amours, but (perhaps more exciting to the common man of the time) concerning his scientific and inventive genius.

This genius frequently appeared to border on witchcraft and more often than not had additional appeal because it resulted in practical applications that made the hard eighteenth-century life more livable. It is already ingrained in American history that he experimented with electricity, but less well known that his insatiable Yankee ingenuity devised a machine for creating electricity, drafts for fireplaces, the Franklin stove, a more satisfactory method of sweeping chimneys, lightning rods, a clock, the harmonica, bifocal glasses, and a ladder chair which was the grandfather of the ladders now used in libraries to reach high shelves. He also was the first to study the Gulf Stream, to introduce medicinal rhubarb, kohlrabi, and Scotch cabbage to this country, and to propose crop insurance and daylight-saving time. When the balloon was still an experiment and the airplane more than a hundred years away, he saw with breathtaking clarity the possibilities of aerial warfare.

He endeared himself even more by two characteristics that have become so commonplace among his countrymen as to be considered typical. He loved tall stories and practical jokes; and he was an inveterate organizer and joiner.

He once wrote a homily on tolerance and, inserting it in his Bible, pawned it off on gullible listeners as the fifty-first chapter of Genesis. To Englishmen he reported solemnly that American sheep were so laden with wool that they had little carts attached to the hindquarters to keep their tails from dragging. Whales chased cod into the upper Great Lakes—"the grand leap of the whale in that chase up the fall of Niagara is esteemed, by all who have seen it, as one of the finest spectacles of nature."

As an organizer and joiner he has seldom been equaled. Among other things, he organized—and joined—his historic Junto, the Union Fire Company of Philadelphia, the American Philosophical Society, the first Pennsylvania militia, and the first American abolition society.

He was seventy when the Revolution began, with long years of diplomacy behind him in London town, but lively as a cricket and ready to win the French over to the American side, which he did without losing any of his charm with the women or forgetting his scientific research or his writings or his sense of humor. And when he decided it was time to pack up and go home, he fooled everybody, including his feminine French admirers, by making the trip without dying and doing research on the Gulf Stream enroute.

He became the oldest and one of the sagest delegates to the Constitutional Convention. He thought youthful thoughts and made young jests till the end, at eighty-four.

Drinking was not, of course, a Franklin monopoly. For it is one of the great illusions of all time that the founding fathers or their fathers before them were any less bibulous than their descendants, each generation, indeed, rivaling the last in its fondness for alcohol, the screams of the Victorians and the resulting Prohibition era to the contrary notwithstanding.

One of the men most disliked by the Pilgrim fathers was the bosun of the *Mayflower*—he ignored William Bradford's pleas for beer when Bradford fell ill on the voyage to America.

The Puritan attitude on liquor may be gathered from the "victuals" supplied his troops when Captain John Mason marched against the Pequots in 1637, his men provided with "good beer, three or four gallons of strong water, and two gallons of sack."

French and Indian warriors were equally well cared for. "None came to prayers," reported Chaplain John Graham during the campaign of 1756, "but they fixed a table without the door of the tent, where a head colonel was posted to make punch in the sight of all, they within drinking, talking and laughing during the whole service." "Over here, as in England," another observer said in the 1760's, "the social life of men was in the taverns. From the richest merchants to the poorest porter, each man had one or two favorites where he was more apt to be found after his work was over than in his own house."

Even so intolerant a soul as Increase Mather, in writing *Woe to Drunkards* viewed bibbing tolerantly. "Drink in itself is a good creature of God," he said, "and to be received with thankfulness. . . . The wine is from God . . . the drunkard is from the Devil."

The pre-Revolutionary attitude farther south was even less strict. Grog shops, wine at meals, and heavy drinking were taken as a matter of course. Toasts were commonplace among high and lowly. After he had round-robined his rebel volunteers, Nat Bacon recorded that he "gave them brandy to wind up the charm," and throughout the country, according to Dr. Daniel Dorchester, a nineteenth-century historian of temperance, "the popular view of alcoholic liquors was that they were beneficial to health, intellectual powers, and social happiness; . . . that men who did not drink rum and cider were not worth much to work and could not endure the extremes of the weather." A keg of rum, he said, was the standard supply to raise a barn; a barrel, to raise a meeting house.

This was wholeheartedly underwritten by Washington, whose attitude toward drinking among the troops may be gathered from a contract he wrote for his gardener before going to the wars. It provided for "a decent suit of clothes, befitting a man in his station; . . . four dollars at Christmas, with which he may be drunk four days and four nights; two dollars at Easter to effect the same purpose; two dollars at Whitsuntide to be drunk two days; . . . a dram in the morning and a drink of grog at dinner at noon." At Valley Forge, he ordered that any man who got drunk must cut a stump, thereby getting a large parade ground cleared in record time.

The average colonial, like his descendants, was not averse to variety in his drinking, but (as to this day) he never sacrificed strength to style in his mixtures. The most popular concoctions were those enabling a man to take his liquor as near straight as possible without choking.

Basic ingredients were homemade brews and white mule, applejack, apple and peach brandies, and rum. Imported wines seldom filtered down to the average citizen, and he regarded them as effeminate.

With his high-proof basics he mixed potions that would have awed a Borgia. The original mint julep, without benefit of ice, was devised on the theory that too much sugar or too little whisky would ruin it. At its (still-authentic) best it consisted of one half tablespoon of sweetening and some crushed mint leaves—plus straight whisky. A Virginia favorite was "Fish House Punch"—one part water, one part rum and brandy, flavored with brown sugar and lemons. A version of this recipe adds judiciously that drinkers should look out for a swelled head next morning. Even more potent was the rum or brandy shrub—one part orange juice to four parts ardent spirits, sweetened with sugar. A concoction employed summer and winter was called hot flip, a mixture of rum and beer, flavored with a spot of molasses.

When in doubt, a man took his rum or brandy straight, chasing it with beer. . . .

A recurrent irony in American history has been that wars for freedom have been followed by reigns of reaction. The Revolutionary GI, having freed himself from Britain's dictatorship, came home to find the domestic scene dominated by the logical, the unemotional, and the cautious who had had the luck or the last-minute presence of mind to celebrate the final victory without sharing any of the long winters of defeat.

Profiteers there were, fat with fortunes they were determined to increase. Aiding and abetting these were men of the old New England theocratic strain, edging back toward control with a brand-new set of taboos and intolerances. Even politically, after a brief, almost blinding glimpse of democracy in action under Jefferson, the common man faced forces of reaction hardly distinguishable, save for the catch phrases they coined, from those against which he had fought so bitterly and at such great sacrifice.

Postwar times were hard for the little people—economically as hard as they had been in the depths of the wartime inflation. Having been stripped of most of their bonus money by Hamilton and his smart business backers, soldiers faced a brief respite before depression struck during the winter of 1785-1786. Save for the shrewd few, the going remained difficult until 1788.

There followed three years of comparatively good living before the speculative collapse of 1791. By this time the people had found a name for it—*panic*—a word quick on the lips of sons whose fathers were caught in the Panic of 1791, as the sons were caught in the Panic of 1819. Big business that year contracted the credit of the Bank of the United States, which big business controlled, leaving those not in the know to the mercies of sheriff sales and the debtor prisons.

Neo-theocrats on the social front rivaled the men of property on the economic. The strings of convention upon women tightened in the settled communities along the eastern seaboard, in sharp contrast to the hands-off view taken of their activities during the Revolution, when wives and sweethearts marched and even fought with the troops, and camp followers were considered as important to morale as rum. Such goings-on were damned by the Puritan-minded and even by Washington, who tried vainly to keep the trollops in his caravan from parading proudly with the troops. The feminine warriors dressed wounds, unblushingly plundered the enemy dead, mended ragged clothing, cooked, and made the hovels of Valley Forge and Morristown more habitable. Women outshone men during Benedict Arnold's invasion of Canada in the bitter fall of 1775, and their contribution to the happiness of the troops everywhere led to relaxation of social conventions. Married or unmarried, the girls did pretty much as they pleased, and their battleground independence was asserted in varying degrees of defiance by their sisters at home.

But during the post-Revolutionary period, restrictions arose, devised by the pious and aggravated by the economics of the times. English common law, which then prevailed in every state save Louisiana, permitted a man to beat his wife without liability. A drunkard could take his wife's clothing to buy rum, and courts would sustain his action. Husbands bothered by nagging wives could have them committed to insane asylums. Men had full legal right to confiscate their wives' earnings.

The post-Revolutionary theocrats heartily approved these conditions. To prove that slavery was ordained by God, the Reverend F. A. Ross of Huntsville, Alabama, compared the Negro's lot to that of the housewife. "O ye wives," quoth he, "I know how superior you are to your husbands in many respects. . . . Nay, I know you may surpass him in his own sphere of boasted prudence and worldly wisdom about dollars and cents. Nevertheless he has authority from God to rule over you." Wives were slaves. "Will you say that you are free, that you will go where you please, do as you please? Why ye dear wives, your husbands may forbid. . . . Will you run away with your stick and your bundle? He can advertise you!" Said the *Presbyterian Magazine:* "Authority must be vested somewhere . . . authority in the human race is vested in man, as the divinely appointed head of creation. 'Wives submit yourselves unto your husbands as unto the Lord.' "

Woman suffrage, which had been common in the colonies, was stamped out in state after state until it was nonexistent. "Even at the middle of the (nineteenth) century," Calhoun sums up in his *A Social History of the American Family*, "Woman had no recognized individuality in any sphere of life. She toiled in domestic obscurity. . . . The boy past twenty-one was free but the girl continued to work without wages. . . . Marriage transferred her services to the husband. . . . Almost every woman had to marry . . . or else become an utter dependent, living after her parents' death with some married relative as family drudge without wage and usually regarded with disrespect by the children. To step out as a wage earner was to lose caste and be barred from the neighborhood functions. . . . It was believed to a great extent that any woman that attempted a vocation outside of domestic service was henceforth unfitted to be a wife and a mother."

As time went by, women rose to publicize woman's inadequacies. By the end of the era, Catherine E. Beecher was to win hosannas by saying that "the more intelligent a woman becomes, the more she can appreciate the wisdom of that ordinance that appointed her subordinate station, and the more her taste will conform to the graceful and dignified retirement and submission it involves."

A wife, ruled the *Ladies Repository*, should regard her husband with affection, reverence, and faithfulness. "Man," declared a feminine writer in the Madison (Georgia) *Visitor*, "is superior to woman," having "a more stately form, stronger nerves and muscles, and, in nine cases out of ten, a more vigorous intellect."

Feminine education went forward accordingly. "When reading was first taught women in America," Calhoun reports, "it is said that opposition arose on the ground that a woman would forge her father's or husband's name if she learned to read or write. Geography was likewise opposed on the score of its tendency to make her dissatisfied with home and desirous of travel. The first public examination of a girl in geometry, given in New York in 1829, raised a cry of disapproval all over the land. College education of women was branded as horrifying and vulgar by both clergy and educators."

While his wife suffered the indignities of near-slavery, her husband, bedeviled by economic stresses, found that even the pleasure of drinking was gaining the disapproval of the blue-noses. He took the attack as a joke for so long that he did not realize its seriousness until it had reached nationwide proportions.

The campaign began as the Revolution ended. The period around 1785, said Dr. Albert G. Lawson, temperance historian, "was the age of drink." Veterans were the worst offenders. In proportion to their numbers, estimated another historian, the post-Revolutionary drinker consumed "a barrel of distilled spirits for every gallon" drunk toward the close of the nineteenth century.

Against such formidable and enthusiastic opposition the drys were forced to move cautiously. When one of the first temperance societies was organized in Moreau, New York, in 1808, moderation was all that was asked, and penalties for violations were mild and alcoholic. Members were fined fifty cents for getting drunk. Another society required a drunken member to buy drinks for the house. A third met in a bar and the newly elected president toasted the membership with a tumbler full of whisky.

But in 1826 came the American Society for the Promotion of Temperance, dedicated to the idea that "if all temperance people could be induced to . . . pledge . . . entire abstinence from ardent spirits, topers would, in time, become an extinct race." A word was coined to keynote the campaign—*T*(for total)-*totaler*. The campaign of the century was on.

The going continued rough. Frances E. Willard, one of its leaders, pointed out that in the 1830's "total abstainers were considered undesirable (insurance) risks, and had to pay more than others, because if exposed to cold they did not take a drink, nor yet as an aid to digestion; because they not only refused the comfort of a good creature of God in health, but insanely declined its magic aid in case of sickness." In the '40's the drive began to have serious influence on the mores of the time, greatly enhanced as it was during that decade by organized campaigns for state prohibition laws and by a horrendous set of drawings devised by Dr. Thomas Sewall of Washington, D. C., purporting to show the effects of alcohol on the human anatomy, drawings which became required equipment in public schools in state after state.

Thus grew a minority that from the Revolution until its ultimate victory in the twentieth century was regarded by the majority of people as a joke but which, despite steadily increasing liquor consumption down through the years, eventually succeeded for a time in forcing its will upon the entire nation.

Regardless of the backward trend of the times toward Puritanism, post-Revolutionary pleasures of all kinds thrived.

Enhanced by steadily improving transportation—stagecoaching

approached its heyday east of the Mississippi about 1828—eastern centers regularly enjoyed the theater, puppet and peep shows, waxwork museums, panoramas, glass-blowing exhibitions, balloon ascensions, freaks, magicians, medicine shows, and circuses.

As early as 1815, a theatrical road show went by wagon from Albany to the headwaters of the Allegheny and thence to towns along the Ohio. Local stock companies entertained at Cincinnati from 1801, and there were professionals in St. Louis in the same year.

Another kind of professionals, singly or by twos or threes, enlivened and enriched the lives of the people, especially on the frontiers. Each an actor in his own way, these were the pedlars, found upon the roads and wilderness paths, a handful traveling in their own elaborate vehicles, a larger handful in stagecoaches or wagons, some few mounted on horse or mule, a vast multitude afoot. Spurred by the same vague, mostly impractical urge that had played a considerable part in bringing them or their forbears to America, while some concentrated grimly on making a fortune and others worked toward a special paradise learned of from relative or friend, most indulged themselves in the undistilled nonchalance of wanderlust, not caring much about the future so long as no man disillusioned them by saying there was no big rock candy mountain, no pot at the end of the rainbow, no endless landscape of fields, each greener than the last.

The majority of them, the wilderness being what it was, were young; not a few were specialists. These filled wagons with spinning wheels, organs, winnowing machines, or corn shellers, carrying them one at a time on their backs from the roadside to the ultimate trailend customer. Sleigh dealers dragged their wares behind the covered wagon that was their home and office. Others specialized in brooms and books and pottery.

"Trunk pedlars" could carry their entire stock on their backs—pins, needles, hooks and eyes, scissors, razors, combs, buttons, spoons, small hardware, lace and perfume and medicines, melodeons and jackknives—Yankee notions of every sort and description.

At gaining the ultimate bargain in "country pay," or bartering, not a few were masters. In Connecticut, from which most of them came, and throughout New England, peddling was long considered the first step to fame or fortune. Collis P. Huntington, who became a railroad magnate in the far west, began his career as a pedlar, as did Jubilee

Jim Fisk and B. T. Babbitt, the soap king. A mendacious vendor of quack medicines who worked unsuccessfully out of Cleveland, Ohio, and who became famous in history for saying, "I cheat my boys every chance I get. I want to make 'em sharp!" was the father of John D. Rockefeller, Sr.

Others made history more closely related to the common folk who were their customers. Among these was that puckish parson, the Reverend Mason Locke Weems, who, when the books he was peddling didn't sell, dreamed up some of his own, thereby becoming one of the nation's first pulp writers and gaining dubious fame for his highly imaginative *Life of Washington*. Actually, Jefferson was a man more to Weems' personal liking, as were Jefferson's common people. The little parson, who could also fiddle, favored taverns, churches, and southern mansions impartially with his wares and his talents.

Stranger, to the point that he became almost as much a legend as a man, was Johnny Appleseed (Jonathan Chapman), a primitive Christian, who appeared in the Ohio valley in 1801 and for decades thereafter distributed apple seeds and saplings to the frontiersmen, seeds which grew into orchards over a hundred thousand middle-western square miles. Small, clothed in rags, barefoot—shoes given him he passed on to movers he considered more needy—he was beloved of animals, Indians, and children. He believed that to kill for food was sinful. Stretched on many a cabin floor, he preached to the listening pioneer family. He died at seventy-two, a stranger in a strange house, mourned by the whole frontier.

Also on the roads were journeymen uninhibited by pedlar packs —dancing masters, fencing masters, colporteurs, preachers, printers, cobblers, metal workers, dentists, artists who could scissor your silhouette in a matter of minutes, singing teachers who could organize a whole community into a chorus, orators who could make of you another Demosthenes for a small consideration.

Between visitations from such geniuses, frontier and town folk alike found pleasures at church meetings, dances, and political rallies. Turkey shoots became a favorite frontier sport, and dueling added excitement to the era. Men drank and gambled in the taverns. Women gossiped and entertained at prodigious feasts. Small girls made samplers of the American eagle or of Adam and Eve and small boys even in the eastern cities had a wilderness within close reach for a playground.

Economic and social restrictions of the settled seaboard reached the frontiers ineffectively or not at all: as was true in the two centuries behind them, freedom-loving men turned in a steady stream toward the wilderness.

If they brought with them anger against the society they had left behind, here they could dissipate it with prodigal indifference. A sort of negative tolerance prevailed—if you couldn't stand your neighbor and his way of doing things, you didn't have to bend him to your way or yourself to his. One or the other of you could move on. Frontiersmen were generally friendly and not undemocratic, faced as they were with the common enemies—native savages and savage nature.

There developed what Calhoun calls "an individualistic democracy akin to anarchy . . . the ax and the rifle 'made all men equally tall.' " Courtship, marriage, and your standing in the community continued free and easy for adults, as did discipline of the children.

And beyond the political and economic frontiers opened up by the Revolution, for each of which the people found a leader, beyond the military pioneering against the British and the pioneering that went into the settlement of the Ohio valley and Kentucky and all the vast area east of the Mississippi—far away and with vast distances but dimly realized stretched other frontiers, political and economic as well as geographic; endless, American, imponderable. . . .

[4]

The Frontiersmen

George Washington

It is the most tragic of farces that so many Americans should insist both that Washington could not tell a lie, and that his chroniclers may not tell the truth.

—RUPERT HUGHES, *George Washington*

> These are the things, which once possess'd
> Will make a life that's truly bless'd—
> A good estate on healthy soil
> Not got by vice, nor yet by toil . . .
> A merry night without much drinking,
> A happy thought without much thinking. . . .
>
> —*Excerpt from a favorite poem*
> *of Washington's boyhood*

All Washingtons are born old.

—GEORGE WILLIAM FAIRFAX

It is unfortunate both for history and for George Washington that his political sponsors and the Victorians who followed froze him in lily-white marble instead of picturing him as the vivid and tragic human being that he was.

Most of the popular facts about him are fiction. He did not cut down a cherry tree—that folk tale sprang from the imagination of happy-go-lucky Parson Weems who hoped that his audience would be amused by his yarn, but hardly expected that they would swallow it whole.

Washington wasn't a military genius unless that term may be applied to a commander who broke all records for accumulating defeats.

The accumulation would have been larger if his staff had not restrained him; yet he loved war. Early in his career he said, "I have heard the bullets whistle; and believe me, there is something charming in the sound," a remark which won from no less a personage than George II the response, "He had not heard many or he would not think them very charming." As was so often the case, George II misjudged his man. Robert E. Lee may have been thinking of the first American commander-in-chief when he said less than a century later: "It is well that war is so terrible, or else we might grow too fond of it." Washington loved war so fondly that all his life, despite his business prudence, he was willing to fight, if need be, for nothing.

Despite his shortcomings at the policy level, Washington was an excellent executive, exacting and formal, but seeking and accepting advice from his subordinates, leading them by outworking them, yet capable of shrewd delegation of powers, winning their admiration and confidence by seldom playing favorites. He never dealt in personalities, including his own. "His integrity was most pure," Jefferson said of him, "his justice the most inflexible I have ever known, no motives of interest or consanguinity, of friendship, or hatred, being able to bias his decision." Not once in his whole career could the charge that he sought self-aggrandizement be made to stick, and he had the genius to keep silent when fiery temperaments opposing him tried to reduce their quarrels with him to an exchange of personal recriminations. He seemed utterly incapable of gossip. "Of the famous and picturesque personages he met, he gave never a line of description," notes Rupert Hughes.

He was neither calm nor unbendingly aloof. He had a hair-trigger temper. Discovering a poacher rowing in the Potomac near Mount Vernon, Washington charged on horseback into the water, jerked the offender from his boat, and beat him resoundingly. In battle he frequently risked capture by abandoning himself to a towering rage. General Charles Scott, a master of profanity, testified that Washington at Monmouth "swore till the leaves shook on the trees, charming, delightful. Never have I enjoyed such swearing . . . like an angel from Heaven."

Most misleading is the portrayal of Washington as a religious man. He was religious only as much as convention demanded, and hunted or drank or went to the theater far more often than he attended

67

church on Sundays. He was once even haled before a justice of peace and fined for Sunday horse trading. It was an age of lengthy dinner hours and many toasts, and Washington loved them, whetting his appetite for more wine after the meal by eating nuts. He was casual about the religious beliefs of others, once saying he didn't care whether a man was a Mohammedan, a Jew, or atheist, so long as he was worth his salt. He died without requesting a clergyman or mentioning God, and did not leave a dime to any religious institution in an age when such bequests were considered mandatory.

He was no dignified spectator of sports, but an enthusiastic and expert participant. As a youth, he excelled in wrestling and weight lifting. Jefferson singled him out in an age of accomplished equestrians as the best and most graceful of them all. He could ride sixty miles in a day if pushed to it. He was inordinately fond of playing catch, and in his prime could bend a horseshoe with his hands.

Though he had a reputation for being formal, impersonal, and humorless even in his own day, he was not without wit. Anticipating Mark Twain by more than a hundred years, he wrote home after Braddock's defeat that he had heard a rumor of his (Washington's) death and dying speech and took "this opportunity of contradicting the first and of assuring you that I have not as yet composed the latter." After the war the king of Spain gave him a donkey for a present, and Washington wrote Rabelaisian letters to Lafayette and others about the donkey's amours. He regarded the breeding adventures of his hounds with similar barroom hilarity. During the war, he once said with wry humor: "The men with me are too few to fight, and not enough to run away with."

His political sponsors built him up as a great statesman, profoundly wise. With rare exceptions, his statesmanship was neutral if not negative; political philosophy bored him; he read little, and most of that was "how to" books on farming and making money.

He made neither an appearance nor a speech before the electorate when first he ran successfully for the Virginia House of Burgesses at twenty-six, a campaign liquor bill of two hundred dollars offsetting his modesty. In the House, during his fifteen years in office, he served on such committees as the one to consider the problems of hogs running wild in the streets of Winchester. He spoke seldom, reluctantly. While such men as Patrick Henry and Jefferson were pioneering political history, Washington was silent and inactive save when, in 1769, he introduced an agreement boycotting British-taxed goods and got his neighbors to sign it. He was silent during the heated debates of the first Continental Congress at Philadelphia in 1774, and thirteen years later still held aloof at the Federal Convention to form a union. Only when he became the first president of the United States did he abandon his noncommittal stand, at last publicly favoring the aristocracy and the men of property.

This surprised none of his contemporaries. Alexander Hamilton—who had been his aide-de-camp during the war, and had gone as far as he dared toward monarchy at the Federal Convention, advocating that the Senate and the president be elected for life and that the latter appoint state governors and have veto power over state legislatures—was named Secretary of the Treasury. Hamilton clashed almost immediately with Jefferson over financial affairs, and Washington, after vainly attempting to remain neutral, sided with his brilliant protégé and the royalists.

Always he had suspected and disliked the masses. He grew up thinking "the common run" (his phrase) contemptible. When he took up his sword to lead the colonials, he was defending his fortune. Had the threat to it been withdrawn, even after the shooting began, he would have renewed his loyalty to the crown.

But, instead, the crown crossed him, ruling in April, 1775, that the title to hard-won lands he had been awarded for his fighting on the frontier was considered null and void, as were other titles he had bought from his troops. He stood to lose more than thirty thousand acres of choice sites scattered along the Ohio valley from Pittsburgh almost to Cincinnati. It was enough to make the most conservative businessman fighting mad.

He did not give up hope, however, of remaining loyal to England. Writing an English friend after the Battle of Lexington, he was careful to blame "the ministerial troops," not the king—a typical tory rationalization that left the door open for a change in Parliament and peace without separation. England, which Washington never saw, he called "home" until long after the Revolution had begun. As late as 1774 he denied hotly that his compatriots were "setting up for independency and what not . . . no such thing is desired by any thinking man in all North America."

69

Toward his inferiors his attitude was always that of any other socially conscious contemporary aristocrat—there were few!—a mixture of paternalistic tolerance darkly cloaked in resignation to one's duty and one's responsibilities, justice edged with impatience, pity, polite interest, and anger bordering on hatred. At times he could be shockingly callous. He once apologized to Governor Dinwiddie of Virginia for hanging instead of shooting soldiers guilty of capital offenses. "It conveys much more terror to others," he explained. He sent French scalps to Dinwiddie from the front, and promoted Indian scalping parties because he considered them more effective than white raiders to terrorize the enemy. The lash and the gallows were busy at his command during the Revolution. Instead of selling disobedient slaves down the river, he punished them with the hell of the West Indies, trading them off for rum and sweetmeats. There is a story that after Yorktown he took one of his black slaves into the woods and made the Negro dance to a horsewhip to celebrate the victory.

He loved fine clothes and fine living. As a bridegroom he wore a deep blue suit, its coat lined with royal red. Trimmings were silver. His vest was of embroidered white satin and he sported golden shoe and knee buckles. His quarters even at Valley Forge and during the equally bitter months the previous winter at Morristown were comfortable if not luxurious. Martha joined him at both encampments, and there were dances and good food and wine and even theater for himself and his officers.

He was vain with a vanity which he hid behind a charming meekness and the manners of an exquisite eighteenth-century gentleman, and which he fed with elaborate pageantry whenever the occasion offered.

He became one of the wealthiest men in America. This he achieved by inheritance, by marriage, by the most painstaking accounting (for years he kept a balance sheet even of his betting), by getting his ultimate dollar's worth of service from his black and white slaves, by pleading near-bankruptcy to dunning friends and relatives, including his mother, and by real-estate speculations during which he drove innocent squatters from his wilderness properties and took advantage of those among his troops who needed cash by buying their veterans' land rights for as little as two cents an acre.

He was a notoriously sharp trader. Once he told Henry Lee he wanted to buy one of Lee's horses, but Lee refused to sell on the grounds that Washington never paid what anything was worth. Washington won the hearts of his countrymen by serving throughout the Revolution without pay, but Congress gave him an expense account. His pay would have figured out to some $51,000. He turned in expenses for $64,000. Later, he offered to work as president for nothing, but some Congressmen remembered his war bargain and prudently recommended a salary of $25,000 annually.

In his view there was nothing hypocritical about this or anything else he did. He subscribed, wholeheartedly and without concealment, to the attitude of his kind, succinctly stated by John Randolph— "I am an aristocrat; I love liberty, I hate equality."

He was, in sum, publicly and personally, the nation's outstanding man of property—confident of the rightness of a God and a society endowing certain able persons like himself with wealth and talent, and equally confident that the capitalistic system is the more nearly universal force for good than any other spiritual or material. Didn't gentlemen of property write the Constitution? Wasn't the country, under their leadership, potentially the greatest monument to material welfare the world had ever seen? Didn't more people, rich and poor, stand to prosper than under any other system?

Personally, his character was typical of his class. He was fully conscious of his responsibilities as a man of property and willing to make sacrifices to meet them. He was profit loving, power loving, luxury loving. He enjoyed a lusty joke. He was bellicose and incredibly enduring and stubborn. Paternalistically benign up to a point, he could also be brutal if crossed. Above all, he was a gambler who loved his stakes high and, when forced to it, could play them with abandon.

Beyond that, at rare, heroic moments he realized an idealism that knows no class and is the treasured possession of that handful of mankind who, given the opportunity for self-aggrandizement, have rejected it in the ennobling hope that by so doing they will bring a greater good to at least some few of their fellow men.

Washington was born, according to the calendar of his day, on February 11, 1732, and, according to the time's standards, to the purple.

71

His birthplace, long since destroyed, was a four-room farmhouse at Bridges' Creek, Westmoreland County, Virginia.

His family had been landed gentry for more than a hundred years. His great-grandfather, John Washington, farmed plantations, served in Governor Berkeley's House of Burgesses and, as a colonel in the Virginia militia, was partner to the murder of six Indian envoys of peace. John had a son named Lawrence and Lawrence had a son named Augustine, born in 1694. Augustine married twice, and his second wife, Mary Ball, gave him George for their first-born.

Augustine was a sober, colorless colonial businessman. He went to school in England, sailed back and forth between England and America for a while, and took over the management of the lands inherited from his father. From him, George may have acquired his passion for figures and balance sheets, for owning land and making money. He might also have acquired his taste for liquor and fine living—Augustine died of gout before George was in his 'teens.

Where he got his love of war is questionable, since his father was too conservative for soldiering and his mother hated it. Told excitedly of her son's victories at Trenton and Princeton (victories after long months of defeat), she is said to have remarked, "This fighting and killing is a sad thing. I wish George would come home and look after his plantation!"

She applied for a pension from Virginia while he was commanding the Continental armies, to his excruciating embarrassment. She had his love for dancing and his high-octane temper. She taught him his exquisite manners and gave him his comeuppance till almost the day she died, only ten years before he did.

George's book learning consisted of reading, writing, and arithmetic taught mostly by a convict servant bought by his father. He matured to an excellent handwriting and to become an indefatigable diarist, letter writer, and accountant. To figure with the zeal of a modern businessman confronted with an after-dinner tablecloth was one of his favorite pastimes, and he wrote thousands of letters in his lifetime, including a long one daily to Congress during the war.

He was slow to learn spelling and grammar. A preposition was something which, if he possibly could, he ended a sentence up with. Schooner he spelled "chooner," news became "knews," treble was

72

"trible," adapted was two words—"a Dapted," New York he called a "matrapolis," dissuaded went down either "diswaded" or "disswaded," monstrous was "monstrious," and proper names he recorded any way his spirit moved him.

He practiced his manners in the homes of transplanted English royalty and Virginia aristocrats, rode to hounds, danced till dawn, gambled, drank, and made love.

He was in and out of love continuously until, at twenty-seven, he married twenty-eight-year-old Martha Dandridge Custis, a wealthy widow. Her holdings added to his made him the richest man in America. Tiny, plump, with hazel eyes and light-brown hair, she managed him and the estate with a calm efficiency which she recorded in spelling more original than his. He called her his "dearest Patsy" and she called him "the Old Man." To the union came children by her first marriage which he guarded as his own and mourned profoundly at death. Martha and George loved to entertain. She followed him to war so faithfully that it was said the British could estimate when the American cannon would begin and cease firing by her departures and arrivals. Theirs was a happy and peaceful match despite the turbulent love affairs which preceded his meeting her, not the least of which, with the vivacious Sally Fairfax, went on almost to the day he was married.

Physically, he grew to be as gigantic as she was petite, six feet two inches tall, broad-shouldered, lean, hard-muscled, and with a physique that stood off the deadly diseases and the brutal hardships of the times with incredible endurance. His hands were remarkably large. He had a long, straight nose, a firm, jutting chin, a tight-lipped mouth nevertheless capable of smiling charmingly, and pale blue eyes that were habitually cold, hinting broadly of their master's shrewdness.

He followed his elementary education with an intensive study of surveying, at which he was precocious—he did creditable work at fourteen—and an excellent craftsman. This led to his first business venture, surveying land to the westward at from $20 to $50 a week, high pay for the period and not bad for a seventeen-year-old in anybody's era. Before he was of age he had saved a sizable stake and owned more than fifteen hundred acres.

His first assignment was followed by one surveying half a million acres in the neighborhood of Pittsburgh for the Ohio Company, in which his family was heavily interested.

Land claimed by the Ohio Company, like most other unsettled areas in the country, was also claimed by others, in this case especially by the French and, in some parts, by Pennsylvania. Robert Dinwiddie, new governor of Virginia, moved promptly against the competition, sending word to the French by wilderness messenger to get out. The messenger failed to deliver, and the governor sought another. Washington, proudly bearing a commission as a colonial adjutant-general, found the French and delivered Dinwiddie's warning in a forty-one-day, five-hundred-mile dead-of-winter trek to what is now northwestern Pennsylvania.

He came back crying warnings of French infiltration, and was rewarded with a lieutenant-colonelcy, an army of fifty tatterdemalions on whom to practice, and the satisfaction of seeing his reports printed (misspellings and grammar unchanged) in London. The French, meantime, ran off soldiers building a British fort at Pittsburgh and built one of their own, Fort Duquesne. Washington got this news as he and his ragged army started west. The French were occupying an area in which Washington had holdings. War had linked arms with business.

His first campaign, which followed, may be taken as typical of his military career. He violated two basic contemporary rules of warfare. He was ignominiously defeated. He was branded an international villain. And when the dust cleared away, he was a hero.

His first mistake came when he and some Indian allies caught up with a party of French and surprised and killed most of them, including one de Jumonville. This led to difficulties, because it turned out that the party was under a flag of truce. Washington, technically, became an assassin, and when the French caught up with him and his little army and made him sign a capitulation, he was so characterized. He pled later that he had signed the document without knowing what the French words meant.

His second error was equally unmilitary. After his raid, he built what he called Fort Necessity at Great Meadows, near what is now Confluence, Pennsylvania. Military experts of the time are agreed

74

with those of today—he could not have chosen a more vulnerable location. One of his contemporaries, Governor Sharpe of Maryland, accurately described it as "a little useless intrenchment between two eminences." The French forced a surrender almost without firing a shot, got Washington's signature to the confession of murdering de Jumonville, publicized it in Europe to discredit the British, and thereby made the twenty-two-year-old amateur who had commanded the Americans an international figure.

Young Washington soon resigned because it was ruled that British officers outranked all colonials, including himself; but his stature remained in the Virginia public mind. The first and one of the most important facets of his personality—an uncanny ability to impress people—had shone forth and was never again to be dimmed.

His military bad luck continued the following year, when General Edward Braddock came over from England to bring order out of chaos. Washington refused a commission, but finally joined Braddock's official family as an aide-de-camp. There followed Braddock's disastrous defeat of July 9, 1755, in which Washington participated by getting out of a sickbed, where he had almost died of fever. Braddock died of wounds the following night. Two more facets of Washington's battlefield genius—blind and blinding courage and almost superhuman physical endurance—flashed through the dust and smoke of defeat. Twice his horse was shot from under him and his coat was riddled with bullets, yet his seemed the only cool head on the field. He got out of bed at four o'clock on the morning of the fight and did not again sleep for seven days. Literally, he gloried in defeat. And again he snatched fame from disaster.

He was unfailing at capitalizing on his left-handed fortune. Four years later, General Forbes, who replaced Braddock, closed in, after painstaking planning, on Fort Duquesne, largely by doing the exact opposite of what Washington advised him to do. But it was Washington who first was able to write home to the authorities that he was camping on the site of the French defenses, after they had been burned and abandoned by the enemy.

A few weeks later he retired to his plantations, not to fight again for nearly twenty years during which many of his countrymen were building up valuable military experience and enviable military records. But in 1775, on the basis of his Fort Necessity-Braddock-Forbes record, it was he who was chosen commander-in-chief of the Revolutionary army.

His record continued consistently bad, rivaled only by his military judgment. When he took command outside Boston in the summer of 1775, the British were under siege in the city. Repeatedly Washington begged his officers to attack, repeatedly they convinced him of his folly. In early spring the British ended the arguments by abandoning the city and sailing away.

Washington moved to New York. Fighting was resumed on June 30, 1776, when Sir William Howe and a flotilla of five hundred troop-filled vessels, including Hessians, moved into Manhattan harbor and encamped on Staten Island. The terrain involved in the fighting that followed may be described roughly as a ball diamond. Staten Island was home plate. Brooklyn Heights, Long Island, was first base, Westchester second, New Jersey third. Water separated everything except second base and the pitcher's box, and when Howe arrived he found Washington standing in the box—lower Manhattan.

Howe decided that he could get a better shot at Washington from first base, and moved in that direction on August 22. Washington elected to keep one foot in the pitcher's box and the other on first. He divided his forces. Worse, those he sent to Long Island failed to protect their in-shore flank. Howe went around it and would have driven the whole force into the East River if he had followed up his victory. Washington staged a masterful retreat back to Manhattan under cover of darkness and fog, but the Battle of Long Island went down in history as an overwhelming British victory.

Howe next decided to move to second base and cut off Washington's only avenue of land escape. This he did on September 15, landing at Kip's Bay (now New York's 34th Street and the East River). Washington's troops, getting wind of it, panicked, and the rage of their commander, trying to whip them in line as he rode frantically up and down in the area today bounded by the New York Public Library and Grand Central Terminal, only served to make them run the faster.

He finally rallied them to make a stand at second base in the Battle of White Plains. Again defeat. A few days later the last American foothold on Manhattan Island, Fort Washington, surrendered.

Washington's ragged and diminishing host retreated to third base, with British advance troops threatening to annihilate them every time they tried to pause for rest. The fateful year of 1776 was nearing a close and Washington's record was unblemished—four defeats, no victories.

The score was even more damaging when considered in military terms. He had played into the British hands not only in his tactics, but in his prebattle planning. American troops fought best as individuals. Washington tried to bludgeon them into fighting Continental style, marching up to the guns of the enemy in perfect formation. American defense screamed for highly mobile units—cavalry. Washington did not like cavalry. He disliked it so much, indeed, that when a unit of mounted volunteers showed up at the last minute for the Battle of Long Island, he told them they could either fight on foot or go home.

The agonizing retreat across New Jersey was marked by bloody footprints in the snow. Men deserted by tens, then by scores. Others dropped out of the line of march, unable to walk. Stragglers were picked off by victory-hungry Hessians. From Philadelphia came word that Congress was abandoning the city, bound for nobody knew where.

But if there is a tide in the affairs of men, Washington's was at full during that December of 1776. It might almost be said that everything he did before that fateful month does not matter and that what he did afterward was anticlimax. Twice within a few days he saved the nation and the war, at the same time establishing perhaps his most noble claims to greatness and his enduring signposts for the conduct of American leadership in the years that lay ahead.

Before Congress left Philadelphia, they notified him that he was in full and dictatorial control of the colonies, a king without a crown. Washington—with a modesty bolstered by his hatred of a monarchy which had so sorely treated one of its most faithful potential servants—promptly refused.

"I with truth declare," he told Congress, "that I have no lust after power, but I wish with as much fervency as any man upon this wide-extended continent for an opportunity of turning the sword into the plowshare."

Nor were his words merely words: as he had before, so now with

77

almost sedulous faithfulness he sought the advice and the approval of the panicky politicians.

His second act was more dramatic but equally revealing of another facet of the man's genius—he did not know how to admit defeat and, faced with it, was at his brilliant best. The blue chips, what few he held, were down. Bigger stakes could not be imagined. Win—and he might win a continent. Lose—disgrace, the Tower of London, the gallows.

"I think the game is pretty near up," he said. But he said also: "My neck does not feel as though it was made for a halter."

True to the finest traditions of his kind, he played with high abandon. He attacked.

The place was Trenton. Washington was across the river from the town, across the Delaware. Trenton was held by Hessians, who had a quaint folk custom, celebrating with wine, song, and revelry a day called Christmas. Washington chose dawn of the day after Christmas to attack, crossing the river above the town in the dead of a crackling cold winter night. The victory was swift, overwhelming, and dramatic. Especially was it dramatic, telling the world that the defeat-ridden colonial cause was not dead.

Retiring across the river, Washington was not satisfied. On a night early in January he struck again. The Hessians had been replaced by British. Cornwallis, at Trenton, was reassured by the high flames of Washington's campfires reflected in the river, and did not know that the Americans were attacking his rear at Princeton, ten miles away, until the cannon roared in the dawn. Cornwallis got to the battlefield too late to engage his elusive enemy, who retired to winter quarters and the bitter hardships of Morristown. Neither, of course, could realize that the tide had at last turned, however slightly —that Washington had retreated to prepare a mightier victory— that Cornwallis was pursuing defeat.

The war dragged on, slowly, with long pauses, apparently endless. Howe and the bulk of the British forces holed up in New York for the rest of the winter, and the spring, and most of the summer. Washington, his impoverished command threatening to dwindle to nothing, could only curb his impatience, encourage the stalemate, and prepare elaborate falsehoods concerning the size of his army.

Howe replied at intervals with yarns about where he would next attack. Among the British plans at the time was one to split New England from the rest of the colonies by coming down the Hudson River to New York from Canada. To this dubious and wilderness task was assigned General John Burgoyne with some eight thousand men, and in the summer of 1777 he started his expedition via Lake Champlain and the Adirondack wilds. To stop Burgoyne, Washington assigned a red-faced, egotistical former British officer whose ambition was exceeded only by his hatred of Washington—General Horatio Gates. One of Howe's most convincing rumors was that he would sail to Boston and go cross-country to combine his forces with Burgoyne. Washington prepared nervously to go north to aid Gates when Howe put to sea, but Howe sailed south and landed in early September some forty miles below Philadelphia, the colonial capital.

Washington by that time was back in his most prevailing military form. He opposed Howe first at Brandywine on September 11, then at Germantown.

At Brandywine military intelligence was worse than inadequate, and again he was flanked. He made no use of the cavalry available to him.

At Germantown, with military intelligence again weak, plans were too elaborate, cavalry again mishandled. The battle achieved a new high in American tactics when two colonial divisions attacked each other, fought desperately—and then both fled in retreat.

Howe marched on unopposed to join Cornwallis in occupying Philadelphia. Washington picked the worst winter quarters in all history and Valley Forge became a household name for hardship. Washington's personal cup reached the dregs with word from the north that the choleric Gates had cornered and captured Burgoyne in so impressive a victory that the French promptly came out publicly in support of the colonials and the American Congress appointed Gates to a military commission which, at least technically, gave him authority over his commander-in-chief. Only Washington's steadfast silence saved him from being discredited by Gates and his followers, who eventually talked themselves out of power and Washington back into complete military leadership.

Winter brought the usual stalemate. Neither Howe nor the colonials moved till the following summer, when Howe decided to return to New York and Washington caught up with him at Monmouth, late in June. Here cavalry would have meant a devastating defeat for the British, strung out over miles of road and laden with plunder and heavy uniforms under a blazing sun. As it was, the fighting ended in a draw. Howe returned to New York, Washington fumed in its environs, and the war in the north was forever ended.

Indeed, no fighting of any note occurred from June, 1778, until a year and a half later, when Howe sent Clinton by sea to the South to ravage the country. Vicious bush warfare followed, with both sides hanging or shooting prisoners almost without exception. By May of 1780, Charleston surrendered to British siege and Cornwallis was sent to take over Clinton's command.

He probably would have succeeded in subduing the entire south had not Washington, in one of his most brilliant executive acts, sent General Nathanael Greene, the Stonewall Jackson of the Revolution and said by many to have devised the attacks on Trenton and Princeton, to take over the American command.

Greene arrived without funds and discovered that he was practically without troops. From such modest beginnings he built up what the colonials had so long needed—a mobile, harrying army that could outmaneuver Cornwallis and draw him into a spot where an attack offered some promise of victory. The spot turned out to be Yorktown. The French won the victory before Cornwallis had admitted it by shutting him off from water-borne aid from New York. By mid-October, 1781, Cornwallis recognized the hopelessness of his situation and surrendered. Washington arrived in time to general the final phases and accept Cornwallis' sword.

Before the British evacuated New York, two years went by—years that Washington spent with troops at Newburgh, on the Hudson above Manhattan, and afterward described as the most boring of his life. The final treaty was signed September 3, 1783, the redcoats departed, and Washington, having ruthlessly beaten down several mutinies among his ragged, unpaid troops, retired to Mount Vernon swearing eternal loyalty to peace, plowshares, and the life of a private citizen.

Nobody took him seriously. Four years later when the federal convention met at Philadelphia to create the Constitution, Washington was elected to preside over the fifty-odd men of property who had come as delegates.

They were his kind of people—neither Tom Paine nor Patrick Henry were there, nor Thomas Jefferson—none of those who, during the war years, had voiced the thoughts of the people. The sessions were secret.

When the gentlemen had written the Constitution to their mutual satisfaction—and advantage—they turned again hopefully to their commander-in-chief. It is difficult to conceive a better or even another choice. He of all the leaders of the Revolution was known and respected by everyone, even the conservative and selfish state factions whose major interest was in protecting their own narrow needs, and who stood ready to remain aloof from the union or leave it if a provocation arose to inspire them. Even a majority of the fiery partisans of democracy recognized that their goals must wait until the goal of unity was reached, and that Washington was the best choice to lead them to it.

Reluctantly, he yielded.

The gentlemen rewarded him with a unanimous vote of the electoral college.

As Thomas Jefferson later pioneered a completely unexplored philosophical frontier of politics, now Washington applied his brilliant executive abilities in pioneering the business of the new government. Again, as always, he fought through to a national success—and a personal failure.

Militarist and aristocrat that he was, he went forward with a conviction which soon flowered into an illusion that, because he had so willed it and so ordered, his was one big happy executive family. The people, it was ordered at the same time, must follow and would do well to keep a still tongue in their heads. Must all not hang together, lest they hang separately? Unquestionably! Therefore—peace, and a pox on dissension!

But even in his executive family this could not be. For while Washington was an aristocrat with ideals and a profound yearning to get out of public office, Hamilton, his Secretary of the Treasury, was something else again; and Jefferson, the Secretary of State, was

81

a radical believer in democracy, if not a Jacobin, the contemporary word for Communist. Inevitably, peace became a more and more distant mirage as time went by.

Washington's journey from Mount Vernon to New York, a feature of which was an arch of victory at Philadelphia from which a wreath was lowered by a wire until it rested on his head, was a triumphal procession. He was inaugurated, appropriately, in the heart of Wall Street.

Immediately, and with his active approval, the men of property moved in. Hamilton fostered the redeeming of continental certificates of indebtedness at par, but left the door wide open for speculators when he blocked efforts to protect original owners of the federal paper. The speculators made millions. Hamilton implemented his idea that "those who own the country ought to govern the country" by launching the Bank of the United States, financed and controlled by big business.

Protests from Jefferson were in vain; Washington backed Hamilton's financial policies and could not understand Jefferson's opposition to them. The President begged the two to cease quarreling for his sake, and in a long declaration showing his respect for Jefferson, refused to accept his resignation. Jefferson reciprocated the respect, but continued to fight for democracy. He could get nowhere. He resigned for good in 1793.

Washington was re-elected, and the reign of dollars continued, surrounded by an ill-concealed love of monarchy on the part of his followers. Martha was called Lady Washington, her husband "His Excellency" and, by some, "His Majesty." Firm as he was against a hereditary ruler, he went along with these ideas to the point of telling Congress when he was first elected that he would prefer to be called "His Mightiness."

Washington did not consider these things monarchial in tone. "He sincerely wished the people to have as much self-government as they were competent to exercise themselves," says Jefferson. The difficulty was that he thought the common man incompetent to govern. "The only point on which he and I differed, was, that I had more confidence than he had in the natural integrity and discretion of the people, and in the safety and extent to which they might trust themselves with a control over their government."

82

Washington—and particularly Hamilton—had precious little confidence in "the common run." And as time went by, the people repaid them in kind. Hardly had his second term begun than the opposition became actively hostile. Tom Paine, in an open letter, summed it up, and if he had long since lost his widespread following among the masses, this time at least, he again voiced their thoughts:

"Monopolies of every kind," he told Washington, "marked your administration almost in the moment of its commencement. The lands obtained by the Revolution were lavished on partisans; the interest of the disbanded soldier was sold to the speculator; injustice was acted under the pretence of faith, and the chief of the army became the patron of fraud."

Washington responded by refusing to run a third time, and issued a Farewell Address, favoring more union at home, no alliances abroad.

Martha's Old Man, who had been born old, was old now, indeed. He was forty-three when he took over the command of the Continental armies at Boston, in the prime of life. With war's end, at fifty-one, he had been understandably weary. One observer estimated that he could have had hardly more than three consecutive hours of sleep in any twenty-four during the eight years of the Revolution. Followed some six years' respite, then eight in the presidency. Now, at sixty-five, he must take the long road home embittered by the ingratitude of a nation he had served so long and so faithfully.

He had not wanted to be president. Now perhaps the thought crossed his mind that he should never have agreed to run, nor to back up Hamilton's machinations, nor (God knows!) appoint Jefferson, that turncoat aristocrat with the philosophy of a fool. Another, searing thought—perhaps he had been a tool of these clever followers of his. Certainly their kind of capitalism was not brightly lighted by his high idealism. They had made a smug symbol of him to reach their own selfish ends. Perhaps, indeed, instead of making history, history had made him.

But it is more likely that he was a man who had no doubts as he made his way home, or willed what doubts there were out of mind as he had during the endless, harrowing nights when he had paced

83

the plains of Jersey, a man alone against Europe's most powerful empire. In this last period of his life he is said to have told King Louis Philippe, then an exile in America: "I have never said anything nor written anything that I cared to recall, nor ever done anything that I regretted."

The welcomes given him by the best people in the towns enroute home were reassuring, as was his Mount Vernon mansion with its richly appointed rooms, and the lawns sloping to the fields and to the wide and misty reaches of the Potomac.

If he was embittered, he spoke no word of it. Admirers came visiting. He was the Virginia gentleman, the perfect host, the gracious conversationalist. He was too old for hate, but not too old to ride his fields, tall in the saddle, poker straight, proud, aristocratic.

He came horseback to the end of the road. Soaked from a cold December rain that had turned to snow before he reached the house, flecking his gray hair with sparkling white, he came down with a cold, then pneumonia. His doctor bled him thrice. Some say that he was bled to death.

He said no prayers and, gentleman to the end, was most thoughtful of those watching over him. A flash of his old passion for numbers showed briefly near the end. His lips moved—he was holding his wrist, counting his pulse.

He summed up for his listeners as death stood closer:

"I die hard," he said, "but I am not afraid to go."

He had died hard in all truth, and he had never been afraid.

The end came late in the evening of December 14, just before the turn of a century he had helped make a landmark in man's struggle against tyranny.

It is America's greatest triumph that this opposition to tyranny so quickly reached the masses. It was George Washington's personal tragedy that it reached the masses almost literally over his dead body.

Thomas Jefferson

I have never had a feeling, politically, that did not spring from the sentiments embodied in the Declaration of Independence . . . which gave liberty not alone to the people of this country, but hope to all the world for all future time . . . which gave promise that in due time the weights would be lifted

from the shoulders of all men, and that all should have an equal chance. . . .
I would rather be assassinated on the spot than surrender it. . . . The principles of Jefferson are the definitions and axioms of a free society.

—ABRAHAM LINCOLN

Resistance to tyrants is obedience to God.

—THOMAS JEFFERSON

Seldom in history are found two men who had so much in common
as Washington and Jefferson—and were so completely different.

Both were born wealthy Virginia aristocrats, and both lost their
fathers in their youth but grew up with every advantage. Both married wealth. Each learned to love the outdoors, women, wine, and fine
living, the land, horses and horsemanship, and athletic prowess. Both
were physical giants.

They were equally slow to oppose England's tyranny, yet both
made their rebellion irrevocable when it came. Each staked his life,
his fortune, and his sacred honor on destroying monarchy in America.

They knew the high ecstasy of public acclaim, and suffered at
the close of their political careers from the dull ache of political
disapproval. Each was a poor speaker, preferring letters to oratory.
Both returned to Virginia to live out their years, sustained and
soothed by the bittersweet of delayed approbation that often comes
to the great after they have ceased the fight that gave them greatness.
In old age, each did what he had striven unsuccessfully for a tempestuous lifetime to do—occupied himself with the peace and pleas-
antries of life as a Virginia farmer gentleman.

But the likenesses are superficial, the contrasts profound. Washington was the durable business frontiersman with a lifetime interest
in big-money land operations, fighting at last to wrest control of
them from the hands of other big-money speculators in Britain. Jefferson, the frontiersman of democracy, saw the evils in these strug-
gles and dreamed of an equality rooted in the land, each man with
sufficient to make him economically independent and politically free.
Washington purchased vast stretches of real estate—for his own
profit. Jefferson made the biggest real-estate deal in history—for
democracy. And beyond these material considerations, Jefferson's
lasting greatness was founded on things of the mind and spirit; he
hated war and power and wealth, he was the first great man of the
people.

He was born eleven years after Washington, on April 13, 1743, at Shadwell, a few miles from Charlottesville, Virginia.

His father was Peter Jefferson, a giant of a man who once pulled down an old shed with one tug on a rope at which three Negroes had been hauling in vain.

Peter was self- and well-educated, with an inordinate intellectual curiosity. A surveyor, he got his lands and his slaves by the sweat of his brow and boasted so often of his lack of family tree that his son took it up, saying in later years that a coat of arms could be purchased as cheaply as any other. It was a jest that the son could make unchallenged, for the father married Jane Randolph when he was thirty-one and she nineteen, and the Randolphs were among the first first families of the Old Dominion.

Young Tom was a replica of Peter in mind and body—one of the many aspects of the Jefferson luck which, unlike Washington's, was more positive than negative. With a brilliant, curious mind, the boy had the excellent fortune to train it under the frontier liberal guidance of his sagacious parent.

The lessons, carried out by slave teachers under Peter's close supervision, were varied and thorough. Tom mastered the three R's and learned Latin, Greek, and French with almost equal ease. He was schooled in music, becoming adept at playing that most ubiquitous of frontier instruments, the fiddle. The Jefferson library was good for the times. The boy did not have to be encouraged to read exhaustively.

He learned also to train and discipline his huge body, riding with his father, canoeing, wrestling, playing frontier games.

He was imbued with the rough democracy of the frontier and, unlike Washington, loved and respected the Indians. The shadow of their dramatic and tragic history fell across his thinking even as an old man. One night the boy heard Outassete, warrior-orator of the Cherokee, speak to his tribesmen.

"I was in his camp when he made his great farewell oration to his people the evening before his departure for England," Jefferson recalled long afterward. "The moon was in full splendor, and to her he seemed to address himself in his prayers for his own safety on the voyage, and that of his people during his absence; his sounding voice, distinct articulation, animated action, and the solemn silence of his people at their several fires, filled me with awe and veneration, although I did not understand a word he uttered."

When Tom was fourteen, his father died, but the boy had already an education far beyond that of most contemporary cultured adults. His luck held. Three years later, at seventeen, he became an undergraduate at William and Mary College and the intellectual protégé of four of the most sophisticated and alert minds in all the colonies.

Most of the faculty were theologians, but Jefferson had the good fortune to attract the friendship of William Small, a Scot, a friend of Erasmus Darwin, and an unorthodox liberal; George Wythe, professor of law and, at thirty-five, one of Virginia's leading attorneys; a professor of mathematics named Smith; and—the most influential man in the colony—Francis Fauquier, its acting governor, lover of good living, scholar, opponent of colonial oppression and, to quote his young protégé, "the ablest man who ever filled that office."

Small "most happily for me, became soon attached to me, and made me his daily companion when not engaged in the school; and from his conversation I got my first views of . . . science." Wythe became his "faithful friend and beloved mentor." Smith added to his liberal viewpoint and Fauquier brought them all together with long, conversational dinners and chamber music at the governor's palace.

As an old man, Jefferson said: "At these dinners I have heard more good sense, more rational and philosophical conversations, than in all my life besides."

He matched this adult, intellectual life by arduous toil as a student. Often he was at his books fifteen hours a day.

He was equally enthusiastic about drinking, dancing, sparking, and gambling. Physically, he attracted attention wherever he went— more than six feet tall, lean of face and figure but broadshouldered, attractively homely. His neck was long and thin, his face reddish, his hair brick red, his eyes hazel under bosky brows.

For two years Jefferson was a student at William and Mary, leaving to study law under Wythe in Williamsburg. Five years later, at twenty-four, he was admitted to the bar.

He practiced for the seven following years, making a good living at it and the while acquiring for law a lifetime scorn.

"Our ancestors," he once remarked drily, "were laborers, not lawyers." He jeered at "lawyerish" verbiage. "Lawyers!" he exploded, "whose trade it is to question everything, yield nothing, and talk by the hour!"

The English law, upon which colonial legal practices were based, was a fortress of technicalities in which enemies of democracy could seek shelter. "Blackstone and Hume," he said, "have made tories of all England," and the Blackstone-Hume "sophistries . . . have done more toward the suppression of the liberties of man than all the millions" fighting with Napoleon.

As president, Jefferson added judges to his collection of legal anathemas. He brought impeachment proceedings against one Supreme Court justice and condemned "crafty" Chief Justice John Marshall for his "twistifications."

While practicing in Williamsburg, Jefferson designed and built Monticello, still a landmark near Charlottesville, and to it brought his bride, Martha Wayles Skelton, daughter of a prominent Williamsburg lawyer, whose beauty and charm were rivaled only by her inheritance which, combined with Jefferson's, made them one of the wealthiest couples in Virginia. Jefferson was twenty-eight, she twenty-one. They were deeply in love. Her death a little more than ten years later, after she had borne him their fifth child, took from him a portion of his great heart. Only by the most bitter struggle did he succeed in saving his mind.

During his decade of marital happiness he wrote the most famous of his political documents, the *Declaration of Independence*. At twenty-six, he had been elected to the House of Burgesses, where he quickly became identified with the radicals as their leading thinker and writer. He gained this reputation largely for *A Summary View of the Rights of British America*, written when he was thirty-one for the rebel congress of the House of Burgesses that met in the summer of 1774 to protest the closing of Boston Harbor after the Tea Party.

On second thought, Jefferson regarded the *Summary* as "too bold"—"Prudence," he noted, "requires to keep front and rear together." A year later, he also lamented with Washington that unfortunate "accident," the Battle of Lexington. "I would rather be in dependence on Great Britain, properly limited," Jefferson said at the time of the second Continental Congress in May, 1775, "than on any nation on earth, or than on no nation."

But toward the end of 1775 he was ready to fight. ". . . by the God that made me," he wrote to a friend, "I will cease to exist before I yield to a connection on such terms as the British . . . propose. . . . We must drub him [General Howe] soundly, before the sceptered tyrant will know we are no more brutes, to crouch under his hand, and kiss the rod with which he designs to scourge us."

In the following summer, at thirty-three, he wrote his best-known masterpiece. Edited by members of the committee assigned by the Continental Congress to work with him, including Benjamin Franklin and John Adams, the *Declaration* is nevertheless Jefferson's in both wording and spirit. He composed it between June 11 and June 28, 1776, at an improvised desk in the second-floor parlor of a German bricklayer's house between Seventh and Eighth streets in Market Street, Philadelphia. It is radiant with his vigorous, flowing style, and into it he wove the basic love of human liberty as opposed to love of property which was to be the cornerstone of the political philosophy that he developed, one phase at a time, in the years that followed.

As Tom Paine had done in his *Common Sense*, Jefferson went boldly beyond the hesitant and propertied thoughts of his contemporaries and composed a document which for all time voiced the slow but unyielding judgment of the common man and a monumental warning to anyone daring to oppose that judgment. Saul K. Padover has appropriately arranged Jefferson's version in blank verse in his *Jefferson*. Delete from it the eighteenth-century issues between the colonials and the king, and you have man's greatest paean to his rights to freedom:

"When in the course of human events
it becomes necessary for one people
to dissolve the political bonds
which have connected them with another,
and to assume
among the powers of the earth
the separate and equal station
to which the laws of nature

and of nature's God
entitle them,
a decent respect to the opinions of mankind requires
that they should declare the causes
which impel them to the separation.

"We hold these truths
to be self-evident,
that all men are created equal,
that they are endowed by their Creator
with inherent and unalienable rights,
that among these
are life, liberty, and the pursuit of happiness;
that to secure these rights
governments are instituted among men,
deriving their just powers
from the consent of the governed;
that when any form of government
becomes destructive of these ends
it is the right of the people
to alter or abolish it
and to institute new government,
laying its foundations on such principles
and organizing its powers in such form
as to them shall seem most likely to effect
their safety and happiness. . . .

"We therefore . . .
utterly dissolve
all political connection . . .
between us
and the people or parliament
of Great Britain;
and finally we do assert and declare
these colonies to be free
and independent states. . . .

"And for the support
of this declaration
we mutually pledge to each other

> our lives,
> our fortunes,
> and our sacred honor."

The Declaration, keynoting the feelings of war-tempered rebels, was addressed to one of the mightiest monarchs on earth. It made the youthful Jefferson an international figure. But it typified neither its author nor his method of spreading the gospel of democracy. A philosopher, he hated war and the violent verbiage promoting war and equally disliked dramatics. Reason he preferred to ranting; peace, to the sword. As his ideas on democracy matured, it became his habit to disseminate them quietly, most often in personal letters or by word of mouth.

Perhaps one reason for this is that his most vivid thoughts on government are so succinct and so few. His philosophy is simplicity itself: The mass of humanity is naturally good, and therefore its own best ruler. Anyone who interferes with this rule—by suppressing freedom of expression or religion, education, or economic equality —is potentially, if not actually, a tyrant. His lot should be eternal hostility. The more rule by the many—the more democracy—the better.

Using Jefferson's own words, the essence of what he said in his letters and other papers is one of the best credos on democracy ever devised:

"Man's sense of right and wrong is as much a part of his nature as the sense of hearing, seeing, feeling; it is the true foundation of morality.

"Nothing is unchangeable but the inherent and inalienable rights of man. The God who gave us life gave us liberty at the same time. Every man, and every body of men on earth, possess the right of self government. They receive it with their being from the hand of nature. Individuals exercise it by their single will; collections of men by that of their majority; for the law of the majority is the natural law of every society of men.

"There is a natural aristocracy among men. The grounds of this are virtue and talent. An aristocracy of wealth is of more harm and danger than benefit to society. No race of kings has ever presented above one man of common sense in twenty generations. Every generous, nay, every just sentiment is absorbed in the thirst for gold; nor have I observed men's honesty to increase with riches. But the natural aristocracy among men I consider as the most precious gift of nature for the instruction, the trusts, and government of society."

"I have sworn upon the altar of God eternal hostility against every form of tyranny over the mind of man.

"I would rather be exposed to the inconvenience attending too much liberty, than those attending too small a degree of it. It behooves every man who values liberty of conscience for himself to resist invasion of it in the case of others. I never will, by any word or act, bow to the shrine of intolerance. Our particular principles of religion are a subject of accountability to our God alone. I inquire after no man's and trouble none with mine.

"Of all the avenues of truth, the most effectual is the freedom of the press. Our liberty depends on the freedom of the press, and that cannot be limited without being lost. To the press alone, chequered as it is with abuses, the world is indebted for all the triumphs which have been gained by reason and humanity over error and oppression. The press is the only tocsin of a nation. Where the press is free, and every man able to read, all is safe.

"No one more sincerely wishes the spread of information among mankind than I do, and none has greater confidence in its effects toward supporting free and good government. In extending to the great mass of mankind the blessings of instruction, I see a prospect of great advancement in the happiness of the human race.

"Whenever people are well-informed, they can be trusted with their own government; whenever things go so far wrong as to attract their notice, they may be relied on to set them to rights. No national crime passes unpunished in the long run.

"Reason and free inquiry are the only effectual agents against error."

"I have great confidence in the common sense of mankind in general—the will of the people is the only legitimate foundation of any government.

"I am not a friend to a very energetic government. It is always oppressive. Every government degenerates when trusted to the rulers alone. The people themselves are its only safe depositories. No government can continue good but under the control of the people. The way to have good and safe government is not to trust it all to one, but to divide it among the many.

. "Believing that a representative government, responsible at short periods of election, is that which produces the greatest sum of happiness to mankind, I feel it a duty to do no act which shall essentially impair that principle.

"My most earnest wish is to see popular control pushed to the maximum of its practicable exercise."

So much for the essence of Jefferson's philosophy, which he confirmed with first-hand observations and at times with bitter comments:

Monarchs were morons: he saw them and the results of their regimes when he was in France from 1784 to 1789. "Of twenty million people supposed to be in France," he reported, "I am of opinion there are nineteen million more wretched, more accursed in every circumstance of human existence than the most conspicuously wretched individual of the whole United States. . . . Every man here (in France) must be either the hammer or the anvil."

The ruling class was immoral and unworthy of rule. "Conjugal love having no existence among them, domestic happiness, of which that is the basis, is utterly unknown. In lieu of this are substituted pursuits which nourish and invigorate all . . . bad passions."

Summarizing contemporary royalty, he said:

". . . take any race of animals, confine them in idleness and inaction, whether in a stye, a stable or a stateroom, pamper them with high diet, gratify all their sexual appetites, immerse them in sensualities, nourish their passions, let everything bend before them, and banish whatever might lead them to think, and in a few generations they become all body and no mind. . . . Such is the regimen in raising kings, and in this way they have gone on for centuries.

"While in Europe, I often amused myself with contemplating the characters of the then reigning sovereigns. . . . Louis XVI was a fool, of my own knowledge. . . . The King of Spain (Charles IV) was a fool, and of Naples (Ferdinand IV) the same. They passed their lives in hunting, and dispatched two couriers a week, one thousand miles, to let each other know what game they had killed the preceding days. The king of Sardinia (Victor Amadeus III) was a fool. All these were Bourbons. The queen of Portugal (the mad Maria), a Braganza, was an idiot by nature. And so was the king of Denmark (Christian VII). Their sons, as regents, exercised the powers of government. The King of Prussia (Frederick William II), successor to the great Frederick, was a mere hog in body as well as in mind. Gustavus (III) of Sweden, and Joseph (II) of Austria, were really crazy, and George (III) of England . . . was in a straight waist-coat. . . . These animals had become without mind and powerless; and so will every hereditary monarch after a few generations. . . . And so endeth the book of kings, from all of whom the Lord deliver us."

The moral for Americans was obvious:

"Send [the American pro-monarchists] to Europe to see something of the trappings of monarchy, and I will undertake that every man shall go back thoroughly cured." Democracy's evils "from this day to the day of judgment" could not match those in France in a week or those in England in a month.

Believing that small landowners could become the backbone of an independent and enlightened electorate, he regarded the "mobs of great cities" like London and Paris as adding "just so much to the support of pure government as sores do to the strength of the human body."

Jefferson saw clearly the unholy alliance between the men of property and the men of piety. Himself a profound Christian, he could not tolerate the church's intolerance. "Of all the systems of morality, ancient or modern, which have come under my observation," he said, "none appear to me so pure as that of Jesus." Again: "Had the doctrines of Jesus been preached always as pure as they came from his lips, the whole civilized world would now have been Christian."

But the theologians devised creeds and these had become "the bane and ruin of the Christian church" and "made of Christendom a slaughter-house." "The sum of all religion as expressed by its best preacher, 'Fear God and love thy neighbor,' contains no mystery, needs no explanation," he noted, adding cynically: "But this won't do. It gives no scope to make dupes; priests could not live by it." They "have so disfigured the simple religion of Jesus that no one who reads the sophistications they have engrafted on it . . . would

94

conceive these could have been fathered on the sublime preacher of the sermon on the mount." Priests are enemies of freedom. "In every country and in every age, the priest has been hostile to liberty. He is always in alliance with the despot, abetting his abuses in return for protection of his own." "My opinion," he states elsewhere, "is that there would never have been an infidel, if there had never been a priest."

His conclusion: "I am for freedom of religion, and against all maneuvers to bring about a legal ascendency of one sect over another. It does me no injury for my neighbor to say there are twenty gods, or no god. It neither picks my pocket nor breaks my leg."

As the war got under way, Jefferson faced one of the crises of his life. It had been well enough for him to put some of his ideas on paper in the Declaration. What he wrote had been helpful in rallying the mass of the people against the king. But to attempt permanently to establish his ideals in the American body politic while there was a war on—it was preposterous!

The people, as Hamilton was later to point out, was a great beast. To champion them ill became a gentleman, much less a Virginia aristocrat. Had Jefferson not done enough already, helping in a few brief months to gain more for the cause of liberty than in all the period since the beginning of time? Was he not established as one of the great liberals of a new nation, if not the world? It was all right to be a philosopher—need he ruin himself by becoming a fool? He wanted to retire to his wife and his growing brood of daughters—then why didn't he? Didn't he know when to leave well enough alone?

These and scores of other arguments must have been hurled at him during the summer after he wrote the Declaration, but to no avail. If he wavered inwardly, there is no record of it. There is ample record that he believed a true follower of democracy must put his words into action. Jefferson attempted to do this almost immediately in Virginia, perhaps the most impregnable fortress of vested interests in the new world.

He proposed three drastic changes—laws breaking up the baronial estates of the colony, free public education, and divorce of the church from government. He could hardly have attracted more powerful and bitter opposition if he had asked that the landed gentry of Virginia turn over their holdings to their Negro slaves. Yet the spirit of the times was such that within three years he had won enough of a following to have himself elected governor and win approval of his most cherished legislation, the Bill for Establishing Religious Freedom.

But the times were also warlike, and the philosopher was nothing if not a man of peace. With Virginia the British target for 1780, and Indians encouraged by the enemy to attack from the Blue Ridge, the new governor tacitly approved drastic cuts in war appropriations. By December, a British fleet had driven him from the state's new capital at Richmond and pillaged it, and the following spring the governor and his legislators had to flee to Charlottesville and beyond. Jefferson narrowly escaped capture at Monticello. In June, with his term coming to a close and despite his gains in democratic reforms, he was under investigation for mishandling the war. Vindicated, he returned the following fall as a legislator from his home county, Albemarle, but soon let it be known that the misgivings of the philosopher had overcome the urges of the man of action.

At thirty-eight, he was through—forever—with public life. At thirty-nine—the following spring—his beloved Martha died. Despair over the ingratitude of man combined with his grief to drive him to the edge of madness.

His incredible luck saved him. In 1784, more to get away from the scenes of his bereavement than to serve his country, he accepted an appointment to help Benjamin Franklin and John Adams negotiate commercial treaties in Paris.

Paris was, as is its genius, brilliantly sophisticated, decadent, progressive, liberal, scientific, and profound, all at one and the same time, and with gaiety. Jefferson found surcease for his sorrow, stimulation for mind and palate, sparkling conversations and sparkling wines and burgeoning bookstalls and Ben Franklin and Lafayette, phosphorous matches and talk of a day when men would fly, admiring thinkers who could philosophize with him around the clock, and women who would flirt or make love. Paris, the perennial temptress, tossed her head at Tom Jefferson, and he was hers.

When the aged and beloved Franklin left for home in 1785, Jefferson took the town by storm with his explanation, "No one can replace him, sir; I am only his successor." He came alive, visiting England, touring southern France and northern Italy and, later, Holland. He took notes on agriculture, bought, stole, or smuggled seeds, sketched architecture and machinery. He fell in and out of love with one Maria Cecilia Cosway, a miniature painter, and already encumbered with a spouse. Ideas struck him and he let them develop with boyish delight. In southern France, tired of bouncing in his carriage, he took off its wheels, mounted it on a barge, and made a leisurely canal trip northward, writing and enjoying the scenery enroute. He discovered central heating in Coblenz, Dutch bridges made of discarded scows, and new wines everywhere.

Alive with him came his philosophy of government. Everywhere he turned, the evils of monarchy assailed his eyes. "The best schools for republicanism," he wrote, "are London, Versailles, Madrid, Vienna, Berlin. . . ." "My God!" he exclaimed, "how little do my countrymen know what precious blessings they are in possession of, and which no other people on earth enjoy. I confess I had no idea of it myself."

As the idea was driven home to him, from overseas came, principally through his faithful lieutenant James Madison, news of the framing of the Constitution. No bill of rights had been included. There were loopholes through which it appeared that the tories could gain a lasting hold upon the government. These faults Jefferson helped combat by mail, but he longed at times to resume the fight in person.

French liberals came to him for advice in launching their own revolution. As a diplomat, he parried them; as an American, his heart turned homeward. "Europe would be a prison to me were it ten times as big," he said in the early summer of 1789.

Washington had just become President. One of his first acts was to invite Jefferson for a visit. The fiction was that Jefferson would stay only long enough to make a report, then return to France, although Washington had already marked him for Secretary of State. Jefferson added his own time-honored fiction—his one wish was to retire.

He arrived in New York to take over his new office in March, 1790.

97

It was low tide for democracy. Government and society alike openly favored a trend toward monarchy, patterned upon Britain's. When Jefferson spoke favorably of the coming revolution in France, he was regarded with horror.

"The courtesies of dinner parties given me as a stranger newly arrived among them," he wrote, "placed me at once in their familiar society. But I cannot describe the wonder and mortification with which the table conversations filled me. Politics were the chief topic and a preference of kingly over republican government was evidently the favorite sentiment." He found himself "for the most part the only advocate" of democracy.

John Adams, the Vice President, and Hamilton, the Secretary of the Treasury, led the monarchists. Hamilton particularly became more outspoken as he became more successful. "Take mankind in general," he said—"they are vicious." Society he divided "into the few and the many. The first are rich and wellborn; the other the mass of the people." The people "seldom judge . . . right. Give, therefore, to the first class a distinct, permanent share in the government."

In his early thirties, brilliant, charming when he wanted to be, opportunistic, a protégé of the great Washington, eager to identify himself with the rich and wellborn because his beginnings had been neither, Hamilton thought Julius Caesar the greatest man in all history, and England's the greatest government.

Adams added to the Hamiltonian chorus: "Democracy never has been and never can be so desirable as aristocracy or monarchy. . . . It soon wastes, exhausts and murders itself."

Hamilton was an expert propagandist before the word had its modern meaning. As his star rose, so also rose his *Gazette of the United States,* a newspaper published in Philadelphia by John Fenno. It prefixed the name of the President and other high government officials with "His Excellency." "Take away thrones and crowns from among men," it stated, "and there will soon be an end of all dominion and justice." Hamilton, in the *Gazette,* became "the highest jewel in Columbia's crown."

He took Jefferson in his stride. When Jefferson objected to one of Hamilton's financial schemes, Hamilton won him over by supporting Jefferson and the southerners in locating the permanent capital at Washington, D. C. In cabinet meetings, suavely appear-

98

ing to bow to Washington's plea that there be no quarreling, he badgered Jefferson with antidemocratic aphorisms. He used his genius for finances to make Jefferson appear stupid and inadequate.

Having routed his opponent in finance, Hamilton attacked in politics and diplomacy. Again he won. Washington ran again in 1792. In those days, the candidate getting the second largest number of electoral votes became Vice President regardless of party. The contest for the vice presidency was left open to Hamilton-Jefferson candidates. The campaign was bitter, and the doughty and sagacious John Adams was re-elected. Hamilton moved boldly on Jefferson's citadel, the State Department.

Until the murderous reports of the French Revolution reached America, Jefferson's position had been unassailable. He had organized his department thoroughly and with far-sighted wisdom. But the revolution widened the breach between the monarchists and the advocates of democracy. The monarchists sided with the beleaguered royalists of France and made capital of their wholesale executions. Jefferson and his followers believed the revolution more than justified. Public opinion wavered as one report of killings followed another, but Jefferson was steadfast.

"In the struggle which was necessary, many guilty persons fell without the forms of trial, and with them some innocent," he admitted. "These I deplore as much as anybody, and shall deplore some of them (many a friend of his Parisian days had fallen) to the day of my death. But I deplore them as I should have done had they fallen in battle. . . . The liberty of the whole earth was depending on the issue of the contest, and was ever such a prize won with so little innocent blood? . . . Rather than it should have failed I would have seen half the earth desolated."

A social outcast by this time—few invited him to dinner as the tensions grew—politically he could have made his position tenable but for the arrival of Edmond Charles Genet in the spring of 1793— "Citizen" Genet, minister of the new French republic. Brilliant, liberal, outspoken, and colorful, Genet was totally lacking in the things Jefferson most needed in a French representative at the time. Genet was a revolutionary, not a diplomat, and he did not care who knew it.

Neither, triumphantly, did Hamilton. Every time Genet opened his mouth—and it was too often—he embarrassed Jefferson. Hamilton publicly mourned the guillotined Louis XVI. The cabinet finally requested that Genet be recalled. Shortly afterward, Jefferson insisted on resigning.

But the Hamiltons and the Adamses were not without their battle-scars and certain misgivings. Toward Hamilton, in the tempestuous months of attacks and counterattacks, Jefferson had taken an attitude of unperturbed silence. Into this silence, in the summer of 1791, was introduced a pro-democratic newspaper, the *National Gazette*. Its editor was Philip Morin Freneau, a poet and an employee of the State Department. Had the *Gazette* become solemnly anti-Hamilton, anti-Adams, anti-monarchist, its victims might not have been roused to public ire. But Freneau chose ridicule as his weapon, advising the monarchists, among other things, to get rid of the Constitution, confer ranks and titles, "follow the English model, harp upon the dangers of mob rule, interest legislators in speculation and speculators in legislation, secure a rich manufacturing class by making laws in its interest."

It was too true to be good and Hamilton finally exploded, blaming the newspaper on Jefferson. The attack was so direct that even Washington winced.

Jefferson continued silent, and resigned.

Hamilton was left in impotent fury, for he and Adams were the first to realize that the thinker, the philosopher, the dreamer of democratic dreams, had become a watchful, shrewd master of politics and was playing on time's side. They realized with equal qualms that politicians of fifty, in the vigor of excellent health, are hardly likely to retire permanently, even to so charming a retreat as Monticello.

Jefferson convincingly concentrated on farming—he needed the income and such then advanced ideas as contour plowing and rotation of crops appealed to his scientific mind. His silence continued.

But that silence was ominous and it was not encouraged by Jeffersonian lieutenants such as young Madison and James Monroe. Letters passed between them. Jefferson also kept in too-casual touch with other political leaders of his viewpoint. A year passed and, among other things, Hamilton and his followers signed a treaty with England guaranteeing American neutrality in Britain's war with France, at the same time allowing the British navy to search American ships and take off any sailors alleged to be Englishmen. Another year—and Hamilton vigorously defended the treaty.

Publicly Jefferson said and did nothing, but privately he master-minded a devastating attack on the pro-British foreign policy. Hamilton and Adams began to feel as if they were opposing a ghost. Then, abruptly, Jefferson came into the open, accepting from his followers the nomination for the presidency.

His opponent was John Adams. The electoral votes gave Adams 71, Jefferson 68. Three votes had lost him the presidency, but time was still on his side. He studied the returns carefully. He had carried the solid South, and the voting had been razor close in Pennsylvania. Still officially wordless, Jefferson ended the campaign with a note of triumph to Madison:

"Let us cultivate Pennsylvania and we need not fear the universe."

John Adams must have realized the threat to himself and his party. He had hardly taken his oath of office before he asked Jefferson, his Vice President, to go to France. Jefferson refused. Madison? Madison, Jefferson suggested solemnly, would refuse, also. The interview was formal, and the men parted politely. They never spoke to each other again while Adams was in office.

Jefferson continued to reap political riches with silence. Emboldened by their victory and scared half out of their wits by the successes of the French Revolution, the monarchists set out to squelch all opposition in America through the Alien and Sedition Acts of 1798, virtually making it a crime to criticize the Adams administration. Jefferson's followers wanted to fight the acts from the beginning, but he overruled them, judging that, if the acts became law, they would lead to abuses of civilian liberties that would backfire, blowing Adams into the discard. The courts did an even better job of persecution than Jefferson had hoped, and the turning tide brought with it a huge wave of resentment.

It was dwarfed only by the higher waves of calumny flung at Jefferson in the campaign of 1800 against Adams. For the first time the dubious art of smear appeared, and Jefferson was the target. Opposition papers started and then tried to keep alive a rumor that he was dead. He was an atheist, "the author of the first attack on Christianity in this country," a coward and a libertine. He had gained his wealth by robbing widows and orphans. Negroes served him for mistresses, and he had sired scores of bastard, half-black offspring. His election would be followed by a dictatorship and wholesale rape, for his followers were "apostles of the race-track and the cock-pit."

By this time, silence had become a mantle, and he wore it with a grace that was its own answer to the libels and slanders hurled at him. Politically, his organization of the campaign—always from behind the scenes and with suggestions rather than orders—was a masterpiece. He won over Adams by 73 to 65 electoral votes.

There followed a period of uncertainty while the pro-Adams retiring Congress considered throwing the election to Jefferson's vice-presidential running mate, Aaron Burr, who had also received 73 votes. Even Hamilton refused to take part in such obvious sabotage. Adams, in turn, refused to attend his enemy's inaugural.

The philosopher had become a leader of men, and for the first time in world history democracy had one of its own at the helm of a nation.

Never has a man pioneered so uncharted a frontier, so fraught with dangers, against such odds.

It is as if this theorist, this man of peace, had suddenly been thrust upon a midnight battlefield to face an army of marksmen frenzied beyond fear.

The night is dark, and the field obscured in shadows. High overhead extend formless shadows, turbulent shadows within shadows.

None has ever experienced what Jefferson experienced; no man in all history can be used as a guide or an example. He knew, and his enemies knew, that the cause of liberty had flamed in France and led to wholesale murders and mob rule and the futility of dictatorship under Napoleon. He was aware that his foes longed for the power-welded security that was the cherished possession—never mind by what injustices—of the British ruling and moneyed class. He was a philosopher and wealthy—he understood these fears and longings.

But he knew also that he was not fighting contemporary foes alone. If he could make luminous the flaming liberty which burned in his soul, its light would reach, a beacon of brightness for all men to see, far down the corridors of time.

Unwavering, against incredible difficulties, Jefferson fought on for eight years, the embodiment of democracy.

Each year the flame grew brighter.

With genius' infinite attention to detail, he seldom did anything, publicly or privately, that was undemocratic. In bold contrast to Adams, who had ridden to his inauguration in a coach and six, Jefferson walked. His speech offered friendship to the defeated who had excoriated him so viciously, democracy to all. Returning to his boarding house, he dined without taking a place of honor. "I am decidedly against" presidential pomp and splendor, he declared. It creates a "distance" between citizen and president "which does not tend to aid the morals of either. I think it a practice which we ought to destroy and must destroy and, therefore, must not adopt as a general thing even for a short time."

Adams and Washington had conducted pompous weekly receptions; Jefferson let it be known that he would hold none. Feminine Washington society came to the White House in force to protest. They were told that the President had gone riding. Formal state dinners were abolished. He entertained privately, the table was round so that nobody headed it, and seating was "pell-mell"—everybody for himself—despite a bitter regal protest from the English ambassador. "We have told him that the principle of society as well as of government, with us, is the equality of the individuals composing it," Jefferson explained. "We might as well attempt to force our principles of equality at St. James'," he added, "as he his principle of precedent here."

He often received important guests in bedroom slippers and old clothes, carelessly draped. Privately and in public he welcomed Tom Paine, a rival in sartorial imperfections and democratic idealism.

Not once did he assume the role of the crusader, the preacher, the perfectionist who demands that all conform to his ideas of perfection. A philosopher, he believed that democracy should make haste slowly.

"I am sensible," he said, "how far I should fall short of effecting all the reformation which reason would suggest, and experience approve, were I free to do whatever I thought best; but when we reflect how difficult it is to move . . . the great machine of society, how impossible to advance the notions of a whole people suddenly to ideal right, we see the wisdom of Solon's remark, that no more good must be attempted than the nation can bear."

His cabinet meetings were open forums, and cabinet members were free to call on him without appointment whenever they desired. "I have no pleasure in the exercise of power," he said. The mind of a free man must be kept free from prejudice; a free people must not be frozen in any governmental strait jacket. Change was the essence of progress. "Political dissension is . . . a less evil than the lethargy of despotism." Even violence should not be a barrier to progress. ". . . a little rebellion, now and then, is a good thing, and as necessary in the political world as storms in the physical. . . . It is medicine necessary for the sound health of government. God forbid we should ever be twenty years without such a rebellion."

He knew that the world looked on. America was acting not for itself alone "but for the whole human race. The event of our experiment is to shew whether man can be trusted with self-government. The eyes of suffering humanity are fixed on us with anxiety as their only hope."

Since his main objective was to establish democracy on a firm foundation, his policy was isolation from the then distant monarchies and their intrigues. He saw, with a prophetic clarity, the evils of power politics and international politicians. "I have ever considered diplomacy as the pest of the peace of the world," he said, "as the workshop in which nearly all the wars of Europe are manufactured."

But his own sense of timing, his profound knowledge of diplomacy and power politics, led him to the greatest achievement of his administration. In 1803, by bluffing Napoleon and playing to the cupidity of Napoleon's advisers, Jefferson engineered the purchase of Louisiana Territory—from the Mississippi to the Rockies and from the Dakotas to Texas and the Mexican border—for some fifteen million dollars.

Domestically, he busied himself with righting the wrongs of the Adams administration and reducing the debts incurred by Hamilton to a minimum. When the monarchists took refuge behind Chief Justice John Marshall and his ultraconservative Supreme Court, which set out to tear to ribbons Jefferson's democratic ideals, the President did not hesitate. He attacked, demanding the impeachment of Justice Samuel Chase. Chase had distinguished himself by enforcing the Alien and Sedition Acts to the hilt. Once he had ordered names removed from the jury panel of "any of those creatures or persons called democrats." The impeachment failed—Jefferson characterized the trial a "farce"—but henceforth the court was more circumspect in its opposition.

The Chase trial was the only instance during his presidency when he fought back at his enemies. No matter how bitterly and unfairly the press attacked, he never protested. Indeed, he took a certain pride in their blasts at the president of the United States. It proved the freedom of the democracy's press. "I have lent myself willingly as the subject of a great experiment," he remarked after he retired, "which was to prove that an administration, conducting itself with integrity and common understanding, cannot be battered down, even by the falsehoods of a licentious press. . . . This experiment was wanting for the world to demonstrate the falsehood of the pretext that freedom of the press is incompatible with orderly government." To Baron Alexander von Humboldt, when the Baron said indignantly that a newspaper he saw in the White House libeling Jefferson should be suppressed, the President replied proudly: "Put that paper in your pocket, and should you hear the freedom of our press questioned, show it and tell where you found it."

Toward the end of his second administration, troubles crowded in from Europe. American shipping was caught in the cross fire between England and Napoleon. Jefferson felt peace the priceless need of his young democracy and tried to embargo trade with both combatants. Commerce suffered, and all business felt the economic blow.

The monarchists had at last a criticism of Jefferson that found popular support. Like Washington, he left the White House under a cloud of public disfavor, although one of his last acts was to repeal the embargo laws. But even these had failed to dim the brightness of his benign administration, to this day a beacon on the nation's long road toward democracy.

Also like Washington, Jefferson found the road home lined with admirers, and for almost a score of years he enjoyed the realization of his lifetime dream—farming at Monticello.

The twilight time was replete with happiness. Martha Jefferson Randolph, his only surviving daughter and his favorite, helped manage the estates. He was the idol of her many children. Visitors came in great numbers, eventually driving him nearly to bankruptcy.

Word of this got out, and before he died he received more than enough from Americans in all walks of life to pay his debts.

He was not idle. He supervised his farms personally, riding even after he was unable to pull himself up in the stirrup. In 1817, aged seventy-four, he began one more campaign—to build a university after his own scientific and democratic ideals. Unsuspecting, the state legislature voted him $15,000. Before the old politico had finished with them he had run up a total of some three hundred thousand dollars. He designed the campus of the University of Virginia himself and lived to see it opened. He considered it, the Declaration, and the Virginia statute for religious freedom the three great achievements of his life.

Life was generous. From out of the past came a visitor, a friend, a fellow-campaigner—Lafayette—and the two old men half staggered, half ran across the lawn at Monticello to fall into each other's arms.

John Adams, a foe of other years and still at heart the doughty royalist, wrote seeking peace and friendship. The two corresponded for years, Jefferson, the perennial optimist, never abandoning the hope that even John Adams could be converted to democracy.

Perhaps the hope was realized. Both died on the same day, the Fourth of July, 1826, Jefferson fighting to live to see it. He was the first to go, dead when his ancient New England friend, unknowing, whispered softly:

"Thomas Jefferson still survives."

No follower of democracy has ever to this day denied the truth of these, John Adams' last words.

Priddy Meeks

All the past we leave behind,
We debouch upon a newer mightier world, better world,
Fresh and strong the world we seize, world of labor and the march,
    Pioneers! O pioneers!

We detachments steady throwing,
Down the edges, through the passes, up the mountains steep,
Conquering, holding, daring, venturing as we go the unknown ways,
    Pioneers! O pioneers!

—WALT WHITMAN

The Aquarius (Plateau of Utah) should be described in blank verse and illustrated upon canvas. The explorer who sits upon the brink of its parapet looking off into the southern and eastern haze, who skirts its lava-cap or clambers up and down its vast ravines, who builds his camp-fire by the borders of its snow-fed lakes or stretches himself beneath its giant pines and spruces, forgets that he is a geologist and feels himself a poet. From numberless lofty standpoints we have seen it afar off, its long, straight crest-line stretched across the sky like the threshold of another world. We have drawn nearer and nearer to it, and seen its mellow blue change day by day to dark sombre gray, and its dull, expressionless ramparts grow upward into walls of majestic proportions and sublime import. The formless undulations of its slopes have changed to gigantic spurs sweeping slowly down into the painted desert and parted by impenetrable ravines. The mottling of light and shadow upon its middle zones is resolved into groves of Pinus ponderosa, and the dark hues at the summit into myriads of spikes, which we know are the storm-loving spruces. . . .

The traveler who has abundant strength and perseverance will be amply rewarded, provided he has chosen his way with prudence and good judgment. . . .

None of the cliffs are lofty, but the grandeur of the spectacle consists in the great number of cliffs rising successively one above and beyond another, like a stairway for the Titans, leading up to a mighty Temple. . . .

—Captain C. E. Dutton

Priddy Meeks, like his father before him, "being inclined to new countries," was a mover, a pioneer.

Like most movers, he hated people who got under foot or pushed him around, but he did not dislike royalty under another name if he chose the king, nor was he angered at seeing other people pushed around if he or his did the pushing.

Had you asked Priddy what kind of national government he preferred, he would have replied that he preferred no government at all—like most pioneers, and despite he joined an organized group, personally Priddy was pretty much a rebel, a rugged individualist—personally he was pretty much a law unto himself.

Priddy's idea of the best way to do anything was his way. What he thought was right was right, and what he thought was wrong was wrong. Anybody disagreeing with him was not only an idiot but a sinner against God. . . .

Of all the Americans who did not believe in doing things by halves, the pioneers took the prize, and Priddy was no exception. He was a mover from cradle to grave, and neither the perils and tribulations and poverty of life nor even old age deterred him.

"My father, Athe Meeks," he said, "being inclined to new countries, left South Carolina and moved to Kentucky. . . . He lived there twelve years, then moved to Indiana, four years after the country was surveyed by the Government." Athe didn't like people under foot: "He passed the inhabitants ten miles before he located" in the Lincoln country "at the mouth of Lake Drain, where it emptied into Little Pigeon Creek."

In April, 1812, when Priddy was sixteen, "three Indians early in the morning crept up behind a fodder stack ten or twelve yards in front of the door, and when my brother Athe got out of bed and passed out of the house and turned the corner with his back toward them, they all fired at him. One ball passed through his kneecap, another ball passed through his arm. . . . Meanwhile, father jumped out of bed, ran to the door to see what was up, and met an Indian . . . who shot him right through the heart. He turned on his heels and tried to say something and fell dead under the bedstead."

Athe, after eluding the Indians, one of whom "seemed like he was practicing" with a tomahawk and Athe the target, came to the house and told his mother and two sisters, Priddy being already in town, to flee to the settlement. "I will kill one Indian before they kill me," he said. "I shall have to die anyway."

"If you die," his mother replied, "I'll die with you. I will not leave you."

They started toward town, Athe repeatedly begging them to leave him to die. They came to two of their horses in a field.

Far from making Athe comfortable before he died, "mother said 'go,' and Athe hobbled along till he got his hands on them, and they never moved out of their tracks." Bridles were made of hickory bark, Athe mounted one horse, the youngest girl the other. All the women carried guns. They "reached the settlement in due time . . . but not without Athe's wanting to . . . lay down and die." His mother was obdurate, and the future bore out her stout stand. Athe "got over his wounds and made a very active man without show of any impediment whatever." Before the three Indians got out of the neighborhood, they were tracked down and killed by settlers.

It never occurred to Priddy and his folks to move back to civilization after this tragedy, no more than it occurred to the thousands of others who met similar tragedy in the wilderness. The Meekses instead went on to the French Island settlement on the Ohio and from there, at twenty, Priddy married and set out on his own. He became a mover by profession, farming and doctoring on the side; when he wasn't working at moving, he traveled for fun.

He settled a while on the Embarrass River in Illinois, fifty miles or so from the nearest inhabitant. "Here I had splendid hunting for honey and wild game, . . . built a horse-mill to grind corn, . . . owned two farms and was a-doing well." But sickness struck his cattle—"cattle and hogs died so fast I scarcely had time to take the hides off." He solved the difficulty after the fashion of movers— packed up and left.

Next stop was on the Illinois River—"a sicklier place I never want to see. Here I bought me a nice little farm, and established a wood-yard." Here also he lost one of his children, Huldah—"she was killed by the doctors, whom I was opposed to having anything to do with her, only the folks over-persuaded me."

After a few side trips, visiting relatives and on business, Priddy moved to a farm near Versailles, Illinois, where events transpired which changed the whole course of his life. Priddy met the Mormons.

This religious group, after being driven out of Missouri, had in 1839 settled on the Illinois side of the Mississippi a few miles above Keokuk, Iowa, and named the place Nauvoo, the capital of the Kingdom of the Lord. "From the beginning," says Bernard de Voto in his *The Year of Decision: 1846,* "they have had the complete smugness of a people on whom a monopoly of truth and virtue were conferred by Almighty God." They considered themselves, in fact, the chosen people. All outsiders they termed "Gentiles."

Priddy attended his first Mormon meeting near Versailles, coming to scoff and remaining to marvel. He went home imbued with the Spirit.

His wife, Sarah, at first skeptical, soon became alarmed. "She would try to reason me out of it," Priddy recalled, "and would shed tears over it which touched my tender spot." He finally suggested that they "fix up and go to Kentucky where her father lived and see all her folks and get away from Mormonism." ("It did not take long to get ready," added this inveterate mover casually, "the distance being about six hundred miles by water.")

When they arrived, a Baptist revival was going on and Priddy couldn't resist the temptation to engage one of the "biggest preachers" in argument. "He was so badly beaten he took sick and had to quit." When Priddy was right he was right, and what he thought was wrong was wrong, and anybody disagreeing with him sinned against God and sickened.

Sarah also capitulated, as did most of Priddy's relatives back in Illinois, "and all," he records, "gathered at Nauvoo," where "I suffered many inconveniences and deprivations of life."

Any lingering misgivings Sarah may have had were justified a thousandfold at Nauvoo. Infuriated at Mormon smugness, Mormon clannishness, and Mormon sharp business practices, and taking advantage of the anarchy of the frontier, Illinois mobs had been attacking Nauvoo with heightening ferocity from almost the day that the settlement had been established.

First phase in the mob war had been what the natives called "wolf hunts"—the faithful were tracked down singly and in groups, beaten, tarred and feathered, and sometimes killed. The Mormons responded by raids of retaliation. The climax came in June, 1844, when Joseph Smith, the Mormon's prophet, was murdered with his brother in a jail at Carthage, Illinois. Brigham Young took over the leadership, and by 1845 the word got around that the Mormons were preparing to flee. The mobs, their hatred sharpened by greed for booty, closed in. Priddy, by then an elder in the church and one of the most prosperous householders in the settlement, describes some of the "inconveniences":

"At a certain time," he says, "the mob was threatening to come upon us. We had to stand guard night and day. We were every man counseled to prepare for the worst." There was a shortage of arms. "I made a spear out of an old table fork and put a handle to it six or seven feet long. . . . I lived more than a mile from the Temple but every man when he heard the drum beat must be at the Temple quick as possible night or day with their weapons of defense. Sometimes the alarm would be given in the dark hours of the night. We were broken of our rest a great deal. I don't know how many days we expected the mob to come every day."

Some, living farther than Priddy from the Temple, were victims of mob "burnings," when natives routed out an isolated Mormon and his family, looted the house, and burned it to the ground before the family's eyes.

Attacks became so violent and frequent that Young and his "Twelve Apostles," aided by advice from the Elders, decided they would be annihilated if they did not leave ahead of their departure schedule, set for the spring of 1846. The great trek west began with crossings in ferries over the Mississippi early in February. A few days after the moving began, the river froze and many were able to flee over solid ice. Those who arrived safely on the far side rendezvoused nine miles inland on Sugar Creek, where huge log fires, lean-to's, and make-shift cabins proved poor shelter against the below-zero weather.

Elder Priddy Meeks was lucky to escape with his life. "While passing through Carthage a mob took me and put me in jail where the blood of Joseph and Hyrum Smith was to be seen." A friendly sheriff arranged his escape, warning as Priddy left:

"Don't look back till you reach the timber or they might suspicion you."

Priddy obeyed instructions to the letter, but "it was a task for me to keep my head straight." When he fled across the river he left behind his "house and lot and all my furniture and stock and books, in fact, everything that I had—and never got anything for it. . . . I crossed the river with my frail wagon and a pair of young bulls under the tongue. Their principal gift was in kicking, which they could do without taking sight or a rest and could hit almost anything aimed at." He added: "While crossing over a ridge seven miles from Nauvoo, we looked back and took a last sight of the Temple. . . . We were sad and sorrowful. . . . We got to Sugar Creek after a night and found plenty of Saints there for they were scattered all along like sheep without a shepherd. . . ."

Priddy had become a mover again at the climax of one of the greatest mass land migrations in the history of the world.

For the Mormons were but a few drops of spray on the tidal wave now inundating the West, a vast multitude of movers for the most part unimpelled by religious persecution, bound from any place you want to name in the East to God only knew where beyond the Mississippi. Volumes have been written explaining what motivated them, conjuring up a heroic medley of reasons dear to orators to this day: With warning of disaster ringing in their ears, with knowledge of past and present proving the utter folly of their course, with hardships in the present and only the vaguest kind of pipe-dream hopes for the future, with everything to lose and nothing tangible in potential gain, these pioneers forged forward toward freedom—toward fortune—toward empire!

Undoubtedly all these things figured in their daydreams and were of paramount significance to the progress of the nation. But their diaries are filled with notes equally significant to their descendants, the modern Americans, be they offsprings of the movers of a century ago or sons and daughters who within the last few decades pioneered their own difficult trails to these shores.

Uppermost in the mover mind was a devil-may-care urge to get away from the humdrum of life, to see what was on the other side of the mountain, to crusade for the sheer joy of crusading, to discover Paradise—pioneers were filled with an unblemished, boyish, exuberant abandon.

Those who had anything less stayed home. Along the eastern seaboard, where cities were abuilding and industrialism was just around the corner, labor-hungry businessmen and conservative politicians warned the sensible away from the frontiers. One senator expressed the pious hope that the Pacific Coast would become populated by a nation friendly to the United States. "Whether half the Oregon immigrants will ever reach St. Louis is at least doubtful," declared the *New England Magazine* in 1832. "Did any white man ever cross the Rocky Mountains, who would say that a white woman could have followed him? . . . All that can be done in Oregon within a hundred years is already done in Maine."

In the Middle West, ex-pioneers who had settled down and wanted their children to settle with them told of the hardships of moving. Men and women who had known the Wilderness Road warned that west of the Mississippi you had no roads whatsoever, fewer landmarks, wide-spaced water holes, no forests filled with game. Stay home, young man, stay home!

And the young men and the sturdy, regardless of age—Priddy

Meeks set out at fifty-one, Sarah being forty-seven—singly or with their women and children continued to move westward.

Anybody could go anywhere he chose and often did, but there were main routes that became famous. Outstanding was the Oregon Trail, well defined by 1841. It ran, roughly, from western Missouri north to Omaha, thence westward along the southern bank of the Platte River to the Green and Snake rivers, and then over Immigrant's Pass to the banks of the Columbia in Oregon. At Fort Bridger in western Wyoming, the Mormons turned south to the Great Salt Lake country. Farther on, at Fort Hall, Idaho, another branch to the southwest led through Nevada and the arid Carson Sink over the mountains south of Lake Tahoe into California. Other routes paralleled these from east to west through Texas, New Mexico, and Arizona (the Santa Fe trail), and through Minnesota, the Dakotas, and Montana.

You left Missouri or somewhere along the Mississippi as early as you dared in the spring. If you were lucky, you got over the last range of mountains in the west before winter set in. If you were lucky. . . .

If you were lucky, you got a good guide, either by joining a party that already had one, or by organizing a party and hiring one on your own. Whether you picked a good one was something that you would not know till journey's end—there was no checking at the outset on the accuracy of what a guide told you, and only your judgment could sort a liar from an honest man. Some were singularly unlucky when it came to guides. An inexperienced and ill-led group ahead of Priddy, called the Donner Party, got caught in the mountains this side of California in the winter of 1846-1847 and more than half died of starvation, many of the rest surviving by cannibalism.

If you were lucky, you also guessed right or took the right advice on equipment. You got yourself an overland wagon, a "prairie schooner"— but not a new one. In new ones, the wood shrank in the heat of the plains, and the wagon fell apart. You learned that if yours was a journey of more than a thousand miles, oxen were better than mules, oxen being cheaper, tougher, less easy to stampede by raiding Indians and—if worst came to worst—more tasty. Another thing, if they stampeded in harness, you learned it was best to let 'em rip: if you tried to pull them up or to one side, they'd fall, break their necks, maybe break yours, and wreck the wagon. Let 'em rip, and in a few minutes they would return to their plodding walk.

Your load, for a long journey, was limited by the capacity of your wagon. Every possible ounce, you learned, should be in food. To count on hunting buffalo or anything else was to court disaster, the trails being as crowded as they were with others counting on the same thing and the buffalo so well aware of it that they avoided the main routes.

You learned to pick and pack your food carefully. If you were lucky, indeed—if your judgment and advice was excellent—you won half the battle before you started, picking and packing your food. Bacon and pork were put in strong sacks and then in boxes lined with bran to protect them from the heat. Butter was preserved by boiling and sealing in tin cans. Dehydrated vegetables were not uncommon even in that distant day. "They are prepared," wrote Rudolf Marcy in his *Handbook for Overland Expeditions,* "by cutting the fresh vegetables into thin slices and subjecting them to a very powerful press, which removes the juice and leaves a solid cake, which, after having been thoroughly dried in an oven, becomes almost as hard as a rock. A small piece of this, about half the size of a man's hand, when boiled, swells up so as to fill a vegetable dish, and is sufficient for four men."

Powdered buffalo meat soaked in grease—pemmican—was also recommended, as were citric acid, grapes, onions, and plenty of salt, coffee, sugar, flour, and yeast.

Stout clothing, rifles and pistols, a generous supply of buckskin— to repair clothing and harness and to make shoes—spare parts for the wagons, tools, "two lariats . . . for every horse and mule," cooking utensils, "green or blue (eye) glasses, inclosed in wire-work" as a protection against the sun, a supply of medicines, blankets, comforters, a spinning wheel, a plow, seeds for the first planting—no matter how lucky you were, you couldn't possibly hope to load everything that would be needed in emergencies on the journey and still not exceed your wagon's capacity twice over.

But with luck you got started reasonably right—only to be faced with any one of innumerable difficulties which the vanguard of the march West mostly learned the hard way. If you overworked your animals early in the journey, they broke down later when you were racing over the mountains against winter; but if you didn't move fast enough through the spring mud, you lost the race anyhow.

Pick a camp site near good water, but also pick one you can defend against Indian raids. And beware of water along the Platte River. It's full of alkali. Drink it, and the next day you'll think you have cholera. You'll be wrong—but the results will be just as fatal.

Speaking of the Platte, beware of quicksand. Teams, wagons, and drivers have disappeared without a trace.

In crossing rivers, plan ahead. Test the crossing first on foot, marking the best route with sticks. Water the animals before you start— otherwise, they're likely to stop in midstream for a drink, holding up and endangering the whole operation. Never start a mule on a crossing without a rope to haul him out if he gets terrified and lies down, which is his habit. If the stream is particulary swift, fix a rope trolley across the water and make a ferry out of a thoroughly caulked wagon bed and barrel floats.

In the far west, there are long stretches without water, and the river beds are often many feet down deep slopes. You may have to kill three or four oxen and splice their hides into ropes to let the wagons down one bank and haul them up the other.

You'll learn that it's often less tiring to walk than to take a beating in the wagon over the rutted trail. Dust will cover your belongings like drifted snow, so thick that you can hardly see the horns of the lead oxen, so thick that you think you will die for want of breath. A burial on the trail must be brief—you must press on or die too. Hunger flanks your march, and dust-crazed thirst, and sudden death. You will know bitter cold as well as heat before you reach the end of the trail if you go all the way, and perhaps tornadoes and floods, and certainly mosquitoes and rattlesnakes. But somehow, if you are lucky, you will find the strength to push on day after day from four or five in the morning till eight at night, not counting sleepless nights on guard duty if you are a man and the Pawnees are threatening or the cattle have stampeded, not counting the long, taut watch over a sick child if you are a woman.

And then, the stark necessity of improvising shelter and foraging food at the beginning of winter and at the end of a trail that will have bankrupt you of everything you possessed except—if you were lucky—a battered wagon, a few head of exhausted oxen, and your own exhausted self.

Had you told one of these movers that he was romantic, he would probably have guffawed, withdrawn into sullen silence, or pushed you half off your feet in a straight-arm gesture of embarrassment. Nor were they stunningly handsome. Occasionally a child would appear along the trail untouched by hardship; rarely would be seen a young man or woman not yet weather- and toil-beaten. For the most part they were as refugees, and hard-bitten.

Priddy Meeks had heavy, sloping shoulders, a large head with high forehead, and a large mouth over a large, firm chin. His unbending rightness and shrewd resourcefulness showed most markedly in his cold eyes. He wore chin whiskers till old age, then a full beard.

Sarah's face was long and narrow, her eyes rather close-set on either side of a long, straight, wide-bridged nose, her mouth tight-lipped from a thousand disappointments and ten thousand hours and days of hardship. Her hair was Indian-straight and remained Indian-black deep into her old age. Her body was sturdy, stout, broad-hipped, broad-shouldered.

But appearance or none, luck or no luck, they and a majority of those who moved West with them were never long without end-of-the-rainbow optimism and exuberant abandon.

Theirs was the same spirit over which Moses Austin puzzled in Tennessee as early as 1796, when he saw "women and children in the Month of December Traveling a Wilderness Through Ice and Snow, passing large rivers and Creeks, without Shoe or Stocking, and barely as many rags as covers their Nakedness, without money or provisions except what the Wilderness affords. . . . Can anything be more Absurd than the conduct of man, here is hundreds Travelling hundreds of Miles, they Know not what for Nor Whither, except it's to Kentucky, passing land almost as good and easy to obtain, the Proprietors of which would gladly give on any terms, but it will not do, its not Kentucky, its not the Promis'd land, its not the goodly inheritance, the Land of Milk and Honey."

He might have added, as did another observer, Eliza Farnham, "I have met many hundred of these moving caravans and scarcely ever saw an unhappy or anxious face among them."

"I could not but esteem this moment of my departure," wrote Captain Meriwether Lewis of the Lewis and Clark expedition on the eve of leaving for the Northwest in 1804, "as among the most happy of my life." Add the editors of *The Oregon Trail*, one of the W.P.A. American Guide Series: "He was voicing the feeling of all who followed him westward."

Indeed, the Lewis and Clark company might be said to have set the tone for all that followed. George W. Fuller in *History of the Pacific Northwest* called the party "the dancing explorers," for they enjoyed themselves and entertained the natives everywhere they went. In their troupe was a Negro who became a one-man sideshow to the Indians, who had never seen one of his color before; a fiddler; an acrobatic dancer; and Lewis often climaxed the show in true medicine-man fashion by passing out ointments, eye water, and liver pills.

The movers who followed saw to it that there was a generous share of entertainment for old and young. "For every person who became a symbol of pioneer tragedy," records *The Oregon Trail*, "there were thousands who enjoyed the overland journey. One emigrant who became wealthy remarked wryly in his later years that he suffered more and had less enjoyment on de luxe hunting trips than he had on his oxcart journey across the plains. A Utah woman who had crossed the country about 1850 remembered the trip as a picnic from beginning to end; how she ran beside the slow-moving cart with her arms full of wild flowers; how she and her playmates played hide-and-seek around the wagons; how her mother knitted placidly, day in and day out, and always had time to tell stories; how in the evening the children ran from one campfire to the other while their parents gossiped and sang. People quarreled, made love, played cards, danced, wrote poetry and letters, honeymooned, joked, and carried on other normal activities under conditions that gave them added zest."

Priddy Meeks, for all his years, echoes and re-echoes this joy of the road. Once on the trail in the spring, he was happy—"not knowing where we were going or what was ahead of us . . . and we did have a good time! notwithstanding the hardships and trials and troubles and sickness." Often it rained steadily all day and the wagons sank hub-deep in the mud, but "we took no thought of the morrow and was as joyful as spring birds."

The men and boys won relief from the trail's monotony on hunting expeditions. Women and children bathed and waded in the streams. Kids raided Indian graves. At night there were campfires and mouth organs, guitars and banjoes, songs, yarning, betting on the distance which would be covered tomorrow or the number of miles to the mountains.

"I had a fiddle," Priddy noted, "and we had a shindig . . . every once in a while. . . . I never felt better in spirit in my life, and my wife was just as faithful as she could be; not a word of murmuring did I hear from her lips."

The great wave of pioneers crested about the time that he went West. In 1842, less than a hundred movers had reached Oregon, less than a thousand in 1843. From then on the numbers mounted, reaching an estimated peak in 1845. By the early 1850's, more than one hundred thousand persons had reached the West Coast overland. In 1849-1850 the gold rush brought high tide to California. Thousands died enroute—five thousand on the Oregon Trail alone in 1852—but other thousands got through.

Areas that had no recorded population in 1830—even Chicago was but a handful of people—were thriving commonwealths thirty years later. Texas led the list with a population of more than 600,000 in 1860, California had 379,000, New Mexico 93,000, distant Oregon 52,000, more distant Washington 11,500. The Priddy Meekses and the Mormons had built up a Promised Land of more than 40,000 souls in Utah.

The end of the trail for Priddy, he thought for a time, was Salt Lake City.

But his trials, like those of many another pioneer turned settler, had just begun. Hardly had he settled and started farming than locusts—he called them "crickets"—ruined his crops. Hunger more severe than he had ever known stalked the countryside. "My family went several months without a satisfying meal of victuals," he recalled. "I went sometimes a mile up Jordan to a patch of wild roses to get the berries to eat which I would eat as rapidly as a hog, stem and all. I shot hawks and crows and they ate well. I would go and search the mire holes and find cattle dead and fleece off what meat I could and eat it."

Finally, the faithful Sarah protesting as usual, Priddy went to the mountains to seek wild game—"as the proverb is, it's root hog or die!"

The trip was a success—as were two others and the next year's crop. For the first time since coming west, Priddy began to prosper handsomely.

Then, in 1851, when he was fifty-six, he answered a call to help increase the population at Parowan, threatened by Indians. A year later and he was off on an exploring expedition to Long Valley. Ten years later he moved again, this time to Harrisburg.

He was in his eighties before he finally settled down.

Another thing that Priddy did not do by halves was marry. His first venture was at twenty when he wed Polly Bartlett, "who lived to have four children, two boys and two girls, and then she died." Priddy "lived single" for three years and then married Sarah Mahurin Smith, a widow with one child, "by whom I had five children."

Sarah was of tougher stuff than Polly—she it was who crossed the plains without complaint—and when her ardor died in her late fifties and one day he set off for Salt Lake City from Parowan, she called after him:

"Don't you come back without another wife!"

"That," said Priddy, "put me to studying, for she never talked that way before; so the more I studied about it the more I was determined to try." After a false start—"a monitory impulse struck me with such force" that he "left quickly, badly whipped, without saying a word to the girl on the subject"—he met Mary Jane McCleave and "they told her I had come for her and she said she would go." Priddy double-checked:

"The red clouds in the west were all that gave light. I thought if I could see her countenance by the light of the red clouds I would knew what to do; and when I was introduced and shook hands with her I was right in the light. I stepped to one side to let the light shine in her face" and "peace sprung up in my troubled soul."

"I then told Mary Jane it was just right."

A neighbor intervened.

"Mary Jane," he said, "if you knew Brother Meeks as well as I do you would not be willing to go with him."

"The fact was," explained Priddy, "he wanted Mary Jane himself and both his boys wanted her" and "the three were so disappointed that they were as cross to her as wet hens."

Well they might have been, for Priddy's new wife was of no common stuff.

"Mary Jane was nearly seventeen years old and I was nearly sixty-two years old," he recorded. "People may say what they please about being mis-mated in age in marriage, but the Lord knows best about these matters. And if there was ever a match consummated by the providences of God this was one; and she has borne me ten children, and if anything they were above the average of smartness, all well formed and intelligent."

Priddy Meeks was at his best as a rugged individualist and a rebel when it came to frontier medicine, which has been admirably depicted in *The Midwest Pioneer, His Ills, Cures and Doctors*, by M. E. Pickard and R. C. Buley, and even more admirably summed up in their dedication. "To the Pioneer Doctor who boldly faced the wilderness," it reads, "and to the Pioneers who bravely faced the Doctor."

Priddy, stricken at the death of Huldah, the daughter who was "killed by the doctors" after folks "over-persuaded" him, began an investigation of the science of medicine on his own. He found unlimited confusion, aggravated by the presence of quacks in great numbers throughout the frontier. It has been estimated that seventeen different varieties of self-appointed healers were active at the time, not to mention anybody resourceful enough to mix something colorful in a bottle with an equally colorful label, give it a fancy "patent" name, and sell it from the back of a wagon, catching the attention of the crowd by describing "symptoms," telling jokes, singing to a banjo and implying—not without truth—that regular doctors didn't know what the hell it was all about.

In this last contention the healers had a deadly ally in that most fearful of frontier diseases, "the milk sick," which carried off thousands of settlers annually, among them the mother of Abraham Lincoln. Also known as sick stomach, the trembles, the slows, and puking fever, it attacked the digestive tract with a violence usually fatal. It sometimes wiped out entire communities. Calomel and bleeding, favorite cure-alls of the regular medics, were as useless in attacking the disease as were such frontier superemetics as lobelia inflata, familiarly known as the puke weed, which became Priddy's favorite nostrum. Everybody had a guess and nobody an answer as to the cause and cure of the disease. Not until the 1920's was it discovered that it came from cattle eating certain plants containing the poison tremetol, for which even today there are no fairly certain antidotes.

With such a disease going unchallenged by the professionals, the amateurs had a field day. Quacks at one time outnumbered approved physicians three to one in Wisconsin. Michigan's high death rate in the 'thirties and the 'forties was blamed on these charlatans. Ohio was condemned as a "paradise of the incompetent," and Priddy Meeks' then home state, Indiana, was adjudged "a sink-hole in medical practice."

Newspapers ran column after column of patent medicine advertising, each concoction more magical than the last. Here are a few as advertised in the Portsmouth, Ohio, *Journal* of January 20, 1824:

"Dr. Balthasar Beckar respectfully informs the public that he is possessed of the genuine ABRACADABRA and understands the true use of the Dandelion flowers.

"He is the inventor of a PILL that will straighten a Roman nose to Grecian; sharpen a bullet-nose to a keen edge; and bring down the most inveterate pug-nose to a reasonable degree of earthly-mindedness. His DROPS are sovereign for all disorders of the teeth; they will extract the future decayed tooth from the gums of a nurse child, with intense delight, and will insert in lieu thereof a piece of polished ivory; they will give the breath any fragrance that the Patient may desire, and change the same at pleasure. Dr. Balthasar Beckar has a portable machine by which he frequently amuses himself with distilling rose water from his own breath. Onion-eaters may be supplied with an apparatus for condensing their breath into Gum Assafoetida at a reasonable price. He has also a LOTION for converting the outer integuments into fur or broadcloth, at the will of the Patient.

"The Unborn Doctor (for so Dr. Balthasar Beckar is commonly termed in the place of his nativity) scorns to make any professions which he is not able to fulfill. As soon as the crowd of Patients will afford him a little leisure, he will endeavor to sell for publication a few of the certificates, with which the gratitude of the world is continually loading the United States' mail. His correspondence is immense, and he had the honor of having under his care at this moment several of the crowned heads of Europe.

"N.B. Cancers cured by inspection. Boots and shoes cleaned and every favor gratefully acknowledged.

"P.S. No cure, no pay.

" * * To prove the security of his professions, Dr. Balthasar Beckar will, on Monday next, precisely at 12 o'clock, standing on the pavement in front of the Athenaeum, swallow one of his own Pills. Practitioners of Medicine, and men of science generally, are invited to attend and witness this heroic achievement."

Into this medical melange Priddy Meeks plunged, and although, "without learning but little only . . . in the backwoods with my gun on my shoulder . . . could not rest satisfied until I got the books; and just two weeks from the day I got the books I put out into the woods to collect the medicine."

The books concerned Thomsonism, runaway favorite of the seventeen different quack systems aforementioned. Its originator was Samuel Thomson, born in 1769 at Alstead, New Hampshire, who, unlike Priddy, saved his daughter when doctors despaired of her recovery from scarlet fever in 1796. Having had a month of formal education, having been turned down on the grounds of ignorance when he applied to a root doctor as an apprentice, and having "a very strong aversion to working on a farm," Samuel Thomson set himself up in the cure-all business. By the early 1820's his system had outstripped all others in a popularity that was unchallenged for nearly two decades.

It was founded on the use of steam baths and vegetable remedies, chiefly lobelia and cayenne pepper. These Priddy seized upon avidly.

After Huldah's death, "when the sickly season of the year came on I visited many of the sick and was very successful in relieving them with leaves and herbs, so much so that the community insisted that I quit work and go doctoring. . . . They said: 'You beat all the doctors.'"

"That expression," he adds modestly, "brought me to my studies and I saw that it was a fact, and I could not deny it."

122

He forthwith treated the ever-loyal Sarah and "made a sound woman of her" and "this gave such an impetus to the anxiety of the people about my success that it seemed like going against wind and tide to withstand their influence . . . and from that time henceforth my labors began with the sick."

He cured frozen feet by a heavy dose of cayenne pepper, inflammatory rheumatism by having the patient take "a little chew of Indian root and half that amount of yellow dock three times a day," bad kidneys with burdock and dandelion, a fractured skull with his beloved lobelia spiced with cayenne pepper, yellow jaundice with a dose of "good strong vinegar and soot or eggshells," and a toothache with the root of the blue flag—"the pain ceases the instant it is chawed."

He created Dr. Meeks' Female Relief Pills—"compounded of those wholesome herbs [including a generous portion of lobelia] that the Lord said in the Word of Wisdom He had ordained for the constitution or nature and use of man and he [Dr. Meeks] has suffered nothing to enter into those pills antagonistic to the Word of Wisdom." Even men could benefit by dosage; the pills were "so compounded and modified as to be adapted to male or female of all ages and in all conditions of life . . . and . . . are designed for common use and common complaints of every name and nature."

Priddy left no record of how the pills helped his patients, but they undoubtedly were of great aid to him during periods of financial distress.

Dr. Meeks went beyond these mundane things from time to time—he explored the supernatural and routed devils and evil spirits.

His first bout with banshees took place shortly after he became a Mormon. Recuperating from an illness, he was so weak that "the spirits of affliction or evil spirits or disembodied spirits or the devil if you please, got possession of me and come near killing me. . . . They would make me work in a horse mill" and "sometimes they would put a pack on my back so heavy I could scarcely stand up under it." But "something" seemed to tell him to put the Doctrine and Covenants, or the Book of Mormons, under his head. Should he do this, all would be well.

Three devils came. Heartened, Priddy confronted one of them:

"I drew back my fist and aimed to strike him right in the belly and said, 'Clear yourselves, you devils, I do not want anything to do with you.'" He was never troubled with them again, but "had considerable to do with them in working against their power over other people."

One of these other people was William Titt, a lad who was "the best hand to look in a seer stone that I was ever acquainted with." William, who lived with the Meekses at the time, was attacked by the devils, and "they told him if it had not been for old Meeks they could have destroyed him." Other devils in woman's form pestered William and once gave him an invisible book to read. "To my astonishment," says Priddy, "it was a passable discourse with language and words that he was not competent to use." But devil's language, withal: "The subject was . . . chaff, no good principles in it."

Priddy fell back on his old cure for these goings-on.

"I told him to put the Doctrine and Covenant under his head and never consent to anything that they would propose to him . . . and they never troubled any more in that way while I was acquainted with him."

Another case concerned a twelve-year-old girl "possessed of evil spirits to such a degree that her feet and legs, hands and arms were drawn up to her body so she could not help herself one particle, and they called it rheumatism." But it was devils. They "would rip and tear all over the house and make a terrible fuss so it could be heard by everyone."

This case was particularly interesting in Dr. Meeks' view because the devils were finally routed by Dr. Phelps Brown's herbal ointment "and the leading ingredient in the ointment," Priddy added triumphantly, "is lobelia."

As he grew older, Priddy himself had "a great many supernatural communications." "In one instance," he relates, "I had a view of an angel in the form of a right white fowl like a swan, high up, flying very regular and steady across the firmament to the southeast. My feelings seemed to signify that it was a messenger with dispatches on important business. I felt both sweet and solemn. . . ."

The spirit reproached Priddy for not publishing his cayenne pepper cure for frozen extremities. Priddy published it, and the spirit came no more.

Another time he saw "a city in the sky," and calling Sarah, they climbed up a ladder to it, and found it inhabited with hogs, all of whom he recognized as certain of his Mormon enemies. Again, his first wife, Polly Bartlett, visited him in the spirit, looking "the most pleasing I ever saw her," and when he asked if she were happy she replied yes, but never so happy as she would be when she was with Priddy once again. . . .

. . . and who is there to scorn these tales of spirits and visions, who to despise Priddy Meeks for believing that what he thought was right was right and what he thought was wrong was wrong and that anybody disagreeing sinned against God? And who can say he had ever known poverty or starvation after so rich a life?

For did not he and that vast host of other pioneers cherish, above all, impossible visions and glory in a vast abandon? Did they not die mourned by many children who were to pick up where their parents left off and, upon these pioneer foundations, and with this heritage of restlessness and strange idealism and stranger abandon, raise a nation to world stature?

And what of Priddy's doctoring?—who is there to look back on it with a patronizing smile? Mary Jane, who followed his treatments, lived to be ninety-three. Priddy himself was ninety-two before he climbed the long ladder to the city in the sky. And did not the faithful and trusting Sarah, of whom with his nostrums the young Dr. Meeks made a sound woman, did not Sarah live to the ripe age of ninety-nine?

[5]

The Years of Expansion
(1832–1865)

There is a phrase which has grown so common in the world's mouth that it has come to seem to have sense and meaning—the sense and meaning implied when it is used; that is the phrase which refers to this or that or the other nation as possibly being "capable of self-government"; and the implied sense of it is, that there has been a nation somewhere, sometime or other, which *wasn't* capable of it—wasn't as able to govern itself as some self-appointed specialists were or would be to govern it. . . .

Men write many fine and plausible arguments in support of monarchy, but the fact remains that when every man in a state has a vote, brutal laws are impossible.

—MARK TWAIN, *A Connecticut Yankee in King Arthur's Court*

These were not the most superlative times the republic was to experience; but they were more than passing so. Nobody who could or dared did anything by halves. All hands fell to, helping the United States to stretch its claims to the Pacific, forge itself into a nation in the crucible of the Civil War, change from a rural to an industrial society and expand every which way, any way you wanted to go, stay home and make a fortune with some new kind of a factory; go west and clean up fabulous sums in gold, gamble, drink, fight, or wander in superlatives; go superlatively broke; be superlatively evil or sanctimonious, democratic or antidemocratic—celebrate as nobody ever celebrated before—mourn as nobody ever did before or since.

Here was a people with the greatest natural unexploited treasure trove in the history of the world, overstocked and undermanned. Here was opportunity beyond the fondest hopes of the wildest dreamer. Here was so much elbow room, so much to keep everybody occupied, that a man could do pretty much as he damn pleased without getting called for it. Seizing the opportunity without much thought of consequences, morals, the other fellow, or historical significance, most people went to town to the best of their abilities, and those without abilities went superlatively to ruin.

In the South, more rapidly to exploit the abundant earth, slaves were imported. In the North, instead of importing slave manpower, Yankee ingenuity devised machines.

This came naturally, since New England stay-at-homes had muscled their wits for a century or more devising things to make living more comfortable at home and sales of the Yankee pedlars more frequent and profitable abroad. Simple things brought big returns. Early colonial combs were whittled from wood. Enoch Noyes at Leominster, Massachusetts, devised a way of fashioning horn combs by machine in 1759, and horn combs soon outsold the wooden ones. Brass, silver, and pewter buttons were the only ones in early America. Enoch figured out a way of making buttons of bone, and again the Yankee traders cleaned up.

Pins were first imported from England, where they were made in two parts. The heads were forever coming off. In 1832, Thomas Ireland Howe of Derby, Connecticut, devised a machine that made pins in one piece and made Howe a fortune. Shoestrings made of leather strips, culled from the tanner's scrap heap, swelled the pedlars' bags. John Bostwick of Sharon, Connecticut, designed better mouse traps. Franklin and Jefferson toyed with the idea of making brooms from broom corn, but got too involved in other affairs. Just before the turn of the century, Levi Dickenson of Hadley, Massachusetts, planted some corn and made a few brooms. By 1810, his neighborhood was turning out seventy-thousand brooms annually and other neighborhoods were competing.

But the needs of the labor-starved nation demanded much more of its inventors. Americans were poorly clothed in homespuns. Food production began to lag behind their lusty demands. The country was huge—horse-powered wagons and man- and sail-powered river craft were not enough to bridge the vast distances.

Inventions to satisfy these needs were thought up, pre-empted, or improved by big and little Americans in a score of fields. James Watts' invention of the steam engine in the eighteenth century was exploited in a multitude of ways by Americans early in the nineteenth. In the mad scramble, some men got credit, some wealth, some abject disappointments and poverty, but always there was progress. Oliver Evans of Delaware harnessed steam to flour-milling machinery and a variety of stationary engines. When a mob, believing that machines were stealing their jobs, wrecked his Philadelphia factory, the shock killed him. Robert Fulton, one of many to develop the steamboat, was more fortunate, successfully powering his famous Clermont in 1807. John Stevens, another steamboat pioneer and one who was born wealthy and made additional fortunes with his inventive genius, had a steam-powered train in operation at Hoboken, New Jersey, as early as 1826. By the 1830's railroads were operating widely; by the 1840's they were one of the phenomenal developments of the nation.

Steam and the ingenuity of the Yankee, not the least of whose talents was a canny ability to swipe another man's idea if it could be converted into a fortune, worked to solve the clothing problem. The first step came in 1793, when a young Yale graduate went South to teach school, heard planters worrying about the high cost of separating cotton from its seed, and—almost overnight—solved the problem with the gin. It was so simple an idea that when Eli Whitney defended his patents, courtrooms were filled with men who took careful notes on the testimony and went out and built gins of their own.

With raw cotton thus in plentiful supply, mass manufacture of yarn was pioneered by Samuel Slater, who located at Pawtucket, Rhode Island, in 1790, his head bulging with facts on the spinning machines at which he had labored in England. Soon he had duplicated and improved them. Soon, too, he married Hannah Wilkinson, said to have been first to substitute cotton for linen in making thread. Others flocked to work under her husband and went forth to build their own factories. By 1809 there were sixty-two mills with 31,000 spindles, and twenty-five additional mills on the way.

The third step—power looms to weave the yarn into cloth—was also pirated from England, this time by a first-family-of-New-England scion, Francis Cabot Lowell, who in 1814 at Waltham, Massachusetts, built the first raw-cotton-to-fabric mill in the nation.

The industrial labor-saving cycle was completed when Elias Howe and others perfected the sewing machine, which Howe patented in 1846.

Still disputed is whether Walter Hunt, an impractical Quaker who finally headquartered in New York City, was not the first American to invent the sewing machine. He unsuccessfully challenged the Howe patents later in the century. Hunt is the undisputed inventor of the safety pin, done in one inspired moment and sold the next for $400. He also invented the first fountain pen, including its name; paper collars (from these he got enough revenue to keep him in his old age); the self-closing inkwell now standard, if dubious, equipment in post offices; the restaurant steam table; the kitchen knife sharpener made of two sets of concentric steel discs, and a pair of suction-soled shoes with which you could walk on a ceiling. He also experimented with, if he did not perfect, breech-loading rifles and the metallic cartridge.

Farming inventions added to the flood of new equipment. In 1833, John Lane, a blacksmith in an Illinois village called Chicago, hit on the idea of facing a wooden plow with an old saw—first step toward metal plowing. By 1844, sulky plows were being built, and about the same time drill planting machines appeared on American farms, copied from English models. English talent also supplied the first reaper, but many engineers in this country developed reapers and the harvest combine far beyond British models. Leading the Americans was Cyrus H. McCormick, a Virginian who built his first reaper in 1834, sold two in 1840, and, in 1848, having established himself in Chicago, was turning out more than five hundred reapers a year.

Other notable inventions helped pace the times. Samuel F. B. Morse, a New England artist, sent his first telegraph message from Washington to Baltimore ("What hath God wrought!") in May, 1844, carefully wording it to answer the screams of certain die-hard clergy, who thought Morse a tool of Satan. God, they contended, would have created telegraph in the beginning if he had wanted man to put words on wires. Richard March Hoe, whose father had converted the hand press to steam power, designed the rotary press. Charles Goodyear of New Haven came out of a debtor's prison to develop the formula for what Daniel Webster named "elastic metal" —vulcanized rubber. Samuel Colt, ex-itinerant lecturer on chemistry, devised a revolver that the army turned down but the West welcomed with itching trigger fingers. And Thomas Blanchard, a Massachusetts lad who invented an apple parer at thirteen and a tack-making machine that revolutionized the industry before he was of age, sealed the fate of craftsmanship and fertilized mass production with a machine lathe that would copy any pattern precisely and quickly. It remained to Thomas A. Edison, later in the century, to invent electric power and lights, and others to perfect the gasoline engine. Then was completed the equipment with which mankind was to ride into the machine age.

Little devices rivaled big in speeding the wheels of progress. In 1829, William A. Burt of Detroit patented the first United States typewriter, the machine which more than any other enabled women to become white-collar workers. A group led by Christopher L. Sholes, a Milwaukee editor, realizing that it would be a boon to women who wanted to earn a living, went on from there. The design on their first model was completed by 1867. Manufacturing rights on an all-caps machine went to E. Remington & Sons, New England gun manufacturers, in 1867. This was produced in quantity in 1873; by 1878, carriage shift made possible caps and lower-case letters.

In 1836, Thomas Edmonson invented the railroad ticket, revolutionizing travel customs. Previously, tickets were written in long-hand and in duplicate, and contained enough miscellaneous information to fill a page and extend customer lines clear around the block. Scalpers were as numerous across from the stations as they are today across from stadiums. Passengers were even described on their tickets —"a girl," "whiskers," "a foreigner." They had to take a specified coach, into which they were locked by the "Captain of the Car," or the "Master of the Cars." This sometimes led to further complications, since the coaches were wooden and, in case of fire, passengers, unable to escape, were roasted to death.

George Bailey, a railroad clerk who had immigrated from England to Canada, adapted Edmonson's ticket; from 1855 the "Bailey" ticket spread over the land.

Shortly after 1800 a Philadelphia perfumer also roused the ire of the clergy when he began to serve soda water with fruit syrup. The syrup was approved, but soda water was of the devil, especially on Sundays.

The mixtures prospered, nevertheless, and were followed by the full flowering of the ice business, brain child of a stubborn Bostonian named Frederic Tudor, who pioneered refrigeration to a point where natural ice could be preserved and shipped long distances. Ice cream, said to date back to Nero, shortly became a national institution. John Mathews of New York then designed and manufactured apparatus for soda fountains, whose proprietors got around ecclesiastical objections by serving sodaless drinks on the seventh day, called sundaes.

A third ice-born innovation, the mint julep, prospered in the South almost from the day ice arrived. . . .

"It is worthy of remark," said Alexander Hamilton, casting a shewd eye toward the future, "that, in general, women and children are rendered more useful, and the latter more early useful, by manufacturing establishments." Southern savants echoed these noble sentiments. Cotton mills, said the head of the Masonic order of South Carolina, would be "a never-failing asylum for the friendless orphan and the bereft widows" employing "the tender services of those who have just sprung from the cradle, as well as those who are tottering to the grave, thus training up the little innocents to early and wholesome habits of honest industry, and smoothing the wrinkled front of decrepitude with the smiles of competency and protection." New England manufacturers did not dissent.

Sam Slater, the spinning machine immigrant from England, let the whole family in on the wholesome values of factory labor. The man of the house signed up for the women and children, as exampled by one Dennis Rier, who contracted for the services of himself, his sister, and their six children—eight workers in all. Total weekly wages received in turn from Mr. Slater were $15.16. New England children up to twelve received from 10 to 25 cents for a twelve-to-sixteen-hour day. Wages of men and women were not appreciably more, and during depressions were noticeably less. In 1820 a Philadelphia laborer got 20 cents a day with board.

Women, who in New England made up from two-thirds to nine-tenths of a factory's personnel, averaged even less than 20 cents a day with board in good times or bad. Board and room was in company-owned houses. By the 1840's, wagons were touring New England villages to recruit girls for the factories, work that turned out to be so ideal that the vehicles won from the fortunate young women the name of "slavers."

When Samuel Colt, coining money from his revolvers, decided to spend some of it on better surroundings, shorter hours, and educational facilities for his workers, New England manufacturers to the last man rose to condemn him as a traitor and an idiot.

As industrialism spread in the 1820's, population began to shift from country to town. Manufacturing labor increased 127 per cent between 1820 and 1840, and the big towns began to grow into giant cities. In 1790, 3 per cent of the population was in towns of 8,000 or more; by 1860, the percentage was sixteen. Seeking to dominate this shifting, confused mass of humanity there arose the most colorful, uncompromising gang of business buccaneers the world has ever seen.

One may be offered as their epitome, Cornelius Vanderbilt, ex-ferryboat captain, waterfront corsair, coastwise shipping magnate, railroad magnate, Hercules in a plug hat, paragon at profanity, and as merciless as he was aggressive.

He differed from some of the youngsters who followed him in that he was physically, as well as mentally, a barroom brawler, while many of his successors became desk and paper pirates only and went to fat. Another thing, he was honest—he had the inclinations and morals of a jungle rat and didn't give a goddamn who knew it, while the next generation went in for piety, patriotic pronunciamentoes, and general hypocrisy.

Otherwise, he was the embodiment of their philosophy, their methods, and their Gargantuan achievements. In the sea trade his custom was to wreck the competition by rate cutting and then knife the public with monopoly charges. Money didn't mean as much to him as power—his wife suffered to the point of insanity from his incessant parsimony. He loved a fight and hated sentiment. His oldest son he considered an idiot and told him so.

He never let down. At fifty-five he hit on the idea of short-cutting sea travel to the west coast by a land hitch through the jungles of Nicaragua. He pioneered the route personally while younger men quailed under the titanic drive of his personality and returned to

132

civilization more aged than he. The route went through and he made a fortune on the travel trade during the gold rush of 1849. At sixty-three, he suddenly decided to hell with shipping, and bought into railroads, thus swelling his fortunes. He lived to be eighty-three, ready to lick his weight in wildcats till the day he died. "What do I care about the law," said the old commodore, "hain't I got the power?" His idea of a good rate of interest was 25 per cent per annum, and he usually got more.

With these and lesser fry to inspire them, there arose toward mid-century a set of young men, most of whom had come up the hard way and were as uncompromisingly piratical as Vanderbilt. Their goal was fortune, and most of them achieved it in a modest degree before the Civil War, when, disdaining to fight, they hired substitutes—and cleaned up.

Jay Cooke made a fortune in commissions selling war bonds, Jay Gould and Jim Fisk in playing the market, John D. Rockefeller, J. P. Morgan, and Philip Armour in selling war supplies and sometimes re-selling them and sometimes selling supplies that were notoriously poor or poisonous. Westward, Collis Huntington and Leland Stanford did all that they could, which was a great deal, toward cornering every resource and utility to their own profit. All fought among themselves and fattened off the land and the people. It was devil take the hindmost, but Satan himself would have been unwise indeed had he chosen to get out ahead and expose his back to these murderous builders of empire.

With greed endowed and unshackled, generosity and idealism lived in a matching turmoil of violence edged with abject poverty, save during the Jackson era and the years blessed by the benign Abraham Lincoln.

As the population shifted to the cities, slums began to blossom. Irish and German immigrants helped handsomely to overcrowd them. Bloodshed was inevitable and, before the Civil War, brawling reached legendary proportions.

New York set the pace for the nation. At one time or another, almost everybody fought in Manhattan, where between 1825 and 1855 Five Points became the worst slums of all time. By the latter year, it was estimated that thirty thousand of the city's population was affiliated in one way or another with a gang. Bowery gangs fought gangs from Five Points and one another and preyed upon the general public. One mob, operating under the happy title of Honeymooners, worked openly at Madison Avenue and Twenty-Ninth Street, beating up and robbing any passer-by who looked worth the clubbing.

Political gangs battled at the polls at election times, rival volunteer fire departments fought while houses burned to the ground, and bar-room brawls were as commonplace as broken heads. Climax of the era came in 1857, when a reform police force, resplendent in top hats, squared off with the old Tammany squads and fought to a draw in City Hall Square.

That year, 1857, notable for a bad depression, was also notable for violence and crime up and down the land, and Chicago first made claim to rivalry with New York in matters of mayhem. It had grown from a village to a city of eighty thousand in two decades, and its police found crime so prevailing and criminals so enthusiastically predatory that they customarily solved the problem by sedulously avoiding any place where they knew violence was impending. Unable to overlook riots, the cops usually came out the worse for wear. The 1857 depression brought a new high in crimes, brothels, and gin hells. Wells Street became one center, a region called the Sands another.

The Sands was on the site of the present Wrigley-Tribune buildings and was a haunt of river rats and canal boatmen. In one week in 1857 it boasted seven murders. When the police finally tightened their belts and raided it, the attack only served to scatter the inhabitants and make crime more widespread throughout the city.

Holding up the honors for the far west was the Barbary Coast in San Francisco. Unlike its sister slums, it was built on the fabulous prosperity of the gold fields, but its mayhem was equally repetitive and picturesque. Poker was considered too slow by the miners, who favored faro. One man achieved brief notoriety by betting—and losing—$200,000 on the turn of a card. The Coast had the most luxurious and the most incredibly filthy bawdy houses of all time, and gun battles were as chronic as fist fights. A man who went out alone at night was considered a fool and usually a woman who went out never came back.

In this turbulent sea of business barracudas and bellicose gangsters, common folk in the cities found it difficult to keep themselves and their mores afloat. Family life was threatened with extinction by the high cost of living, the low grade of tenement housing, and—most deadly—the almost total lack of sanitation. Hogs nuzzled garbage and other waste in New York and Philadelphia, and New Orleans between 1840 and 1860 established a national if not a world record for being the dirtiest and unhealthiest of cities. Yellow fever, cholera, and other plagues struck with monotonous regularity, sometimes taking a toll as high as one out of every three persons.

Once the cholera spread from New Orleans to the nation, threatening to decimate urban populations. This was in 1849. River towns were hardest hit. Panacea preventives made fortunes for their owners. Small boys and women smoked unabashed, others chewed garlic, houses reeked with the odor of gunpowder, and handkerchiefs with the redolence of vinegar. Still the death tolls mounted. In mid-July in New York, the count reached 1,400 in a single week. Cincinnati and St. Louis reached highs of 6,000 each. Graveyards overflowed and wholesale burials followed, cart drivers going through the streets chanting, "Bring out your dead! Bring out your dead!"

Whether it was this constant threat of death, or the sanguine sadness which followed with the Civil War, whether the ugliness of the towns-grown-overnight-into-cities and the bleak ugliness of the frontier settlements, or the rise of industrialism and the disappearance of pastoral civilization and the blasted hope of its return—whatever the cause, the times were marked by a strange and all-pervading preoccupation with death. It might be said, indeed, that contemplation of death was the chief pleasure of the era. It was the one thing that nobody, rich or poor, intellectual or ignoramus, did by halves.

It found its highest expression in the literature of Nathaniel Hawthorne and Edgar Allan Poe, in the plaintive music of Stephen Foster, in the somber personality of Abraham Lincoln, and in the macabre pageantry of his funeral, perhaps the most prolonged folk liturgy in all history.

In retrospect, it was amusing:

"They had pictures hung on the wall," says Mark Twain through the eyes of Huck Finn, summing it up as only he could. "There were some that were called crayons, which one of the daughters which was dead made her own self when she was only fifteen years old. . . . One was of a woman in a slim black dress . . . and she was leaning pensive on a tombstone on her right elbow, under a weeping willow, and her other hand hanging down her side holding a white handkerchief and a reticule, and underneath the picture it said, 'Shall I Never See Thee More Alas.' Another one was a young lady with her hair all combed up straight to the top of her head, and knotted there in front of a comb like a chairback, and she was crying into a handkerchief and had a dead bird laying on its back in her other hand with its heels up and underneath the picture it said, 'I Shall Never Hear Thy Sweet Chirrup More Alas.' There was one where a young lady was at a window looking up at the moon, and tears running down her cheeks; and she had an open letter in one hand with black sealing-wax showing on one edge of it, and she was mashing a locket with a chain to it against her mouth, and underneath the picture it said, 'And Art Thou Gone Yes Thou Art Gone Alas.' . . . Everybody was sorry she died, because she had laid out a lot more of these pictures to do. . . ."

But at the time, a time generally indifferent to life, there was a pervading concentration on death and mourning that would not down and that contrasted sharply with the other pleasures of the people.

These, paradoxically, were almost numberless, offering diversion to all strata of society. Perhaps allied with the delight taken in death and mourning was another preoccupation that led to endless vicarious pleasures—pleasures enjoyed by Americans to this day.

As communications became more national in scope, so did the accounts of murders, and the people seized happily on the best of them and converted them into street-corner folklore. First to gain national prominence was the case of Dr. George Parkman, wealthy old Bostonian and one of the founders of Massachusetts Medical College. Dr. Parkman disappeared. Then, thanks to the school's janitor, an amateur detective, the doctor's body was found in a secret vault in the basement of the college and Dr. John W. Webster, a professor of chemistry at Harvard, was convicted of the crime.

This was a winter wonder compared only to the doings in March, 1860, of one Albert E. Hicks, a Five Points free-lance gangster, who was shanghaied onto a sloop and retaliated by murdering its crew with an ax. Apprehended, "Hicksey" died on the gallows to the accompaniment of reams of publicity, ably needled by a young man named P. T. Barnum. The public watched, fascinated, till the end.

Less sanguine pleasures also developed during the era. Sunday crowds were thrilled with street races between fine horses, drawing rigs in the summertime and sleighs in the winter, and always risking the necks of the daring drivers. Children, until then helpless under the long and soporiferous duty of attending church, thrilled at the invention of Sunday School by Francis Asbury in Virginia in 1786, a device which by 1830 boasted a membership of 350,000.

And there arose for the enjoyment of one and all the first national master of hokum, P. T. Barnum, grandfather and author of The Word for every press agent and public-relations counsel down to this day.

"At the outset of my career," Barnum said, "I saw that everything depended upon getting people to think and talk and become envious and excited about me. It was my monomania to make men and women wonder and, as a practical result, go to my Museum."

He contended that everybody from showmen to railroad presidents and college professors depended, more or less, upon public support.

"This principle applies to all kinds of business," he said. "The public is wiser than many imagine."

In an era of superlatives, he did everything super-superlative. When he took over the American Museum in New York, he spent all first-year profits on ballyhoo.

"Advertising is like learning," he said. "A little is a dangerous thing."

His attitude was the same toward all propaganda.

He developed rules for his game of kidding the public. One rule was that conflict makes news. He found this true on his first major venture, a Negress named Joice Heath, whom he bought in 1835. She had been midwife at the birth of George Washington and was 116 years old—that was her story and Barnum stuck to it. Skeptics were answered with indignation and alleged documentary proofs. The arguments pro and con drew crowds who paid to see her.

Later he warred on Henry Bennett, owner of Peale's, rival of the American Museum. By this time conflict was second nature to him.

He finally bought out Bennett, but part of the deal was that no announcement would be made and that Bennett would stay as figurehead at Peale's so that the war could continue.

"If you want to quarrel, it's your affair," he told a couple of giants on his payroll when he discovered them planning a duel. "But it must be advertised and must take place on the Museum stage."

Another of his axioms grew out of a battle with the vestrymen of St. Paul's church, petulantly viewing his blatantly noisy Museum from their sanctuary across the street. Barnum attracted a record crowd and silenced the church fathers permanently one Fourth of July after stringing a set of flags from his building to a St. Paul tree. Vestrymen ordered the banners down. P. T. countered by daring them to touch "the Stars and Stripes on this great birthday of American freedom!" The crowd cheered and followed Barnum as he led them away from conflict to the paid entrance of the Museum, thereby adding hundreds of dollars to his growing fortune and patriotism to his list of propaganda musts.

Prestige was another item near the top of the list. Barnum knew that if Mr. and Mrs. Social Register went somewhere, the world would follow. Desire for prestige publicity was behind General Tom Thumb's visit to President and Mrs. Polk in the White House in 1847, and inspired a similar call, paid by Commodore Nutt, another Barnum midget, to President Lincoln during a special cabinet meeting at the height of the Civil War. And prestige was the reason for Barnum's having Jenny Lind give a farewell concert in England before sailing for the States—"to add the *éclat* of that side to the excitement of this."

He learned early in his career the value of tying whatever interested him to news that happened to be headlines; equally important, he always kept in tune with the trends of the times.

He was a Jackson Democrat, a Lincoln Republican, and a temperance lecturer when the occasion seemed auspicious.

He was also a past master of the bizarre as an attention-getter. Anything that set people talking, never mind what, helped business. For weeks an elephant plowed a field by the railroad into Bridgeport, Connecticut, P. T.'s home town. Thousands speculated excitedly—until P. T. moved the pachyderm to his Museum. He sailed Tom Thumb in a balloon over theater audiences, and when the novelty of that wore off the balloon (almost) got away from those holding it. Both stunts made headlines.

In everything he did, he displayed the public morals of a Methodist deacon, a hide as thick as a rhino's, a shrewd ken of mass psychology and mass entertainment, and the enterprise of an ambulance chaser. For decades the public waited breathlessly for his next hoax—and loved it.

The somber tones became more pronounced as time clocked the era to its close and the people, all the people, stumbled tragically toward the greatest superlatives of the century—the superlatives of a war in which brother fought brother and men hated farther beyond reason than they had ever hated before. At the heart of the turbulent social whirlpool was slavery, and in the end all were caught in its dizzy madness.

It began happily enough and within the bounds of innocence as set by the standards of the times. African coast-wise traders found it profitable to pick up a few natives, already enslaved by local chieftains, and retail them, beginning as early as 1619 at Jamestown, in colonial America. The chieftains were as pleased with the trinkets they received as were the traders at their easy profits. American buyers, already trading in indentured whites, first indentured the blacks for life. Not until 1661 were they legally designated as slaves, their children being thus also enslaved. But even then it was only a minor social item—there were only about three hundred black slaves in the country in 1650.

The trade continued casual until the rise of the tobacco plantations, which created an enlarged demand for cheap labor which, in 1672, England answered by chartering the Royal African Company to furnish a supply. American free-lancers joined in the trade as the profits became evident. But even then the lot of the slave was considered a not unhappy one. Was he not being released from the brutal rule of the savage native chieftains by Christians whose civilization was by far the most superior in the world? When a master died in many a tribe in Africa, his slaves were put to death with him; was not the American custom of perpetuating responsibility for them from father to son much more humane?

Whatever the ethical arguments, the slave trade blossomed into one of the most profitable trades in the colonies during the century before the Revolution. By 1730, the Royal African Company was spectacularly prosperous. By 1771, it had more than two hundred ships in the trade, more than seventy were operating under colonial management, and routes had been established on a golden triangle each point of which minted money.

Ships embarked from New England laden with rum, calico, and Yankee notions. These were exchanged on the African coast for Mandingoes, Senegalese, Coromantees, Whydahs, Nagoes, Pawpaws —any enslaved tribesman that could be rounded up by an ambitious chief. For as little as $5.00 for a male and $3.50 for a female, these were marched aboard the slaver, thirty or forty in a batch strung together with leather thongs around their necks. Slaves were sold for from $70 to $100 in the West Indies in those days, for as much as $300 in the colonies. Doctors bought for a discount the "culls," those who had become ill enroute but not too ill to jettison, and cured them up for market. Everybody prospered. Some of the profits of the Indies sales were converted into molasses which, in New England, was converted—also at a profit—into rum. A ship could net from $35,000 to $100,000 in one round trip and make as many as five before it had to be abandoned.

Any semblance of happiness or innocence disappeared as the interest in big profits became paramount. First trouble, ironically, arose among the whites—the Royal African Company and others experienced difficulties with their agents, who showed too enthusiastic an interest in getting their share of the take. Native chieftains, who formerly had sold only slaves picked up in the normal course of tribal warfare, became equally enthusiastic, raiding as far as a thousand miles inland. The trade became such that it attracted captains and crews who could be careless of the health of their cargo if profits hung in the balance and who became acutely conscious of the fact that the more numerous the cargo—comfort and sanitation be damned—the larger the returns.

But if morality had to walk the plank, returns on investments brightened the voyages as business boomed. Some authorities have estimated that more blacks than whites came west across the Atlantic between the 1730's and 1800—between 50,000 and 100,000 Negroes annually, the majority to the Indies trade, but nearly 400,000 to the colonies. By Revolutionary times the importation of slaves had become so odorous that all but those who were profiting so handsomely by it had begun to realize that it must be stopped.

Jefferson, shrewdly putting the blame on the king, tried to condemn the slave trade in the Declaration of Independence. George had "violated the most sacred rights of life and liberty of a distant people, who never offended him, captivating them into slavery in another hemisphere, or to incur miserable death in their transportation thither." But delegates from South Carolina and Georgia objected, saying they "had never attempted to restrain the importation of slaves and . . . still wished to continue it" while "our Northern brethren also I believe felt a little tender under these censures." They had, Jefferson observed drily, "very few slaves," but had been "pretty considerable carriers of them." Slave-freeing, even in the South, became mildly popular during the Revolution, but no permanent step against the evil was taken till the Constitution was drawn. The decision, even then, was negative; no law against importation could be written until 1808.

Before that time, most states had legislated against the slave trade; the national law of 1808 made it unanimous. With the South cooperating willingly to stamp out slavery's greatest curse, the eleventh hour struck without bloodshed.

Before midnight, reasoning men of both North and South were to be overwhelmed by ironies and by the screaming exaggerations of their minorities.

Most poignant of the ironies was the mutual respect which had grown up between many a white man and many a Negro. The Negro had proved himself a common man of rare, uncommon tolerances. The tribes had been sorted out in the minds of the whites by 1800, and none was found wanting. All were affectionate and lovable. If the Mandingoes proved more prone than average to petty thievery, they were gentle far beyond the average. Senegalese, the most intelligent, had developed into craftsmen of high merit. Coromangees from the Gold Coast were hardy and stalwart in mind and body, and the Whydahs, Nagoes, and Pawpaws were noted for their industry, cheerfulness, and obedience. When the master was a good master, they loved him and his mistress and his children to a point beyond slavery. As the master regarded them as his personal, patriarchal responsibility, so did they regard him as one whom they would serve even though they had their freedom.

Northward, another irony oiled the southern flame of hatred and disrespect. Slavery in the factory towns rivaled the slavery of the plantations.

But most bitter of the ironies was that the legislation against importation only served to aggravate the evil. From a social menace, slavery suddenly blossomed into an international scandal. The South, against importation, was blamed for the bootleg importers, mostly Yankees, who came into the trade when it was outlawed, and plummeted it to a new low in bestiality. Slave trade incidents were played up to underline the evils of the whole system. The majority of Southerners, who had been glad to vote the business out of existence, blazed in proud anger when they were charged with perpetuating it.

The evil persisted and grew redolent and stank to high heaven. The trade was a wide-open gamble now, the stakes high. Win, and you made a fortune; lose, and (after 1820) the penalty was death. 'Tween-decks on a trader became narrower and narrower to accommodate more and more slaves. On some ships, the clearance was as little as eighteen inches. The *Maria*, only fifty feet long and sixteen wide, captured in 1847, had 230 slaves aboard, plus crew. The human cargoes were packed so tightly that disease could sweep a ship like a hurricane, and naval officers patrolling the coast reported that they could smell a slaver farther than she could be seen on a clear night.

Sensational cases rose to haunt the nation. In 1781, the *Zong*, with 440 slaves aboard, ran low on water. Disease broke out among the blacks. The captain, remembering that his insurance covered jettisoned cargo, threw more than a hundred of the living Negroes to the sharks. Plague broke out in another hold and the captain attempted to solve the problem by battening down the hatches. In this hellhole all died, for the disease spread abovedecks, and the crew abandoned ship without freeing any of the blacks who may have still been living.

The voices of the masses began to be raised in chorus with the voices of the righteous minorities shouting that the southern many were responsible for the inhumanities of the few.

Both sides became hysterical, both were led by the clergy. The northern pulpits rang with invective, followed shortly by pleas for a holy war to wipe the evil from the land. A preacher's daughter, and the sister of two of the most famous preachers of the time, Harriet Beecher Stowe, wrote a book called *Uncle Tom's Cabin* that swept the North like a prairie fire.

Clergymen in the South outdid themselves in Biblical justifications for their stand. They attended in a body an antiabolition meeting in Charleston, South Carolina, in 1835, and in the same year the ministers of Richmond, Virginia, "earnestly" deprecated as "highly improper" the interference of "the people of any other state with the domestic relations of master and slave." They added: "The example of our Lord Jesus and his apostles, in not interfering with the question of slavery, but uniformly recognizing the relation of master and servant . . . is worthy of imitation of all ministers of the gospel." "Slavery is not a moral evil," declared the ministers of the Methodist Episcopal church at the Georgia annual state conference of 1838. The Rev. J. C. Postell embroidered the point. "Far from being a moral evil," he declared, "it is a merciful visitation, . . . the Lord's doings, and marvellous in our eyes."

Midnight was striking, and the roar of cannon spewing more bloodshed than the Republic had ever known could be heard above the contending voices. . . .

[6]

The Men of Democracy

Andrew Jackson

I think better of the people the more I meet with them. I have tried them in every way, and never found them faithless.

—Nathaniel Macon

Beware of all enterprises that require new clothes.

—Henry David Thoreau

. . . the Hon Major General andrew Jackson is gone and his voice are heard no moore on earth. But his name still lives in the heart of the American people. . . .

—*From the diary of the Negro freedman*, Michael Shiner

The thoughtful friends of democracy hung on the horns of a dilemma. They could sum it up in the words of their great hero, the sage of Monticello.

"I feel much alarmed," he said in 1824, "at the prospect of seeing General Jackson President. He is one of the most unfit men I know for such a place . . . (a) military chief. His passions are terrible . . . no doubt cooler now . . . , but he is a dangerous man." If elected, he would be the embodiment of what Jeffersonians had dreaded—the day "when . . . government shall be drawn to Washington as the center of all power."

The other horn of the dilemma was Hamiltonianism—"We can pay off his debt in fifteen years," the sage had predicted, "but we can never get rid of his financial system." The system had remained, and the men of property gained new powers under it. During the post-Jefferson era, unable to win at the polls, they had lulled the leaders of democracy with the sloganized "American system" of national harmony, the "Era of Good Feeling" under which everybody got along with everybody else so long as the propertied prospered. The heads were knocked out of the drums of Jeffersonian democracy, big business thumping loudly the while for Jefferson's opposition to centralized government and playing up how wrong he had been to envision a pastoral democracy when all signs pointed toward an urban industrialism. Centralizing the powers of property was, of course, not questioned.

In driving the money changers from the temple, would Jackson seize so much power that democracy, too, would be destroyed? Should the Jeffersonians risk a dictatorship under a militarist—or see it extended under the banner of big business?

They studied the man's record more closely, and were more afraid. When he had not been garnering fame as a man of war, he had for the most part been a frontier man of property. He undoubtedly had the empassioned friendship of the people, but no matter how carefully his career was edited, no matter how cleverly his heroic achievements were played up and his terrible temper played down, no matter how assiduously he cultivated urbanity and made peace with his enemies, certain inescapable facts remained. Andy Jackson was, to view it bluntly, a border baron, a half-horse-half-alligator man possessing much of the arrogance and none of the suavity of Hamilton, a frontier warrior with the fierce, blind, rudimentary pride of a feuding mountaineer, the uncompromising clan loyalty of an Irish chieftain, the legendary drinking capacity of Paul Bunyan, and the calm, serene reasoning ability, when roused, of a cornered wildcat.

During the early 1820's, Jefferson and the Jeffersonians looked on the political scene and Andrew Jackson, hoping for the best and expecting the worst.

Jackson had come by his reputation as naturally as he had acquired his red hair, blazing blue eyes, and lank, wiry body.

He knew hardship and conflict from the day of his birth, March 15, 1767, the son of north-of-Ireland immigrants who had settled in a log cabin near the dividing line between North and South Carolina. (Both states claim him.)

His father died a few days before he was born. In 1781, when

Andy was fourteen and already a veteran of the Revolutionary War, his mother died of disease contracted nursing Continental prisoners at Charleston, South Carolina. The date of her death and her grave were unmarked.

"Make friends by being honest, keep them by being steadfast," she told him as she left home for the last time. "Andy," she said, "never tell a lie nor take what is not your own, nor sue for slander. Settle them cases yourself."

Humorless, embittered against the British and the world at large, boyishly romantic concerning his heroic mother and women in general and mottoed codes of honor, Andy faced the world defiantly. From his youthful experiences, he would have been sanguine indeed to expect that life would give him anything but a fight, and the frontier communities in which he grew to manhood did not disappoint him. He quickly learned to respond in kind, thereby launching a career more unhappy than Jefferson's, more warlike than Washington's, and thorny with the disappointments in men and events that is the galling diet of the heroically romantic.

He grew up the hard way, without parents, unaided by notable mentors, the ease that comes with a sizable inheritance, or the security of a fireside; but sparks of genius flashed from him almost before he walked.

He read at five, wrote a neat hand at eight, and, at nine, was the public reader for the community, thirty or forty of whom first heard, broadcast in his shrill tenor from a Philadelphia paper, the Declaration of Independence.

He was born to the saddle, and as a courier helped neighborhood soldiers conduct guerilla warfare during the British invasion of the South. Captured, he so guided the enemy toward Continental troops as to give warning. He refused to black an English officer's boots on the grounds that he, Andy, was a prisoner of war, and he received for his pains sword wounds on his left hand and his head which he carried to his grave.

After his mother's death, his formal training was sporadic. He was apprenticed for six months to a saddler. He attended, to quote Marquis James, "several schools, if all claims advanced in behalf of casual educational institutions of that frontier are valid."

Informally, his progress was spectacular. He knew while still in his teens how to train a cock for a fight, a horse for a race, to drink, gamble, enjoy women, and hurl a challenge.

At fifteen, he was so tall and precocious that he threatened to kill a grown man with whom he quarreled. Soon afterward he attained his full height of more than six feet. His hair was Irish red and his face, pale and pockmarked from a childhood bout with smallpox, was lean, expressive, strange, and wild as an Irish god's, alight with intense, piercing blue eyes.

Inheriting a few hundred pounds from a grandfather in the old country, he went to Charleston to claim it and gambled it away in a few weeks. Enroute northward, he stopped to teach and attend school for a few months, finally coming to a pause at Salisbury, North Carolina, where he arranged to read law in a local office. At this point he was seventeen and, to quote a contemporary, "the most roaring, rollicking, game-cocking, horse-racing, card-playing, mischievous fellow that ever lived in Salisbury . . . more in the stable than in the office." He broke up a Christmas ball by issuing invitations to the only two white prostitutes in town, kept himself in debt with fine clothes and a fine horse, gave his temper and the back of his hand to anyone who crossed him, and, at twenty, was admitted to the bar.

Less than a year later he was heading west equipped with two pistols and a prize rifle, and trailed by a pack of hunting dogs. Pausing long enough to argue a few cases and challenge one of North Carolina's most prominent lawyers (the duel ended with both men firing into the air), Attorney Jackson went on to Nashville, where he became a court prosecutor for the then Western District of North Carolina.

He was twenty-one. In Nashville, as James puts it, "debtors, defying the law's machinery, had banded together to run the town. Andrew Jackson espoused the cause of the creditors." Within a month the young prosecutor enforced seventy writs and the court's reputation was permanently established. By siding with the men of property, he became one. Real estate was legal tender—fees made him. "Almost before he knew it," he was a large landholder. Thenceforth, in Tennessee, Schlesinger notes in *The Age of Jackson,* Jackson "normally acted with the landholding aristocracy both against the financial aristocracy and the canebrake democracy."

147

He also found a tavern to suit his tastes, quarters to suit his needs, horses and horsemen to match his standards and, before many months, enough trouble to keep any normal man occupied for a lifetime.

He fell in love with Rachel Donelson Robards.

Clouds of gossip and slander still swirl around her name as they did when she lived, thickening as the accounts reach Jackson's rise to national prominence. But had she linked her life with a less tempestuous career, she would probably have come down to posterity as did many another by family word-of-mouth, a frontier gentlewoman, more beautiful than average in her youth, who made amends for a girlhood error by becoming far more cultured than most of her neighboring contemporaries, and unrivaled in loyalty and in long-suffering.

The youthful mistake was Captain Lewis Robards, hyper-jealous and temperamental, whom she chose from among numerous rivals when she was eighteen. Repeatedly she tried to make a go of their marriage. They finally parted with Robards' promise that he would get a divorce.

Jackson, being a lawyer, may be said to have compounded Rachel's original error by not making certain that the divorce had been granted. For more than two years he and Rachel lived in technical adultery, she a bigamist, until Robards sued in the Virginia courts. The Jacksons promptly remarried. But for all Jackson's pretensions to maturity, it might be said in his defense that at the time of their first vows he was only twenty-four, he was in love for the first and only time of his life, and the bride—"she was irresistible to men" observed a woman who knew her well—the bride was beautiful.

Beautiful or no, in light of what followed she certainly deserves more from history than a reputation as an obese, barefooted pipe smoker (thousands of women of the times smoked pipes, including Washington's mother), a frowsy cabin woman with the manners of a scullery maid.

For her, Jackson built more than one mansion, each "Hermitage" a frontier masterpiece more stately than the last. Over them she presided with the skill of one used to managing large households and many guests under frontier handicaps.

While he was occupied with war and politics, she managed the plantations he acquired. Childless, she reared four adopted children, giving one his name, and over the years she sheltered nearly a score of others.

She wrote to him when absent in a style even now as fresh and heart-borne as the day it was penned, pastoral literature vividly contrasting to the stilted pap flowing from the honeyed, "cultured" pens of many a sophisticated eastern contemporary. A glance at her letters is enough to blast forever the legend of her illiteracy. "Your letter . . . was everything to me," she wrote when first he took the field in the War of 1812. "Where'er I go, where'er I turn, my thoughts, my fears, my doubts distress me. Then a little hope revives me again and that keeps me alive. . . . Do not my beloved husband let love of country, fame and honor, make you forget (me). . . . You will say that this is not the language of a patriot, but it is the language of a faithful wife. . . . Our little Andrew often does he ask me in bed not to cry, papa will come again and I feel my cheeks to know that I am shedding tears. . . ."

She loved, with equal depth, God, peace, and kindliness. . . .

They prospered, and politically he gained minor national prominence. He got all the legal practice that he could handle. Often he was paid in real estate. One plantation was added to another and he acquired many slaves to work the land.

He sold some property for six thousand dollars in long-term notes to a Philadelphian who later, having resold the land, failed. Jackson could not get back the land and had to pay off the notes to an eastern bank. Again, eastern merchants overcharged him and sent him poor products to stock a trading post he had opened. He acquired a distaste for eastern businessmen and bankers. It was the aversion of a man of property for another who had bettered him.

He got a first-hand look at the east when he was twenty-nine. ("Make friends by being honest," his mother had said, "keep them by being steadfast"—he had many friends.) In 1796, when Tennessee was admitted to the union, he was elected as the only congressman from the new state. A year later, when a senatorial post was open, he was appointed, but in a few months he resigned. In neither office did he say or do anything that attracted notice. He didn't like politics and wanted to get back to his plantations and to Rachel.

Another maternal admonition which resulted in action concerned her advice against suing for slander—"Settle them cases yourself." One case, involving a political rival who had allegedly slandered Rachel, ended in a near-duel. A second, involving Charles Dickinson, the best pistol shot in Tennessee, who also slandered Rachel, ended in Dickinson's death. He got in the first shot, but though Jackson was severely wounded, he kept his feet. "I would have stood up long enough to kill him if he had put a bullet in my brain," said Andy afterward.

For a time, all slander ceased. Mr. Jackson became Judge Jackson of the Tennessee supreme court. While he was chronically land-poor, he achieved enough prosperity to breed and race thorough-breds. One, Truxton, became a champion west of the Blue Ridge and won his master many a fat purse, accompanied at times by enough drinking and quarreling to keep an edge on the Jackson temper. Rachel gathered foster children around her and there was good wine and the strange new whisky made of corn, and fulsome feasts on the rich provender of the frontier, served amid gaiety by candle-light. Peace—Jackson style, liberally salted with local controversy—reigned at the Hermitage.

Then war struck the nation and Jackson, who had found time to identify himself as a leader in the local militia, blazed into action.

Contemporary records indicate that, so far as he was concerned, the War of 1812 was a God-sent opportunity to renew his boyhood feud with the British. The nation having called for fifty thousand volunteers, Major General Jackson took up the challenge and in March, 1812, called for an equal number.

Adventure—travel to far, romantic places—conquest—war's most tempting lures were offered to the troops. The campaign was to be toward Canada. "Youth is the season for martial exploits," he trumpeted. "How pleasing the prospect" of the "grand evolutions of an army of fifty thousand men. To view the stupendous works of nature . . . Niagara . . . Montmorenci . . . carrying the republican standard to the heights of Abraham"—what more could a man desire? "Perhaps from a feeling of delicacy for Tennessee's pride in its military prowess," Marquis James comments, "the General omitted to mention that the invitation to whip England had been extended to other states as well." With the generosity which always marked his dealings with friends, he was willing to let his neighbors share in his private war, but the rest of the nation in his estimation was only something that had to be defended by Andrew Jackson and the fighting men of Tennessee.

By fall, his enthusiasm had been dampened to a smoldering impatience, recruiting and national and army politics being what they were. Some two thousand troops rallied to his call. He was offered no command in the regular army. Another general was sent against Canada, to wage a losing campaign, and a second—James Wilkinson—was put in command at New Orleans.

Not until December was Jackson, still with state-militia rank, ordered to Natchez to play a minor role in the defense of the lower Mississippi. Arriving with his Tennesseans on the double-quick, he was soon told by Wilkinson to disband his little army. Jackson refused. He'd led his boys into the field; winter and wilderness be damned, he'd lead 'em back. It was a cruel march, but no man in the line endured more than his general. Andy Jackson returned home without military glory, but with a new name. Watching him by day and by night on the long trek over the Natchez Trace, the troops had rechristened him "Old Hickory."

The impatient warrior filled the idle hours at home with feuding, this time engaging a life-long friend and admirer, Thomas Hart Benton. Trouble began, as a matter of fact, while Benton was in Washington trying to forward General Jackson's military fortunes.

Jesse Benton, Tom's brother, fought a duel with a young blade named Billy Carroll, seconded (after protesting that, at forty-six, he was too old) by Jackson. The affair might have resulted favorably enough to keep Tom Benton's temper below the boil save that Billy Carroll won by plugging brother Jesse in the seat of his pants. Tom kept the feud flaming, and incendiary frontier tongues aggravated the blaze.

Old Hickory finally let it be known that he would horsewhip Tom Benton on sight. The two men and their followers met in the Nashville Court House Square on September 4, 1813, Jackson opening with the promised horsewhip and everybody joining in with pistols, swords, dirks, fists, and profanity. How anybody escaped alive is to be wondered, and the brawl took on miraculous proportions when none died. Tom Benton, unharmed but fair game for all Jackson's friends, fled town. Jackson, with numerous wounds, his left shoulder shattered, almost bled to death. From that day, ill health, which had bothered him intermittently, became chronic.

As Jackson fought for his life, the opportunity for which he had been waiting arrived. The Creeks, encouraged by British successes, went on the warpath. Would he be able to lead against them?

"The health of your general," Jackson informed his men from his sickbed, "is restored. He will command in person" against the Creeks, marching in nine days. He made no mention of the duel, but his troops understood: bullets had softened and failed against the iron heart of the hickory.

The Indian campaigns repeated the hardships that Washington had known, plus the special hardships of the Georgia and Alabama wilderness. Volunteers whose time did not run out were constantly threatening to desert. Supplies were short or nonexistent. Dishonest contractors short-changed the troops; honest suppliers found it difficult to keep up with Jackson's lightning moves. Malaria and dysentery were the only camp followers who never fell behind.

To all these things Old Hickory responded by keeping constantly on the offensive. "I am determined to push forward if I have to live upon acorns," he said early in the campaign. On November 9, 1813, a little more than two months from the day he had fallen in the Benton feud at Nashville Square, he led his men into the battle of Talledega on empty stomachs. Having won, he held them together four days without food. When the troops mutinied, he blocked the road home and threatened to shoot the first deserter. One of Old Hickory's arms was still in a sling from feuding wounds, but no man moved. Again, he stopped them by blocking their retreat with cannon. Only once in battle did these raw recruits retreat, to be returned to the attack by their general's shrill voice, purple with profanity. By spring he had wiped out the last organized Indian resistance at Tohopeka, and by summer had exacted half the ancient Creek domain in the terms of surrender, half of that belonging to Indians who had fought on the side of the whites. The Indians' name for Jackson was Sharp Knife.

Washington at last rewarded him with a major generalship in the regular army, and command of the South. His return from the field to Nashville was a triumphal march.

Elsewhere, with a few outstanding exceptions, the war went badly. With Napoleon's exile to Elba, the British were able to devote undivided attention to America. New England was invaded, Cape Cod sacked or put under tribute, and forays reached as far as Long Island. Antiwar New Englanders prepared for a convention at Hartford to get out of the union and the war. Farther south, Washington was raided and the White House burned. The British then prepared to move on the south by sea.

Jackson was there ahead of them, having in November captured Pensacola, Florida, a British base though in Spanish territory, and done his best to fortify the whole coast line. He first believed that the British would land at Mobile, but also had a wary eye on New Orleans, where he had declared martial law.

Unschooled in military matters, he was the first great American general to insist on fullest information concerning terrain and enemy strength and movements—thorough intelligence. He also planned elaborately for any alternative.

Six water routes could be used as approaches to New Orleans, and he ordered them all blocked. One blockade was done carelessly, and the British got through. Jackson meantime reinforced his army with pale clerks drafted from New Orleans shops and counting houses, troops rushed in from out of town, and a band of pirates under Jean Laffite, whom Jackson had first condemned and then recruited.

His plan for defense was simple: let the British attack him along the route they must travel to reach New Orleans, at a spot of his own choosing. The spot gave him a right-flank anchor on the river, with a swamp at the left. The British must come at him head-on.

Nor did he make Washington's perennial error of trying to fight British-style. Hunters and Indian fighters, by reflex his men sought cover and shot afterward when danger threatened. Jackson provided the cover by throwing up a dirt rampart, and waited for the British to attack. This they did, outnumbering the Americans two to one, on the fog-fringed morning of January 8, 1815. James, in *The Life of Andrew Jackson*, describes it:

"General Jackson was standing on the parapet when a caprice of the wind unmasked the British advance. They were immediately in front, not more than six hundred and fifty yards away, and headed straight for the point behind which Jackson had massed his reserve. . . . A heavy frost had embossed the cane stubble with silver. Across this shining carpet moved a field of red tunics latticed by white cross-belts, and a pulsing hedge of bayonets that gave an impression of infinity."

Twenty minutes later the field was a shambles, the men in the picture-book ranks having been picked off "like teeth snapping from a comb." Survivors fled the field. "That leaden torrent," said one British lieutenant, "no man on earth could face."

The British losses were two thousand dead and wounded. Jackson had thirteen casualties—seven killed, six wounded. It was the most astounding victory in American history.

Proudly, Rachel, who joined him to take part in the celebration, began calling him "the General" instead of "Mr. Jackson."

Old Hickory bore adulation modestly. But as if foreseeing the fears of the Jeffersonians and wishing to document them, he clashed repeatedly with civilian authorities, domestic and foreign, in the years between his spectacular victory and his nomination for the presidency.

Having driven off the British, for more than two months he ignored the howls of protest from New Orleans civilians and continued to enforce martial law on the grounds that he had no word of peace and no assurance that the redcoats might not return to the attack. Three years later, eagerly accepting an invitation to quell a Seminole rebellion near the border of Spanish-owned Florida, he crossed over the line, seized Pensacola, and tried and executed a couple of British intriguers who got under foot. Military governor of the territory of Florida after its purchase from Spain, he wrangled with civilian authorities from the day he arrived until the day he left, in October, 1821.

Two years later he was elected to the Senate from Tennessee, and in 1824 he was a candidate for the presidency.

If a presidential campaign ever surpasses all others in make-believe, the one it will have to beat is that of 1824.

There were five candidates. Perhaps anticipating the storm that was to come in the eighteen thirties, and fearing to face it, all were more or less noncommittal on the issues—tariff, internal improvements, and banking.

Liberal misgivings in Jackson crystallized and the old-line democrats followed Jefferson in backing Secretary of the Treasury William H. Crawford. This put Crawford in the precampaign lead, but he later suffered a stroke that kept him helpless and in hiding, while his supporters protested loudly that he was in the pink.

A second candidate, Secretary of State John Quincy Adams, himself admitted privately that he appealed to the general public much as a statue appeals to pigeons. Two others—Secretary of War John C. Calhoun and Speaker of the House Henry Clay—were unblushing politicos who stayed in the race after being certain of defeat, hoping for a thimblerigged finish or, at worst, a handsome consolation prize. Andrew Jackson, the man whom everyone expected to furnish the campaign fireworks, spent his days protesting that he had been forced into the fracas under protest. He affected an urbane silence and went around making friends with old enemies.

All the candidates got together in Washington. Jackson—again by his friends—had been elected senator from Tennessee as part of his presidential build-up. Next to him in the Senate chambers sat Tom Benton, and they shook hands and made up. John Quincy Adams entertained Old Hickory on the anniversary of New Orleans. Calhoun, Jackson, and Clay wined and dined one another. Rachel visited Washington, and was accepted socially.

As a final fillip to reality, Jackson won with ninety-nine electorals to Adams' eighty-four, with Crawford and Clay third and fourth; but without a majority, as then required, the decision was left to the Congress and went to Adams. Clay had wanted to bargain votes for Jackson in exchange for a promise of the secretaryship of state, and Jackson had refused. Adams went to the White House, Clay to the State Department.

Jackson carried his urbanity home with him, but he had been double-crossed and he knew it; anger smoldered near the surface. It hardened to determination as the people rallied round, people who had voted for him because he was a colorful military hero, but who now sought him out because he was the symbol of their own betrayal. He had won this vast army of friends by being steadfast—steadfastly he prepared to redeem their loss and avenge himself in 1828.

He had an issue now—popular sovereignty. It was worthy of his temperament and his energies. Frontier and feud-loving rugged individualist, lawyer-planter who more often than not had sided with men of property, dictatorial militarist, indifferent politician—Andy Jackson had at last become a man of the people. They "called him," says Schlesinger, "and he came, like the great folk-heroes, to lead them out of captivity and bondage."

Jackson resigned from the Senate in 1825 to devote his full time to the campaign. His passions, despite Jefferson's observation, were no longer terrible, and if they were dangerous, their threat was to the enemies of democracy. Jeffersonians buried their doubts and flocked to his banner. To his loyal Tennessee following was added Crawford supporters led by the most able politician of the era, Martin Van Buren of New York.

"Say nothing and plant cotton," Old Hickory was advised, and he obeyed. He did not have to speak. He was the embodiment of an electorate that had been wronged.

The opposition, and especially Clay, who was fighting for his political existence, quickly realized Jackson's strength. The amenities of 1824 were jettisoned as the men of property hoisted full sail to catch up with their prey. The second harvest of libel, slander, and innuendo—to become a bumper crop a century later—went to market. A handbill proclaimed that Jackson had spent his best years gambling, cock-fighting, and horse-racing, "and to cap all tore from a husband the wife of his bosom." Even before Robards had had time to sue for divorce, Jackson and Rachel "slept under the same blanket." Jackson himself was of dubious origin—his mother a prostitute, his father a mulatto.

Jackson's friends replied with matching fictions, declaring that Old Hickory never played cards and never, never swore. He was persuaded to make the only campaign tour of his life—to New Orleans with Rachel for the thirteenth anniversary of his greatest battle.

The election was too decisive to necessitate a congressional decision—178 electorals to 83. The defeated candidate was John Quincy Adams. Revenge was complete.

Rachel died almost as soon as she knew that Mr. Jackson was to be Mr. President. The legend is that, having been miraculously sheltered from knowledge of the campaign slander, a gossip revealed it to her, and her heart failed.

For the first time in the memory of all who knew him, Old Hickory wept.

"In the presence of this dear saint," he said at her grave, "I can and do forgive all my enemies."

A few days later he re-phrased it:

"May God Almighty forgive her murderers as I know she forgave them. I never can. . . ."

Perhaps it was her death which so markedly changed him; perhaps it was the change that comes to many men on succeeding to the presidency.

His hair was snow-white, a bristling banner of defiance, his face seamed with ill health and hard living and the agony of his loss, his body lean almost to emaciation. He was sixty-one; his enemies studied him with hopeful eyes and surmised that he was dying.

Other things seemed to indicate that at least the fires of battle in him had faded to embers. His urbanity had grown into a suave, Southern-gentleman calm laced with politeness. Women were amazed at his gallant demeanor, and men at his quiet poise. Daniel Webster, who had come from a visit to Monticello to spread the word that Jefferson opposed Jackson, now admitted Old Hickory's manners "more presidential than those of any of the candidates." Mrs. Webster agreed.

To be sure, he still smoked a Powhatan pipe like an angry Indian and brought with him the penchant of the west for chewing tobacco and salting his language with profanity. But now when his temper flared, it was obviously under control—he made of it a weapon rather than let it victimize him. Behind his blue eyes and the soldierly way he carried his lean, towering body lurked a hidden surety, a strength that exasperated his enemies to bitter anger and held the loyalty of his friends like a vise.

157

He had set out alone for Washington, but he had not been alone. Everywhere he was given deep sympathy and Godspeed, and his strength was renewed; for the common man, as Van Buren observed, had become "his blood relations—the only blood relations he had," giving him a confidence and a strength beyond reckoning.

The times, like his own tragic life, were infinitely perplexing. In a social sea made tempestuous by the hurricane winds of industrialism, he must navigate the ship of state from charts outmoded by the new and violent conditions.

As is often the case during a stressful era in a society, minorities threatened to enslave the opposing political parties and the nation.

This was particularly true of the men of property, who were divided, roughly, into three factions.

One was made up of eastern banker-industrialists, who took their traditional stand against change—in this case change leading to expansion in the west. If the west expanded, it would offer alluring opportunities to eastern laborers, thinning their ranks and forcing eastern businessmen to raise wages or be short-handed. Western communities would grow into states having uncontrolled and hostile votes. Eastern capitalists therefore opposed easy loans and expanded currency. They wanted to keep money scarce and under their control.

Rising men of property in the west did not like this, nor did many in the east who, outside the magic circle of the most favored few, could not get loans to expand their factories or other enterprises. These formed another, loosely knit faction.

The third was the southern planter group, who admired the eastern banker-industrialists but hated their control. Southerners regarded industrialism with the same jaundiced eye that they cast upon the west, where new states threatened to be slave-free, liberty-loving, rebellious.

All three factions, by the nature of their interests, were forced to unite for a time on one thing—defense of the Bank of the United States, which controlled the finances of the nation.

The bank, in turn, was controlled by a handful of men, led by Nicholas Biddle of Philadelphia, who represented only a minority of the propertied interests, and a fanatical minority at that. But men

158

of property knew that if they turned on Biddle singly or in a small group, he would wreck them. In the beginning, they considered him better—anything was better—than Jackson. They resigned themselves to the tyranny of the Biddle minority.

Conservative as well as radical democratic minorities were equally embarrassing to Jackson. Like Franklin D. Roosevelt, he needed the support of both but could accomplish nothing if he yielded completely to the pleas of either.

All the men of good will in the party were united in their desire to extend Jeffersonian democracy. Far from being discarded, it was expanded to meet industrialism's challenge to freedom. In attacking the rising social evils, the democrats accepted the Jacksonian trend toward a government centralized and strong enough to cope with the centralized strength of capital. They were equally united in believing that monopolies must be stamped out, that wealth was secondary to labor, that human rights were more important than property rights, and that economic equality was as important as political equality.

But the conservatives in the party opposed most if not all of these ideas; and among the liberals were minorities whose theories on how to implement the program were as numerous as the sands.

Typical was a group which became identified with Jackson and his "radical" government and was held up to ridicule by the opposition. It was led by Robert Owen, a wealthy Scottish manufacturer, who came from England preaching the value of labor over capital and the right of labor to share equally in all profits. It was the philosophy of Karl Marx a generation before he was heard from, and it made the men of property scream the louder because one of their own propounded it. Their anger was matched only by their satisfaction when Owen's socialistic community at New Harmony, Indiana, signally failed.

Variations of Jefferson's pastoral democracy rose to haunt the Jacksonians. Most popular was the scheme of F. M. C. Fourier, championed in America by Albert Brisbane. This panacea divided incomes, personalities, and society in general by neat mathematical formulae, breaking up the world into groups of 1,620 picked people —no more, no less—and thus eliminating class conflicts to bring on the millennium. Fourierism attracted a wide following, especially in the east, and, while frequently identified with Jackson, more often than not failed to support him or embarrassed him with downright opposition.

History was meantime being made by individuals in the liberal wing of the party. Under Jefferson, democracy had been lucky to have a handful of leaders; under Jackson was a whole army of men and women, brilliant, opinionated, crusading, and each with his peculiar concept of how democracy should go forward.

Fanny Wright, one of the first great women political leaders, fought against slavery, for labor, against the church, for communism. She supported Jackson, and he was by some held answerable for her most radical ideas, distorted into fantasy by the opposition. Ely Moore, first president of the typographical union, favored universal education, equal taxation on property, strikes—all radical ideas for the times. To his left were rabble-rousing labor leaders who screamed anarchy—and supported Jackson.

Colonel Richard M. Johnson of Kentucky campaigned against the organized church and imprisonment for debts. George Bancroft and a score of others battled with industrial barons and machine politicians in New England. William Cullen Bryant, poet-editor of the New York *Post*, typified the liberal literary leaders.

Almost without exception, these men and women objected to one or another facet of the Jackson program, while Jackson had to answer to the opposition for every facet of theirs. At one time or another, all were targets for the conservatives; Jackson was always the bull's-eye.

Jackson therefore had nearly a score of strong factions to consider in conducting his fight against the entrenched financial interests— the subtly varied branches of the conservative opposition, plus all the variegated groups from right to left among his followers. Even if he succeeded, he must face the blame of one and all, for it was inconceivable that he could wrest monopoly from the eastern financiers without a business panic. The political poker table to which he sat down was crowded with opponents, both friends and foes. The foes had marked the deck.

As if his entire life had been a preparation for the struggle, Old Hickory joined the game in silence and began to play with the cunning of a frontier lawyer-politician and with an Indian fighter's genius for picking his enemy's weakest points. Before anyone realized what he was up to, he launched an attack on the Bank of the United States.

The bank had been rechartered in 1816 for twenty years—the charter would have to be renewed, at the latest, by 1836. Nicholas Biddle, who unblushingly campaigned on the floor of the Senate, elected to raise the issue in 1829. The battle continued in decelerated intensity for more than a decade, although Jackson had won it before the end of his second term and his political career.

Some of the bank's capital was government subscribed, but it could take public funds and use them without interest, issue all the bank notes it desired, could not be taxed, and could not have a competitor. Only five of its twenty-five directors were government appointees, and toward these and Washington, Biddle was peremptory. "No officer of the government, from the President downwards, has the least right, the least authority, the least pretence, for interference in the concerns of the bank," he ruled. Bank officers "should be at all times prepared to execute the orders of the board, in direct opposition, if need be, to the personal interests and wishes of the President and every officer of the government."

How this arrogance was tolerated at the time, how it has been softened since by some observers into righteous indignation at the attacks of "King Andrew" on the freedom of private citizens, is one of history's minor mysteries.

In the House, Henry Clay led the fight for the bank. Daniel Webster was its outstanding defender in the Senate, his golden oratory made real in more ways than one by substantial loans from Biddle. Scores of other senators, congressmen, and their relatives also turned out to be heavily obligated to the Philadelphian.

Thomas Hart Benton, Old Hickory's ancient enemy and now a staunch supporter, led the opposition in stalling for time—a quick vote meant certain Biddle victory. Biddle swept him aside. Patriot that he professed to be, he threw a Fourth of July party for his henchmen to celebrate victory, which came in the Senate by a vote of 28-20, passing the House 107-85.

Old Hickory, receiving the bill and pondering it, waited until July 10, vetoed it, and broke his silence. His veto message buried forever any doubts as to whose side he was on, and electrified the country.

Gone was the profane invective at which he was a master, gone the passion that once reduced conflicts to terms of personalities. Andrew Jackson spoke as a statesman championing the ideals of the common man.

"It is to be regretted," he said, "that the rich and powerful too often bend the acts of government to their selfish purposes. Distinctions in society will always exist under every just government. Equality of talents, of education, or of wealth can not be produced by human institutions. In the full enjoyment of the gifts of Heaven and the fruits of superior industry, economy, and virtue, every man is equally entitled to protection by law; but when the laws undertake to add to these natural and just advantages artificial distinctions . . . to make the rich richer and the potent more powerful, the humble members of society—the farmers, mechanics, and laborers—who have neither the time nor the means of securing like favors to themselves, have a right to complain of the injustice of their government."

Biddle tried to brush it off as he had brushed aside Benton. The message was "really a manifesto of anarchy, such as Marat or Robespierre (oh, shades of Hamilton!) might have issued to the mob." Jackson was a "chained panther, biting the bars of his cage." Rallying his forces, Biddle returned to the attack, not realizing that he had been reading his own funeral oration, incapable of foreseeing that he was marching inevitably, not toward victory, but toward criminal indictment and the opposition of the men of property whom he supposed were his allies.

If nothing else had done it, the Jackson veto and his accompanying statement led to a fireworks of reforms. It was undoubtedly the fear of these that made the conservatives launch one of the filthiest campaigns in American history against him in 1832.

He was a murderer many times over, a wife stealer, an anti-Christ. A majority of newspapers, encouraged by wealthy advertisers, supported the bank. To elect him, declared the opposition, was to risk having your wives and daughters violated and your home confiscated. Because he had replaced many old-line Adams politicos with his own men, he was branded with inventing the "spoils system." Death was frankly hoped for before and after the campaign. During the 1832 cholera epidemic, Henry C. Carey, a Philadelphia publisher,

162

said that if it could carry off the President "I would submit to all the inconveniences of it for a month or two." Said the Boston *Courier* in a post-election editorial: ". . . there is one comfort left: God has promised that the days of the wicked shall be short . . . he may die before he can be elected" by the electoral college. "It is the duty of every good Christian to pray to our Maker to have pity on us."

Jacksonian Christianity, based on the naïve idea that Christ believed in loving thy neighbor, and the golden rule, was a favorite target. Liberal Christians were branded "atheists" by the pious parsons of the well-to-do, operating under the "widespread assumption," in Schlesinger's words, "that God was a disciple of Alexander Hamilton." Jackson was the anti-Christ. "One New York preacher roundly condemned the men who broached 'the pompous doctrine that all men are born free and equal' in the teeth 'of all the providence of God, in whose unsearchable wisdom, one is born in a manger and another on a throne.' 'The axiom of equal rights,' this gentleman continued, 'is infidel, not Christian, and strikes at all that is beautiful in civil, or sacred in divine institutions.' "

But there was no way to destroy Old Hickory's popularity among the people. Henry Clay, Jackson's nearest opponent, lost by a large majority.

Reform flowered. In 1832 a bill abolishing imprisonment for debts passed House and Senate and within a decade nearly all the states had followed suit. Jackson himself led the fight against the conservatives of the Supreme Court, appointing men who sided with the people rather than with property, as had been the case under John Marshall. Opposing state rebellion against national trends, notably in South Carolina's incipient revolt against the tariff, he strengthened both federal powers and respect for the office of the presidency. While Old Hickory advised from the sidelines, Van Buren, his White House successor, put through an executive order limiting federal workers to a ten-hour day without wage reduction.

If his reforms were to be jettisoned in the turmoil of the Civil War and forgotten for decades afterward under reactionary rule by the men of property, nevertheless he had nailed up signposts for future progress that neither time nor distortions could obliterate.

He lived until June 8, 1845, a Sunday. He died to the mournful chant of the slaves at the Hermitage who, like common folk everywhere, sensed that his going was a bitter loss to the cause of freedom.

He was buried by the side of his beloved Rachel in the garden of the Hermitage, where at last they found the peace which for a turbulent lifetime had eluded them.

Abraham Lincoln

... And God talked with him, saying ... thy name shall be Abraham; for a father of many nations have I made thee.

—GENESIS, 17: 3-5

... slavery and the tremulous spreading of hands to protect it, and the stern opposition to it which shall never cease or the speaking of tongues and the moving of lips cease.

—WALT WHITMAN

There is a very holy and very terrible isolation for the conscience of every man who seeks to read the destiny in the affairs for others as well as for himself, for a nation as well as for individuals. That privacy no man can intrude upon. That lonely search of the spirit for the right perhaps no man can assist. This strange child of the cabin kept company with invisible things, was born into no intimacy but that of its own silently assembling and deploying thoughts.

—WOODROW WILSON

Abraham Lincoln was born of pioneer stock near Elizabethtown, Kentucky, February 12, 1809.

When he was about three, his folks moved to a farm near Knob Creek, Kentucky, where the valley soil was richer and the living easier. Tall wilderness hills flanked the valley with sylvan silence.

When Abe was seven, the Lincolns penetrated a hundred miles of wilderness to clear farm land along Little Pigeon Creek, in Indiana.

Here he got his frontier schooling and lived and worked till he was twenty-one save when, at nineteen, he hired out for a few months on the crew of a flatboat to New Orleans.

At twenty-one he drove the oxen when the family moved to Illinois. Abe didn't like farming, so he hired out for another trip to New Orleans. Then he settled at New Salem, Illinois, on the Sangamon River. Here he was a store clerk, surveyor, postmaster, finally a politician. At twenty-three he ran for the state legislature and lost;

at twenty-five he ran and won. He also served in the Black Hawk War, which turned out to be mostly a camping trip for Lincoln and the local boys, who elected him a captain in the Illinois militia.

Lincoln became engaged to Ann Rutledge, nineteen-year-old daughter of a New Salem tavern keeper, but shortly afterward she contracted malaria and died.

He represented New Salem in the state legislature till he moved to Springfield and began studying and practicing law, at twenty-eight.

At thirty-one he became engaged to Mary Todd, ten years his junior, of Kentucky and Springfield frontier society. After an off-and-on love affair, they were married when he was thirty-three. They had four sons during the next ten years.

When Lincoln was thirty-eight to forty, he served without distinction in the national Congress as a Whig.

He returned to Springfield to practice law and dabble in politics. In October, 1854, when he was forty-five, he made a speech at Peoria, Illinois, challenging Senator Stephen A. Douglas of Illinois, already a national figure, and Douglas' support of the Kansas-Nebraska Act, which opened the northwest territories to slavery.

A little more than ten years later he was dead.

Thus for forty-five years of his life he was just another frontier lawyer-politician. He was a national figure for slightly more than ten years, a world figure for less than six, in which brief time he accomplished more with fewer words than any American statesman before or since. Despite unbelievably incompetent assistance, in his administration was fashioned an army unrivaled for the time. The Union was saved, slaves freed, and, in addition to leading the way in all these matters, Lincoln found time to carve in granite, rules for democratic progress to be followed by generations to come.

Yet perhaps his more difficult task was during the forty-five years of his obscurity when in his loneliness he molded his own most complex personality into genius.

Our greatest man of the people, he was also the most lonely.
Loneliness was his heritage. His mother, Nancy Hanks Lincoln, said by some to have been born out of wedlock, at times must have known the isolation that is a bastard's peculiar gift from society. She

165

was besides, in Carl Sandburg's words in *Abraham Lincoln, The Prairie Years,* "sad with sorrows like dark stars in blue mist." Thomas Lincoln, Abraham's father, was a frontiersman to whom loneliness was as much a trade as a goal.

Mother and son were close. When he was less than nine, she died.

Few events are more lonely in all the gamut of human experience than a child going to a strange community. Twice as a wilding, once when he was old enough to know the bitter hurt of it, Abe Lincoln faced children who, as is their way, ringed him in a hostile circle to gaze unblinking at this gaunt and suspect alien.

He learned well, Sandburg notes, the deep loneliness of the wilderness: "Silence found him; he met silence. In the making of him as he was, the element of silence was immense."

As he matured, to his loneliness was added a profound melancholy. Both were aggravated by the death of Ann Rutledge, with whom he spent a last hour alone two days before she died, and long hours afterward at her grave and wandering lorn along the banks of the Sangamon. As his melancholy matured, there came blue spells that sank him into baffling, kithless reveries, blinding and deafening him to those near by, his face unutterably sad.

His favorite poem went like this:

> Oh, why should the spirit of mortal be proud?
> Like a swift-fleeting meteor, a fast-flying cloud,
> A flash of the lightning, a break of the wave,
> He passes from life to his rest in the grave.
>
> The hand of the king that the sceptre hath borne
> The brow of the priest that the mitre hath worn . .
> The beggar who wandered in search of his bread,
> Have faded away like the grass that we tread.
>
> 'Tis the wink of an eye—'tis the draught of a breath—
> From the blossom of health to the paleness of death,
> From the gilded saloon to the bier and the shroud
> Oh, why should the spirit of mortal be proud?

"There goes old Mr. Lincoln!" a boy called after him once.

"They commenced it when I was scarcely thirty years old," Mr. Lincoln remarked to a friend.

166

Out of the depths of him came strange, mystical imaginings and a conviction that he was acting as the tool of some higher intelligence whose goals were too inscrutable for human understanding. He considered himself "a humble instrument in the hands of our Heavenly Father." Should he fail, "I must believe that for some purpose unknown to me, He wills it otherwise." "God wills this contest, and wills that it shall not end yet," he said at one point in the war. A vestige of the frontier folkways with which he had grown up was his belief that folk superstitions had their roots in reality, and dreams and visions had their meanings. Before leaving Springfield, he saw a double reflection of himself in a mirror, one reflection ghostly pale. He would be elected twice to the presidency, was his interpretation, but would not survive the second term. A few days before his assassination he dreamed that the White House was filled with sobbing people who told him that they mourned the President's death. . . .

Physically, Lincoln was a dour, awe-inspiring giant, almost a monster of a man, six-feet-four-inches tall and "not merely tall, but longish," with more than their share of the height in his "spider-like legs, and with "rake-handle" arms. His gaunt homely face was notable, says Sandburg, for a mouth and eyes that "masked a thousand shades of meaning" and in the eyes as nowhere else appeared his tremendous diversity, their expression ranging from "rapid twinkles of darting hazel that won the hearts of children" to "a fixed baffling gray that the shrewdest lawyers and politicians could not read."

A contrasting and equally vivid dominant of his physique was its humor. He shook hands, said Herman Melville, "working hard at it like a man sawing wood at so much per cord." When walking rapidly, another observer reported, he looked like "a crane in a bulrush swamp." He wore formal clothes and particularly white gloves like a comic in a minstrel show. John Hay, one of the White House secretaries, describes him early in the war "calmly looking out of the window at the smoke of two strange steamers puffing up the way, resting the end of his telescope on his toes sublime." Reviewing troops from the saddle, Lincoln dropped his legs "halfway between the under part of the girth and the ground," reported the newspaperman A. K. McClure, and "his long arms could have guided the horse by the ears."

One night General Ben Butler and Gustavus Asa Fox, Assistant Secretary of War, got the President out of bed to report a minor victory. "He immediately came in in his nightshirt," Butler reported, "and he seemed very much taller in that garment; and Fox was about five feet nothing. Fox communicated the news and then he and Lincoln fell into each other's arms. That is, Fox put his arms around Lincoln about as high as the hips, Lincoln reached down over him so that his arms were pretty near the floor, and thus holding each other they flew around the room once or twice, and the nightshirt was considerably agitated."

Lincoln hid his loneliness and taught himself to live with it by mental as well as physical humor, a facade of polite graciousness, frontier yarning, and frequent sophisticated wit. No less an authority than Ralph Waldo Emerson saw in Lincoln "a grace . . . a simplicity which is the perfection of manners." Edward Everett, another Boston elegant, concurred by characterizing the backwoods lawyer whom most of New England's socially elite labeled with such epithets as "baboon," as "a gentleman in the finest sense of the word." A casual White House visitor, ordered by an aide to drop behind the Chief Executive when they went to the portico to greet a regiment, was quickly put at ease by Lincoln: "You see, they might not know who was President!" To a courier overcome with embarrassment after running head-on into the President one night at the War Department, Lincoln said with equal kindly wit: "I wish the whole army would charge like that!"

As a frontier storyteller, his reputation was legendary in Illinois during the years he practiced law around the state circuits. It became all-embracing when he rose to national stature. Every Joe Miller gag that could be, was credited to Lincoln, as well as most of the folk humor of the time. He took no credit: "I remember a good story when I hear it, but I never invented anything original. I am only a retail dealer." But it was his lifetime habit to be reminded of a story and, in the telling, to give it his own peculiar twist.

Many of these stories were forced, many too earthy for print. Still others, encouraged in an era when the pun was considered side-splitting, would have been smothered at birth today. Of a man named T. R. Strong, he said: "T. R. Strong, but coffee is stronger." And again: "Gentlemen, this is a day of fast, and I am pleased to observe you are working as fast as you can."

At its spontaneous best, his dry, penetrating wit has seldom been equaled. He could be reminded of a story of devastating pertinence on occasion. When a Kentucky peace delegation came to him in the spring of 1861, proposing appeasement to end the war, Lincoln said:

"Well, I will . . . answer . . . by telling you a little anecdote from Aesop's fables. . . . There was a lion once that was desperately in love with a beautiful lady . . . and the lady . . . agreed to marry him, and the old people were asked for their consent. They were afraid of the lion . . . and they said to him . . . 'our daughter is frail and delicate, and we hope that you will submit to have your claws cut off and your tusks drawn, because they might do very serious injury to her.' The lion submitted, being very much in love . . . and they took clubs then and knocked him on the head."

The demands of the South reminded him of his sons Tad and Willie. One had a toy, the other yelled for it. When told he should give it up to quiet his brother, the possessor said, "No, sir, I must keep it to quiet myself."

Urged to violence in a diplomatic quarrel with England, Lincoln said: "Two roughs were playing cards for high stakes out west, when one of them, suspecting his adversary of foul play, straightway drew a bowie knife from his belt and pinned the hand of the other player to the table, exclaiming: 'If you haven't got the ace of spades under your palm, I'll apologize!' "

When Lincoln was a lawyer, a New York firm wrote for financial information on a Springfield man. Lincoln replied:

"Yours of the tenth received. First of all, he has a wife and a baby; together they ought to be worth $500,000 to any man. Secondly, he has an office in which there is a table worth $1.50 and three chairs worth, say, $1. Last of all, there is in one corner a large rat-hole, which will bear looking into."

He had a talent for humorously characterizing a man or an institution, and for whittling a pretentious one down to size. Two of his most dignified and self-important cabinet members—choleric Secretary of War Edwin M. Stanton and long-bearded Secretary of the Navy Gideon Welles—Lincoln dubbed "Mars" and "Neptune." A reporter from the London *Times* was introduced to the President, who said: "The London *Times* is one of the greatest powers in the world—in fact, I don't know anything that has much more power —except perhaps the Mississippi."

Seeing a flourishing John Hancock of a signature, he remarked that it was like a "short-legged man in a big overcoat, the tail of which is so long that it wipes out his footprints in the snow." Someone was eulogizing a profound historian, doubting whether "any man of our generation has plunged more deeply in the sacred font of learning," when Lincoln cut in with, "Yes, or come up dryer."

Another man reminded him of Jim Jett's brother—"the damndest scoundrel that ever lived, but in the infinite mercy of Providence, also the damndest fool." A committee objecting to Grant's drinking got from Lincoln the most famous of his retorts—"If I can find out the brand of whisky Grant drinks, I'll send every general in the field a barrel of it." Of the procrastinating and supply-hungry Mc-Clellan, Lincoln remarked, "If I gave him all the men he asked for, they'd have to sleep standing up."

He was equally aspic concerning pestiferous office seekers. "Gentlemen," he said to one delegation wishing a man appointed on the grounds that he was in ill health, "there are eight other applicants for that place, and they are all sicker than your candidate." Another office seeker was described by his friends as "pre-eminently qualified for the position. No honor, sir, could be showered on him that could elevate him higher" in their estimation. Lincoln replied, "To appoint so good and excellent a gentleman to a paltry place like this would be an act of injustice to him. I shall reserve the office for some poor politician who needs it." "Why I am one of those who made you President!" one petitioner protested. "Yes," retorted Lincoln, "and it's a pretty mess you got me into."

He could be positive as well as negative in his humorous approach to office seekers. A committee denied one Billy Patterson a commission because they thought him "ignorant and insolent" when answering their question, "Who was Oliver Cromwell?" with "I don't know and don't care a damn; I ain't hunting his job." Ruled Lincoln: "This seems to have become a sort of triangular contest between Charles Stuart, Oliver Cromwell, and Billy Patterson. It is generally believed hereabouts that Charles and Oliver are dead. If the committee upon investigation finds this to be the fact, give the appointment to Billy

Patterson." "This man wants work," he wrote to one of his secretaries—"so uncommon a want that I think it ought to be gratified."

He was a man of paradoxes, of mecurial moods. Intimates and casual observers alike, after describing his lank figure and gaunt face, spoke of the changing attitudes of both—the body awkward and amusing in gesturing a joke, bulging oaken strength in a moment of crisis, incredibly tall in anger, sagging to its marrow in times of discouragement or fatigue. The face was capable of an animated dazzling joyfulness a moment after it had been remote, inanimate, and leathern in solemn thought. One observer at the White House saw him petulant, infinitely sad, argumentative, brusque, dictatorial, and joyful almost in as many minutes.

He was a politician in the best rough-and-tumble, dog-eat-dog, ward-heeler sense of the word. "Without the cunning of a fox, without a wilderness sagacity, without natural instincts such as those guiding wild geese on thousand-mile flights, he would have gone down and under in stalking a presidential nomination," Sandburg says. Seward, rival for the nomination and later Lincoln's Secretary of State, credited him with a political "cunning that was genius." Peopling his cabinet with politicos, Mr. Lincoln was characterized as "more of a politician" than all of them "put together," by Senator William P. Fessenden.

Yet it was Fessenden who also, like many another, observed that Lincoln had a "tenderness of heart . . . fatal to his efficiency in times like these." "He never assumed superiority over anybody in the ordinary intercourse of life," said Horace White of the Chicago *Tribune*. "His democracy was of the unconscious kind." At the height of the war he found time to visit four soldiers repairing the White House plumbing and tell them, "If you can't fix that thing right off, I don't suppose I'll get any grub today." "Pigeon hearted," he called himself when it came to pardons—he pardoned hundreds who sent him a plausible plea by a man, and he pardoned almost anybody, North or South, whose advocate was a tearful woman.

Despite the incredible load he carried at the White House, he devoted long hours to hearing personally the requests of any and every petitioner who could get by his secretariat. His "public opinion baths" he called them—"I feel, though the tax on my time is heavy, that no hours of my day are better employed than those which bring me again within the direct contact and atmosphere of . . . the people. Men moving in an official circle are apt to become merely official—not to say arbitrary—in their ideas, and are apter with each passing day to forget that they only hold power in a representative capacity." The effect of his contacts with the people, he felt, was "renovating and invigorating."

Lincoln's diverse and oft-time conflicting characteristics were forged into an integrated personality by his oaken will, bound in the toughest iron of reticence and of faith in himself and God.

His reticence was remarkable when it is considered that his major addresses and messages can be counted on your fingers. He never made a speech during a presidential campaign. His drive for the presidential nomination of 1860 was based on two speeches, the "House Divided" in 1858 to accept the Republican nomination to run against Douglas for the Senate, and the Cooper Union speech in February, 1860. He made no other addresses till his first inaugural. During his first term he sent messages to Congress in July and December of 1861, and in December of 1862-3-4. In addition, he delivered the so-called Lincoln's Gettysburg Address, more important as historic literature than at the time it was given, when it passed almost unnoticed. There was his second inaugural. And that is all.

He began his campaigning with a challenge to Douglas in the fall of 1854. Two years later he spoke before the state Republican convention, and then, in 1858, delivered his "House Divided" speech. This last, stripped of oratorical verbiage and clearly stating the problem facing the nation, was his first statesmanlike address and won him national attention which he never afterward lost.

From its opening, it riddled the arguments of the compromisers and laid bare the fundamental issue:

"If we could first know where we are, and whither we are trending," he said, "we could better judge what to do, and how to do it. We are now far into the fifth year since a policy was initiated with the avowed object and confident promise of putting an end to slavery agitation. Under the operation of that policy, that agitation has not only not ceased, but has constantly augmented. In my opinion, it will not cease until a crisis shall have been reached and passed. 'A house

172

divided against itself cannot stand.' I believe this government cannot endure permanently half slave and half free. I do not expect the house to fall—but I do expect it will cease to be divided. It will become all one thing, or all the other.

"Either the opponents of slavery will arrest the further spread of it, and place it where the public mind shall rest in the belief that it is in the course of ultimate extinction; or its advocates will push it forward till it shall become alike lawful in all the States, old as well as new, North as well as South."

He lost the election to Douglas following a series of campaign debates which were pure politicking but out of which Lincoln emerged with a larger popular following than his opponent. They established him as a candidate for the 1860 Republican nomination. His chances were enhanced shortly after his fifty-first birthday when he spoke at Cooper Union in New York City, directly challenging the Southern slave partisans:

"Wrong as we think slavery is," he reasoned, "we can yet afford to let it alone where it is, because that much is due to necessity arising from its actual presence in the nation; but can we, while our votes will prevent it, allow it to spread into the national territories and to overrun us here in the free states? If our sense of duty forbids this, let us stand by our duty fearlessly and effectively." He concluded with the classic sentence: "Let us have faith that right makes might; and in that faith let us to the end dare to do our duty as we understand it."

After his nomination, he stayed at home and stood on his record: "Those who will not read or heed what I have already publicly said would not read or heed a repetition of it."

Once elected and in Washington, with office seekers doing everything but mob him, with his insistence on seeing the general public regularly, with Northern business leaders offering all kinds of advice and no assistance, with Congress cut to ribbons by the desertion of its Southern membership and rancid from the political machinations of those who stayed behind, with tragedy stalking his personal life, Lincoln for the next two years suffered the most unrelenting mental, spiritual, and physical strain ever experienced by a great leader in all history.

It began with silence, climaxed on a spring day in 1861. Fort Sumter had fallen and he had called for seventy-five thousand troops to defend the Union.

No troops came, no word, nothing. Washington was isolated, its wires cut, its railroads blocked. Most of its guardsmen had deserted to the Confederacy. Maryland wavered between the opposing forces. Virginia prepared to side against the Union. In the words of Henry Villard, of the New York *Herald*, "it was as though the government of a great nation had been suddenly removed to an island in mid-ocean in a state of entire isolation." "I think, sir," said aged General Winfield Scott, then in command of the Northern armies, "that Fort Washington could be taken now with a bottle of whisky."

Should word come from the North, there was no assurance that it would be encouraging. New York, which might have been considered its capital, if not in popularity at least in financial and newspaper editorial leadership, had when last heard from been toying with the proposal of its mayor that it secede from the Union, become a free city, and sell war supplies to the North in the same fashion that it had for months been selling them to the South.

Lincoln had stopped off enroute to Washington, and Manhattan's millionaires—spiritual sons of the money- and power-hungry men who had opposed Jackson, uninterested in democracy, peace, and the people so long as they could turn a whacking profit—New York's financial leaders had entertained Lincoln at breakfast. So pretentious was the affair that William H. Aspinwall, a railroad magnate, told the President-elect that he would not see so many millionaires together at any other table in the city. Lincoln replied casually that he was a millionaire—in votes. Nobody present thought the remark amusing.

Lincoln continued his way to Washington and the crisis at Sumter and the beginning of the war which, in April, appeared to be developing into a contest between the formidable army recruiting under the leadership of Robert E. Lee—and one A. Lincoln. "I don't believe there is any North!" he burst out to John Hay at one point. Again, after walking the floor alone in silent thought for nearly half an hour, he cried in anguish: "Why don't they come! Why don't they come!" Daily the situation became more tense and the President more isolated. Carl Schurz describes the President's most lonely moments:

"One afternoon after he had issued his call for troops . . . a feel-

174

ing came over him as if he were utterly deserted and helpless. He thought any moderately strong body of secessionist troops, if there were any in the neighborhood, might come over the 'long bridge' across the Potomac, and just take him and the members of the cabinet —the whole lot of them. Then he suddenly heard a sound like the boom of a cannon. 'There they are!' he said to himself. He expected every moment somebody would rush in with the report of an attack. The White House attendants, whom he interrogated, had heard nothing. But nobody came, and all remained still.

"Then he thought he would look after the thing himself. So he walked out, and walked, and walked, until he got to the Arsenal. There he found the doors all open, and not a soul to guard them. Anybody might have gone in and helped himself to the arms. There was perfect solitude and stillness all around. . . ."

There followed defeat. First to command the Army of the Potomac was General Irvin McDowell, a West Pointer who yielded to the clamor of the public and the politicians, not excluding the President, and led green troops into the first battle of Bull Run on a Sunday in July of 1861. Washington society, in carriages and with picnic lunches, went out into Virginia to see the show, so decisive a defeat that Beauregard, the Southern commander, could have taken Washington with a skirmish had he followed up his victory.

Then came delay, personified by George B. McClellan, a jackanapes who framed his orders in Napoleonic phrases and posed like Bonaparte for photographers. Young, handsome, politically ambitious, he wrote his wife, "Who would have thought, when we were married, that I should be so soon called upon to save my country?" One night he walked by Lincoln and Seward, waiting in the McClellan living room, marched upstairs, and sent word down half an hour later, in response to a query, that he had retired. He ran the Army of the Potomac as he had run the Ohio and Mississippi Railroad, with efficiency, with arrogance, and without taking any chances. He demanded and received a plethora of supplies and men, and trained the men to battle pitch. And then—he demanded more of everything.

While the President fought off a growing swarm of critics and waited for McClellan to sit out the winter, difficulties assailed him from elsewhere. His political troubles rivaled those with the military.

He set out to staff his cabinet with the best men available, and they set out as promptly to show him how to run the government. He was told, "They will eat you up." "They will be just as likely to eat each other up," he replied. They tried to do both.

At least two of them had presidential ambitions. William H. Seward of New York had been Lincoln's strongest rival for the 1860 Republican nomination and there was a prolonged struggle before Seward, as Secretary of State, learned that he was not to run the government and finally came to admit, "the President is the best of us."

Not so Salmon P. Chase of Ohio, Secretary of the Treasury, of whom it was said he bowed to his mirror murmuring, "Mr. President." Chase early formed an alliance with a young, hard-bitten Philadelphia financier, Jay Cooke, who organized bond-selling for the government, performing what was then considered miracles of money-raising from the general public. He also tried as intensively to make presidential timber of Salmon P. Chase. Chase was an undercover candidate for the nomination until the eve of the 1864 Republican convention.

To add to the cabinet difficulties was Simon Cameron, a Pennsylvania politico who, until replaced by Stanton in early 1862, kept the War Department on the verge of scandal.

At home was Mrs. Lincoln, termagargantuan in her criticisms of the men surrounding Lincoln and the more difficult for him because she was diabolically accurate in her characterizations. Seward was not to be trusted. If Chase "thought he could make anything by it, he would betray you tomorrow." McClellan was "a humbug"—all talk, no action.

Patiently he parried her, because of all who knew her he understood her best. And she, pursued by a blinding madness that attacked her with renewed intensity in February of 1862, sought shelter in his understanding lest she go under. So it was that when the war was less than a year old and the Union cause growing steadily worse, to his multitudinous burdens was added the weight of her downfall.

Events seemed to have conspired to climax the tragedy that was the life of Mary Lincoln. She was a stickler for petty formalities, and overweeningly proud and ambitious. Mr. Lincoln should never answer the door, it was the servant's duty. He should never come to the table in his shirtsleeves or dip into the butter with his own knife, he shouldn't mess up the house or stretch out full length on the parlor floor. He should put on style. Comb your hair, Mr. Lincoln, it looks like a haystack. Lift me up on a chair so I can straighten your tie. Why is it, Mr. Lincoln, that you refuse to pay me any nevermind?

Publicly, her pride and ambition dominated. "Mr. Lincoln is to be the President of the United States one day," she said a decade before he gained national prominence. "If I had not thought so, I would not have married him—you can see he isn't pretty." Another time she said, "Look at him! Doesn't he look as if he would make a magnificent President?"

She was tiny alongside him, plump, with beautiful arms and shoulders, her face animated by sparkling shrewd blue eyes and her tongue by a torrential temper. She knew quality, and if she was so indiscriminating as to put formalities and fine feathers ahead of fundamentals, she recognized the fundamentals when she saw them. "His heart is as large as his arms are long," she told a friend. And if he didn't join a church, he was nevertheless deeply religious; it was "a kind of poetry in his nature."

They shared a poetry of deep reciprocal affection at times between her tempers. They also shared always their love of children. Perhaps their greatest happiness together was in their enjoyment of the Lincoln boys.

One had died before they went to Washington; three were living. Robert, the oldest, was a student at Harvard, prevented from joining the army by his mother's hysterical fears. Thomas, "Tad," the youngest, was old enough to know the thrill of moving into the White House, and Willie, at ten, was in the prime of small boyhood. Studious, he read books and wrote poetry of fallen heroes—"His country has her part to play, To'rds those he left behind; His widow and his children all, She must always keep in mind." He was a man of business, sending his verse to the editor of the *National Republican* with a crisp note, "Dear Sir: I enclose you my first attempt at poetry. Yours truly, William W. Lincoln." He was a man of action, riding his own pony and organizing a company which, he wrote a friend, "is in a high state of efficiency and discipline"; he was as well a man of the world who traveled and shared a hotel room with the President of the United States. Oh, Willie was the apple of his parents' eye, and another thing they shared beside their love for him and Tad was a dream of taking the children on a tour of Europe before returning to the peace of Springfield, where the mother and father, long ago, had shared the hobby of studying the stars. . . .

Mary's tragedy was that, once they had reached the goal she had so passionately desired, she found it ill-starred and not at all as she had dreamed it. The small-town, girlish socialite and housewife made a shopping trip east after the presidential campaign, and eastern society watched with an avid interest that soon changed to amusement. Enroute home she stopped off in Chicago, where it was arranged to send a sewing machine to the White House. The sewing machine had a solid rosewood case, richly silver-plated and ornamented with inlaid pearl and enamel, and Mary thought it gorgeous.

When eastern society mocked her, she fought back. Gowned each time more elaborately than the last, she gave balls and receptions at the White House. Some failed because the politicos and the general public who attended stripped the party rooms like locusts, in desperate grabs for souvenirs. Others, for which she issued carefully seeded invitations, failed because Washington society, led by the beautiful and sophisticated Kate Chase, daughter of the Secretary of the Treasury, either did not come or came under ill-concealed protest. Even the loyal support of her husband's old rival, Stephen A. Douglas, failed to salve the hurt of it, and although she found some consolation in advising her husband and in caring for their beloved boys, she was too proud to give up. She announced a reception and ball for an evening in February, 1862. Washington society responded with more regrets than ever before, and the fates added the final touch—Willie caught cold riding his pony and became dangerously ill.

She and Lincoln went through the ghastly mockery of the ball, she disappearing repeatedly during the evening to visit Willie upstairs.

A few days later he was dead.

Society's smug scorn of her role in this tragedy and of her social pretensions and her extravagant clothes clamored in her imagination to an insane pitch. Only the firm understanding of the President saved her from the madness that later, after his death, bore her away.

The most insistent political question haunting Lincoln's nights and days was slavery. Stubbornly he strode around it, seeking a solution. If the house could not be divided, if the North refused to see slavery spread—what then? In his first inaugural he warned the South that their solution—disunion—would be rejected. To preserve the Union was a more vital issue than to solve the slavery problem. "To the extent of my ability," he warned, "I shall take care . . . that the laws of the Union be faithfully executed in all states." And if there be bloodshed, the Southern insurgents must accept the blame. "In your hands, my dissatisfied fellow-countrymen, and not in mine, is the momentous issue of civil war. The government will not assail you. You can have no conflict without being yourselves the aggressor."

His first message to Congress in July requested funds to support the conflict that had now begun, and he touched upon slavery only obliquely. But in December, 1861, he harked back to his "House Divided" speech. "The present struggle between the North and South," he said, "is . . . a struggle between two social systems, the system of slavery and the system of free labor. Because the two systems can no longer live side by side on the North American continent, the struggle has broken out. It can only be ended by the victory of the one or the other system." Disloyal slaveholders forfeited their ownership of slaves under the Confiscation Act. But no permanent solution of the problem was offered.

Again, in August of 1862, replying to a letter from Horace Greeley charging Lincoln with vacillating and confusing tactics, the slavery issue was brushed aside. "I would save the Union," he said bluntly. And in italics: "My paramount object in this struggle is to save the Union, and is not either to save or to destroy slavery."

But the slavery issue was, nonetheless, still the paramount political problem confronting him.

He was in the midst of his struggle for a solution and to save Mary's sanity when military disaster again rose to haunt him. The fighting—it would have been comic opera if it had not been so sanguinary—was resumed along the Potomac under John Pope, an ex-

Indian fighter fresh from minor victories against the Confederacy in the Mississippi valley. Pope talked big: "Success and glory are in the advance, disaster and shame lurk in the rear," and "I have come to you from the West, where we have always seen the backs of our enemies."

But in the East he saw only the second Battle of Bull Run in August, 1862, differing from the first in that there were no picnickers and that the Confederate leaders, whose backs Pope never saw, were those wily and intuitive masters of warfare, Robert E. Lee and Thomas J. ("Stonewall") Jackson. Pope's report on the battle punctured his own prefight bombast: "Unless something can be done to restore the tone of the Army," he dispatched Lincoln, "it will melt before you know it."

His back to the wall, Lincoln responded by putting McClellan back in command, agonized to see him win but fail to capitalize upon a resounding victory over Lee at Antietam in September, and in the same month bolstered the sagging morale of the North by moving boldly upon the slavery problem with his Emancipation Proclamation, issued on September 22, 1862, which declared all slaves free as of the first of the coming January. He then replaced McClellan with A. E. Burnside.

Thirty-nine, a tailor turned soldier when a relative got him into West Point, and a friend of McClellan, Burnside had only one admirable quality to meet the occasion which confronted him: he possessed a painful honesty, saying that he was "not competent to command so large an army." He confirmed it in December, 1862, by a frontal attack in broad daylight on Lee's battlements at Fredericksburg, Virginia. Lee, with a lesser force, succeeded in curbing his astonishment long enough to take a toll of 12,000 Union troops and win another smashing victory.

Even Burnside's fantastic ineptness was outdone by his successor, Joseph ("Fighting Joe") Hooker, handsome, blond, debonaire, blarney-tongued, who waited till May of 1863 to present the Union with its most crushing defeat, Chancellorsville. Lee and Stonewall Jackson did the honors for the South.

It is not that these men were incompetent, or cowardly, or insincere. McClellan had two horses shot from under him in one battle and, once on a hunting trip when he was cornered with an empty gun, clubbed a charging panther to death. Pope was dashing and valorous in battle, Burnside a man of highest integrity, and Fighting Joe Hooker had earned his nickname by bravery in the Mexican War. Each in his way was a good officer and courageous, and if vanity or braggadocio or funk seized them in the hour of high leadership, each may be excused in that he knew all too well Lee's West-Point-trained genius. That they faced it without flinching is enough —it was too much to expect them to face it without misgivings and without error.

If this was true of the flower of Northern generalship, what of their commander-in-chief, whose knowledge of war when he came to the presidency consisted of his Black Hawk junket as a youth? For this unbroken record of one squandered victory and five bloody defeats —for Bull Run, the Peninsula campaign, Bull Run again, the lost victory of Antietam, Fredericksburg, Chancellorsville—for all of them he bore the brunt of the blame.

We glimpse him groping his way, picking up a little military knowledge here, a little there, uncertain and easily swayed because he admittedly knew little of the so-called science of war of which his advisers and his generals spoke so glibly, drawing farther into himself and becoming more alone with the mortal hurt of each disaster and the crushing task of building from its ruins, and shuddering at the overflowing hospitals, the sight of the wounded and diseased, and the fevered cries of the mangled going in ambulances through the streets at night, and endlessly the wagons heaped with dead.

But while the military leaders had then or later explanations for their failures, Lincoln not once offered an excuse and too often protected his generals and humbled himself.

"I will hold McClellan's horse if he will only bring success," he remarked early in the war. After first Bull Run, churchmen blamed defeat on fighting the battle on a Sunday. The military blamed the politicians and vice versa, and the nation's greatest editor, Horace Greeley of the New York *Tribune*, wrote the President confidentially, begging that the Union sue for peace. But Lincoln spent his days and nights trying to assure McDowell of his confidence, visiting the troops to win them from mutiny, laboriously outlining plans for an offensive.

During second Bull Run, he sat up late night after night and, toward the end, till dawn. "The bottom is out of the tub!" he despaired. Afterward, residents of Washington began to desert the city in panic as the wounded poured in. Lincoln made no move, no further outcry, no accusations.

Fredericksburg left him "heartbroken," but he "was very careful," Henry Villard reported, "not to ask anything so as to imply criticism of anybody."

The disaster at Chancellorsville, according to Noah Brooks, found him "ashen . . . piteous . . . broken . . . ghostlike"; but he hastened to the front to cheer Hooker, not to chide him.

At long last, although the storm continued, the tide turned. As Burnside had erred at Fredericksburg, Lee, in an inexplicable lapse of genius, fed men into the maws of Union cannon at Gettysburg early in July of 1863. The Northern command was George S. Meade, veteran of all the battles fought by the Army of the Potomac and Lincoln's eleventh-hour choice to replace Hooker. Lee was driven back into Virginia and for the first time in the east the Confederacy suffered decisive defeat.

Schooled the hard way and emboldened, Lincoln took the whip hand for the first time, replacing Meade for not following up his victory. He threw aside the advice and warnings of the experts and teamed his luck with an ex-West-Pointer whom alcoholism had driven from the army before the Civil War, and who had joined the fight as a drill-master. Stocky, bearded, short-spoken, Ulysses S. Grant had since shown a mulish incapacity to quit until he had won —and the luck to win. He had begun with capturing Fort Donelson on the Cumberland early in 1862, and went on to take Nashville and Shiloh in northern Mississippi, where only his stubbornness had saved him from rout. Other land and water forces completed the western spring campaign by taking all Confederate ports on the Mississippi except Vicksburg. Grant superintended taking that after a bitter siege. Then he was transferred to Tennessee and broke the siege of Chattanooga in the fall of 1863.

He arrived in Washington for the first time in his life the following spring to take over. Appointing William Tecumseh Sherman to head the Army of the Cumberland at Chattanooga, he ordered him to invade the South, with Atlanta as his goal. Sherman set out and for long months was heard from only sporadically. Grant turned toward

Lee and Richmond. Bludgeoning his way in some of the most bloody fighting of the war, he bottled Lee up in the Confederate capital by June of 1864 and announced, "I propose to fight it out on this line if it takes all summer." But summer was too soon for the final collapse of a South that fought valiantly long after defeat was a foregone conclusion. Not until Sherman had taken Atlanta and come north pillaging the Carolinas did Lee's starving army flee Richmond, to be run down at Appomattox Court House.

In the fall of 1864, McClellan ran against Lincoln on a platform notable for its criticism of the administration's management of the war. As the campaign progressed, Sherman marched through Georgia and Grant lay siege to Richmond. McClellan made many speeches to cheering crowds. Lincoln made none. He carried all but three states.

The storm had ended.

Through it all he spoke to the people as they had never been spoken to before, not with the crusading assurance of Tom Paine, not in the polished phrases of the scholarly Jefferson, nor yet in the partisan oratory of Jackson the warrior, but as one of them, a puzzled man trying in the confusion of issues to see the right and, once seeing, to pursue it unwaveringly. In a time when oratory was considered good only when it was flamboyant, and a public figure was supposed to toss off a speech at the drop of a hat, Lincoln's economy of words and his meticulous avoidance of emotion were as strange as the fact that he spoke so seldom.

His pronouncements are sprinkled with gems of political literature. The Gettysburg address was one of these. And in his first inaugural he gave his philosophy of democracy, rejecting alike the anarchy and despotism of the frontier, of big business and of the rebellious Southern planter:

"A majority held in restraint by constitutional checks and limitations, and always changing easily with deliberate changes of popular opinion and sentiments, is the only true sovereignty of a free people. Whoever rejects it does, of necessity, fly to anarchy or to despotism. Unanimity is impossible; the rule of a minority, as a permanent arrangement, is wholly inadmissible; so that, rejecting the majority principle, anarchy or despotism in some form is left."

He said also in the same address:

"Why should there not be a patient confidence in the ultimate justice of the people? Is there any better or equal hope in the world?"

In the message to Congress of December, 1861, he said:

"It is assumed that labor is available only in connection with capital; that nobody labors unless somebody else, owning capital, somehow by the use of it induced him to labor. This assumed, it is next considered whether it is best that capital shall hire laborers, and thus induce them to work by their own consent, or buy them, and drive them to it without their consent. Having proceeded so far, it is naturally concluded that all laborers are either hired laborers or what we call slaves. And, further, it is assumed that whoever is once a hired laborer is fixed in that condition for life.

"Now, there is no such relation between capital and labor as assumed, nor is there any such thing as a free man being fixed for life in the condition of a hired laborer. Both these assumptions are false, and all inferences from them are groundless.

"Labor is prior to, and independent of, capital. Capital is only the fruit of labor, and could never have existed if labor had not first existed. Labor is the superior of capital, and deserves much the higher consideration."

And there comes to us with ever-green verity his declaration to Congress in December, 1862:

"Fellow citizens, we cannot escape history. We . . . will be remembered in spite of ourselves. . . . The fiery trial through which we pass will light us down, in honor or dishonor, to the latest generation."

Perhaps his masterpiece in tolerance and understanding, and his greatest portrayal of the Civil War and of himself and his philosophy, was his last great speech, the second inaugural:

"Fellow countrymen:

"At this second appearing to take the oath of the presidential office, there is less occasion for an extended address than there was at the first. Then a statement, somewhat in detail, of a course to be pursued, seemed fitting and proper. Now, at the expiration of four years, during which public declarations have been constantly called forth on every point and phase of the great contest which still absorbs the attentions and engrosses the energies of the nation, little that is new could be presented. The progress of our arms, upon which all else chiefly depends, is as well known to the public as to myself; and it is, I trust, reasonably satisfactory and encouraging to all. With high hope for the future, no prediction in regard to it is ventured.

"On the occasion corresponding to this four years ago, all thoughts were anxiously directed to an impending civil war. All dreaded it—all sought to avert it. While the inaugural address was being delivered from this place, devoted altogether to saving the Union without war, insurgent agents were in the city seeking to destroy it without war—seeking to dissolve the Union, and divide effects, by negotiation. Both parties deprecated war; but one of them would make war rather than let the nation survive; and the other would accept war rather than let it perish. And the war came.

"One-eighth of the whole population were colored slaves, not distributed generally over the Union, but localized in the Southern part of it. These slaves constituted a peculiar and powerful interest. All knew that this interest was, somehow, the cause of the war. To strengthen, perpetuate, and extend this interest was the object for which the insurgents would rend the union, even by war; while the government claimed no right to do more than to restrict the territorial enlargement of it.

"Neither party expected for the war the magnitude or the duration which it has already attained. Neither anticipated that the cause of the conflict might cease with, or even before, the conflict itself should cease. Each looked for an easy triumph, and a result less fundamental and astounding. Both read the same Bible, and pray to the same God; and each invoked His aid against the other. It may seem strange that any men should dare to ask a just God's assistance in wringing their bread from the sweat of other men's faces; but let us judge not, that we be not judged. The prayers of both could not be answered—that of neither has been answered fully.

"The Almighty has his own purposes. 'Woe unto the world because of offenses! for it must needs be that offenses come; but woe to that man by whom the offense cometh.' If we shall suppose that American slavery is one of those offenses which, in the providence of God, must needs come, but which, having continued through his appointed time, he now wills to remove, and that he gives both the North and the South this terrible war, as the woe due to those by whom the offense came, shall we discern therein any departure from those divine attributes which the believers in a living God always ascribe to Him?

"Fondly do we hope—fervently de we pray—that this mighty scourge of war may speedily pass away. Yet if God wills that it continue until all the wealth piled by the bondman's two hundred and fifty years of unrequited toil shall be sunk, and until every drop of blood drawn with the lash shall be paid by another drawn with the sword, as was said three thousand years ago, so still it must be said, 'The judgments of the Lord are true and righteous altogether.'

"With malice toward none; with charity for all; with firmness in the right as God gives us to see the right, let us strive on to finish the work we are in; to bind up the nation's wounds; to care for him who shall have borne the battle and for his widow, and his orphan—to do all which may achieve and cherish a just and lasting peace among ourselves, and with all nations."

This message had scarcely reached his countrymen in the hinterlands before his death, from an assassin's bullet in Ford's Theatre, Washington, on the night of April 14-15, 1865.

The record shows that during those hours of tragedy, fiery tempered Secretary of War Stanton was a paragon of statesmanship. He re-established security, telegraphed assurances hither and yon, made a resonant statement—"Now he belongs to the ages"—and generally did all he could to save the nation from the panic he so anxiously anticipated.

But he need not have worried; indeed, it would not have mattered particularly had he sat staring at his hands. The Union was mortised and solid and firm—Mr. Lincoln had seen to that. Now, after the hard fight, he belonged not merely to the ages: he belonged, as always, to the people, and had simply returned to the heart of the people, whence he had come.

[7]

The Dollar Decades
(1865–1910)

Why is it that American business has become identified in the public mind as
opposed to everything that spells greater security, wellbeing, or peace of
mind for the little guy? . . . I think the answers are pretty clear. We (businessmen) got the reputation we have because, by and large, we earned it . . .
Where on the record is there a single example to show that big business ever
initiated a legislative program of benefits for the workers? Is it not clear that
they have always waited until they were forced or asked to do something?
—CHARLES LUCKMAN

When the common workingman, bewildered and unaware of the
significance of his role, walked timidly into the American spotlight
after the Civil War, he was greeted by catcalls, brickbats, and old
vegetables. Wild throws hit with equal effectiveness the so-called and
more submissive middle class.

The play in which the two starred was destined some fifty years
later to reach its climax with the common man in the leading role;
but during the first act, he was booed off the stage more often than
not, and what little applause he received, coming from the galleries
only, was considered by the best critics of the times as too raucous
to merit attention.

These were tempestuous times, during which industrial America
revised Victorianism to meet its own lusty needs with results wonderful for a laborer to behold. He was supposed to fear God and expect the worst. He was seldom disappointed.

During nearly half of the period, he was, as usual, haunted by depressions. In 1884, Ulysses S. Grant, the ex-President, and member
of the firm of Grant and Ward, New York, went bankrupt. It took

the country more than three years to recover, with wages reaching a low in 1887, and unemployment reaching an estimated high of a million. Prosperity was returning when, in 1890, the international banking house of Baring Brothers failed. Business went from bad to worse, reaching an acute stage in the winter of 1893-1894. Wages again plummeted and jobs were not to be found.

The poor workingman during both decades was deluged with competition from abroad, encouraged alike by padrones and by American industry. Immigration mounted to new highs annually until, by 1900, the total had piled up to 36½ million persons born either in a European environment or of foreign parentage—within 3 million persons of being half the population in the nation. Of more vital economic significance, the balance of immigrants shifted from comparatively high-priced laborers from the north and west of Europe to the dirt-cheap workers from the south and east. Prior to 1883, 85 per cent were northerners; by 1907, 80 per cent were southerners.

By means of these, the padrone got his 10 per cent, the native and imported laborer his comeuppance, and big business a system of two-men-for-every-job that makes the Grapes-of-Wrath labor racketeering in modern times seem like penny ante. A group of Chicago Bulgarians were sent to Arkansas with the promise of jobs. They paid in advance their railroad fares, employment agency commissions, and 10 per cent of their hypothetical first month's wages to their padrone. Reaching Arkansas, they found that four times more men than needed had been sent out similarly. The unlucky ones walked back to Chicago, saved enough for another try by working in sweatshops, and were shipped to Oklahoma. Again they had to walk home. Helpless without their padrone, who spoke American, which they did not, they had to take this treatment or die in a sweatshop. If they landed a job, they were often fired at the end of a month to be replaced by more commissionable labor.

Once at work, they were deadly competition to natives who might want to cry out for more equitable wages. "It is a common opinion in the district," a report on Pittsburgh steel mill labor conditions stated, "that some employers of labor give Slavs and Italians preference because of their docility, their habit of silent submission . . . and their willingness to work overtime without a murmur. Foreigners as a rule earn the lowest wages and work the full stint of hours."

The laborer's woes were further aggravated from 1890, when the United States census reported that "the unsettled area (of the nation) has been so broken into by isolated bodies of settlement that there can hardly be said to be a frontier line." Native-born and immigrant alike henceforth more often than not were forced to sit tight wherever they were and take it. Those who protested were branded anarchists, the catch-all derogatory of the times.

The vanishing frontier, industrialism, immigration, and poverty among farmers created another population problem, the city slums. Between 1880 and 1900, following decades of slow growth, the small towns of pre-Civil-War days became huge cities. Population in New York increased more than a million and a half; that of Chicago more than trebled; Philadelphia picked up nearly half a million, and St. Louis and Pittsburgh two hundred thousand each.

Jacob Riis reported that in New York "three quarters of its people live in tenements, and the nineteenth century drift of population to the cities is sending ever-increasing multitudes to crowd them. The 15,000 tenant houses that were the despair of the sanitarian in the last generation have swelled into 37,000." In Chicago, Jane Addams pictured the streets as inexpressibly dirty, ill-lit, ill-paved, and flanked by firetrap wooden tenements hundreds of which were unconnected with street sewers and were without water supply. Blind Man's Alley, near Chatham Square, New York, had interiors so matted with dank filth, according to police reports, that, far from being a firetrap, nothing could set them ablaze. Summer temperatures in these buildings reached 115 degrees. Riis describes one room "not thirteen feet either way" where slept twelve men and women, two or three in bunks, the rest on the floor. "A kerosene lamp burned dimly in the fearful atmosphere, probably to guide other and later arrivals to their 'beds.'"

Acute housing shortage throughout the period made the big city an owner's paradise.

"Goddamn it!" one replied when a tenant pointed out that the rent was exorbitant. "You keep talking like that to me and I'll throw your stuff into the street and you and your family after it!"

When Andrew Carnegie bought Painter's Mill in Pittsburgh he made history modernizing its equipment but spent not a dime on Painter's Row, company living quarters for workers and their families and notable for "back-to-back houses, without ventilation, having cellar kitchens, dark, over-crowded sleeping quarters, no drinking water whatsoever, and no sanitary accommodations worth the name."

Daniel Murphy, who made a fortune out of firetraps, was indignant when the New York Board of Health threatened to padlock the worst of his houses if he did not rid them of pests.

"My monument stands waiting for me in Calvary!" Daniel said. "These people are not fit to live in a nice house!"

In 1884, when a young New York assemblyman named Theodore Roosevelt successfully supported legislation curbing sweatshops in city tenements, the State Court of Appeals declared the bill unconstitutional. If enforced, the court ruled, the regulation would take a man from his home and "its hallowed associations and beneficent influences."

Disease was commonplace, epidemics were chronic, and crime, aided by politics, began to declare macabre dividends—again at the expense of the working classes. "The Bend" block of Mulberry Street, New York, had a child mortality rate more than 20 per cent ahead of the rest of the city. Scarlet fever, smallpox, measles, pneumonia, tuberculosis, and rickets all took their toll. Crime held a field day. Gangs, which until after the Civil War had been comparatively disorganized, now took on the aspects of big business, and the slums became post-graduate schools for the mobsters who were to put lawlessness into the headlines in later decades. New York's notorious Fourth Ward tenement area turned out more criminals in 1870-1890 than the rest of the city combined. Chicago slums were comparably productive, and San Francisco's Barbary Coast ran wide open.

Manhattan streets "swarmed with prowling bands of homeless boys and girls," Herbert Asbury records. Many were adult-coached. Classic was the case of David Smith, who, after burning a wound in the arm of fourteen-year-old Edward Mulhearn and aggravating it with acid, trained the child to be a beggar, following him closely to collect the profits. The boy received bad food and worse treatment as a reward.

Others were less unfortunate. The Fourth Ward's Little Daybreak

Boys attacked a boating party in the harbor and sold their plunder to a junkman. A youth named Crazy Butch trained his dog to snatch purses and later organized a gang of pickpockets who operated successfully upon crowds which gathered after Crazy Butch created a rumpus by bumping into an innocent pedestrian with his bicycle and then showering the victim with Billingsgate. By the 1890's many of these youngsters had grown in power and viciousness, and the city was divided into districts. These were ruled systematically then and later by such schooled experts as Monk Eastman, who boasted gallantly that he always removed his brass knuckles before striking a lady; One-Lung Curran, who created a feminine style in Hell's Kitchen by knocking out a policeman and presenting the officer's jacket to his moll; and Happy Jack Mulraney, who got his name from a facial deformity and eventually went to prison for shooting one of his best friends who had asked him why he didn't laugh on the other side of his face.

The more resourceful of these gentlemen laid the groundwork for hijacking, bootlegging, and other twentieth-century criminal refinements, in the meantime cornering the traffic in narcotics, murder, mayhem, and women, and preying pettily on their neighbors. Prices were standardized. Toughs would beat up a man for two dollars, break his nose and jaw for ten dollars, and so on to murder, at a hundred dollars and up.

White slavers held regular weekly meetings to discuss the market and swap products. The age of consent under most state laws was thirteen, and traffickers used that as a point of departure. Chicago police found one child, who had been a house prostitute for six months, clutching a toy in her arms. Women plied their trade for small change in San Francisco's Barbary Coast. Factory girls, their resistance at zero after working all night, were waylaid by pimps in both cities and elsewhere. Those who could not be taken by subterfuge were treated with knock-out drops. Others volunteered, for next to children, women were the most abused victims in the labor marts.

In 1893 there were approximately forty thousand prostitutes in New York, ten thousand in Chicago, and a proportionate number in smaller cities, with only a handful of places to which they could turn for help if they desired to escape. As one girl retorted when a reformer quoted Christ and advised her to go and sin no more: "Go where?"

The average daily income of 150,000 female workers in New York in 1890 was estimated at sixty cents, from a high of two dollars as cashier in a department store to a low of thirty cents as a thread-puller in an East Side factory. Chicago women often fared worse. Female sweatshop workers in Chicago during the depression years of the 1890's got as little as a nickel a day for twelve hours of sewing.

Department-store girls worked under a system of fines for minor infractions, assessed arbitrarily by the superintendent and the time-keeper. When reformers fought through a bill requiring stores to supply rest benches for clerks, the benches were installed and anyone who used them was fined handsomely. In one set of stores, where "girls fainted daily" and "looked like corpses," they were discharged as soon as they had worked in the shop long enough to expect a raise. The management frankly stated that as the reason for dismissal.

Domestic help got from three to four dollars on an average per week for women, seven to eight dollars for men. Work included all washing, ironing, cleaning, cooking, baking, sewing, and mending for many a hired girl, and her dates, dress, and morals were closely super-vised. One weekday night off was allowed for good behavior.

Children of five were considered employable under most state laws. Parents, and especially the foreign born, sped this practice when they found it less difficult to get jobs for half a dozen offspring than for one adult. Massachusetts and New York had some labor leg-islation, but it was embryonic. In New England, labor got from three to thirteen dollars for a sixty-hour week during the 1880's. Factories in the same area were paying dividends up to 95 per cent.

Living costs were of course less, but not in anything like the same proportion. The average workingman's budget in Massachusetts in 1883 was based on an income of $754, of which $372 went for food, $149 for rent, and $32 for fuel, leaving less than $150 for clothing, doctors' bills and incidentals. This was comparatively high for the nation. Wages in the South were much less. Rural wages generally were so low that migrating from cities presented a dubious solution to the problem of the unemployed.

All wage figures were subject to revision downward at the first rumor of a depression. A male sweatshop worker receiving $1.50 a day in 1884 was lucky if he got sixty cents a day three years later, and the high cost of living got higher. Another worker, paid by a first-class uptown New York house, received from $7.58 to $9.60 per week for working from 6 A.M. to 11 P.M. A suspender maker, helped by his wife and eighteen-year-old daughter, made as much as $15 a week during three good months of the year. The other nine months he averaged from $3 to $4. His rent was $10 a month, he paid 10 cents for a small pail of coal, meat was 12 cents a pound, milk (half water and untested) 4 or 5 cents a quart.

Opposition to labor legislation was intense. Cries of socialism greeted proposals for workmen's accident compensation. Asked why he did not put a leak-proof roof over his factory, one New England manufacturer remarked, "Men are cheaper than shingles." An eight-hour-day law for women in Illinois was passed and then declared unconstitutional. In the same state, child labor legislation was opposed by glass manufacturers, who declared that barring children from their plants would bankrupt the industry.

Of course, the laborer had friends who tried to help him; and he tried to help himself. In 1881-1885, the number of strikes mounted to a then new high average of five hundred annually. Two—the Pullman strike in the Chicago area and the Homestead strike in Pittsburgh—were sensational.

To call the Homestead, in 1892, a strike, is to misrepresent the facts, since H. C. Frick locked the workmen out in the belief that they were going to make trouble when he announced a wage cut. The company at the time was coining money, but Frick claimed it was in the red. His objective was to break the steel-workers' union by slashing wages without giving labor leaders an opportunity to arbitrate. He turned Carnegie Steel's plant into an armed camp defended by Pinkerton guards. In the ensuing clash, hot steam was turned on the workers. Eighteen persons were killed and many wounded before it was over. The war ended with workers taking a 20 per cent cut.

The Pullman strike, two years later, involved all United States mine workers and American Railway union men, a total of 750,000 employees. George M. Pullman, whose paint-brush whiskers tufted a stubborn chin, refused to arbitrate. He claimed that he had built a model town for his employees. They were unappreciative anarchists to oppose him. That his wages were miserable and that Pullman residents, among other things, paid a model price of $2.25 per thousand feet for gas bought by their benefactor for 33 cents, was not mentioned.

Grover Cleveland, as sincere and honest a public servant as ever held office, was president. Pullman staunchly supported anti-Cleveland Republican war chests. Governor Altgeld of Illinois was a liberal. Everything pointed toward victory for labor until railway workers meddled with United States mail, and Cleveland moved in with the National Guard. The strike collapsed.

Pullman drove the leaders out of town and had them blacklisted among employers from coast to coast for the rest of their lives. The Federation of Organized Trade and Labor Unions never recovered from the blow. The American Federation of Labor absorbed the Unions' group in 1886, but long after the turn of the century the workingman continued to take a terrific beating.

When Frick cabled Carnegie that Homestead was settled, he added exuberantly that he did not think Carnegie Steel would "ever have any serious labor trouble again." His millionaire boss, who had risen from a textile-mill bobbin boy and believed in letting other men do his hard work, cabled back: "How pretty Italia!"

Those were the good old days! "The distinctive characteristics of this people," says Mark Sullivan with nostalgia, "included . . . a vigilance against encroachment by government on the individual [and] a freedom of stratification into castes, social or industrial, accompanied by the absence from the country's political system of any permanent or important labor or otherwse radical political party." Anyone who was unemployed was either a radical or a tramp. One was as bad as the other. "The American tramp," declared a group of Chicago businessmen when asked to aid unemployed in the depression winter of 1893, "would not work if work were offered to him. He deserves not the tear but the lash. The toe of a boot by day and a cold stone floor by night—these be the leading courses in the curriculum by which we would educate into self-respect such tramps as are capable of it. The tramp is a pariah and we ought to keep him such." The Chicago *Tribune* backed up these sentiments with an editorial recommending that chronic unemployed be eliminated by poisoning.

The man of money was staunchly defended. William Graham Sumner, to this day hailed by some for his "liberal" mind, gave as his reason for defending the "millions of the millionaire, that I love my own wife and children and that I know no way in which to get the defense of society for my hundreds, except to give my help, as a member of society, to protect his millions." Pointing out that every age is "befooled by the notions which are in fashion in it," Sumner declared that "ours is befooled by democracy." In 1894, writing upon "The Absurd Effort to Make the World Over," he argued that "democracy never has done anything, either in politics, social affairs, or industry, to prove its power to bless mankind," and asked: "Where is the rich man who is oppressing anybody?"

Metropolitan newspapers, with a few heroic exceptions, voiced similar noble sentiments throughout the era, and with justification. "They are all owned and controlled," W. T. Stead remarked from Chicago in the early nineties, "by men who have sunk thousands of dollars in their journalistic investment, and who do not want to get left if they can possibly help it. . . . To lead public opinion may be glorious, but it is not always profitable."

While the apologists acted their parts thus loyally upon the stage, heroes of high finance worked industriously upon the audience. The Astors, beginning before the Civil War and continuing into the middle eighties, parlayed a pittance of $20 million into a jackpot of $200 million. Armour, Rockefeller, and Jay Gould cleaned up modestly on the Civil War and then came on to amass fortunes beyond the imaginings of the Pharoahs. James J. Hill—"after the grasshoppers, we had Jim Hill," said the farmers of Red River Valley— got his by railroading and importing immigrants, and lived to bemoan the antitrust attacks of Theodore Roosevelt, saying, "It really seems hard . . . that we should be compelled to fight for our lives against political adventurers who have never done anything but pose and draw a salary."

Politically, things were less "hard"—for everyone but the workingman. There was considerable give and take, but the great American underdog wound up nationally doing the taking. In 1880, the Republicans won. It was a colorless campaign. Grover Cleveland, victorious in 1884, fought big business during his term and saw the Republicans returned to the White House with Benjamin Harrison in 1888 for his pains.

Cleveland won again in 1892, and big business leaders, their alarm heightened when the Democrats came up with William Jennings Bryan in 1896, prepared to shoot the works. They nominated McKinley. Marcus A. Hanna, the Ohio capitalist and McKinley's manager, told the monied interests to sit tight, and one of the notable political battles of the century was on.

"The East and the moneyed interests everywhere were whipped to a frenzy by terror," recalls James Truslow Adams in *The Epic of America.* He describes "the members of the Stock Exchange marching in a body up Broadway, and the general sense of untold horrors overhanging the whole country if Bryan were elected. I have never known another such wave of emotion catching up whole communities, not even our entry into the Great War or Armistice Day."

Bryan did not have enough stature to breast the tide. As my father used to put it, "That man could get more votes with a speech and lose more at a ballot box than any other candidate in American history." Marc Hanna went around taking levies. He assessed the beef trust $400,000, collected $250,000 from Standard Oil, and so on down the list, telling those who expressed fright, "You make me think of a lot of scared hens!" Jim Hill abandoned the Democrats and bought a paper in St. Paul to keep it out of the hands of the Bryanites. One of the campaign arguments was that if Bryan were elected, all employ-ment would cease. Thanks perhaps more to the Republican cam-paign chest than to Bryan's lack of ability, McKinley won, $7,000,000 to $300,000.

The money rulers also beat the American worker to the punch in matters holy. Devout J. P. Morgan gave half a million to the Episco-palians in a lump sum. Hill, though a Protestant, donated a million to the Catholics. John D. Rockefeller, Sr., topped them both with his largess to the Baptists.

The Reverend Frederick T. Gates of Minneapolis reciprocated by dubbing the Union Pacific "the most magnificent railroad property in the world," and the pastor of Euclid Avenue Baptist Church,

Cleveland, approached the subject with more frankness if not finesse when he declared: "People charge Mr. Rockefeller with stealing the money he gave to the church, but he has laid it on the altar and thus sanctified it."

"If Christ came to Chicago," wrote W. T. Stead in 1893 in the book he called, *If Christ Came to Chicago*, "he would find the spectacle of the greatest of all His churches [the Catholic] doing ecclesiastical goosesteps in the parade ground, but refusing to go forth to battle against the powers of wickedness in high places, and against all the tyrannies which oppress the poor, because . . . it might endanger the church and create difficulties even with some of its own members.

"The various [Protestant] churches are wealthy, comfortable, served by able and zealous ministers, and sung to by choirs of ecclesiastical nightingales." But for the most part they "have succumbed to the temptation of 'being at ease in Zion.' . . . Ministers [are] needed who will do more than make faces at the devil from behind the pulpit. . . . Instead of regarding church members as saved souls, the tendency is to regard them as members of a select club."

This worm's-eye view may appear distorted to some, especially if they were contemporaries and not worms. Justifiable protests are due especially from small businessmen of the times who sincerely believed in "rugged individualism" in the finest sense of the phrase, and struggled tragically to offset the ruthlessness of the combine builders by being fair to their labor and scrupulous in their dealings with everyone.

It is equally true that for the workingman there were numerous persons to whom he could and did turn for help, and many things which he could do to find surcease for his troubles.

If nothing else, he could go out and, for as little as two cents, drink beer gathered from old barrels and needled so effectively that one glass was enough to make him completely unconscious or crazy or both. He not only could, he did. "Forty per cent of the distress among the poor," according to an official report of the times, "is due to drunkenness." In 1890, New York had one saloon for every two hundred inhabitants. San Francisco had one for every ninety-six, not to mention unnumbered blind pigs. Activities of the blue noses seemed to stimulate bibbing. In 1878, it was up to 1,250 million gallons, a per capita increase of from 8 to 17 gallons. Saloons ruled the slums, being "the only places in the neighborhood where [a man] could hold his social gatherings, and where he could celebrate such innocent occasions as weddings and christenings."

Since the daughters of the poor and unemployed were being lured in great numbers by pimps, it follows that the sons found a plethora of brothels in which to debauch themselves. There were also dope dens in increasing numbers during the era.

More innocent pleasures could be worked in, if one were employed and lucky—this last being a necessary qualification, as witness the unfortunate Chicagoan who, after toiling twelve hours for six days in the week, met his boss in the park of a Sunday and was taken to task for not having busied himself with home work over the week end. Steamboat excursions could be enjoyed for moderate sums. Picnics, often sponsored handsomely by politicians, were frequent. There were songs—"The Sidewalks of New York," "Little Annie Roonie," "The Bowery," "Where Did You Get That Hat?" —to robe one's lot in a pleasant, rhyming sentimentality.

In the spring of 1894, the workingman was able vicariously to enjoy the spectacle of quixotic Jacob S. Coxey and his 20,000 unemployed followers making an abortive march on Washington; and although football was for the cultured and baseball not yet a national pastime, working folk had one man who symbolized all that was athletic—and more—in the epic person of John L. Sullivan.

John L. never let them down. In the last bare-fist bout for the heavyweight title and with the temperature at 120, he whipped Jake Kilrain, "the Artful Dodger," at Richburg, Mississippi, in seventy-five rounds, between which he refused to sit down. "What's the use of settin' down?" he called to protesting friends. "I gotta git up again, ain't I?" Although he lost the title three years later to Gentleman Jim Corbett, he roared through the nineties, usually drunk, generally colorful, and invariably vocal. For the delectation of his followers he said: "I believe in fights everywhere but funerals." He said: "Corbett can't punch a hole through a pound of butter." He refused to pay for an oil painting he had ordered for himself. "Judge," he argued to the court, "look at the thing. It ain't art." He trained on "a haircut and a shave." When it looked as if he might be deserting his worshippers by going on the wagon and a temperance lecture tour, actually it turned out that he was only giving them a new set of anecdotes over which to chortle. He repeatedly quarreled with the mine-run temperance leaders and lectured them in his matchless style on the fundamentals of democracy and the clean life.

Nor did the lack of movies and radio leave ordinary folk destitute of other pleasures—bands, torchlight processions, fires, Chautauqua orators running sweat beside a sweating pitcher of ice water under the dead heat of an open-sided tent. And best of all, there was that masterpiece, so admirably described by Harry Birdoff in his *The World's Greatest Hit*, the play which revolutionized theater-going in America and ran continually for more than ninety years—the stupendous, magnificent, great, and moral *Uncle Tom's Cabin!!!*

First appearing at Troy, New York, in 1852, it became a hit that broke all records there to this day, moving on to New York and spreading through stock companies to the entire North before the end of the Civil War. Pronounced dying at that point, it revived as Southerners came north to see it and Northerners trouped south to play it.

"Tommers" covered the country, their pre-play parade of dogs, slaves, villains, and angels as familiar to small towns as spring.

As the years went by, any resemblance to the original became purely coincidental. When Harriet Beecher Stowe finally saw one version, she was shocked at the language, had to have the plot explained, and left in high dudgeon.

But for the first time in American history a play broke the opposition of church-goers to the theater, drowning out the pious protests of the preachers with equally pious ballyhoo. *Uncle Tom's Cabin* introduced onto the American stage the one-show program as distinct from the lengthy melange of five-act tragedy, two- or three-act melodrama, and burlesque afterpiece which, until Tom's advent, had been standard theatrical fare. It brought spirituals to the fore in America and introduced the matinee and popular prices.

Whole families made up stock companies playing the show, some boys graduating from Little Eva through Topsy to adult roles and ending their careers, without acting in another show, as Uncle Tom.

Each decade the theatrical world prepared for the play's demise; each decade some new interest or audience turned up to perpetuate it. It went west with the pioneers and played to packed houses in the gold rushes. It drew crowds because of its political potency, its moralizing, and its mechanical difficulties—often and again Little Eva entered Heaven feet first or dangled in mid-air till the curtain could be dropped for a rescue. Sometimes the dogs beat Eliza in her desperate race across the ice. Again, overtaking her, they showered her with affection.

Mrs. Stowe got not a dime of royalties from the play and the man who first dramatized it in Troy, one George L. Aiken, received a forty-dollar gold watch. It became the greatest hit of all time.

For the rest, common men of the dollar decades could turn to that small but growing coterie of sincere Americans whose heroic leadership paved the way for twentieth-century democracy's advances.

Do not mistake this generalization. It does not refer to those who played sweet charity as if it were charades, nor yet to the militants who attacked the spangled branches of the tree of social evil and did nothing toward blasting its roots. Working folk got patronizing and holiday aid from such organizations as the Ladies' Aid and the King's Daughters, just as they were belabored for their moral shortcomings by the New York Society for the Suppression of Vice and the Anti-Saloon League—Victorian legions which Thomas Beer in *The Mauve Decade* summarized with a personality, a woman, "a grotesque shape in hot black silk screaming threats at naked children in a clear river, with her companionable ministers and reformers at heel."

"A gorgeous materialism had made a cavern for voices of the nation," he added, "and the noise blended in a roar."

Jane Addams, with less sophistication and more tolerance, summed up, in *Twenty Years at Hull House*, in different words by characterizing the period as one "of propaganda as over against constructive social effort; the moment for marching and carrying banners, for stating general principles and making a demonstration, rather than the time for uncovering the situation and for providing the legal measures and the civic organization through which new social hopes might make themselves felt."

If the poor man and his kin, regardless of where he lived, had had no one else during the era upon whom to pin his hopes, he had Jane Addams. Tolerant, patient, incredibly persistent, she believed simply that Abraham Lincoln had cleared the title to democracy, that he had made plain "once for all that democratic government, associated as it is with all the mistakes and shortcomings of the common people, still remains the most valuable contribution America has made to the moral life of the world."

"Private beneficence," she added, serving notice alike to Victorian charity, greedy politicians, and cathedral-doning businessmen, "is totally inadequate to deal with the vast numbers of the city's disinherited."

If she was not the first to found a slum settlement, at least she can be said to have set the standard with Hull House, which opened between a morgue and a saloon in 1889 and became a Chicago landmark before the next decade ended. Lillian Wald undertook a similar task in New York. Others followed. The now National Conference of Social Workers was founded in 1873 under the name of the National Conference of Charities and Corrections, and both the Society for the Prevention of Cruelty to Children and the Children's Aid Society were well organized and active throughout the two decades.

There were other personalities. Joseph Pulitzer bought the New York *World* from Jay Gould in 1883 and promptly took a stand favoring taxes against the rich and opposing corruption, monopolies, vote buying, and ballot-pressure of employers upon employees. Similarly, Charles Evans Hughes became a national figure at the turn of the century by exposing corruption among insurance companies.

In Washington, Theodore Roosevelt fought monopoly and succeeded in establishing pure food laws despite protests by the manufacturers that their liberties were being trampled.

A high-pressure shoe salesman became an evangelist, song writer, and warrior opposed to theological hairsplitting, made a fortune touring England and America, and willed it all to the poor whom he had spent a lifetime helping. This was Dwight L. Moody, who died near the end of the era leaving behind him a high standard for sawdust-trail Christianity that too many of his imitators failed to follow.

There were Henry George and Eugene V. Debs, persistent voices crying in a wilderness, plus scores of others, large and small, fighting or laying the foundations for a future fight against the monied interests and for social justice.

And Walt Whitman; and one who called himself Neshan the Terrible. . . .

[8]

The Evangels

Neshan the Terrible

General William Booth Enters Into Heaven (to be sung to the tune of "The
Blood of the Lamb" with indicated instrument):

(Bass drum beaten loudly.)

Booth led boldly with his big bass drum—
(Are you washed in the blood of the Lamb?)
The Saints smiled gravely and they said: "He's come."
(Are you washed in the blood of the Lamb?)
Walking lepers followed, rank on rank,
Lurching bravos from the ditches dank,
Drabs from the alleyways and drug fiends pale—
Minds still passion-ridden, soul-powers frail:—
Vermin-eaten saints with moldy breath,
Unwashed legions with the ways of Death—
(Are you washed in the blood of the Lamb?) . . .

(Bass drum louder.)

Drabs and vixens in a flash made whole!
Gone was the weasel-head, the snout, the jowl!
Sages and sibyls now, and athletes clean,
Rulers of empire, and of forests green! . . .

(Reverently sung, no instruments. . . .)

And . . . Christ came gently with a robe and crown
For Booth the soldier, while the throng knelt down.
He saw King Jesus. They were face to face,
And he knelt a-weeping in that holy place.
Are you washed in the blood of the Lamb?
—VACHEL LINDSAY, *Collected Poems*

Joe the Turk was six-feet-two, and before he joined the Salvation Army he was known to his neighbors as "the Walking Terror," than which it would be difficult to conceive anything more potent in the way of a compliment, considering that the time was the 1880's and the place San Francisco's Barbary Coast. "To show you the kind of a man I was," he explained later, "I got sore with my best friend and he was six months in the French Hospital and eighteen in the City and County Hospital."

Joe had gigantic shoulders, arms, and hands, and an enormous chest, above which were the short, thick neck and the cannon-ball head of a wrestler. His eyes were big and dark and questioning, his mustachios magnificent to behold. He had a voice which was an improvement on the fabled bull of Bashan, and the heart of a lion. The story goes that once when a mob was about to hang a Salvation Army officer on a bridge near Green Bay, Wisconsin, Joe left a frightened group of comrades standing hopelessly on the outskirts of the crowd, approached the bridge, boomed, "Open up in the name of the Lord!" walked calmly to his man, took him by the arm, and led him off to a train before the mob recovered from its astonishment.

Self-educated, Joe achieved heights as a musician, a designer, and for his originality generally. In the opinion of a reporter on the Beloit, Wisconsin, *Morning Citizen*, Joe had "a lip for a cornet like a circus player, although when he tried to sing the consequences were hard to describe." Oratory was another of his fortes, despite the handicap of a broad accent. He was equally effective conversationally. "When he steps up to a man and begins to talk . . . with his rapid tongue and peculiar accent," one witness testified, "it's enough to frighten a mummy."

As a showman he was seldom surpassed, possessing, in the conservative estimation of Salvation Army writer William G. Harris "the color of the East, the showmanship of the West, the passion of the Latins, the fervency of the colored folk, the determination of the Scot, the pertinacity of the Norseman, and the enthusiasm of the Irish."

During his career, and among many other things, Joe credited himself or was credited with having been the first man in a Santa Claus uniform to solicit Salvation Army funds on New York streets, with introducing the saxophone into this country, and with having been arrested "fifty-seven times for Jesus."

Even in pre-Army days, Joe's inventive talents flowered. He designed a hole-in-the-wall arrangement in his Barbary Coast shoe shop so that instead of having to walk out of his own establishment and into the saloon next door, all he had to do was bang on the wall, where an aperture connected directly with the back of the bar. Salvationism stimulated these talents. When the Army took over the saloon, Joe led in covering its walls with mottoes in poster colors, and did the front over in red, yellow, and blue. Into the wooden walk in front of the place with brass nails he hammered the legend, "Are you saved?" and every shoe he repaired henceforth had a brass-nailed "S" on the sole, regardless of whether the customer was an Army man.

Joe designed his own uniform, with bloomer-like pants in firehouse scarlet, a scarlet jacket trimmed in gold braid, and a matching fez. As Paul Waitt put it in the Boston *Transcript*, Joe was a "human circus poster garbed in flaming red," his fez like "a pink gumdrop atop a watermelon," the effect made the more radiant by a smile that "resembled a sunset."

Joe's was also the genius behind a glass coffin which appeared in one Army parade filled with liquor bottles upon which was draped an imitation snake, with the caption, "Drunkard's Doom."

When he took to traveling, his bag bore the gold-lettered motto "Salvation or Damnation."

He designed innumerable posters, signs, and cartoons, and an umbrella which for a time became, with his uniform, a personal trademark. The umbrella was made of felt on which were worked mottoes in gold. From its gold fringe dangled handpainted likenesses of Army leaders. The creation was wired with yellow, green, blue, and red lights and atop it perched a small replica of the Statue of Liberty.

In addition to his other talents, Joe the Turk was a philosopher notable for the simplicity of his tenets and for the stubbornness with which he clung to them.

"When I was in Constantinople," he said, "I thought that America was just like Heaven. I thought that every man who walked the streets was upright and good." He had no sooner landed in New

York than one of these angels stole his baggage, but he spent a lifetime struggling to make his illusion come true. America, he learned, believed in freedom of assembly and freedom of speech. Fifteen years of opposition by Americans who disagreed with him failed to cool his own belief in these freedoms. His theology was the essence of brevity: "There's hope for the whosoever." And after seeing the Army parade for the first time, he spoke of "the big drum talking of the Judgment Day. . . ."

His name was not Joe, nor was he a Turk. He was born Neshan Garabedean, an Armenian. This name he Americanized to Joseph Garabed, and Americans, observing his swarthy complexion and mustache and hearing his accent, made the ultimate simplification.

Born in Tallas, Turkey, he was the son of an Armenian priest who died when Joe was an infant. Joe picked up his English at a United States mission school in his home town and went to Constantinople when he was seventeen as a cobbler's apprentice. He prospered, then fell upon hard times in the economic backwash of the Russo-Turkish War. An older brother wrote of the wonders of America from Worcester, Massachusetts, and Joe scraped together enough money for the trip.

Later in life he said that he got his first glimpse of the Army when his boat touched at Liverpool. One of the first questions he said he asked his brother was, "Where's the Salvation Army?" only to learn with disappointment that the organization did not then operate in the United States.

There are reasons to believe that this story is imaginary, at least so far as Joe's disappointment was concerned. He sought out no other religious group in Worcester, finally settling in the world's least promising locality for a man seeking religious associations.

Indeed, the Barbary Coast of San Francisco is probably the only place in all history where a man staged a campaign against righteousness, using all the tactics of the anti-vice crusaders in reverse. He was Happy Jack Harrigan who, having been converted, for a time went straight, thereby (according to his testimony) losing his shirt. Returning to the Barbary Coast, he announced a lecture on "The True Inwardness of the Temperance Movement, or, The Potato Peeled," in the course of which he declared, "I stand before you a frightful example of the destructive effects of temperance. But though crushed to earth, I will rise again!"

He did, becoming the owner of the Opera Comique, at Jackson and Kearny streets, otherwise known as Murderer's Corner. The Comique was notorious as the bawdiest concert saloon of its day. Its owner was equally renowned as a Beau Brummell and for a silken mustache with ends so long that Jack could knot them under his chin.

Competition was keen. The Bull Run, the Thunderbolt, Every Man Welcome, the Tulip, and the Morgue were among the scores of places which tried to rival the Comique. One enterprising owner packed them in by having his waitresses dress in short skirts, silk stockings, slippers—and nothing more—an innovation that was topped by a competitor whose feminine help appeared in short red jackets from the bottoms of which the ensemble skipped to the knees.

Gambling joints, opium dens, bawds, thieves, murderers, pimps, clipsters, hoodlums, and disease all operated at full throttle. If they were not aided, they were at least abetted, by the police. Lush-workers preyed like jackals on drunkards. It was considered dangerous for law-abiding citizens to cross Kearny Street in broad daylight.

Criminals were the Coast's heroes. The word "hoodlum" was born there and gangs of them roved the streets of the area, attacking and robbing anyone they dared. Billy Smith, one of their leaders, boasted a following of two hundred toughs. Chinese criminals included in their number one of the first big-time gangsters of the nation, Fung Jing Toy, or Little Pete, who was responsible for the bloodiest tong war in all history, and who amassed a fortune in opium and white-slave traffic which he doubled by fixing west coast horse races.

Commercialized lust was a gigantic trade, with parlor houses, "cribs," and "cow-yards" operating at capacity at prices ranging from twenty-five cents to thirty dollars.

Joe opened a shoe-repair shop at 48 Sacramento Street. He took a room at Jack Finnegan's place near by. He made his arrangements with the saloon next door, found business thriving, took out his first papers, and settled down to enjoy himself. But not for long.

"One night I was in a beer saloon on the corner of Kearny and Sacramento streets, when I saw some men coming down the street and one of them was beating a big drum."

Joe, impressed, asked who they were.

"The Salvation Army," somebody said.

Everybody laughed; Joe returned to his beer; but after he went home he could not sleep.

He was haunted by the big drum talking of the Judgment Day.

The following evening he inquired his way to the Salvation Army hall in Commercial Street, but came away unimpressed.

"It was all praying and singing and I didn't want any of it, so I went back to the beer hall."

But night after night the big drum kept talking of the Judgment Day, and Joe finally gave himself up to John Milsaps, captain of the San Francisco corps.

"I was never so happy in my life," Joe related later. "Mrs. Finnegan said I was crazy and I wouldn't stick for two weeks. I said I was crazy to have spent so much money on whisky and I closed the hole in the wall with a Salvation Almanac."

His joy was again short-lived, ending abruptly when Captain Milsaps ordered Joe to march with the rest of the Army. Joe protested. The Barbary Coast boys would take him apart if they saw him parading around with a lot of religious chumps. Besides, it made his ears red. He'd stay behind and guard the barracks.

The captain persisted until one night Joe gave in. He marched for a block or so, then dropped out.

When the captain returned he gave Joe a long lecture. If Joe wanted to be a soldier—he did want to be a soldier, didn't he?—he must shirk no responsibilities. It was his sacred duty to march with his comrades. If he refused, they would think him a coward.

Joe, like Priddy Meeks, became "over-persuaded."

The Army leader did more. To make certain that Joe would not drop out of the ranks before the parade was fairly started, and at the same time to lure him outside the barracks, Captain Milsaps did an inspired thing, indeed.

He let Joe carry the big bass drum.

It is possible that neither man realized it at the time, but this was perhaps the most important moment in Joe's life. From that moment forward he was bold, brave, dominating, creative, inspired.

Joe marched forth a soldier of the King.

The early version of the Salvation Army was the New Deal of its day. Its leaders were "General" William Booth (he gave himself the prefix by telescoping his title of general manager of a Soho mission in London early in his career); and his wife, Catherine Mumford Booth. Although they were Victorian English, their methods were lusty American.

Both crusaded against social evils under a banner of "Soap, Soup, and Salvation." Christian charity, they claimed, was not enough, aimed as it was at helping only "the aristocracy of the miserable." White slavery was not the fault of the slaves but of the smug society that did nothing to rescue them. Child labor was a social evil, underpaid labor a social crime. "The more the working people can be banded together in voluntary organizations, created and administered by themselves for the protection of their own interests, the better . . . for their own interests [and] for every other section of the community." Unorganized, the workingman was helpless in a society believing "that when once a man is down, the supreme duty of a self-regarding society is to jump upon him." Negro slavery was a mild crime compared to the economic slavery of "civilized" society. "The ivory raiders who brutally traffic in the unfortunate denizens of the forest glade, what are they to the publicans who flourish on the weakness of our poor?" With masterful irony, the General proposed that, as a remedy of the lot of England's "submerged tenth," their economic standard be raised to that "of the London cab horse," a standard "at present absolutely unattainable by millions . . . of our fellow men and women."

That his attacks were opposed both in England and America goes without saying. For years, Salvationists never paraded without violence. Their appearance and spread in this country was one long chronicle of bloodshed, not allayed by infrequent visits from the General. Working on the theory that conflict led to converts and even to contributions, he, indeed, urged his followers on to riot after riot. He shrewdly capitalized on every battle. "Nothing," he said in a youthful letter to his future wife, "moves people like the terrific!" Each new attack upon himself and his folk he hailed as "good advertising." After one of the worst of the riots, in Sheffield, England, in 1882, when his blood-spattered legion finally found refuge behind barricaded mission doors, his first words from the pulpit were, "Now's the time to get your pictures taken!"

He and Catherine were a truly great team. She achieved greatness in spite of a frail physique, the General's colorful and dominating personality, and the upbringing of a recluse.

She was three months older than the General. She was much smaller than he—five feet, six inches tall, with small hands and feet, in contrast to his bearded, lank, large-limbed body. She carried her head and shoulders with a hint of arrogance. She was modestly pretty, with brown hair and small brown eyes that were intensely alive. She was active in a genteel, lower-middle-class way, doing church work at the time the General met her, but for all her façade of assurance and opinionated attitudes, she was as inexperienced as a novitiate at a nunnery. It would be difficult to imagine a less suitable mate for him. Yet, as things turned out, it would be equally difficult to conceive a more ideal partner for the venture.

This frail woman, unschooled in poverty, in worldliness, or in hard work, and apparently poorly equipped even for motherhood, in her day became more famous than her distinguished husband, and packed her life full of more work than any half dozen average women of her, or any, time.

She reared and tutored eight children. "We are not sending any of the children to school," she said once: "I hate schools." By outside activities, for years she financed her husband's slum work and the household expenses. In public life she was far ahead of her times. The only serious pre-marital quarrel she had with the General, for instance, concerned equal rights for women. She refused to marry "one who was not prepared to give woman her proper due."

While most of her earnings were from preaching, she did not take to the platform until she was twenty-nine, three years married, and the mother of three children. She preached because the General urged her to—she was frightened half out of her wits at the thought of addressing a large gathering. Yet she lived to become internationally famous as a speaker.

Shortly after she began preaching, the General had a complete breakdown from overwork and had to retire to a sanitarium. Her three children came down with whooping cough. She herself was half sick with a sore throat and chest cold. Again, the first six months of 1870 was "a season of peculiar trial," notes Booth-Tucker in *The Life of Catherine Booth*. "Early in the year Mr. Booth fell ill and was for three months completely laid aside." Catherine ran the household, the slum work, kept a heavy schedule of speaking engagements, sat up nights nursing her husband and Bramwell (who was down with rheumatic fever) and Emma (a crushed hand), and found time to write "The Use of Trials," an essay pointing the moral of her tribulations.

Between these extremes, except when she herself was too ill to walk, she observed a routine which kept her occupied from eighteen to twenty hours a day.

It was she, not her husband, who first championed the poor working girl turned streetwalker as being more sinned against than sinning. She reared her children in London's slums without one of them becoming tainted by the sordid environment.

She loved the General dearly. Her indomitable spirit did not waver until he was firmly established as one of the leaders of his time. Only then, in her mid-fifties, did she relent and put herself into the hands of doctors. She realized that she was seriously ill and insisted that they tell her frankly what her chances were. They summed up with a word—cancer.

Her first remark was that she did not regret missing the fame and the glory—she had hoped only that she might be at her husband's side to comfort him when he died, and now it could not be. . . .

From these leaders, Joe the Turk, starting as a Salvation drummer on a warm evening in 1885, was to gain the courage and inspiration to start a nation-wide campaign of his own in the United States, championing another right peculiar to the people—the right of assembly and free speech. Like the Booths, he immediately became a target for most of the toughs and the law-enforcement officials of the nation. Booth-fashion, he made no effort to dodge the attacks, rather going out of his way to seek trouble. He found it in great abundance. His 1885 parade through the streets of the Barbary Coast set the tempo of his life for years to come.

For a block or so on that historic night, the big Turk only excited curiosity and laughter. Then the little procession swung into Kearny Street and a friend recognized him. There were catcalls, jeers, and somebody shied a brick. A contemporary *War Cry*, Salvation Army house organ, heightened the drama of the incident:

"Rocks flew thick and fast and one of them hit the drummer in the head

Causing a Terrible Gash

from which the blood flowed so freely as to fill his boots. He was in a desperate fix. He could not start to run away with the drum strapped on him. If he did, the hoodlums would murder him. He could not get rid of the drum, so he had to stand."

Captain Milsaps and a couple of Army lassies managed to quiet the mob long enough to carry Joe off between them and get him back to Army barracks, where the captain watched over him hopelessly, assuming that Joe's enthusiasm for the Army and the drum would never survive the beating. The captain misjudged his man. As soon as Joe was able to talk, he announced he'd stick.

He volunteered for the post of doorkeeper at the meetings after his wound healed, leaving an ugly scar. Other scars were added with his new duties, in those days involving fights almost nightly. His nose was broken. In a brawl on the waterfront one night his coat was cut to shreds. He was stabbed in the chest. "I'd get one black eye fixed up and look in a mirror and there'd be another one." His shop was repeatedly wrecked. But his prayers, according to contemporaries, could be heard from one end of the Barbary Coast to the other, and the truculent police eventually became so impressed with these, or his durability, or the fact that they were in fights nightly on his account, that they thought they might as well be in on the beginning of them; and so they offered to help him keep order at meetings and to patrol parades. The worst of the Barbary Coast battles was over.

In April, 1887, there was a call for volunteers to open a campaign in Los Angeles. Joe was the first to step forward and his long record of arrests began.

A barrage of publicity was laid down in the Los Angeles press before the Army's arrival, and citizens took it verbatim. The stories said "Army," and Los Angeles thought "army." Wholesalers came, offering to handle food contracts; stable owners wanted the job of feeding the horses; and when Joe and the other Salvationist with him delayed by announcing that they would have a parade and then talk business, 10,000 of the city's 12,000 inhabitants turned out to jam the line of march.

His partner, somewhat awed by this misunderstanding, talked of retreat, but Joe donned his uniform, took a clarinet, armed his fellow-soldier with a drum, and started out.

At first the crowd thought they were an advance guard, but when it became apparent that they were the entire "Army," spectators began to close in. Joe and partner escaped by dropping through a trap door into a cellar, where they hid until the angry mob broke up.

The Army duo went boldly forward with plans for a tent meeting on the outskirts of the city. Hoodlums cut the tent ropes, almost setting the canvas afire when it fell against the oil lamps, and sacked a smaller tent which the Salvationists were using as living quarters. Police dispersed the mob and promised Joe & Company that they would be arrested if they paraded or preached in Los Angeles again.

Joe responded the next morning by marching through the business section in a red shirt on the front of which in yellow letters was "Prepare to Meet Your God" and on the back, "Salvation or Damnation." The chief of police followed this ensemble thoughtfully for a couple of blocks, then stopped Joe.

"You're under arrest!" he said.

"Why?" asked Joe.

The chief surveyed the Garabed outfit a moment more to verify his first judgment and then announced it firmly:

"For being a parade."

Joe accepted his sentence with "Hallelujah! Praise the Lord!" and went happily off to jail, whose inmates he organized into a clean-up squad, work being followed by revival meetings lasting most of the night and so audible that a reporter called to ask questions. Joe responded with a description of sanitary conditions in the jail, which were distinctly gamey. A prominent local lawyer offered Joe his services. Joe refused.

"The Lord got me in here," he said, looking down his nose at the attorney, "and the Lord will get me out."

The lawyer went to work, however, and demanded a trial. The chief of police changed his charge to "creating a disturbance by tooting a horn," an act which, the court decided, was no crime. Case dismissed.

Joe closed the proceedings by kneeling in the courtroom, offering up a prayer for the judge, and begging forgiveness for the misguided chief of police.

The chief in Santa Ana, Joe's next stop, profiting by the experiences of his Los Angeles colleague, looked up Joe and offered to furnish protection at meetings. Before he could get away, Joe had relieved him of a dollar as the first contribution toward a new drum, a gift which Joe publicized to the chief's embarrassment.

At San Bernardino, which even Joe, with his Barbary Coast background, described as a "tough old hole" in 1888, the local boys came to the first meeting armed with clubs and guns. One of them, the son of a leading citizen, tried to start trouble by heckling the chairman of the gathering and was almost literally knocked out of his clothes by what Joe mildly characterized as "restoring order." The rest of the trouble makers sat through the services in awed silence as Joe patrolled the aisles, while the son of the leading citizen went home in his underwear by back alleys and swore out a warrant. Joe countered the next day by insisting on a trial, gambling on the fact that the leading citizen would want to avoid publicity.

He was right. Even the judge had been instructed to soft pedal the affair. Emboldened, Joe agreed to let the matter drop if the judge, in turn, would swear out warrants for the hoodlums who had been disturbing the meetings. This was done and the local Army workers were able to proceed with their activities unmolested.

Joe went on to East Portland, Oregon, and to one of the epic chapters of his career. A drunken judge sentenced him to ten days and twenty dollars for disturbing the peace.

"Praise the Lord!" Joe boomed.

"Fifteen days extra," the judge retorted.

He was soon to regret it. Joe moved into and cleaned up the jail, held a meeting, and then looked around for something further to occupy his enforced idleness. Not infrequently in those days it was the custom for itinerant journeymen to turn themselves in at a jail to get a night's lodging, and upon one of these, a house painter with a kit full of equipment, Joe pounced. The two worked all night and at dawn the whitewashed walls of the bull pen blazoned with scripture texts. The jailer threatened to call for help. Joe demanded to see the judge, who arrived before noon accompanied by the mayor.

Joe replied to questioning by preaching a lengthy sermon based on two of the wall legends—"Jesus Is the Drunkard's Friend" and "Remember Mother's Prayer." The judge listened patiently.

"All right," he said as the harangue ended. "If I let you off, will you leave town?"

Joe shook his head.

"I demand a trial," he said. "You're always drunk, judge. Jesus is the friend you need."

He got his trial and another opportunity to preach, this time to a packed courtroom.

This adventure was a favorite sermon subject of his in later years, the moral being that, after Joe had gone on to other battlefields, the judge one day "cried to God for mercy while in his basement cleaning out ashes" and a few minutes later rushed to his wife and said he'd met the Lord.

He swore off drinking and joined the Army, serving faithfully in its ranks for years.

Joe's fame spread eastward and he moved his base of operation to Chicago about 1890. At times and at first, the Middle West seemed to receive him with disappointing calm.

At Moberly, Missouri, a contemporary newspaper story related that "it was thought by many that when they [the Army] came out to parade the streets, they would halt and pray and their arrest would follow." No arrests were made.

"The Salvation Army has so far not created any great stir in Duluth," an editor noted coldly during one of Joe's visits, "because the conditions necessary for the successful campaign of a Salvation Army do not exist here. The street paraders have been allowed to go unmolested. . . . The devil has been assailed with torch and drum . . . but no one has been disturbed unless, perhaps, the old gentleman himself."

In Detroit, Michigan, paraders were treated with surprising tolerance although "they blew their horns so loud and discordantly that they frightened the street car horses."

But these receptions turned out to be the exception rather than the rule.

In 1891, trouble reached the boiling point at Chicago. Salvationists found themselves caught between hoodlums and the police. Army quarters were bombarded by rocks, meetings broken up by toughs, and there was no protection. On the contrary, open-air meetings invariably resulted in arrests, following which Army officers were held in jail over night "to cool out," and then dismissed with the traditional:

"You boys wanta go home now?"

Answered with the equally traditional tired nod, the matter would be concluded with:

"All right, go ahead."

Joe took the situation in at a glance, and promptly applied for an outdoor meeting permit. The application was denied. Joe gave careful instructions to the local Salvationists and went ahead with a meeting anyhow.

"If they ask for a permit, send them to me," he had told his cohorts, and when the police came to him he turned his cornet on them and blasted as loudly as his lungs and lips allowed. Meantime, following his instructions, Salvation lassies formed a ring around the flat-feet and sang "Oh, Yes, There's Salvation for You!" The police fled, blushing.

Joe, arrested elsewhere in Chicago, demanded a trial when asked if he wanted to go home the next morning.

"Trial?" sputtered the astonished desk sergeant. "We don't give trials in Chicago!"

Joe stuck to his guns and enlisted the interest of a prominent Chicago lawyer. Before he got through with the police, ten of their number were suspended for sixty days and fined sixty dollars each for molesting the Army, and orders went out from headquarters to handle the Salvationists as if they were thin-shelled eggs.

Joe departed for Macomb, Illinois, and more trouble.

A crisis had been brewing in Macomb for some time. It became known to national Army headquarters when an order was sent to the captain and lieutenant in charge at Macomb, ordering them to transfer to another post. Both wrote back that they would be glad to obey—if they could. It seemed that they had been arrested for parading and disturbing the peace and fined eight dollars each. True to Salvation Army policy of the time, they refused to pay the fines, offering to serve jail sentences instead.

To this Mayor A. B. Lightner agreed, and then hung them neatly on a technicality. They could not be locked up by any but the proper official, the city marshal, who was out of town. When he returned, they could begin serving their fourteen days. In the meantime, they were under orders not to go beyond the city limits.

Joe, accompanied by the captain and the lieutenant, promptly buttonholed the mayor. A long argument ensued, with the inevitable finale—the mayor collapsed under Joe's barrage of broken English. The captain and lieutenant went to the Bridewell, and Joe stayed on to manage their affairs until their time was up.

If anybody except Joe had been doing the pinch-hitting, that would probably have been an end to the matter. But he was never one to let a lily go unpainted. During his brief visit he had uncovered a number of facts that tempted him to further action. According to Army standards, the mayor and his followers were shameless sinners, and were known to foregather and drink of an evening at the mayor's office in city hall, under whose roof was also the jail. What could be more appropriate than for the Army, led by Joe, to make hallelujah from this situation by marching in a body to city hall when festivities at the mayor's club were at their height, and serenade the imprisoned Salvation leaders with appropriate songs? What, indeed!

The Army marched.

Instead of brickbats or arrests, they were met by more serious opposition which brought the affair to a dramatic climax. In the midst of one of the songs—"Washed in the Blood of the Lamb," Joe's favorite—Mayor Lightner burst from his quarters and told the soldiers of the Lord to move on.

Joe, with Ed Coffman, a molder by trade but a Salvationist by profession, protested. The mayor whipped out a revolver, leveled it point-blank at Coffman, and pulled the trigger.

By chance—Joe promptly dubbed it a miracle—the weapon missed fire. The mayor tried again. Again—another miracle—the gun failed to go off. Friends on both sides intervened. Coffman was arrested, charged with creating a disturbance and resisting an officer, somebody put up bail, and again the affair assumed a routine pattern.

But not for long. The following day, the editor of the Macomb *Weekly Eagle* published an account of the incident in which Mayor Lightner was portrayed as the villain and his ·gunplay characterized as "atrociously uncalled for."

The day after that, the mayor and the editor quarreled on a downtown street. The editor countered in his next issue:

"We made no illusion [sic] last week," he wrote, "to Mr. Lightner's private character and only assailed his public acts as ·mayor of the city of Macomb. Since he has publicly attacked us on the street and has written a letter insinuating things which we dare him to follow up, we will give him his heart's content of personal matters, and without fear of his revolver or threats in other directions. We say that it was a cowardly and uncalled-for act on his part to draw a revolver and attempt to use it in a crowd." If Mayor Lightner wanted to make anything of it, let him remember also that "we are not made of stuff to be frightened by man or beast [and] the only reason we have not·denounced [the mayor] sooner is that we dislike to couple the name of our fair little city with the acts of such an official."

How much the editor knew concerning "personal matters" was not revealed, but it must have been plenty, because Lightner beat a retreat that, urged on by Joe, turned into a rout. The mayor freed the captain and the lieutenant. Joe countered with a series of Hallalujah meetings that soon took on the aspects of political .rallies under a slogan of "Get Lightner." Red-hot salvation became so flaming as far as the mayor was concerned that he finally had to step down in favor of a rival administration.

The finale is somewhat obscured, partly owing to the paucity of the records, partly because of Joe's brilliant memory. His version was that, "with becoming modesty," he offered to act as mayor himself and was accepted, and he appointed the local Army captain city marshal. Only by pleading for weeks was he able to relinquish his duties, bid farewell to the ever-grateful citizens, and return to the wars, thenceforth self-labeled, "Joe the Turk, ex-mayor of Macomb, Illinois."

Joe undoubtedly made capital of the designation till the day he died. But that he was ever mayor, according to L. F. Gumbart, a Macombite who was a contemporary, is "a gross canard."

At least Joe left in a blaze of glory, as witness the story written by the editor of the *Eagle* on the eve of departure:

"EVERBODY CELEBRATED
POLITICAL, MILITARY, AND RELIGIOUS
EXCITEMENT, LAST NIGHT

"Macomb was a hot-bed of excitement, Tuesday evening. Music from band, army corps, and lusty Salvationists filled the air and smoke from hundreds of torches and a couple of cannon blinded the eyes of the man in the moon."

It was the kind of prose that Joe liked so well that he saved it among his favorite souvenirs.

With a sense of the dramatic, the epic, that would have made Shakespeare cry out in envy, in the summer of 1893, at the height of the season, Joe went to Saratoga Springs, New York.

Saratoga in the summertime and in the nineties boasted Pierpont Morgan and Bet-a-Million Gates. Elihu Root and the president of the New York Phoenix National Bank, Eugene Dutlih, with his wife, and the president of any other bank you want to name with (or without) *his* wife, were regular visitors. And there were George W. Pullman, with Pullmantown profits and two years of strikeless paradise to go, and Berry Wall, who in a year was to return with a bride to whom the Prince of Wales had asked to be presented, and Captain Warren Beach, each morning giving his wife a bouquet of freshly gathered sweet peas with an elaborate gesture where all could see, and General Daniel E. Sicle, who lost his leg at Gettysburg and saved his neck when tried for killing his wife's lover, and half a world or more of other notables with mistresses diamond laden.

These celebrities gambled fortunes on the horses by day and at the tables by night. They stared at Lillian Russell in a Victoria whose matched pair were exquisitely harnessed in the whitest of doeskin. Everyone watched gaily from the verandah of the United States Hotel as Barnum's Circus, its master but recently dead, staged its annual parade. Everyone listened posed in lush tableaux while wafted through the trees from the baton of Professor Stub came the latest tune of Victor Herbert or—fantastic prelude to a night of debauch! —the haunting strains of "Nearer My God to Thee!"

And there was the one who was to be Saratoga's king, the thirty-eight-year-old son of a quiet, hardworking Congregationalist couple of New Bedford, Massachusetts, a square, solid man, known to a choice few like J. P. Morgan as an authority on history, religion, and art, but publicly famous for his knowledge in the less ethereal fields of women and gambling. To the former he gave his favors, all worldly; to the latter, his name—Canfield. Dick Canfield was there in 1893, his first two-dollar-a-week shipping-clerk job at Jordan, Marsh and Company's Boston department store forgotten, and his New York gambling houses but dimly remembered as he dreamed of converting Saratoga Club House into a fabulous fairyland where the white poker chips in the private rooms would be valued at $100, the red $500, the blue $1,000, and the sky the limit; where the house would have a million dollars in cash in the safe to pay off on a bad night, and where you could dine like a god, pointing out the trout you wanted in a pool in the patio and having it cooked to order. . . . Dick Canfield, dreaming a dream that the following year was to come true and to continue for what Hugh Bradley calls the "most dazzling decade in the history of Saratoga as well as in the history of gambling."

Dazzling Saratoga in the summertime and in ninety-three—Saratoga—and Joe the Turk!

It was an unenviable assignment. He found competition for even his gaudy uniform. John Graham, the New York criminal lawyer, was there before him and Graham, short, fat, with a round, red face, was notable for patent leathers with cloth tops, trousers that matched a tightly buttoned blue sack coat trimmed with two-inch white silk braid, a large white collar, a heavily knotted tie as blatant as Joe's cornet, and a white derby with a black band; added to which was a willingness rivaling Joe's to parade these wonders.

Joe, arriving July second, promptly gathered the Army faithful about him, instructed them briefly, and went to town. "Never," as the editors of the *Daily Saratogian* put it the next day, "has such a scene been presented as the one on Broadway last evening."

Leading his small corps, Joe stopped in front of the Grand Union

Hotel. A crowd gathered and blocked traffic. An officer approached. Joe blew his cornet in the face of the law. The officer compromised by breaking up the crowd. Joe lingered on, then moved to the corner of Phila Street, where he tuned up again. This time the law closed in.

The police asked the usual question:

"Have you ever been arrested before?"

"Fourteen times for Jesus," Joe replied.

He was charged with blocking traffic. A packed courtroom heard him deliver a sermon, plead not guilty, and demand a trial. The story went on the wires. It was picked up with hilarity from coast to coast, especially in places where Joe was known.

The Saratoga board of street commissioners promptly met and passed a new bylaw, which they admitted was "designed to prevent any repetition of the excitement occasioned . . . by the arrest of Joe the Turk." Next day the case was dismissed, but the court warned Joe that he must obey the new bylaw. Joe listened without comment. A coaching party passed down Broadway and a bugle sounded merrily.

"All right," Joe thundered, "arrest them, too!"

The court reddened and ordered the room cleared.

That night Joe violated the new law and half a dozen others. Three Army lassies were also arrested. They were dismissed with a reprimand, and Joe was let out on bail pending trial at the end of the month.

The trial would undoubtedly have played to a packed house, regardless, but in the interim Joe and others built it up to sensational proportions and the case was so widely discussed that there was great difficulty getting for jury duty anyone who would admit himself unprejudiced.

Barnum's Circus came to town, and to that colorful kite Joe appended himself as a dramatic tail:

"I had two donkeys harnessed to a cart, in which rode Captain Gaynor and Lieutenant Young carrying my umbrella. The donkeys were decorated with Stars and Stripes signs bearing Gospel invitations. Then we had a wagon covered with large banners, and in a surrey rode some Schuylerville comrades, wearing Stars and Stripes sashes. I then had another donkey, which I rode myself.

"As soon as the circus procession had passed, we fell in line down

Broadway. Great excitement prevailed, and people who had come to see the devil had the privilege of seeing something to make them think of Christ and eternity. We marched all the way to the circus grounds and back."

At this point the village fathers again stepped in, ruling that Joe could make no public appearance of any sort without a permit.

"Nearly every day, though," Joe reported modestly to New York City headquarters, "there is some kind of parade with brass band, banners, etc., and they march through the streets unmolested. No wonder the Salvation Army gets in jail here. Hallelujah!"

The trial was a seven-day wonder. It was held at Ballston Spa, the county seat, a few miles from Saratoga, and attendance at even the races dropped off as the summer folk turned out for the show.

Village Attorney James T. Brusnihan had called in the district attorney, John Person, to bolster his dignity, which had not been helped by an anonymous letter warning him to drop the charges, they displeased Almighty God, the terrific thunderstorms of the past week were visitations of His wrath, and didn't Brusnihan know that the proprietor of a large hotel who had sworn against the Salvationists had since seen his mother and sister seriously injured by the cars, one of them fatally?

Brusnihan became exasperated as the trial got under way. Will W. Smith, a prominent up-state lawyer, appeared for the defense and spoke eloquently on the Bill of Rights. When the accused took the stand he spoke so confidently of former victories that the village attorney finally cut in.

"You haven't won here yet!"

"No," Joe retorted, "but I expect to!"

Even the jury laughed at that one.

"We find him guilty but recommend a suspended sentence," was their verdict.

The court fined Joe fifteen dollars. He appealed. Brusnihan and Person, worn out, continued the fight, but their hearts were not in it. Joe won.

To understand that there was a method behind his madness, it is necessary to remember Joe's fundamental belief in democracy and to understand the early American Salvation Army. Each time Joe was arrested, he pulled back the curtain of his mind and revealed his major objective, but it was usually lost in the dazzling color of his personality if not his regalia. Invariably, after demanding a trial, he would say:

"And I'm going to take this to the Supreme Court of the United States if I have to."

He never had to. But he meant it, and the Army was back of him. Nor was he sent from town to town simply to make trouble. Nine times out of ten his job was to build up a test case in the state in which he was working, win it, and thereby leave Salvationists within the state's borders free to continue their activities unmolested.

The problem was one that haunts the nation to this day—to go over the heads of petty local officials and bring them to terms by a decision from a superior court.

Undoubtedly, most of the local boys needed teaching. Some of the decisions which Joe was handed in the lower courts are still classics in reactionary literature. Hear ye the solemn words of Judge Stanley Woodward in Wilkes-Barre, Pennsylvania, a decision, be it noted, dated November, 1898, when almost everyone else had ruled that Joe was in the right. Said Judge Woodward:

"As the questions raised in this case partake of a religious nature, and have been treated as such in the arguments of the learned counsel for the defendant, we conclude our opinion with a few quotations from the Holy Scriptures which seem to be pertinent.

"In the Epistle of Paul to Titus, chapter three, we find this command: 'Put them in mind to be subject to principalities and powers, to obey magistrates, to be ready to do every good work.'

"In the Epistle General of Peter, chapter two: 'Submit yourselves to every ordinance of man for the Lord's sake, whether it be to the king as supreme, or unto governors, as unto them that are sent by him for the punishment of evil doers, and for the praise of them that do well.'

"And in Romans, chapter thirteen: 'Let every soul be subject unto the highest powers; for there is no power but of God; the powers that be are ordained of God.'

"Judgment will be entered for the plaintiff upon the case, fine $6 and costs."

Joe appealed.

Joe won.

Joe always won. . . .

By the turn of the century he was armed with decisions from superior courts in a dozen key states and was able to reel off the gist of them the minute he strode into a courtroom. Salvationists were equally well informed. Some of the rulings were so militantly pro-Army that the most obtuse of local benchmen hesitated to rule against them. A decision of the state supreme court of Wisconsin on Joe's arrest in Portage is typical:

"The [Portage] ordinance," the Court stated, ". . . is entirely un-American and in conflict with the principles of our institutions and all modern ideas of civil liberties.

"The people do not hold rights as important and well settled as the right to assemble and to have public parades and processions with music and banners and shouting and songs in support of any laudable or lawful cause. . . . These principles, well established by the courts . . . have become a part of the supreme law of the land, so that no official body or lawful authority can 'deny to any person the equal protection of the laws.' It is plain that the ordinance in question is illegal and void."

With 1900 it became even plainer that Joe the Turk, the Army Alexander, had no more worlds to conquer.

Life became, by comparison, a walk and a whisper. And dignified. Late in 1899, even the New York *Times* editorialized concerning Joe —Joe, who, it seemed, had been visiting none other than the Secretary of State to plead the case of United States citizens desiring to visit Turkey.

Joe had three speeches—"Twenty-Five Days in Jail for Jesus," "Closing the Hole in the Wall," and "The Wonderful Conversion of the Judge." These grew more mellow and imaginative with the years. He had his favorite concert piece, "Washed in the Blood of the Lamb," and his favorite warm-up song, a tune that went—

"The blood of my Savior now fills me with shouting,
The faith of my Savior now keeps me from doubting—
The blood is a cure for the dumps!"

At which point Joe would interpolate:
"Now everybody yell, 'Dumps!' "
Everybody yelled, "Dumps!"

He traveled hundreds of thousands of miles, visiting Salvation Army posts and outposts from one end of the country to the other. He became a fixture at Army conventions. In 1917, in Lewiston, Maine, the *Evening Journal* pictured him baldish and graying after an eight years' absence. A half-page article typifies the change that had come over his world. The editors, speaking for the town folk, said they were "glad to see him and glad to welcome again this picturesque warrior for the Christian faith."

He was still traveling in 1922, but pictures indicated that his mustache was turning white. In 1923, at 68, he was definitely classed as a patriarch. A story in the Boston *Traveler* told of Joe's fight for permission to parade there "thirty years ago one balmy June evening in Malden Square." In 1924, headline writers were dignifying him with the title, "Lecturer."

Joe retired from active duty in 1925. Toward the end of 1928, the New York *World* noted that "a few weeks ago, Staff-Captain Joseph Garabed, alias 'Joe the Turk,' sounded farewell from the tower of the Salvation Army building on Fourteenth Street, at whose dedication he blew the bugle thirty-two years ago. To make way for new skyscrapers, the old building must move on, as Joe the Turk has so often had to do."

He died on October 11, 1937, at 120 West Third Street, New York, aged eighty-two. Metropolitan newspapers ran a two-paragraph story on the funeral, and the *Times* concluded:

"The services, which were attended by one hundred Salvation Army officers and friends of the Salvationist, were conducted by Commissioner Alexander M. Damon, territorial commander."

Joe must not have liked that. Having the commissioner was an honor, sure, Hallelujah, but the reporter should also have said something of the fights for freedom of assembly and of speech, the work in the prisons, the General and the General's Lady, red-hot salvation, battling for the Lord—and the big drum talking of the Judgment Day.

Walt Whitman

If one advances confidently in the direction of his dreams, and endeavors to live the life which he has imagined, he will meet with a success unexpected in common hours.
                                                    —HENRY DAVID THOREAU

The Boston People were willing to learn, but only if one recognized how much they knew already. Their minds were closed on certain lines, and they did not like "originality."
                                                    —VAN WYCK BROOKS[1]

Before his contemporary critics made of Walt Whitman a great beast, he was mostly a newspaperman—warm, friendly, rather humorless, a hater of hypocrisy, a lover and a defender of little people —one with the eye and the first-hand knowledge of a schooled realist and the futility of an economic inhibitant. As is the way with newspapermen, his dream was to tell the boss where to go, and off somewhere to put on paper exactly what was on the Whitman mind.

He was born Walter Whitman, Junior, near Huntington, Long Island, New York, May 31, 1819, the second of eight children. His father was a Quaker, a carpenter, and dour, but politically alert, a Jacksonian democrat who named one son after Old Hickory, another after Jefferson, and schooled them all sternly in the writings of Tom Paine. Walt's mother, born Louisa Van Velsor, was of Dutch-Welsh extraction.

Besides Walt, she had two moderately successful sons—George, who became an officer in the Civil War, and Jeff (Walt's favorite and admirer), an engineer in the Brooklyn waterworks. Her oldest son died in an asylum, one of the girls married a drunkard, another boy died of tuberculosis and his wife became a whore, and the youngest, a boy, was feeble-minded. Understandably, Walt was her favorite. She never knew what he was driving at—she found him and Longfellow in comparable "muddles," saying that if *Hiawatha* is poetry, "perhaps Walt's is." But she understood Walt, her son. She let him roam the streets of Brooklyn at will when the family moved there, about the time he learned to walk, and spoiled him unstintingly

[1] From *The Flowering of New England*, published and copyright 1936 by E. P. Dutton & Co., Inc., New York.

when he was at home till the day she died. "Farewell my dear beloved Walter" were the last words she wrote.

He rewarded her with life-long affection—he once said that the two great loves of his life were his mother and the wounded of the Civil War—and, in his youth, by making of himself a boy wonder. Printer's devil on the *Long Island Patriot* at fourteen, he was his own publisher and editor at nineteen (the Huntington *Long Islander*). He taught school at intervals between newspaper jobs. He figured as a New York and Brooklyn orator in the campaign for Van Buren when he was twenty-one, and at twenty-three had written and sold a novel, *Franklin Evans, or the Inebriate,* a horrendous tale on the evils of drink. He also freelanced not unsuccessfully with short stories, equally horrendous or lachrymose, in the spirit of the times.

Before he was thirty, he had become a leader in the school of personal journalism soon to reach its full bloom. It was an era in which Captain Henry King, editor of the St. Louis *Globe-Democrat,* declared that if you banished the words "blackguard, liar, and villain from our newspapers . . . even the 'good and useful' Greeley would quit in disgust." Greeley, in his prime as editor of the New York *Tribune* during the Civil War, used all these epithets freely, called Governor Seymour a liar point-blank, impugned the motives of Abraham Lincoln at the height of the Civil War, said in an editorial to William Cullen Bryant of the New York *Evening Post*, "You lie, you villain, you sinfully, wickedly, basely lie," and tilted with Henry J. Raymond of the New York *Times* concerning everything from high national policy to bets about the total circulations of their respective sheets. James Gordon Bennett routed both of them in the circulation controversy by frowning piously on gambling and remarking that they had "exhibited very little morality in the conduct of their journals." Truth is, nobody knows to this day who had the most circulation.

Western editors swelled the chorus. Outstanding was James King, who started the San Francisco *Bulletin* in 1855. He was so outspoken and so specific—David Broderick he labeled "boss of the most dastardly set of politicians that ever infested a city"—that he was murdered by the political mob, two of whom were hanged for it by vigilantes.

The newspaper spirit of the times was summed up toward the end of the era by one of its masters, Henry Watterson of the Louisville *Courier-Journal*, who, when rebuked for aspersing the governor of his native Kentucky, responded:

> "Things have come to a heluva pass
> When a man can't cudget his own jackass."

Although never one of the leaders in the field, Walt Whitman as the twenty-seven-year-old editor of the Brooklyn *Eagle* in 1846 had his high moments of editorial ire. Tall, lean, big-boned and muscular, he dressed his role as well as wrote it, sporting a stick and a bowler, chin whiskers and the clothes of a dandy.

At times he castigated prominent nobodies who came under his observation and again, generalizing, horsewhipped whole groups and strata of society.

"Still the black-hearted traitors who ply this work (of importing slaves)," he wrote, "go forth with their armed bands and swoop down on defenseless villages, and bring their load of human trophy, chained and gagged, and sell them as so much merchandise." Nor should white labor submit to slavery: 'We call upon every mechanic . . . carpenter . . . mason . . . every hard-working man—to speak in a voice whose great reverberations shall tell all quarters that the workingmen of the free United States, and their business, are not to be put on the level of Negro slaves."

"American aristocrats," on the other hand, were "that most contemptible phase of aristocracy in the whole world!" Jacob Astor was better off dead, and Grace Church, New York, was an unholy haven for moneyed snobs. ". . . the rustling silks and gaudy colors in which wealthy bad taste loves to publish its innate coarseness—the pompous tread, and the endeavor to 'look grand'—how disgustingly frequent are all these at Grace Church. Ah, there is no religion *there*."

At the end of a year, Walt broke with the publisher of the *Eagle* after kicking downstairs a political friend of the boss for objecting to the Whitman (anti-boss) stand favoring free soil.

From the *Eagle*, Walt went to the New Orleans *Crescent*, having met its publisher by accident in New York. Fired, doubtless for having made a mistress of an octaroon, he returned north a few months later to start a free-soil weekly of his own in Brooklyn.

He called it the *Freeman*, built it into a daily despite early difficulties, including a fire that wiped out his printing plant, and then walked out on it, almost a year from the day when he began publication.

The legend is that a phrenologist told him he was a born poet, but it is difficult to imagine his pursuing, without wavering for the rest of his life, a career so casually inspired. The phrenologist merely crystallized what Walt had been cogitating upon a long time.

For six years, from age thirty to thirty-six, he worked intermittently for his father as a carpenter, probably at the old man's insistence, investing intervals wandering along the shores of Long Island, floating lazily in the sea, dozing under a tree, shouting poetry to the waves, and jotting notes in a handmade scratch pad, notes hammered out a word at a time, revising, revising, revising.

The result was the first or 1855 edition of *Leaves of Grass*, the title suggesting his newspaper background, "grass" in those days meaning a part-time worker in a composing room, and "leaves" being what is now known as "galley proofs."

Walt worked on the forms himself, and peddled the book at a dollar a bound copy. (It now sells for $5,000.) Some phrenologist friends also distributed it, and even advertised it, as well as sent copies to reviewers. With one exception, reviewers were so virulent against the author that the distributors became frightened.

"This book should find no place where humanity urges any claim to respect," said the Boston *Intelligencer*, "and the author should be kicked from all decent society as below the level of the brute. There is neither wit nor method in his disjointed babbling, and it seems to us he must be some escaped lunatic, raving in pitiable delirium."

"He is the poet who brought the slop-pail into the parlor," said another critic, while Charles Eliot Norton—whom Carlyle called "the Unitarian pope" and Emerson "the tyrant of the Cambridge Parnassus"—Norton, admitting that some passages were "most vigorous and vivid writing," dismissed *Leaves* as combining "the characteristics of a Concord philosopher with those of a New York fireman." Parts of it were "disgustingly coarse," and he warned "that one cannot leave it about for chance readers, and [he] would be sorry to know that any woman had looked into it past the title page."

Total sales and review copies reached only about fifty, despite the reviews. To the second edition, a year later, preface omitted, the critics were more passionately opposed. His salesmen friends returned all copies to the author.

There were multitudinous reasons for this opposition, the chief being that the men and mores of literary America could not have been more remote from Walt if they had been located on Parnassus in fact—or on the moon. A tight little monopoly with its capital in Boston and its suburbs stretching as far as New York, it was led by Ralph Waldo Emerson, a former Unitarian minister, a Harvard graduate, and a lecturer and essayist to America at large.

Here was a world mountainously moral, blind to its faults because convinced of its utter righteousness, well mannered, and, viewed across the vista of America's most tempestuous century of growth, misty with the charm of lavender and old lace, Latin puns, Useful Knowledge Societies, crinoline hoopskirts, inlaid fans, Dickensian collars and cravats, and rich old Madeira.

Among the youth, education was the watchword, lectures the fashion. "They read Keats and Tennyson together," notes Van Wyck Brooks, "copied their own poems in manuscript books, which they passed from hand to hand, and talked about women's rights and socialism. The girls composed flower-pieces and painted in water colors. The young men read St. Augustine and Plato" and wintered in Rome and summered in Paris. "The young girls read the young men's character by holding the young men's letters against their foreheads. It was all rather bashful and indirect, as if they were a little ashamed to confess that they were interested in these mundane matters. . . . They made all kinds of discoveries, as that sometimes words came into one's mind that had a deep meaning for oneself, although they conveyed nothing to anyone else. . . . The strange, dire planet called Human Nature, hitherto so dark and baleful, had swum into their ken." (*The Flowering of New England.*)

Here flowered men whose names and writings became household words in the following decades—James Russell Lowell, Dr. Oliver Wendell Holmes, Longfellow, Emerson and Thoreau, and the historians Sparks, Prescott, Motley, Parkman, and Bancroft. Here Longfellow wrote that life is real and life is earnest and we must be up and doing; created the village blacksmith who owed not any man, the children's hour, the little girl who had a little curl, the midnight ride of Paul Revere, and such lyric folk-verse as

> ". . . the night shall be filled with music
> And the cares, that infest the day,
> Shall fold their tents like the Arabs,
> And silently steal away."

And there was Dr. Oliver Wendell Holmes—"Paris sandwiched between two slices of New England"—with a wit as sharp as it was inoffensive, taking in sideshows and horse races with the same sparrow and dilettante savor with which he dissected blue-nosed reformers. And Bronson Alcott, the greatest dilettante of them all, who reached the pinnacle of his career with the eight-year rise and fall of Brook Farm and ended his life copying gravestone inscriptions from New England cemeteries. Elizabeth Peabody, who pioneered kindergartens in this country, was one of them, and Margaret Fuller, an Amazon of a woman with the "true Boston passion for putting everything in its proper place" and with an urge to form "a true temple of culture, as unmistakable as a Boston bank."

And there were Whittier and Hawthorne; George Ticknor, who could always recognize genius if it appeared among his friends or men of good breeding; Edward Tyrrel Channing, who fathered most of the New England writers in his classes at Harvard and most of New England's reforms of the time in prisons, education, and immigrant aid; Edward Everett, Emerson's professor of Greek at Harvard, who made a career of oratory and whom Francis Parkman characterized as the most finished example of New England scholarship—"void of blood, bone, sinew, nerves and muscle." (Everett, whose oratorical masterpiece lasted one hour and fifty-seven minutes and made a huge audience cheer his flamboyant periods to the echo; a speech followed by a five-minute dedicatory postscript by one A. Lincoln: to go down in history as the Gettysburg address.)

And, in the foothills of Parnassus, there were the literary periodicals, appealing to America's sophisticates with articles emphasizing good manners, broad irony, platitudes, love among the chaste, and occasional resoundingly good fiction and essays by the Boston leaders—everything liberally interlarded with classical references, whether pertinent or dog-eared from being dragged in.

Typical is an issue of *Harper's New Monthly Magazine* at about the time Whitman stormed Parnassus with his earthy, unstyled, sex-frank lightning.

"Of all heroic attributes," says the issue's Ironist, "none commands so universally the respect and admiration of mankind as courage. . . . Whose heart has not leaped when Christian nimbly reached out his `sword to give Apollyon the last victorious thrust? . . . The favorite pursuit of man, civilized and barbarian, Christian and heathen, is to make hash and mincemeat of each other."

"Some people sneer at perfumes," says the author of another article, "call them foppish, effeminate, a waste of money, and a foolish gratification of sensual appetite." But not so! "So long as men have noses, it will be as well to use them; and so long as they are used, or rather fed, in moderation, it will be idle for Cato to turn up his own at the habit."

Any illusion that penny-dreadful fiction and the stage were the sole Victorian repositories for bad writing is here dispelled.

"No, Luke," says Milicent, in a short story of that title, "it is because I would have neither of us miserable that I am resolved to end our engagement."

Luke, after "a few turns in the room," replies angrily and departs, to be replaced by a Mr. Halford, who would make Milicent his bride and free her from supporting her invalid sister.

"You would buy a slave, not win a wife!" Milicent tells him. "Never! Never! . . . Let this suffice you, Mr. Halford; my will is fixed. Yes: any misery, even to desolation. . . ."

And then—Luke returns. The author concludes:

". . . and if I yield to my bent, and describe at length the happiness of their after-life . . . it might . . . throw the doubt of fiction over all."

The editor is more abrupt. The story of Milicent is followed in the same column by an article titled "Wanted—a Healthy Wife," complaining that women work too little, eat too much, and drive their husbands to Delmonico's and drink.

An editorial deals with the low pay among preachers, averaging from $200 to $600 annually, concluding with the pious wish that "kind Providence would send some constructive organizing intelligence who can bring into the administration of religion the same largeness, method and consistency that have done such marvels in the world of . . . commerce. The counting room needs to learn many things from the church, but the church has something to learn of the counting room."

The editor is bitter in another editorial against any person who waves pocket-handkerchiefs, especially at Barnum's diorama. Elsewhere, he opposes teetotalers for condemning wine drinking at meals, puts himself on record as favoring commonsense, and indicates, after considerable narrative circumlocution, that he is not opposed to giving alms to (old) beggars.

For Parnassus was not without its social defenses, staunchly guarded by men like Daniel Webster, and indeed symbolized by that magnificent spokesman for the Boston merchant—Webster, whose every word weighed a pound, "a small cathedral by himself."

The *North American Review*, Boston's leading literary periodical in the early decades of the century, as was the *Atlantic Monthly* from 1857, left, according to Brooks' report, "no doubt about its conservatism . . . with all the temperamental limitations that marked Webster's class of 'solid men.' . . . In literature it had a marked aversion for the notes of the new age."

The *Atlantic Monthly* followed in the *Review's* footsteps, from the beginning plumping for hard money and against such things as federal controls and the "musical Jew-brokers" allegedly controlling New York's opera world. Henry Ward Beecher was hailed as a "national institution."

Fiction was lachrymose. The *Atlantic's* leading short story in the first issue, by Harriet Beecher Stowe, titled "The Mourning Veil," told of a child dying of burns and saying, "Yes, I suffer, but only a short pain. We must all suffer something. My Father thinks a very little enough for me. . . . Oh, mamma, that [mourning] veil was for you; don't refuse it; our Father sent it, and He knows best. Perhaps you will see Heaven through that veil." Quoth the mother after the funeral: "Ah, this mourning veil has indeed opened my eyes. . . ." And, in the end: "There, by the smiling visage of the lost one— by the curls of her glossy hair—by the faded flower taken from her bier, was laid in solemn thankfulness the Mourning Veil."

Little wonder that this world, so alien to everything Whitman was trying to tell them, should reject him with animus, Whittier expressing the consensus by throwing *Leaves of Grass* into the fireplace, and the rest, excepting Emerson, following Longfellow's motto,

"Write on your doors the saying wise and old,
   "Be bold! Be bold!" and everywhere—"Be bold;
Be not too bold!"

Walt had been too bold, indeed. To the chaste moralizing of the Whittiers, the Longfellows, and the Lowells, as well as to the youthful, he said "all were lacking if sex were lacking. . . . Without shame the man I like knows and avows the deliciousness of his sex, without shame the woman I like knows and avows hers." To the solid men of literature he said, "Listen, I will be honest with you. I do not offer the old smooth prizes but offer rough new prizes. . . . you shall not heap up what is call'd riches, you shall scatter with lavish hand all that you earn or achieve."

The well mannered he dismissed with a caricature and heavy irony. "The little plentiful manikins skipping around in collars and tail'd coats," he called them, adding: "I am aware who they are (they are positively not worms or fleas)."

"Boston," as Brooks points out, "was controlled by an oligarchy, an unofficial caste of leading men for whom a 'republic' and a 'democracy' had next to nothing in common." But Whitman uttered "the word Democratic, the word en-masse," and to the barons of the churches and the counting rooms he said:

"I think I could turn and live with animals, they're
     so placid and self-contain'd,
I stand and look at them long and long.

"They do not sweat and whine about their condition,
They do not lie awake in the dark and weep for their sins,
They do not make me sick discussing their duty to God,
Not one is dissatisfied, not one is demented with
     the mania of owning things,
Not one kneels to another, nor to his kind that lived
     thousands of years ago,
Not one is respectable or unhappy over the whole earth."

The miracle that Whitman was not lynched for publishing his book is matched only by the miracle that Emerson immediately recognized its worth and, unlike all the other critics, hailed it as "the most extraordinary piece of wit and wisdom that America has yet contributed. . . . I have great joy in it. I find incomparable things said incomparably well. . . . I greet you at the beginning of a great career."

For while both men glorified man, and both visioned the nation marching toward a great destiny, Emerson was an integral part of Boston and all it represented, despite he was regarded by many of his fellow Bostonians as "an atheist and worse," a writer of "conceited, laborious nonsense." To compare or bracket him with Whitman is to class a brilliant and rebellious scholar with a sincere and integrated genius.

At best, Emerson was the master phrase-coiner and popular philosopher of his time, with a penchant for piquant aphorisms:

"Hitch your wagon to a star."

"A foolish consistency is the hobgoblin of little minds, adored by little statesmen and philosophers and divines."

"There is properly no History, only Biography."

"An institution is the lengthened shadow of one man."

"Travelling is a fool's paradise. We owe it to our first journeys the discovery that place is nothing."

"All mankind loves a lover."

"Happy is the house that shelters a friend. A friend may well be reckoned the masterpiece of nature. I do then with my friends as I do with my books. I would have them where I can find them, but I seldom use them."

"Every hero becomes a bore at last."

"The hearing ear is always found close to the speaking tongue."

"Coal is a portable climate."

"There is always a best way of doing everything, if it be to boil an egg."

"Beauty without grace is the hook without the bait.

"Next to the originator of a good sentence is the first to quote it."

He moralized with equal facility. "The only reward of virtue is virtue," and "The reward of a thing well done, is to have done it." Into every life a little rain must fall, you've got to take the bitter with the sweet. "The dice of God are always loaded. The world looks like a multiplication-table, or mathematical equasion, which, turn it how you will, balances itself. Take what figure you will, its exact value, nor more nor less, returns to you. You cannot do wrong without suffering wrong. Always pay; for the first or last you must pay your entire debt. Go put your creed into your deed, nor speak with double tongue. The only gift is a portion of thyself."

Would you be great? Be virtuous—and humble. "The essence of greatness is the perception that virtue is enough. A great man is always willing to be little." Brains aren't everything. "Heroism feels and never reasons and therefore is always right," and "nothing astonishes men so much as commonsense and plain dealing."

Material possessions help—and don't let the sophisticates tell you different. "Money, which represents the prose of life, and which is hardly spoken of in parlors without an apology, is, in effects and laws, as beautiful as roses. The world is his, who has money to go over it." Nor is this unjust, for money represents toil. "The farmer is covetous of his dollar, and with reasons. He knows how many strokes of labor it represents."

Honest labor is more to be sought than a career in the mire of politics. "The political parties meet in numerous conventions . . . the young patriot feels himself stronger than before by a new thousand of eyes and arms. . . . But not so O friends. . . . It is only as a man puts off from himself all external support and stands alone that I see him to be strong and to prevail. He is weaker by every recruit to his banner." The nation's highest political office undermines character. ". . . the President has paid dear for his White House. It has commonly cost him all his peace, and the best of his manly attributes . . . he is content to eat dust before the real masters who stand erect behind the throne." In sum, "the less government we have, the better."

Mind triumphs over matter; money, while beautiful as roses, isn't everything.

"Great men are they who see that spiritual is stronger than any material force; that thoughts rule the world. There is no beautifyer of complexion, or form, or behavior, like the wish to scatter joy and not pain around us."

Therefore be not dismayed if your material success lags behind your deeds. "If you serve an ungrateful master, serve him the more. Put God in your debt. Every stroke shall be repaid. Let the great soul incarnate in some woman's form . . . go out to service and sweep chambers and scour floors, and its effulgent day-beams can not be muffled or hid, but to sweep and scour will instantly appear supreme and beautiful actions . . . and all people will get mops and brooms."

And if the rewards still lag behind the deeds? Be nonchalant, be philosophic: "Keep cool: it will all be one a hundred years hence."

Emerson watched the nation's parade toward its destiny, always with sidelong glances at his own particular audience. Walt marched in the vanguard, shouting. Emerson's love of the common man was hedged about by thorny New England mores, and was correspondingly synthetic. Friendship was Nature's masterpiece, to be sure, and Emerson did not "wish to treat friendships daintily, but with roughest courage. I much prefer the company of playboys and tin-pedlars to the silkened and perfumed amity which only celebrates its day of encounter by a frivolous display, by rides in a curricle and dinners at the best taverns." Yet for hours one day he walked Whitman on the Boston Common rather than suffer the embarrassment of inviting him to the Emerson home, and when Emerson visited Walt in New York, he returned shocked by Walt's noisy firemen friends.

Less than a year after he praised Walt's *Leaves* to Walt, he wrote Carlyle that the Englishman could light his pipe with the book "if you think, as you may, that it is only an auctioneer's inventory of a warehouse." And as for friendship, when you come right down to it, "we walk alone in the world. Friendship, like the immortality of the soul, is too good to be believed. Friends such as we desire are dreams and fables." Only in some future time, when we are finished men, "shall we grasp heroic hands in heroic hands."

He talked a great game, Emerson.

Whitman looked about him, Emerson retreated within himself.

"Let the age and wars of other nations be chanted and that finish the verse," said Whitman, and, the verse being finished, he turned to his "greatest poem, the United States themselves." "I can find Greece, Palestine, Italy, Spain and the Islands . . . in my own mind," said Emerson. Repeatedly, he recommended solitude: "The soul environs itself with friends that it may enter into a grander self-acquaintance or solitude. . . . The heroic cannot be the common, nor the common the heroic. . . . We must go alone. Isolation must precede true society. I like the silent church before the service begins. . . . How far off, how cool, how chaste the persons look, begirt each one with a precinct of sanctity. So let us always sit. . . . I see not any road of perfect peace which a man can walk, but to take counsel of his own bosom. Let him quit too much association."

Emerson defined prudence as "the art of securing a present well-being." Said Whitman: "He has prudence who has learnt to prefer real long-lived things, and favors body and soul the same, and perceives what evil or good he does leaping onward and waiting to meet him again, and whose spirit in any emergency whatever neither hurries or avoids death."

Whitman glorified physical love, but Emerson, "looking at these aims with which two persons, a man and a woman . . . are shut up in a house to spend in the nuptial society forty or fifty years," did not wonder at "the profuse beauty with which the instincts deck the nuptial bower. . . . Thus are we put in training for a love which at best knows no sex . . . but which seeketh virtue and wisdom everywhere, to the end of increasing virtue and wisdom."

Emerson of the pretty little hymns for the more reedy registers of a melodeon was never to be compared with Whitman, who orchestrated symphonies with emphases on the kettle-drums and brass.

After his first and second editions of *Leaves of Grass* were returned to him by the distributors, Walt took heart only from himself. He began to haunt Charlie Pfaff's, a beer cellar on Broadway near Bleecker street, New York, and wrote a few additional poems for the third edition of his masterpiece. During the winters he picked up a few dollars driving stages for disabled friends, but generally he was insolvent and his only fame was the dubious recognition given him by Pfaff when Walt came to bask in the warmth of Charlie's standard greeting—"Ah, there comes the unclean cub of the wilderness!"—plus a mug of beer, usually on the house.

And then, in 1862, at forty-three, Walt was abruptly pulled into the maelstrom of the Civil War.

He began the venture as an errand and ended it as a career. His brother George had written Mother Whitman that he had been wounded, and there had been no further word. Walt went in search of him and found that the wound was minor—a cut cheek, healed before Walt arrived. But during his search, he visited a number of hospitals in and around Washington, and, deeply moved by the needs of the wounded, he stayed on to serve them, keeping himself alive with a part-time job a friend secured for him in the federal paymaster's office.

Wounded had been turned away from hospitals in the capital during the awful spring and summer of 1862. When they asked feebly where they should go, they were answered with a shake of the head. The entire city was a hospital, and filled beyond capacity. Tents were pitched along the flats of the Potomac and fevered men desperately gulped the muddy and infectious bottom water. After the second battle of Bull Run, in August, floors of the Capitol and the Patent Office were cleared for the endless line of stretchers pouring into the city. Museums, art galleries, churches, and private houses were pressed into service.

Doctors and surgeons were volunteers but poorly organized, and there were no organized nurses, who, according to the customs of the times, and allowing for the notable exceptions of Clara Barton and her handful of followers, were men. Posters were broadcast for these male nurses, urging them to come bringing a bottle of brandy, a bucket, and a tin cup. Of those answering the calls, the majority got to the front carrying their brandy in their bellies, their cups and buckets lost somewhere beside the road. One group of two hundred dwindled to sixteen before it reached the battlefield; another fell off from one thousand to seventy-five.

Wounded lay where they had fallen for days at a time unattended. At the field hospitals, there were chronic shortages of surgeons, lint, linen, bandages, and liquor. This last was the contemporary anesthetic—amputations were performed after the patient had a shot of strong liquor, if available. He was held or tied down as the operation went forward. Patients not infrequently fainted or went out of their minds. "Many of the amputations have to be done over again," Walt wrote his mother. "Many of the poor afflicted young men are crazy. Every ward has some in it that are wandering."

Surgery near the battlefields was wholesale. Outside a field hospital, at the foot of a tree, "I noticed a heap of amputated feet, legs, arms, hands, etc., a full load for a one-horse cart." Flies swarmed on wounded and helpers alike in season.

Historic irony drapes like a black fog over the fact that Lord Lister, professor of surgery at Glasgow, Scotland, did not begin his researches which opened the door to modern sterile surgery until 1860, completing them in the summer of 1865, Civil War years during which approximately half of America's youthful soldier amputees suffered the incredible pain of surgery only to die of gangrene or other infectious causes. And although the other great forward step in surgical history—anaesthetics—had been successfully employed as early as 1842 by a Jackson County, Georgia, country doctor named Crawford W. Long; although it got world-wide publicity and professional acceptance through dramatic demonstrations by the Boston dental surgeon W. T. G. Morton as early as 1846; and although Morton conducted a one-man crusade at the battlefronts during the Civil War, winning belated praise and dying in poverty for his pains— despite all these things, ether was almost unknown to Civil War wounded.

Said one surgeon at a Union field hospital: "I'd rather be in hell with a broken back trying to eat soup out of a bottle with a fork than be in this damn hole."

Day and night, day and night, Washington streets were filled with the rumble of ambulances and the groans and screams of the wounded and fevered. Day and night Walt ministered to them, black or white, friend or enemy, stealing spare moments from his rounds and his work to write to his mother, friends, and New York newspapers to tell the awful story of the hospitals and solicit funds and supplies.

He lived in a shabby room, top floor back, at E and Sixth streets, his furniture a bed, two chairs, a pine table, a sheet-iron stove, and a small packing box, upended, for a cupboard. He had so few dishes that he used a paper bag for a sugar bowl and a strip of brown paper for a butter plate. Carl Sandburg goes the rounds with him in *Abraham Lincoln: The War Years:*

He "gave fruit, paper and envelopes for writing letters, tobacco, newspapers, books, to fellows who lay with swamp fever or dysentery or bullet paths in their young bodies. At some beds Whitman spoke greetings and passed the time as if he were an uncle or a brother just from home and the folks. . . . Whitman might read from the New Testament or Shakespeare but never from his own works; he did not let on he wrote poetry." Most of the boys never knew his last name. To them he was simply "Walt."

"Here is a characteristic scene in a ward," he wrote the New York *Times* in December of 1864. "It is Sunday afternoon. . . . I am taking care of a critical case, now lying in a half lethargy. Near where I sit is a suffering Rebel from the Eighth Louisiana . . . He has been here a long time, badly wounded, and lately had his leg amputated. It is not doing very well. Right opposite me is a sick soldier boy laid down with his clothes on, sleeping, looking much wasted. . . ." And to his mother: "One soldier brought here about fifteen days ago, very low with typhoid fever . . I have particularly stuck to, as I found him to be in what appeared a dying condition, from negligence and a horrible journey of about forty miles, bad roads and fast driving; and then after he got here, as he is a simple country boy, very shy and silent, and made no complaint, they neglected him. . . . I called the doctor's attention to him, shook up the nurses, had him bathed in spirits, gave him lumps of ice, and ice to his head; he had a fearful bursting pain in his head, and his body was like fire. . . . He did not want to die, and I had to lie to him. . . ."

In the end, he became one of them, suffering from malarial fever, a poisoned cut on his hand from helping a surgeon amputate a gangrenous leg, and exhaustion. This last led eventually to a stroke in January, 1873, a bitter night during which Walt almost died before help discovered him.

These years in Washington were the golden days of his manhood, when Whitman, the mature and most human being, brought into full flower, to the limit of his abilities, the precepts of Whitman, the youthful poet-idealist.

Here, at his prime, was a man become Olympian in mind and body. "The first thing about him that struck me was the physical immensity and magnificent proportions of the man, and next the picturesque majesty of his presence as a whole," wrote a young Scotch physician on meeting him. "His head is set with leonine grace and dignity upon his broad, square shoulders, and entirely covered with long, fine hair. . . . There is an irresistible magnetism in his sweet, aromatic presence, which seems to exhale sanity, purity and naturalness, and exercised over me an attraction which positively astonished me, producing an exaltation of mind and soul which no man's presence ever did before. I felt that I was here face to face with the living embodiment of all that was good, noble and lovable in humanity."

It was a cleanliness not without honor when it came to the most controversial aspect of his life, his writings on sex and his personal sexual affairs. He was accused of perversion and of advocating it in his writings, usually by men perverted themselves by lack of a healthy approach to sex, or who attacked him on those grounds that everything for which he stood might be discredited.

For his part, Walt was as puzzled as had been Benjamin Franklin by beings so wayward that they returned from battles boasting unblushingly of mass murder, but hid in shame and darkness to perform the act of creating life.

The facts of his sex ventures are obscure. It may be assumed that he had an affair with a woman in his youth in New Orleans. In Washington, he was more than normally friendly with Peter Doyle, a young, uneducated street-car conductor. His Washington diary notes speak in code of a love affair that has, unwanted, intruded on his life. Anne Gilchrist, an English writer and liberal, decided when Walt was in his early fifties that he was the love of her lifetime, and threw herself upon him in an empassioned and extended correspondence. Walt temporized—and finally ducked. When eventually, over his emphatic protests, she came to the States, the affair reached a Platonic compromise. For a year they visited back and forth between their homes in Camden and Philadelphia. After some three years, Anne returned to England, and they ceased corresponding.

But although the details of his sex life are lacking, this can be said: not once in his entire career did he indulge in the nastinesses which marred the writings of many another man, not once did he indulge in the Rotary braggings of sex conquest that is one of the marks of sexual maladjustment or lack of sexual satisfaction. His mind was clean and he was, by eye-witness testimony, strikingly clean of body. It may be assumed that his love life was notable for a sweet cleanliness and fulsome realization.

Walt himself summed up in his old age, not without humor, saying, "My life, young manhood, mid-age, times South, etc., have been jolly bodily, and doubtless open to criticism. Though unmarried I have had six children—two are dead—one living Southern grandchild, fine boy, writes to me occasionally—circumstances have separated me from intimate relations." There is no evidence whatsoever of the children, but the attitude is unmistakably not that of a man whose personality has been marred by a lifetime of perversion.

That he was a practiced liar was one of the sidelights of his personality. During his entire life "as a press agent he remained as bad," notes Frances Winwar, "as the poet was great." Walt consistently ballyhooed Walt, let truth fall where it may.

"Death in a Schoolroom," one of his early and horrendous short stories, became, as he looked back across the years, a sensation which was repeatedly reprinted. The author of *Franklin Evans, or the Inebriate* (as portrayed by the author) was "one of the best novelists of this country . . . a pioneer in this department of literature." As editor of the Brooklyn *Eagle* in 1846 he gave a Fourth of July Ode a big typographical play, but the author's name got even better treatment: "Walter Whitman." And when the 1855 edition of *Leaves* fell upon hard ways, he wrote an anonymous article contrasting Whitman to Tennyson, to Tennyson's loss. "An American bard at last!" he hailed himself.

He unblushingly passed Emerson's letter of praise to an editor for publication without bothering to get Emerson's permission, and wrote to Emerson with equal lack of embarrassment that the first edition was a sell-out—"a few years and the average annual call for my poems" would be ten or twenty thousand copies—"more, quite likely."

Reviews, character sketches, articles designed slyly to start controversies over Whitman—these were produced during his life by himself in far more prolific outpourings than ever characterized his poems. "His manner," said Walt of Walt, "was at first sight coldly quiet, but you soon felt a magnetism and felt stirred. His great figure was clothed in gray, with white vest, no necktie, and his beard was as unshorn as ever. His voice is magnificent and is to be mentioned with nature's oceans and the music of forest and hills." In 1876 he bespoke himself on how Whitman had been neglected. In 1889 he posed for the birthday edition of *Leaves of Grass* in winter clothes but with a butterfly tied to his finger. All his life he affected clothing that attracted attention—as a young editor, the dandy; as a poet of the people, the man in working clothes. When he moved from Washington to Camden to live out his old age, he had himself listed in the city directory as "Whitman, Walt, poet," and he spent thousands of dollars on his own tomb out of a budget that remained lean till his dying day.

It might be said that *Leaves* finally came into its own despite these goings on. Seldom has a book been more unlucky. Thayer and Eldridge of Boston brought out a well-promoted and well-advertised third edition in Boston in 1860. In 1861, the Civil War drove them out of business and the book off the market. A fourth edition did not appear until 1867, a fifth in 1871. *Drum-Taps*, war poems that had been first published separately, were incorporated in the 1867 offering. But not until the sixth, in two volumes, in 1876, were there encouraging sales.

The seventh, thanks to a ban by the Society for the Prevention of Vice, broke a record for 1882 by selling three thousand copies in one day, and the book began at last to gain a wide audience.

Its author, who had launched it as a young man of thirty-six, was now sixty-two.

It was his only book. He wrote and published others from time to time, but in the end he combined the best of them in *Leaves*.

Never once in all the years did he whine, not once indulge in self-pity, never did he waver. "When the book aroused such a tempest of anger and condemnation everywhere," he once said, discussing the first edition, "I went off to the east end of Long Island, and spent the summer—the happiest of my life—around Shelter Island and Peconic Bay, then came back to New York with the confirmed resolution from which I never afterward wavered, to go on with my poetic enterprise in my own way, and finish it as well as I could."

Outstripping the neglect of *Leaves* was the neglect of its preface, which even Walt apparently discounted. He dropped it from the second edition, in 1856, and did not restore it till the seventh, more than a quarter of a century later. Hardly a contemporary critic took note of it, and it has gone unnoticed by many in more recent times.

Yet these are words too resoundingly classic to have for so long remained so obscure. The Preface gets greener with the years, as pertinent for today's form-proof novelists and the Hollywood writers with their sick-sweet mess of pottage as it was when it first appeared to confound the Whittiers, the Lowells, and the Stowes.

We have been imitators too long, says Whitman; too long have we cherished form and cuteness and Cinderella. When will our writing men come up to the high formless breathtaking and magnificent heights set for them by the nation that begot them? We have outlived our literary youth, too often squandering it in literary whoredom. Have we not waited long enough, is not now the time for world-amazing manhood?

Were his poems to be forgotten, Whitman would remain among the American immortals for this preface, one of the nation's greatest masterpieces.

In their full-length magnificence, or abridged and rearranged in places for emphasis as they are here, Walt's words rank with Tom Jefferson's as a credo for American democracy:

The Americans, of all nations and at any time upon the earth, have probably the fullest poetical nature . . . and the United States themselves are essentially the greatest poem.

Here is not merely a nation, but a teeming nation of nations. Here is action magnificently moving in vast masses . . . the hospitality which forever indicates heroes . . . here the roughs and beards and space and ruggedness and nonchalance and prolific and splendid extravagance.

Other states indicate themselves in their deputies . . . but the genius of the United States is not best or most in its executives or legislatures, nor in its ambassadors or authors or colleges or churches or parlors, nor even in its newspapers or inventors . . . but always most in the common people.

Their manners, speech, dress, friendship—the freshness and candor of their physiognomy—the picturesque looseness of their carriage . . .

Their deathless attachment to freedom—their aversion to anything indecorous or soft or mean—the fierceness of their roused resentment—their curiosity and welcome of novelty—their self-esteem and wonderful sympathy—their susceptibility to a slight—the air they have of persons who never knew how it felt to stand in the presence of superiors—the fluency of their speech—their delight in music, the sure symptom of masculine tenderness and native elegance of soul . . .

Their good temper and open-handedness—the terrible significance of their elections—the President's taking his hat off to them, they not to him—

These common people await the gigantic and generous treatment worthy of them.

An American bard is to be commensurate with the people. His spirit responds to his country's spirit . . . he incarnates its geography and natural life and rivers and lakes—

Mississippi with annual freshets and changing chutes, Missouri and Columbia and Ohio and St. Lawrence with the falls, and beautiful, masculine Hudson . . .

The blue breath of the inland sea of Virginia and Maryland and the sea off Massachusetts and Maine and over Manhattan bay and over Champlain and Erie and over Ontario and Huron and Michigan and Superior, and over the Texan and Mexican and Floridian and Cuban seas and over the seas off California and Oregon . . .

And when the long Atlantic coast stretches longer and the Pacific coast stretches longer, the poet easily stretches with them north and south . . . he spans between them also from east to west and reflects what is between them . . .

The growths of pine and cedar and hemlock and live-oak and forests coated with transparent ice, and icicles hanging from the boughs and crackling in the wind . . . and sides and peaks of mountains . . . and pasturage sweet and free as savannahs or upland or prairie with flights and songs and screams that answer those of the wild pigeon and high-hold and orchard oriole and coot and buzzard and condor and eagle.

Into the American poet enter the essence of the real things and past and present events—the tribes of red aborigines—the weather-beaten vessels entering new ports or making landings on rocky coasts—the first settlements north or south—the rapid stature and muscle—the haughty defiance of '76, and the war and peace and formation of the constitution . . .

The union always surrounded by blatherers and always calm and impregnable—the perpetual coming of immigrants—the wharf-hem'd cities—the unsurveyed interior—the log houses and clearings and wild animals and hunters and trappers . . .

The free commerce—the noble character of the young mechanics and of all free American workmen and workwomen—the fluid movement of the population—the Yankee swap—the Southern plantation life—slavery and the tremulous spreading of hands to protect it, and the stern opposition to it which shall never cease till it ceases or the speaking of tongues and the moving of lips cease.

246

For such, the expression of the American poet is to be transcendent and new.

Let the age and wars of other nations be chanted and that finish the verse— as if it were necessary to trot back generation after generation to the eastern records! As if the opening of the western continent by discovery and what has transpired since in North and South America were less than the small theatre of the antique or the aimless sleep-walking of the Middle Ages!

Not so the great psalm of the republic. Here the theme is creative and has vista.

The direct trial of him who would be the greatest poet is today. If he does not flood himself with the immediate age as with vast oceanic tides . . . and if he does not attract his own land, body and soul, to himself and hold on its neck with incomparable love and plunge his semitic muscles into its merits and demerits . . . and if he be not himself the age transfigured . . . let him merge into the general run and wait his development. . . .

Of all nations the United States, with veins full of poetical stuff, needs poets and will doubtless have the greatest and use them the greatest.

Their Presidents shall not be their common referee so much as their poets shall.

There will soon be no more priests. Their work is done. They may wait awhile . . . perhaps a generation or two . . . dropping off by degrees. A superior breed shall take their place. A new order shall arise and they shall be the priests of man, and every man shall be his own priest. Through the divinity of themselves shall the cosmos and the new breed of poets be interpreters of men and women and of all events and things. They shall find their inspiration in real objects today, symptoms of the past and future. . . . They shall not deign to defend immortality or God or the perfection of things or liberty or the exquisite beauty and reality of the soul. They shall arise in America and be responded to from the remainder of the earth.

Exact science and its practical movements are no checks on the greatest poet, but always his encouragement and support . . . the atomist, chemist, astronomer, geologist, mathematician, historian, and lexicographer are not poets but they are the law-givers of poets and their construction underlies the structure of every perfect poem . . . always of their fatherstuff must be begotten the sinewy race of the bards.

Of all mankind, the greatest poet is the equable man. He is the equalizer of his age and land . . . he supplies what wants supplying and checks what what wants checking. If peace is the routine, out of him speaks the spirit of peace. In war he is the most deadly force of war . . . he can make every word he speaks draw blood. Whatever stagnates in the flat of custom or obedience or legislation, he never stagnates.

He judges not as the judges judge, but as the sun falling around a helpless thing. As he sees the farthest, he has the most faith . . . he sees eternity in men and women . . . he does not see men or women as dreams or dots. There is that indescribable freshness and unconsciousness about an illiterate person that humbles and mocks the power of the noblest expressive genius. The poet sees for a certainty how one not a great artist may be just as sacred as the greatest artist. The others are as good as he, only he sees it and they do not.

The messages of great poets to each man and woman are, Come to us on equal terms, Only then can you understand us, We are no better than you, What we enclose, you enclose, What we enjoy, you may enjoy. Did you suppose that there could be only one Supreme? We affirm that there can be unnumbered Supremes, and that one does not countervail another any more than one eyesight countervails another . . . and that men can be good or grand only if conscious of the supremacy within them. The master knows that he is unspeakably great and that all are unspeakably great . . . that nothing, for instance, is greater than to conceive children and bring them up well . . . that to be is just as great as to perceive or tell.

It is not consistent with the reality of the soul to admit that there is anything in the known universe more divine than men and women.

The poetic quality is not marshalled in rhyme or uniformity of abstract addresses to things nor in melancholy complaints or good precepts, but is the life of these and much else and is in the soul. The best singer is not the one who has the most lithe and powerful organ . . . the pleasure of poems is not in them that take the handsomest measure and simile and sound.

The rhyme and uniformity of perfect poems show the free growth of metrical laws and bud from them as unerringly and loosely as lilacs or roses on a bush, and take shapes as compact as the shapes of chestnuts and oranges and melons and pears, and shed the perfume impalpable to form. . . .

Who troubles himself about his ornaments or fluency is lost. The fact will prevail through the universe . . . but the gaggery and gilt of a million years will not prevail. Most works are most beautiful without ornament. Great genius and the people of these states must never be demeaned to romances. As soon as histories are properly told there is no more need of romances.

The art of art is simplicity. The greatest poet swears to his art, I will not be meddlesome, I will not have in my writing any elegance or effect or originality to hang in the way between me and the rest like curtains. I will have nothing hang in the way, not the richest curtains. What I experience or portray shall go from my composition without a shred of my composition. You shall stand by my side and look in the mirror with me.

The great poets are also to be known by the absence in them of tricks and by perfect personal candor.

How beautiful is candor! All faults may be forgiven him who has perfect candor. Henceforth let no man of us lie, for we have seen that never, since our earth gathered itself in a mass, have deceit or subterfuge or prevarication attracted its smallest particle or the faintest tinge of a shade—and that through the enveloping wealth and rank of a state or the whole republic of states a sneak or sly person shall be discovered and despised . . . and that the soul has never been once fooled and never can be fooled . . . and there never grew

248

up in any of the continents of the globe a being whose instinct hated the truth.

It has been thought that the prudent citizen was the citizen who applied himself to solid gains and did well for himself and his family and completed a lawful life without debt or crime.

Beyond the independence of a little sum laid aside for burial money, and of a few clapboards around and shingles overhead on a lot of American soil owned, and the easy dollars that supply the year's plain clothing and meals, it is melancholy prudence for such a great being as a man to devote himself to the toss and pallor of money-making, with all their scorching days and icy nights and all their stifling deceits and underhand dodgings, and shameless stuffing while others starve . . . and all the loss of the bloom and odor of the earth and of the flowers and atmosphere and of the sea and of the true taste of the women and men you pass or have to do with in youth or middle age . . . and the issuing sickness and desperate revolt at the close of a life without elevation or naivete, and the ghastly chatter of a death without serenity or majesty—these are the great fraud upon modern civilization and forethought.

The prudence of the mere wealth and respectability of the most esteemed life appears too faint for the eye to observe at the thought of the prudence suitable for immortality.

He has prudence who has learnt to prefer long-lived things, and favors body and soul the same, and perceives what evil or good he does leaping onward and waiting to meet him again, and whose spirit in any emergency whatever neither hurries or avoids death.

The prescient poet projects himself centuries ahead and judges performer or performance after the changes of time. A great poem is for ages and ages in common and for all degrees and complexions and all departments and sects and for a woman as much as a man and a man as much as a woman . . . the greatest poet brings neither cessation or sheltered fatness and ease. The touch of him tells in action. Whom he takes, he takes with firm, sure grasp into live regions previously unattained . . . thenceforth is no rest.

The universe has one complete lover, and that is the greatest poet. His love above all love has leisure and expanse . . . he leaves room ahead of himself. He is no irresolute or suspicious lover . . . he is sure . . . he scorns intervals. Nothing can jar him . . . suffering and darkness cannot—death and fear cannot. To him complaint and jealousy and envy are corpses buried and rotten in the earth . . . he saw them buried. The sea is not surer of the shore or the shore of the sea than he is of the fruition of his love and of all perfection and beauty.

And liberty is indispensable. The attitude of great poets is to cheer up slaves and horrify despots. Liberty is poorly served by men whose good intent is quelled from one failure or two failures or any number of failures, or from the casual indifference or ingratitude of the people, or from the sharp show of the tushes of power, or the bringing to bear soldiers and cannon or any penal statutes.

Liberty relies upon itself, invites no one, promises nothing, sits in calmness and light, is positive and composed, and knows no discouragement. The battle rages with many a loud alarm and frequent advance and retreat . . . the enemy triumphs . . . the prison, the handcuffs, the iron necklace and anklet, the scaffold, garrotte and leadball do their work . . . the cause is asleep . . . the strong throats are choked with their own blood . . . the young men drop their eyelashes toward the ground when they pass each other . . . and liberty is gone out of that place? No—never!

When liberty goes, it is not the first to go nor the second nor the third to go . . . it waits for all the rest to go . . . it is the last.

When memories of the old martyrs are faded utterly away . . . when children are christened after tyrants and traitors . . . when I and you walk upon the earth elated with noble joy at the sight of slaves . . . when the soul retires in the cool communion of the night and surveys its experience and has much ecstasy over the word and deed that put a helpless, innocent person into any cruel inferiority . . . when the swarms of cringers, suckers, doughfaces, lice of politics, sly planners for their own preferment to city offices or state legislatures or the judiciary or congress or the presidency, obtain a response of love and natural deference from the people whether they get the offices or no . . . when it is better to be a bound booby in office at a high salary than the poorest free mechanic or farmer with his hat unmoved from his head and firm eyes and a candid and generous heart—or rather when all life and all the souls of men and women are discharged from any part of the earth—then only shall the instinct of liberty be discharged from that part of the earth.

This is what you shall do: Love the earth and sun and the animals, despise riches, give alms to everyone that asks, stand up for the stupid and crazy, devote your income and labor to others, hate tyrants, argue not concerning God, have patience and indulgence toward the people, take off your hat to nothing known or unknown or to any man or number of men, go freely with powerful, uneducated persons and with the young and with the mothers of families, re-examine all you have been told at school or church or in any book, dismiss whatever insults your own soul, and your very flesh shall be a great poem and have the richest fluency, not only in its words but in the silent line of its lips and face and between the lashes of your eyes and in every motion and joint of your body. . . .

For no great literature can long elude the jealous and passionate instinct of American standards.

America prepares with composure and good-will for the sons and daughters who are to come. Only toward as good as itself and toward the like of itself will it advance halfway. An individual is as superb as a nation when he has the qualities which make a superb nation. The proof of a poet is that his country absorbs him as affectionately as he has absorbed it.

After he had recovered sufficiently from the stroke he suffered in Washington at fifty-three, Walt went to live with his brother George in Camden, New Jersey. Ten years later, when George moved west, Walt had sufficient funds to buy his own house in Mickle Street.

He lived out his newspaperman dream to the end, his quarters a masterpiece of masculine husbandry. Dusting and straightening up were taboo and nothing was ever thrown away. Furnishings included packing-box tables, editions of *Leaves of Grass*, newspapers, books, clippings, a bust of his long-remembered Quaker evangelist, Elias Hicks, another of Grover Cleveland, a figurine of himself in which ants nested, and a coal-oil stove.

In 1885, when he was sixty-six, there arrived Mrs. Mary Davis, a sailor's widow, bringing with her a profound admiration for Walt, a few pieces of furniture, and a canary. Despite gossip—by this time it served only to amuse him—this liaison lasted seven years. She kept him more tidy. He never permitted her to dust and ordered his breakfast by pounding on the floor of his upstairs bedroom with a heavy cane. He was habitually late for other meals. He was given a phaeton and horse by public subscription, and drove at a brisk trot with Mrs. Davis unabashed through the streets of Camden and Philadelphia. He eked out a not barren living from royalties on *Leaves* and from an anniversary lecture on Lincoln on the date of the assassination begun when Walt was sixty and subsidized annually by admirers.

His worldly chronicle shows that he died March 26, 1892. But he lives now and will continue to live in the souls of men and women who learn from him to love the earth and the sun and animals, despise riches, give alms to everyone that asks, stand up for the stupid and crazy, hate tyrants, have patience and indulgence toward the people, take off their hats to nothing known or unknown or to any man or number of men, go freely with powerful, uneducated persons and with the young and with the mothers of families, re-examine all that they have been told at school or church or in any book, and dismiss whatever insults their souls.

The Rainbow Boys

In the Big Rock Candy Mountains,
You never change your socks,
And the little streams of alkyhol
Come trickling down the rocks.

The shacks all have to tip their hats
And the railroad bulls are blind,
There's a lake of stew and of whisky, too,
You can paddle all around in a big canoe,
In the Big Rock Candy Mountains.

In the Big Rock Candy Mountains,
The jails are made of tin,
And you can bust right out again
As soon as they put you in.
There ain't no shorthandled shovels,
No axes, saws or picks—
I'm a-going to stay where you sleep all day—
Oh, they boil in oil the inventor of toil
In the Big Rock Candy Mountains.

Oh, come with me, and we'll go see
The Big Rock Candy Mountains.

—American Hobo Song

I declare there is less effrontery in what I am doing than in the mock-modesty of the common run of magnates who hire a hack to write them up, and spread abroad mercenary lies to ingratiate them with the public. If you call me impudent, what word would you find for the honorable hypocrite chuckling at his own portrait and striking attitudes as his venal publicist lauds him to the skies as the sum of all virtues? Go and tell him that puffing cannot make a frog into a bull, and that it is lost labor whitewashing an Ethiope! If need be I can fall back on the old proverb that a man must need praise himself if he has no kind neighbors.

—ERASMUS (1508), *The Praise of Folly* translated from the Latin by
HARRY CARTER

It is very common in this country to find great facility of expression, and common, though not so common, to find great lucidity of thought. The combination of the two in one person is uncommon indeed.

—ABRAHAM LINCOLN

. . . there was something very engaging about these great simple-hearted creatures, something attractive and lovable. There did not seem to be brains enough in the entire nursery, so to speak, to bait a fish-hook with; but you didn't seem to mind that, after a little, because you soon saw that brains were not needed in a society like that, and indeed would have marred it, hindered it, spoiled its symmetry—perhaps rendered its existence impossible.

—MARK TWAIN, *A Connecticut Yankee in King Arthur's Court*

Men came to America bearing in their hearts a legend of the big rock candy mountains and a land where freedom's fondest dreams came true.

Too occupied with surviving the conflicts of a frontier civilization, they soon abandoned making the legend a reality. But it slept in their hearts, and lightly; and it was a song in the hearts of their children.

Often and again the nation strove, under strong, sincere leaders, toward realization of the legend. Gradually, molded in the crucible of the conflict, it began to take on at least the outlines of the hopes that fathered it.

But the way was long and hard, and some leaders there were who—either from selfish reasons or because they found for their impatience a matching restlessness among many of the people—some clothed the legend in strange and wonderful trappings, at times more unreal than the original dream.

These evangels of the pot at the end of the rainbow wakened the legend in the hearts of many, and the people would follow them until the rainbow of their promises faded in the hot mists of actuality. The people sometimes turned away in disgust or struck out in anger; sometimes, with good-natured tolerance, they dismissed the evangel as harmless.

But who, knowing the legend sleeping in his and every American's heart, can condemn the people for following the strange and wonderful evangels? Who can condemn the strange and wonderful evangels, knowing of the common legend in their hearts, so easily wakened?

Whether by choice or accident, the rainbow boys usually appeared in pursuits yielding blue chips.

When preachers were considered the epitome of achievement, Henry Ward Beecher was a minister. Harry Reichenbach gained success in press agenting while it and advertising were changing from modest enterprises to gigantic gold mines of opportunity for young men trying to get ahead in the world. Huey Long rose to political prominence as politics became one of the nation's major professions. . . .

Henry Ward Beecher dates back to the Civil War and before. A pulpit in those days could be a national hook-up, a movie hit, a best-seller, and a political campaign headquarters all rolled into one, and the man who occupied it could do no wrong. Henry Ward was always right, even when wavering, as was his habit, on matters of national import until he could discover which side the most people were on; or when caught betraying his best friends.

In his essence and at his best, he was not an evangel of Christianity nor even of emancipation, but of a highly emotional and sentimental opportunism—a big-rock-candy-mountain man in the robes of a cleric. He was the embodiment of the philosophy of the brass ring. "Do the right thing just once at the right time and dramatically," his career shouted blatantly. "After that you can go on indefinitely getting away with murder!" And the people applauded and flocked to his church and bought his books and made such a hero of him, withal, that he was one of the highest-paid orators and writers of his time, regardless of his mediocre talents in either field.

Henry Ward was born in 1813, and in his defense it should be emphasized that he began life shadowed by a number of clouds. One was his father, Lyman Beecher, to become president of Lane Theological Seminary at Cincinnati, and already famous for his stern theology and chill morality. He was anti-liquor, anti-democracy, anti-tolerance. With Jonathan Edwards he agreed that children were vipers and infinitely more hateful than vipers, and trained his with a discipline, to quote Catherine Beecher, "so severe that it was thoroughly remembered and feared." Henry Ward, cherub-faced and not, in contrast with some of the other children, especially bright, was a particularly venomous reptile in the old man's mind.

To add to the boy's difficulties were several other clouds, including half-brother Thomas K. Beecher, who grew to be a gentleman, a liberal, and a scholar; sister Catherine, well-known religious writer and spic crusader against woman suffrage, and sister Harriet, who became Harriet Beecher Stowe, author of *Uncle Tom's Cabin*.

In this unaffectionate environment, it is little wonder that—between household chores and unproductive sessions at seminaries, often run by his sisters and populated with girls—Henry Ward sought solace in long walks and loneliness.

Finally graduating from Amherst, he studied for the ministry under his father at Lane Seminary, finishing at twenty-four. Shortly afterward he accepted his first church, at Lawrenceburg, Indiana, and married Eunice Bullard, from New England, where his father had first flowered. Two years later, he accepted a call to a new church in Indianapolis. In 1847, at thirty-four, he went to Plymouth

Congregational church in Brooklyn. It was this pulpit that he spent the rest of his life making the most famous in the nation.

The dumpy boy had grown to be a man noticeably prone to plumpness, but with a radiant personality, a gift for telling jokes, an oratorical style that made up in emotions what it lacked in polish, a brilliant smile, and, behind all this (perhaps confirming his father's theories) the wily wisdom of a serpent.

For a time his success, though local, was not spectacular. The man who had called him to the new church, Henry C. Bowen, became one of two close personal friends. Bowen was also publisher of *The Independent*, one of the most successful national magazines of the time.

Beecher's other friend was *The Independent's* editor—Theodore Tilton, a youthful worshiper at the Beecher throne. Bowen gave Henry Ward an excellent pulpit; Tilton gave him access to the pages of a national publication. Henry Ward was on the high road to success.

He made other influential connections. Henchmen of Tammany Hall political boss William Marcy Tweed were in his congregation, as were big businessmen, including friends of Jay Cooke, who one day was to pay Henry Ward $15,000 in stocks for influencing, both from the Beecher pulpit and in print, the public mind in favor of Cooke speculations. Discreetly, Beecher jockeyed on public issues, including slavery, blasting instead at such hole-proof evils as sin, French literature, and the theater. His approach to life was not entirely negative. "His favorite theme," says the Encyclopaedia Britannica is one of its most brilliantly misleading understatements, "was love."

On the eve of the Civil War, a brass ring flashed before his eyes and Henry Ward grabbed for it blindly. Blind is the word for his entire approach to the most important question of the day—slavery—on which he had, up till then, taken about every possible stand that verbiage and a shrewd ability at phrasing could support. Now, with the North screaming abolition, Henry leaped dramatically on the bandwagon. From his pulpit he auctioned off a beautiful mulatto girl from Staunton, Virginia, buying her freedom with the money, jewelry, and heirlooms which his congregation poured at her feet as he whipped them to hysteria with his oratory. Henry Ward became a national figure overnight.

He knew how to hold the limelight once he had succeeded in gaining it. During the war, he went to England, taking huge credit for converting the British public to the Union cause, a cause with which they had been sympathetic from the beginning. He wrote an incredibly bad novel and sold it for the then incredibly large sum of $24,-000. He wrote testimonials for sewing machines, Sapolio, and a truss to cure ruptures. A casual correspondence with Lincoln he built up from his pulpit into a mirage that led people to believe the President considered him one of his closest advisers. (Old Abe decidedly did not.) And he continued to preach about love.

It was not something that he found in his own home, where Eunice, his wife, had developed maternal techniques matching old Lyman Beecher's. Old Lyman himself, who had also joined the household, made life so miserable that they finally had to put him up in a separate residence, and from Henry Ward's home his sister Catherine plotted campaigns against those awful women, the suffragettes. Eunice as a wife was, it appears, about as warm as an iced corpse. Further, she did not like the gregarious habit Henry had of bringing a friend home for dinner. Further, she did not approve of a lot of other things he did, never mentioned between them. Henry Ward summed his home up as the "vainest, the most vapid, the most juiceless, the most unsaccharine of all things" and said he dreaded daily to go back to it.

Finally, he quit going. He turned first to the wife of one of his best friends, Henry C. Bowen. When she confessed to it on her deathbed —she was thirty-eight and the mother of ten children and beloved by Bowen—Beecher managed to avoid public exposal, although almost immediately Bowen, as publisher of *The Independent,* forced Henry Ward off the editorial staff. A few years later, unabashed, Beecher seduced Libby Tilton, wife of his other best friend and his most faithful admirer, *The Independent's* editor. Theodore Tilton, after a long delay during which Beecher valiantly worked at propaganda designed to discredit Tilton and any testimony he might give —Tilton took the case to court.

It was, needless to say, the trial of the century. Attention of the nation centered on City Court, Brooklyn, during the 112 days of testimony, examination, and cross-examination, and waited breathlessly for the jury's decision. It was inconclusive—the jury disagreed.

"The world will never forgive you," a friend told Tilton, "for having condoned your wife's crime." Incredible as it may seem, Henry Ward had sold that idea to the public and, aided by unlimited legal talent, to twelve of his peers. His greatest victory was won.

He soon had another. Henry C. Bowen, after the long years of silence, asked the Plymouth congregation to hear charges he wished to bring against its pastor. Without naming his dead wife, he rose and accused Beecher point-blank of adultery. He was promptly thrown out of the church. Henry Ward Beecher, Casanova of the Cross, reigned supreme.

He packed 'em in at the church. He went on a triumphant tour, getting as much as $1,000 a lecture. He figured in political campaigns. He became more and more outspoken, more and more arrogant. No need now to hedge his oratory—Henry Ward Beecher could get away with anything and had proved it. "Is the great working class oppressed?" he asked. "Yes, undoubtedly it is" for "God has intended the great to be great and the little to be little." Again he said: "The man who cannot live on bread and water is not fit to live." Himself, he was fit to make $40,000 or more a year and sway every audience that he faced.

But though he was perhaps too thick-skinned by then for it to touch him, the tide had subtly turned. Other leaders spoke against him, and spoke bluntly. Henry Watterson of the Louisville *Courier-Journal* called Beecher "a dunghill covered with flowers." "Henry Ward Beecher," said Charles A. Dana of the New York *Sun*, "is an adulterer, a perjurer, and a fraud; and his great genius and his Christian pretenses only make his sins the more horrible and revolting." "Mankind fell in Adam, and has been falling ever since," remarked another editor, "but never touched bottom till it got to Henry Ward Beecher."

Half-brother Thomas K. Beecher had never been a Henryphile. Once, filling Henry's pulpit, some of the audience had started to leave as Thomas began the sermon. "Those who came here to worship Henry Ward Beecher," Thomas said smilingly, "are excused. Those who wish to worship God will remain." Now he summed up the case for the less spectacular clergy. "Henry," he said, "is following his slippery doctrines of expediency and . . . has sacrificed clear, exact, ideal integrity."

But Henry heeded not, continued to follow, continued to sacrifice. Till he died of apoplexy at seventy-three, he played his bluff hand—and won.

Few but sensation-seeking women attended the funeral. The nation failed wholeheartedly to mourn. More puzzled than disgusted by Henry Ward's performance, they were perhaps too close to the footlights to' realize his contribution to history. It took an observer of a later generation to put it into words for them.

"Though we speak with the brisk quack of the radio," said Sinclair Lewis, "our words are still too often the lordly lard of Henry Ward Beecher."

In his youth, Harry Reichenbach spoke not with the tongues of angels but in the gamin dialect of the street corner; nor did he possess Henry Ward's pompous hypocrisy.

His goal was clearly and honestly stated time and again.

"Ladeez and gentlemen," he said in effect, "the big rock candy mountain is hokum and I'm the man to deck it in tinsel and spangles and sell it with Gargantuan humor. You'll get ballyhoo for your money, but if you go home with empty pockets, you'll also go home laughing."

Unlike Barnum, he did not discover miracles for the world's amaze. He was not a manager, an entrepreneur, a proprietor of museums full of freaks. He considered management too mundane and unexciting for his talents. He was the unadulterated son of ballyhoo. "He starred at making people talk," said Walter Winchell after Reichenbach's death. "No matter what the product or the person or the place, when Reichenbach was engaged to exploit it the subject became known—often internationally."

Reichenbach said in *Anatomy of Ballyhoo: Phantom Fame:* "Publicity is the nervous system of the world." If he sometimes put it ahead of the product he was promoting, it was not out of dishonesty, but because, as one of the world's greatest ballyhoo artists, *his* product, publicity, always had to be unrivaled in its spectacular excellence. If, toward the end, he united in historic wedlock the ballyhoo of the sideshow to the publicity of big business, thereby paving the way for the hypocrisy of modern public-relations counseling, he did it with the naïveté that often marks a pioneer, not with malice aforethought.

He was born in 1884 and died, at forty-nine, in 1933. He could hardly have packed more into his life had he lived to twice that age.

His education was of the informal sort that could be got only in America. The son of an unsuccessful store- and saloon-proprietor in Maryland and West Virginia coal towns, Harry was an invalid from his second to his ninth year, and, during the last of these, read voluminously of Frank Reade, Junior. Frank Merriwell was his hero from then until he was grown.

"I never saw the inside of a school," Harry said, years later. Becoming exuberantly healthy in his teens, he ran away from home with a carnival, and there went to college, largely under one Doc Crosby, a medicine man, carnival dentist and savant. Doc's philosophy could be summed up in a paragraph, part of his lecture on fair dealing and pharmaceutics.

"Honesty," he told Harry, "is the best policy. Dr. Crosby's Wonder Tonic and Immortal Beverage has been a standard product for over twenty years—and you know why? Because I've never adulterated it. I've always stuck honestly to the same formula—from sixty-five to ninety percent water . . . water is Nature's gift to man!"

Reichenbach also credits Crosby with the classic, "Never give a sucker an even break," and from Bill Swanson, proprietor of the show, gained moral justification for this motto. "The worst thieves," Bill used to say indignantly, "are those who cheat their own neighbors every week in the year. A carnival man is always considerate. He cheats a new clientele every week and at that, he gyps them of very little."

With this excellent counsel, plus the motherly guidance of Millie-Christine, the show's Siamese twin—"there was a fine, big-sister quality in both of her"—plus jail sessions for brawling and vagrancy, plus hoboing and riding freights when times were bad, plus spieling for a high-diver while carnival pickpockets plied their trade, and sundry other experiences—thoroughly equipped, young Harry finally qualified as the advance man and press agent for Reynard the Great. "The fabulous magician and handcuff king," Riechenbach described him, "who could step out of sealed boxes, open locked safes, break through bolted prison cells and walk through brick walls with ease, but who couldn't get out of his own hotel room because I had absent-mindedly locked him in." Here Reichenbach got his graduate degree in his craft, for Reynard "made the tricks of the carnival and circus look like games in a kindergarten."

The handcuff trick was easy—Reynard could pick any conventional manacle with a hairpin. To spring himself from jail cells, he had a large collection of keys which he concealed on his person or pinned to the back of a guard, later getting the right one by reaching through the bars. He would take a hospital strait-jacket and struggle out, exchanging it by legerdemain for one of his own which came apart by pulling a string. The struggle was not faked—"he was really trying to hold the jacket together, because once he pulled the string, it was as loose as a nightgown."

Sometimes there were difficulties, as when a blacksmith spent a year designing a pair of Reynard-proof handcuffs. Reynard got wind of it and his wife accused the blacksmith of making improper advances; he was rushed out of the theater in disgrace. Nailed in a pine coffin, Reynard normally got out because Harry furnished the nails, too short to withstand pressure when the magician, behind a protecting screen, pushed on the boards, extricated himself, and then slapped the coffin back into shape. One night a customer came with veritable spikes, and Reynard was caught. But Harry sprinkled a few drops of chloroform on the coffin, yelled foul play, and opened the box in feverish haste. Sure enough, Reynard was unconscious.

At Rutland, Vermont, advance reports were that business was the worst in years. Harry, after an exploratory look around, had the good luck to discover that the town fathers were confronted with the problem of finding a child who was either lost or had been kidnaped. Reynard appeared, and, blindfolded, led the police to a shack where the lost child was sleeping. The mother babbled gratitude but never betrayed that Harry had paid her for the stunt.

Reynard finally became so successful that he made for New York, and there he and Harry parted company.

The boy was a man—"a child," to use his now dated phrase for an artist in his craft, "of the ram's horn"—a Ph.D. of ballyhoo. He set out on his own and, although the going was at first not lucrative, crowded into the following years some of the greatest publicity stunts of all time.

Allowing for a certain professional pride and a chronic professional genius at exaggeration, Reichenbach credits himself in these salad days with making "September Morn" a national sensation. He bribed small boys to stare at it while they made bawdy remarks, and then invited Anthony Comstock, the anti-vice virago, to witness the immoral scene. He turned Elinor Glynn's *Three Weeks* from a flop to a best-seller by encouraging post-office bluenoses to rage. Finally, he stumbled into his field of greatest achievement and his greatest love—the movies.

You have only to see an early silent picture to realize that here was the ideal media for Reichenbach's talents. Moving pictures were in the realm of make believe. They were new. They cried for the patronage of the masses. They cried also for ballyhoo because, even as a novelty, they were incredibly bad entertainment.

Reichenbach changed all that. Gradually, of course, the movies improved, but he was way ahead of them. He sold the public on the idea that they were indispensable before they were out of the laboratory stage. He sold critics on the idea that they should be reviewed when critics, rightly, believed that they were worse than hokum. He sold theater managers on running them when it was a liability to do so. All this he did with one thing—ballyhoo.

One of his early successes was "The Virgin of Stamboul," a 1919 atrocity produced by Universal. A Turkish maiden, Priscilla Dean, was abducted by a villain, Wallace Beery, and then rescued. As it stood, it was, in Reichenbach's honest estimate, "a menace to the box office." He dug up a delegation of Turks from New York's East Side —"the gang," said O. O. McIntyre, then press agent for the Hotel Majestic, where they were installed in regal splendor, "not only looked like Turks but they smelled like Turks"—and let it be known, especially to the press, that they were looking for the abducted virgin of Stamboul. By the time Boyden Sparkes, too good a newspaperman to be carried away, exposed the hoax, it had won hundreds of columns in the papers, and his exposure only served to inspire hundreds more. The picture was a sellout.

Fox brought out a turkey called "Over the Hill to the Poor House," which attracted sufficient persons to fill the balconies, but left the expensive seats empty. Reichenbach hired actors in top hats to stage arguments on Broadway street corners on the merits of the picture, and finally settle their dispute by going to "Over the Hill." The downstairs seats were soon at a premium.

He established a Tarzan following that is good to this day by clothing a trained ape in full dress and turning him loose of a Saturday evening in a hotel lobby. The lobby of the theater where Tarzan was showing was made into a jungle, complete with chattering monkeys. A Professor T. R. Zann checked in at another hotel with a lion.

"We polled," Reichenbach said modestly after this stunt, "over twenty-five thousand columns in news stories and established the film as a national hit."

Stars as well as shows claimed his attention. Douglas Fairbanks, Senior, Marguerite Clark, Clara Kimball Young, Alice Brady, Charles Ray, Gloria Swanson, Wally Reid, Barbara LaMarr, Rudolph Valentino, and Francis X. Bushman were among those who benefited from his genius. When Valentino's popularity slipped, Harry needled the star back into national prominence by having him grow a beard, and then, after violent protests from the Master Barbers Association of America, having him cut it off. This lily was gilded when the shaven beard was dedicated to a museum of moving pictures. Harry got Clara Kimball Young national headlines after a hurricane in Chicago to which Harry, in the windy city at the time, rushed relief in her name. He tells the story of his best stunt for Bushman:

"He had been receiving only $250 a week in Chicago. I wanted to raise his salary to a commanding figure. When we got off at Grand Central (New York) I had my coat pockets loaded with two thousand pennies. As Bushman and I walked along Forty-second Street toward the Metro office I dropped handfuls of pennies in our line of march. At first children followed us to pick up the coins, then grown-ups, then everybody grew curious and joined in the parade. By the time we reached Metro, streets were black with milling crowds, and the police unable to disperse them. When the officers of Metro looked out of the window they judged Bushman's popularity by the vast throngs that had followed us and he received a thousand dollars a week without any argument."

Between times, Harry made a couple of trips abroad, one to South America, where he managed a bloodless revolution, and one to England, where he bet that American ballyhoo could be effective there and, to the embarrassment of some of the most stuffy dignitaries of the Empire, won.

The South American junket started out as a promotion stunt for a Sarah Bernhardt movie which flopped. To get his fare home, Harry (he says here) wound up in Uruguay as press agent for one Dr. Crispo, leader of the opposition. Harry organized a campaign for a new election under the slogan, "Men of Uruguay, are you men or monkeys?" and Crispo was swept into the presidency so precipitously that he paid Harry to leave the country for fear he would take up with the competition.

The English venture was less political, Harry going there for Carl Laemmle to attempt to get approval from the British censors for the suppressed *Outside the Law*. This he did without much difficulty and went on to bet Guy Newall, a young British producer, that he could gain for Newall's picture, *The Bigamist*, British prominence by American methods. Sir Charles Higham, a British publisher, sauced the bet by saying that Harry's efforts would be a waste of time.

Reichenbach started by announcing that he was going to project a stereoptican advertisement on Buckingham palace, which started tongues wagging, and then sent out scented letters, to Sir Charles among others, from a girl signed "I. D." saying she was in a lot of trouble and, in light of their intimate associations, how about helping her out? After referring their letters to their solicitors, British bigwigs learned that I. D. was Miss Ivy Duke, co-star of *The Bigamist*. Harry put up posters offering a reward for the apprehension of another character in the play, which so upset Scotland Yard that those worthies finally publicly begged him to lay off. He then planted an advertisement in rolls at a banquet presided over by the Bishop of Birmingham, who ate half of his handout before he realized what he was doing. Ballyhoo's harvest was such a bumper crop that even Sir Charles admitted defeat.

It was World War I that changed Reichenbach from a ballyhoo artist to a full-fledged public relations counsel. Whether or not he was conscious of the significance of what he did, he dressed up his circus techniques till they blended into the suave double-talk that today is dispensed in tremendous quantity by hirelings of big and little business and government. Movies had, by subtle transition, changed from a sideshow to a (more or less) dignified industry; and the prophet of movies was Reichenbach. "It is the greatest force in propaganda," said Harry. During the first World War, he helped make propaganda come of age.

He went to work for the Committee on Public Information under George Creel and overnight quit making ballyhoo and began making history.

Morale on the Italian front reached successive depressing lows. Harry projected a movie screen on mountainsides along the Alpine front, ostensibly to win over the Germans. It was of tremendous morale value to the Italian troops, who also saw it. With the help of others, he devised endless propaganda to drop over the German lines, including a diploma entitling a German private to an Allied commission if he would surrender. He devised a Bible for German consumption, wording it to promote the Allied cause. He took old Doc Crosby's philosophy—and Reynard's—to war.

He came back to continue, for plush fees, the work of other years. There was nothing he could not do. One time he took a girl, a perfect unknown and incompetent whom Caruso said had "the only female baritone I have ever heard, if there is such a thing," and made her a celebrity on a bet. He carried ballyhoo, forever, out of the realm of the carnival into the realm of the respectable.

But it is perhaps no exaggeration to say that he would have laughed, like the showman he was, at the public-relations counsels who, taking their cue from him, stepped on a more modern stage and made hypocrisy a profession. For Harry Reichenbach was no hypocrite; he was a carnival spieler, rampant on a field of spangles, piping a gay tune for the rock candy mountain boys, that they might laugh with him, even if the joke was on them.

Huey Pierce Long was of more serious stuff; he thumbed his nose at the men of property and that which, in their hypocrisy and for their convenience, they chose to call democracy. Huey knew that it was as phoney as an ape in a top hat, and he proceeded to burlesque it at a profit, beating them at their own racket. Men of the people and friends of democracy reserve for him a special hate, but he did much for them, exposing the falseness of the "democracy" of the moneyed few. And he willed them a warning.

Life for him from the beginning was no laughing matter. He came from a bailiwick of bitterly disillusioned rock candy mountain boys, "the Free State of Winn," a parish—Louisiana for county—where a man would skin a flea for the hide and tallow, and the land was as poor as gulch dirt. The only luxury was rebellion and the consequences of rebellion could be made to appear mild when contrasted with the stark, poverty-stricken realities of keeping a body and soul together. Huey was weaned on rebellion, as his father before him.

"There wants to be a revolution," declared Huey's old man. "I seen this domination of capital, seen it for seventy years. What do these rich folks care for the poor man? They care nothing—not for his pains, nor his sickness, nor his death. They'd sooner speak to a nigger than a poor white."

Older folk in the parish had supported post-Civil War Republicanism, William Jennings Bryan, Eugene V. Debs, the I. W. W.'s, and Socialism. Always they lost to the medieval hierarchy of moneyed men who ruled New Orleans and state politics and controlled scores of newspapers and banks. Fascism breeds on poverty and ignorance, just as a democracy thrives on economic and political equality and education. Louisiana had for long been a dictatorship without a dictator. Huey supplied that lack and dramatized the whole sorry spectacle.

He was born in 1893, the eighth of nine children. His father managed with luck to send six of them to college, but when Huey's turn came, it was up to him. He was not one to hanker for the hard labor and skinny rewards that went with working Winn Parish soil. At fourteen he auctioned books on street corners, at fifteen learned to set type. Studying style from Baptist revivalists and downstate politicians, he finally concentrated on the spoken word. "I can't remember back to a time when my mouth wasn't open whenever there was a chance to make a speech," he said.

Everything he learned he put promptly to work. A quarrel arose between him and his high-school principal. Pamphlets and oratory by Huey, aged fifteen, succeeded in ousting the principal. His oratory he applied to salesmanship. "I can sell anything," he bragged. He became a drummer for Cottolene, a vegetable shortening. Instead of spending his nights yarning with other drummers in small-town hotel lobbies, he put up at farmer's houses. He helped the wives cook and do the dishes. It was cheaper, and he made friends as well as sales. He was careful to make friends. Even then, a sassy kid, he had a pretty good idea where he was going. "I was born into politics, a wedded man, with a storm for my bride," he said afterward. Like most things he said, it wasn't exactly true, but close enough—and dramatic.

He made enough money to start attending Oklahoma State University Law School and almost enough trouble campaigning for Champ Clark against Woodrow Wilson to get thrown out. Marrying Rose McConnell of Shreveport, he went on to Tulane University, where he set an all-time scholastic record by completing the school's three-year law course in eight months.

He began practicing in Winnfield, Winn Parish. He was twenty-one. One of his first cases was defending a state senator who, after World War I began, was indicted for suggesting that wealth as well as men be conscripted. Huey won. He was draft age but gained exemption as a man with a wife and child.

Louisiana law limited most of its high offices to men over thirty. There were a few exceptions, and Huey picked one, membership on the Railroad Commission. Violating all the campaign cliches of his region—he rode in a snappy car, dressed fit to kill, and got farmers out of bed to solicit their votes—he won by a narrow margin. He used the post to attack big business and ballyhoo Long until he was old enough to run for governor.

At that time he was twenty-four and notable for an upturned nose, a wide grin, wild brown eyes, towsled red hair, a dumpy figure going to fat, and a gift of gab. A lot of people laughed at him. When he attacked Standard Oil and Standard Oil knocked him kicking, the laughter became cynical. But Huey knew that a blow against him was shared in imagination by all the Winn Parish folk in the state and that they loved him for it. He was going along all right so far—a young man of the people.

Gradually he came to the conclusion that he could not only sell anything, he could do anything. In 1923, thirty years old, he set out noisily to prove it by running for governor. He lost—and the laughter rose to a roar. But Huey kept talking, selling, seeing folks, at the same time devoting himself to fat corporation legal cases—"Why not? I admit I'm the best lawyer in Louisiana!" He was learning about the state's phoney democracy—and fast. He took care to make political friends in New Orleans and Catholic southern Louisiana, where he had been weak in 1923.

Maybe it was the legal practice he accepted that won them over, maybe his willingness to play ball, maybe the roughneck salesmanship of the man, maybe because there seemed no other way of stopping him. Whatever the reasons, some of the medieval hierarchy decided that so long as Huey was out for Huey and democracy was just part of his sales talk, he was one of their kind of people. They backed him. If they regretted it later, it was for at least one of the same reasons—he turned out to be their kind of people with a vengeance.

The campaign brought a new high in a lot of things, notably promises and invective. "Every Man a King," was the campaign motto (borrowed without credit from William Jennings Bryan)— "but No Man Wears a Crown." He promised free school books, good roads, free bridges, lower utility rates. He called his opponents everything he could lay his tongue to, depending on the sex and temper of his audience. At thirty-five, he became the state's second-youngest and first poor-white governor. Immediately he went to work— not for the people, but for Huey. "Stick by me," he told his boys. "We'll show 'em who's boss. I'm gonna be President some day."

Because he wanted to build votes for himself, he kept his promises about the roads, the books, the bridges. But the boys all took a handsome cut on the work, and so did Huey. Utility rates were not reduced. He cleaned out public servants from top to bottom regardless of merit and put in his own gang—regardless of merit. He had a "sonofabitch book" and everybody in it got "stomped."

Raiding New Orleans vice dens for downstate approval, he trampled the rights of individuals under martial law. (The dives reopened after patronage had been channeled to the right people—Huey's boys —and Huey frequented them often.)

If there was any further question as to where he was heading, it was answered when somebody confronted him with the state constitution. "I'm the constitution around here now," he said. He backed it up by supervising voting machines in the legislature so that they habitually showed a winning score for whatever Huey wanted.

His night life, his highhanded attitude toward state constitution and laws, and the enthusiasm with which he and his henchmen dipped into state funds became such an open scandal that the opposition tried to impeach him on nineteen counts.

But the fascism that had grown rank for so long in the state was too strong a weapon in Huey's hands. Was it not known that newspapers were the tools of the New Orleans hierarchy? Well, then— all papers were venal. "Two cents a lie!" said Huey, and the people refused to believe the printed truth that was so damaging to their hero. Who said anything about democracy—hadn't legislators, too, been owned since time immemorial by the state's medieval money men? So, okay—buy 'em to work for Huey. He bought "The Famous Fifteen," rewarding them later with some of the fattest political appointments in the state. The impeachment proceedings flopped, and Huey resumed doing everything with which he had been charged—packing a gun, having opponents beat up, robbing, bribing, fixing ballot boxes and votes, carousing and shouting in no uncertain Anglo-Saxon words that he was running Louisiana and God damn anybody who got in his way.

Newspapermen were slugged, photographers had their cameras broken. As if to prove that the press was venal and to caricature its freedom, he started a paper of his own, the *Progress*, dedicated to slandering his enemies. State employees subscribed—or else!—and the paper prospered.

He ran for the United States Senate. An irate husband wanted to introduce into the campaign charges that Huey had broken up his home. He was kidnaped until after the voting was over. Elected, Huey refused to give up the governorship until time to go to the Senate.

As appeasement had put him into power in Louisiana, it smoothed his way in the Senate. He violated every rule that had ever been conceived for a freshman senator and got away with it. And with him onto the national scene he brought two sure-fire national issues— God and share-the-wealth. It took Washington less than a day to discover that he was for both of them.

While he preached a democratic rule of the people for the nation, he made no bones about tightening his one-man dictatorship in the state. During visits back home, he bellowed orders to legislators from the floor at the Capitol. To Oscar K. Allen, Huey's governor now that Huey was gone, he once said before a crowd, "Goddamn you, Oscar, don't you stall around with me. I made you and I kin break you."

With increasing speed, the Long steamroller crushed all opposition. "In one year," Harnett T. Kane records in *Louisiana Hayride*, "his political servants were summoned seven times to Baton Rouge to adopt measures that turned Louisiana into Huey's Reich." He ordered a 2 per cent tax on big newspapers, notably those opposing him in New Orleans. The governor was authorized to call out the militia without interference. State police personnel could be increased limitlessly—Huey's Gestapo.

Huey and his men moved in on city governments that met with their disapproval, throwing them out, putting Long henchmen in. A committee controlled balloting and ballot counting. Big business had to play along and pay the new senator from Louisiana fat fees or suffer consequences. Labor was told by Huey himself that "the prevailing wage is as low as we can get men to take it." Another committee passed on all school employees, regardless of civil service.

Jefferson's sacred trust in education as symbolized by his concept of the University of Virginia had been sold down the river by money-inspired collegiate folkways demanding a professoriate with due respect for the powers that controlled the purse strings, and a circumspect approach to the truth, especially as it concerned real democracy. A university gained standing by the size of its buildings, its gifts from men of property, its football team. So okay, Huey built the "goddamnest" university that ever was.

To hell with Tulane—it had overlooked giving him an honorary degree and its higher echelons included political enemies—he would concentrate on Louisiana State University. Was bigness a criterion? Huey and his mob increased the student population from 1,600 to 8,500. Lots of buildings? He built 'em like crazy, each more fancy than the last, topping it off with a swimming pool supposed to be the longest in the world. When it turned out to be a few feet short, Huey ordered it stretched. He topped that by buying the kids a neighboring country club.

Football team? Orders went out to find the best players in the country, and two airplanes were bought to go get them. A band was built to match. If collegiate conventions provided that a young man or woman go to college even if he had a doorknob for a head, Huey was the man to take care of that one, too. It was estimated at the height of his reign that half the students were on his payroll, and all the good ones in Huey's eyes—the football stars were favorites—could look forward to political appointments on graduation.

As for the faculty, Huey followed the folkways of the academic world—except that he did not try to kid anybody. Many a proper-tied college board before him had appointed a completely innocuous president guaranteed to please, raise a few funds, perhaps, but above all do no thinking which would clash with the board's conservative ideas. Huey did the same by choosing James Monroe Smith, a Louisiana farm boy with a doctor's degree but no discoverable claim to learning. Then he broke with convention by advertising "Doc" Smith's singular talents.

"There ain't a straight bone in Jim's body, but he does what I want him to, and he's a good president," said Huey. Again he said: "Jim's got a hide as thick as an elephant." There is no question that Jim—like many another college head—needed it, especially after Huey died, when "Doc" Smith's thimble wits convinced him that he could make a fortune in the stock market and he spent half a million dollars of state funds and a term in prison before he was convinced that he was wrong.

Nationally, though he opposed Roosevelt, Huey's dubious liberalism is credited by some with having pushed the New Deal into such efforts as increased high-bracket income taxes and the National Youth Administration.

However sound this speculation, it is true that the national administration looked with trepidation on the Huey Long Share-the-Wealth campaign which the Kingfish, now a senator, began in anticipation of the 1936 election, ably assisted by national radio hookups, a huge war chest from "friends" in Louisiana, and a voice almost as persuasive as his own belonging to an old-time revival preacher, Gerald L. K. Smith of Shreveport. Millionaires' fortunes should be limited to $5,000,000, shouted Huey; families should be guaranteed an annual income of from $2,000 to $2,500; every child should get a college education free; every home should have a radio, an automobile, and perhaps an electric refrigerator. All this would be brought about by the rich giving their all to the government and the poor dividing it up and taking it home.

Even had the scheme been economically sound and practical, it was obviously unworkable under Huey's gentle plan of management—"don't tolerate no opposition from the old-gang politicians, the legislatures, the courts, the corporations or anybody!"

Before he was through he was claiming a membership of from two to nine million and threatening to steal huge blocks of votes from the Democrats. He had no illusions that his was an uphill fight, but neither was he pessimistic of the future. "Nineteen-forty will be my real year," he boasted.

On Sunday, September 8, 1935, Dr. Carl Austin Weiss, a young doctor of Baton Rouge, a Tulane graduate and a hater of dictators, mortally wounded Huey at the state capitol. Senator Long fought bitterly for two days, dying on September tenth. There is still more than a suspicion that one of Huey's guards, not Weiss, fired the fatal shot. No autopsy was performed.

The big rock candy mountain boys and their women and children sincerely mourned Huey Pierce Long. His birthday anniversary is even now a legal holiday in Louisiana. He had kept more promises than any man who had preceded him in the state, giving the people benefits which to this day many of them regard as more important than all the disastrous violence he did to what in Louisiana was cynically known, long before his time, as "democracy," but which in fact was a dictatorship of the men of property.

Nor should believers in real democracy dismiss him with unadulterated hatred. His brutal, blatant career showed unequivocally that if democracy—economic as well as political—is seriously lacking in a state, in that state exists rich soil from which a dictator may spring.

If, in a future time, another demagogue arises, and, owing to undemocratic conditions, reaches the heights for which Long strove, only the believers in true democracy who permit it will be to blame.

They will not be able to say that Huey and the medieval hierarchy did not give them fair warning.

271

. . . and the dreams will not die, the dreams live on despite the shoddy of the strange and wonderful Beechers, Reichenbachs, and Longs—the strange and wonderful evangel host of big rock candy mountain boys.

[9]

The Era of Superlatives
(1910–1945)

It is not observed in history that families improve with time. It is rather discovered that the whole matter is like a comet, of which the brightest part is the head; and the tail, although long and luminous, is gradually shaded into obscurity. Yet, by a singular compensation, the pride of ancestry increases in the ratio of distance.

—GEORGE WILLIAM CURTIS, *Prue and I*

I hold that if the Almighty had ever made a set of men that should do all the eating and none of the work, He would have made them with mouths only and no hands; and if He had ever made another class that He intended to do all the work and no eating, He would have made them with hands only and no mouth.

—ABRAHAM LINCOLN

> A train of soldiers passes.
> The khaki lads cheer, laugh, sing, and the flag goes by.
> They are young and the young time is the time to be gay, to sing, laugh, cheer,
>   even out of car windows on the way to mine strike duty.
> Some of the boys will be laid out stiff and flags drape their coffins.
> Some of the mine strikers will be laid out stiff and flags drape their coffins.
> Faraway owners of the mines will read about it in morning papers alongside
>   breakfast.

—CARL SANDBURG, *The People, Yes*

Now more than ever there was no halfway about it—everything was in superlatives. As if to test the sinews of the Republic, opinions, folkways, and events swung repeatedly to a wide variety of extremes and back again.

William Howard Taft's soft administration gave way to the vivid idealism of Woodrow Wilson. Wilson's great heart had hardly stilled before A. Mitchell Palmer, attorney general of the United States, began a vicious witch-hunt among immigrants, accompanied by murderous flouting of civil liberties. The Ku Klux Klan was his handmaiden, and William J. Burns, private detective who had become head of the Federal Bureau of Investigation, baited labor with one hand and covered up for the Harding Ohio gang with the other. There followed the subnormalcy of Calvin Coolidge, the greatest stock market boom and bust in history, the greatest depression—and then new heights of national achievement under Franklin D. Roosevelt.

The 1910-1945 era brought to America its largest concentration of wealth, the most brutal opposition to and the greatest flowering of organized labor, the most spectacular production records, the largest collection of liberal laws, the Prohibition amendment, heavy drinking, gangsterism, fantastically extravagant funerals and parties, two wars each more terrible than the last, a new era in entertainment and organized sports, the rise of the automobile, the radio and the airplane, gadgets galore, synthetics galore, Lucky Strike and Listerine ads galore, frenetic fads, whoopee, jazz, woman suffrage, Amos'n'-Andy, the New Deal, the Blue Eagle, Herbert Hoover, Tom Girdler, Phil Murray, Bruce Barton and God, Howard C. Hopson and the Wall Street confidence men, Huey Long, Mrs. Franklin D. Roosevelt, labor wars, all-out unity in the two national emergencies, bumper crops, unequaled restlessness and confusion and progress—bigger, more, and better everything than the world had ever seen, accompanied by shoutings and alarums, retreats, attacks, and counter-attacks, lusty accusations and recriminations, near-revolutions, bloodshed, bickerings, and daily declarations by all and sundry that the country was going to hell in a handbasket.

The period began innocently enough—on the surface. "The Rosary" sold more than ever before or since—1,300,000 copies from 1911 through 1917. Other song hits included "Sweet Adeline," "The End of a Perfect Day," "She's Only a Bird in a Gilded Cage," "Mother Machree," "Moonlight Bay," and "My Little Grey Home in the West."

If there were still others—"Every Little Movement Has a Meaning All Its Own," "Alexander's Rag-time Band," "My Wife's Gone to the Country, Hurrah, Hurrah!" and even so daring a ditty as "If You Talk in Your Sleep Don't Mention My Name"—they were more than offset by the mores of the times. Women's feet still peeked from beneath voluminous skirts, hair was long and primly dressed, men wore decorous black-and-white, high collars were the vogue of both sexes, and at least an appearance of piety was a social must. In 1912, Percy Hammond, a Chicago dramatic critic, noted a dangerous trend in musical comedies, saying, "the human knee is a joint and not an entertainment." Chautauqua lectures in summer and Y. M. C. A. lectures in winter were a vogue. Revival meetings thrived. New York's five hundred nickelodeons, precursors of the movie theater, were attacked from the pulpit.

Top men of property, their campaign for power accelerated by industrialism, were consolidating last-generation gains into fewer and fewer hands, toward a day when Ferdinand Lundberg, in *America's 60 Families*, would declare that the nation's natural and financial resources were owned by no more than sixty families, buttressed by four-hundred-odd others—a "government . . . absolutist and plutocratic in its lineaments . . . the government of money in a dollar democracy. . . ."

To many a second-decade common man, trying to earn enough to keep body and soul together by the sweat of his brow, this must have appeared as an understatement; democracy was as remote and alien from the life he led as were the lives of the men who employed him and the Myth with which he was bedeviled.

For during the 1910's and 1920's the Great American Myth— that the early English-speaking comers to this country and their children are the custodians and defenders of all that is best in the Republic—grew superlatively portentious.

Ignored was the fact that even the most simple things considered typically American were brought here by newcomers. Swedes imported the log cabin. The onion is Egyptian, the hot dog German, firecrackers are Chinese. Tobacco was introduced to the whites by the Indians. The Christmas tree, Santa Claus, the circus, the zoo—all are immigrant ideas from the north of Europe. A German-born cartoonist, Thomas Nast, originated the Tammany tiger, the Democratic donkey, and the Republican elephant. The story is that the man who introduced the ready-made cigarette was a naturalized American named Anargyros, fresh from Greece. Kalle, Swedish for Charlie, was the original name of the great McCarthy who, with Edgar Bergen, is a second-generation Swede.

Throughout the nation's history, those who most cherished the Myth did most to prove it false. From the day that Jefferson was charged—not without justice—with drawing his strength from among newly arrived Jacobins and foreigners, until Franklin D. Roosevelt was portrayed as a cat's-paw of Ellis Island Communists, followers of the Myth have fought democracy and fostered such classically un-American, reactionary, property-loving, common-man-hating groups as the Klan and the Daughters of the American Revolution.

As a group, their democratic heroes have all been dead heroes, handsomely embalmed to destroy evidence of the democracy that made them great. Their love for the living has generally been reserved for the Hardings and the Coolidges, the Tafts and the Byrds, the Morgans, Rockefellers, Lodges, Fords, Whitneys, Vanderbilts, Mellons, duPonts, Astors, Pattersons, McLeans, Drexels, and Hearsts.

The Myth folk try to overlook such additional facts as that more foreigners have come to this country since than before 1900, when nearly half the population were immigrants or the sons and daughters of immigrants—that 1910-1945 saw the greatest flowering of the newcomers.

All immigrants coming here after 1882 were superior to the majority who came first. In 1882, United States laws barred criminals among others, while full many a colonial early bird was dumped on these shores because he also happened to be a jailbird. Newcomers were even more superior after 1885, when the Victorian equivalent of indentured servants—"contract laborers"—were also barred.

These immigrants were superior candidates for democracy. Unlike the colonials, they knew if only vaguely the meaning and promise of democracy. In many cases, they had seen in their homelands efforts on the part of the common man toward realizing at least an approximation of the democratic ideal. They found here, despite handicaps, educational facilities and other channels of enlightenment far ahead of those in frontier America. They were more quick to win their voting franchise.

The immigrant contributed his share of the reactionaries, criminals, and misfits. This has been emphasized by the Myth folk. But the most important contribution of the newcomers and their children and their children's children has been an eagerness in large numbers to swell the ranks of the people in their fight for democracy. Steadily, always, they have been powerful factors in advancing Walt Whitman's teeming nation of nations.

Yet the more the nation of nations flowered and bore fruit, the stronger grew the Myth.

Labor drew heavily on the newcomers for leadership. Samuel Gompers, who pioneered the American Federation of Labor, was an immigrant from London; John L. Lewis is a second-generation Welsh-American; Philip Murray came here as a boy from Scotland. Rank and filers early in the century—organized or unorganized— were newcomers more often than not. And the Myth was conjured up to haunt them and their fellow Americans, at times with deadly results.

Labor was on the march. Almost from the day the gates were closed, not on immigrants, but on contract labor, the star of the organized workingman began to rise. The American Federation of Labor was organized in Pittsburgh in 1881, its membership jumping from 70,000 in 1889 to 200,000 in 1900. It and other groups, among them the powerful International Workers of the World, claimed a membership of more than two million by 1910.

There followed thirty years of murderous warfare led off by the heyday of the strikebreaker, who went by any other name, usually working under the banner of a private detective agency. Among these were Big Jim Farley's outfit (no connection with F.D.R.'s politico), Pinkerton's, R. J. Coach of Cleveland, the William J. Burns International Detective Agency, the Joy Detective Agency, the Baldwin-Felts Agency, Railway Audits and Inspection Company, and a series of agencies run by Pearl (his mother had wanted a girl!) Bergoff, self-styled "king of the strikebreakers."

Big Jim Farley and Allan Pinkerton were among the pioneers, Big Jim specializing in street railway strikes at the turn of the century. Huge, gasconading and surrounded by strong-arm men, he was credited with driving the first streetcar through a mob of strikers.

Allan Pinkerton's men won undying notoriety during the Homestead steel strike of 1892 and the Pullman strike of 1894. After Homestead, Robert Bruce, a United States Secret Service agent, characterized the Pinkerton operators as the scum of the earth and testified that nine out of ten of them would commit murder for hire.

Pinkerton, Farley, and others were so successful that by 1910 there were hundreds of agencies eager to offer their services as spies, thugs, and strikebreakers against labor. The National Association of Manufacturers organized its own group of specialists. By 1916 it was estimated that there were some 200,000 strikebreakers of various talents available in the nation, and 115,000 were assembled that year when the Brotherhood of Locomotive Engineers threatened to strike.

"There's more money in industry than there ever was in crime," R. J. Coach of Cleveland once said, and big business paid fabulous sums to prove him correct. Bergoff estimated in 1925 that for ten years his annual salary had been $100,000, plus from twice to four times than in bonuses. He and two others in the firm took out approximately $10,000,000 from 1907 to 1925. Management for the Brooklyn Rapid Transit Company paid $2,483,483 to strikebreakers in 1920. In 1916, Interborough spent more than two million.

Top men in the agencies took half the fees. Once a strike was on and the breakers were besieged on a company's property, agency leaders took additional tolls, charging exhorbitant fees to scabs for clothing, food, beds, cigarettes, and gambling privileges. Often the mine-run strikebreakers were hired under false pretenses, held prisoners during the strike, and paid off with a small percentage of what they had been promised.

In the McKees Rocks strike against the Pressed Steel Car Company, Bergoff misinformed most of the men he hired, kept them prisoners after the strike got under way, beat up those who protested, and robbed them all. Labor won the strike—after bloody, Bergoff-inspired rioting—because his own men fled the company plant at the first opportunity. While this murderous war was going on, F. N. Hoffstot, Pressed Steel president, who had brought on the strike by refusing to talk with the men, spoke from New York: "The reports of the disturbances," he declared, "are exaggerated."

Men of property during the period all tried to make it appear that it was the strikers who were bloodthirsty. The criminal records and the murderous performances of the hirelings were overlooked.

Strikebreakers were trained to make trouble and then blame it on the strikers. "You give me twenty-five good guards with clubs and guns," said French Joe, a strikebreaking expert, "and put 'em in wagons, and give me a couple of stool-pigeons with guns to run through the crowds and fire at the wagons to give us a chance to start, and we'll go through the crowds . . . in a day."

Strikebreakers habitually arrived on the scene of trouble armed to the teeth, and as soon as it was established that they would be protected by courts and companies, no attempt was made to conceal the arsenals.

"We don't want no machine guns," declared Bergoff during a textile strike in Georgia in 1934. "We always go prepared. Why, I shipped some tear gas down there by airplane." A strikebreak gangster, Benjamin Mann, was once asked if he was packing a gun while testifying before Judge Keyes Winters of New York. Mann said sure he was packing a gun—he had expected to go directly to work.

In the Philadelphia streetcar strike of 1910, women and children were beaten by strikebreakers, who once livened things up by running two cars through town shooting from the windows. A sleeping baby was among those wounded. Sixteen men, women, and children were killed in streetcar accidents in less than two months.

In the early spring of 1914, under the unctuous auspices of the John D. Rockefellers, Baldwin-Felts gangsters attacked a tent village occupied by strikers against the Colorado Fuel and Iron Company at Ludlow, Colorado. The tents were soaked in gasoline and then set fire. Seven women and children, who sought shelter from the flames in a dugout, smothered to death. Twelve children were murdered. An eleven-year-old boy took his crying sister in his arms to reassure her. His brains were shot out. His bewildered father, William Snyder, appealed to a Baldwin-Felts guard for help. "You red-necked son of a bitch," said the guard, "I have a notion to kill you." John D., Junior, was more cultured in his comments. "Father," he reported, watched the strike "with unusual interest and satisfaction."

Action by the courts almost invariably freed the strikebreakers. One judge went out of his way to compliment Pearl Bergoff on his

279

"masterly activities on behalf of large corporations." Laws were passed against agencies and strikebreakers, but company lawyers invariably found loopholes. Leading Americans approved. Charles W. Eliot, president of Harvard, called the strikebreaker "the hero of American industry." For every strike whose horrors reached the headlines, scores passed unpublicized and scores more were never called in fear of the gangster hirelings of the men of property.

The twenties saw a revival of the Myth in the war against the foreigners in labor's ranks, a nation-wide witch-hunt against "Reds" under the auspices of such notables as Attorney General Palmer, the Daughters of the American Revolution, and the Ku Klux Klan. This war reached its climax in 1927, when two newcomers, Nicola Sacco and Bartolomeo Vanzetti, were sentenced to death in Massachusetts for a 1921 crime they never committed.

Judge Webster Thayer had ruled against them following a trial designed to publicize their radicalism and their foreign origins rather than to prove any criminal charges. Supreme Court Justice Felix Frankfurter, in *The Case of Sacco and Vanzetti*, called Judge Thayer's opinion on the case "a farrago of misquotations, misrepresentations, suppressions and mutilations," but the Thayer sentence was upheld by a committee including A. Lawrence Lowell, president of Harvard University.

Efforts by men of good will all over the world failed to shake Thayer and his backers, and he listened unmoved as Bartolomeo Vanzetti made his final statement to the court. Said Vanzetti:

"I have talked a great deal of myself
but I even forgot to name Sacco.
Sacco too is a worker,
from his boyhood a skilled worker, a lover of work,
with a good job and pay,
a bank account, a good and lovely wife,
two beautiful children and a neat little home
at the verge of a wood, near a brook. . . .

"Oh, yes, I may be more witful, as some have put it;
I am a better babbler than he is, but many, many times
in hearing his heartful voice singing a faith sublime . . .

I felt small at the presence of his greatness
and found myself compelled to fight back
from my eyes the tears,
and quanch my heart
trobling to my throat to not weep before him:
this man called thief and assassin and doomed.

"But Sacco's name will live in the heart of the people
and in their gratitude when . . . yours will be dispersed by time;
when your name . . . your laws, institutions,
and your false God are but a dim remembering
of a cursed past in which man was wolf
to the man. . . .

"If it had not been for these things
I might have lived out my life
talking at street corners to scorning men.
I might have died, unmarked, unknown, a failure.
Now we are not a failure.
This is our career and our triumph. Never
in our full life could we hope to do such work
for tolerance, for justice, for man's understanding of man, as now
    we do by accident.

"Our words, our lives, our pains—nothing!
the taking of our lives—lives of a good shoemaker and a poor
    fish peddler—
All! The last moment belongs to us—
that agony is our triumph."

He and Sacco were electrocuted August 23, 1927. "From now on," inquired Heywood Broun bitterly in the New York *World*, "will the institution of learning in Cambridge which once was called Harvard be known as Hangman's House?" The Myth took a new lease on life.

It lives to this day. Speakers stride to platform and microphone, writers praise, the children of First Families bow to the homage paid them as defenders of democracy. There is applause, solemn, dignified. Nobody boos. Nobody laughs. He who would cry out does so at risk of being branded a subversive foreigner who had better go back where he came from.

The most recent campaign in labor's long war began with a fair omen. Under Section 7-A of the National Recovery Act of 1933—N.R.A.—workingmen were encouraged to organize.

This was opposed by the men of property with cries of un-Americanism, with skillfully devised and heavily subsidized company unions, and by agency and company thugs.

Worse, old-line A.F.L. leadership, secure in the control of their comparatively small craft-union membership, feared they would be thrown out of power if big industries were organized into huge groups led by young, aggressive men. Craft-union membership had won their war, and, understandably, did not want another. William Green went farther, sending word down the line to oppose industrial unionism. Labor suffered from a new form of sabotage—by labor.

This attitude led to failure of the 1934 steel strike—never called—centering in Pittsburgh, under the direction of the A.F.L. Amalgamated Association of Iron, Steel, and Tin Workers (M. J. "Grandmother" Tighe, chief saboteur). Similar lack of A.F.L. progress was notable in the rubber industry (Coleman C. Claherty), and in the automobile industry, where the only union of any size was A.F.L.'s tool-and-die group, which wanted no part of mass organization.

It also left the door open for the Iron and Steel Institute, sparked by $40,000-a-year Arthur Young and actually aided by the American Federation, to launch a drive for company unions. The rubber industry managed to keep the average wages of its workers, counting layoffs, at approximately less than a thousand dollars a year. The automobile industry in Detroit refused to hire known labor organization men, letting them swell the rolls of the city's unemployed, while unorganized Southern workers were imported to man the assembly lines. In the fall of 1935, employment in some of the plants increased as much as 100 per cent; relief rolls dropped only about 20 per cent.

Workingmen who wanted to organize were further handicapped by lack of skilled leadership, making them inept if not helpless when they attempted to better their conditions.

The men finally invented new weapons and made a clean break with the A.F.L., in most instances skilled leaders coming along to captain the new groups.

John L. Lewis, president of the United Mine Workers, was thrown out of the federation, after Philip Murray, a Lewis lieutenant, had paved the way with the Steel Workers Organizing Committee. Out of the Committee for Industrial Organization grew rubber, automobile, and other unions, and the Congress of Industrial Organizations, now the largest labor group in the nation. Independents, notably that led among seamen and longshoremen by Harry Bridges on the West Coast, joined up.

Perhaps as important as any of these things was the discovery of the new weapons—the sit-down strike and the quickie. With the sit-down, the men could tie up an assembly line with a minimum of arguments and broken heads, and it drew members to the new organizations like bees to honey. The quickie brought a brief tie-up at a time when rapid production made it imperative for management to make an equally rapid concession.

The men of property answered with an estimated $80,000,000 a year in brutality, tear gas, machine guns, and propaganda extolling the American way of doing things. "I have never sought to prevent our men from joining an association—no one who believes in American freedom would do that," intoned Henry Ford. Ford thugs maimed scores of organizers and union workers almost as he uttered the words. Big industry hired strikebreakers in 108 plants between 1934 and 1939; between 1933 and 1937 they spent more than half a million dollars for tear gas. Local police often co-operated with the companies. Chicago police in 1939 murdered ten and maimed scores at a peaceful Memorial Day meeting against Tom Girdler and the Republic Steel Corporation. For two days in Canton, Ohio, company guards ran wild in armored cars, scattering buckshot and tear gas so indiscriminately that school children were among the victims.

Sometimes the antics of management reached new highs in the ridiculous. The die-hard steel men of property, invited to Washington to go over a labor code with so mild a labor leader as William Green, refused even to be introduced to him. "I felt," Secretary of Labor Frances Perkins later noted, "as though I had entertained eleven-year-old boys at their first party rather than men to whom the most important industry in the United States had been committed."

But labor would not be stopped. Steel finally submitted to C.I.O. Younger leaders in management favored less violent opposition. Typical of the change, one day Edsel, son of Henry Ford, sat down with C.I.O. organizers and talked terms with friendliness and apparent pleasure. A few days later the Ford Gestapo was disbanded.

By 1945, labor had an organized membership estimated at eight million, four times the 1910 figure, and labor and management were trending toward arbitration rather than strikes.

A truce? Will labor be able to hold its hard-won gains? Will the C.I.O. become as conservative toward future progress as did some A.F.L. leaders in the 1930's? Will the two combine and demand more benefits from society than is their right? What will be the government's role? Will capital make a new bid for control through political channels—attempt to nationalize the industrial fascism which has for so long been their favorite weapon? Or will they submit to democratic processes?

Only the tumultuous future can tell; only the inscrutable will of all the people can, in the end, give the answer.

Accompanying the labor-management war, during which both sides frequently predicted a collapse of production in all fields, American production became superlatively huge, and to say that the people enjoyed its fruits with superlative abandon is to put it mildly. His ability quickly to recover from the bludgeonings of economic debacles and wars, plus a bent to be in all things extravagant, gave the average American—when he could raise the price—an unflagging capacity for indulging himself.

In 1910, he drank 163 million gallons of hard liquor. By 1935, despite or perhaps because of prohibition, the figure was up to 474 million. Cigarette consumption leaped from a modest amount in 1910 to 47½ billion in 1920 and approximately 218 billion in 1941. The nickelodeon of 1908 had grown to the neighborhood movie and the handsome movie palace of the 1940's, attracting billions of customers annually.

Nor is this to imply that church attendance had fallen off; it rose, in the thirties, to some 56 million. Everything burgeoned. Attendance at spectator sports hit new highs. Baseball, football, boxing, bowling, tennis—all sand-lot enterprises in 1910—became tremendous businesses.

There were some 24,000 automobiles and 750 trucks in 1910. In

1941 there were 3,700,000 passenger cars, more than a million trucks. In 1919 there were no radios; in 1941 they were being produced—and bought—at the rate of more than a million a month. Bank deposits increased from 19 billion dollars in 1915 to 107 billion dollars in 1943. The federal government joined in the largesse by building the most magnificent collection of power dams in the history of the world—Boulder, Grand Coulee, Hetch Hetchy, Owyhee, Diablo, Arrowrock and Shoshone, Kensico, Santee, Cherokee, and Saluda, to name a few—not to mention the world's biggest army, navy, air force, war production machine, and relief and social security programs.

The people were equally spread-eagle in indulging their tastes in styles. From a flat-footed start, women's skirts climbed to above the knees and she learned (after 1920) to rouge, wave her hair, to smoke and drink in public, and to dance with increasing abandon. Her boy friend's bathing suit was progressively reduced to a loin cloth, hers to a pair of strategically placed pocket handkerchiefs.

In 1910, bridge whist was popular. Down through the years, other fads added their fillips to the times. There was contract bridge, Mah Jong, sex, crossword puzzles, miniature golf, Eugenie hats, and technocracy, hip flasks, petting, necking, short (and shorter) skirts, bobby socks, and the big apple. There were songs like "Yes, We Have No Bananas," "Stardust," and "The Music Goes Round and Round." There were bands like Paul Whiteman's, singers like Rudy Vallee, Bing Crosby, and Frank Sinatra, sports heroes like Jack Dempsey and Red Grange and Babe Ruth. There were movie stars from Rudolph Valentino to Clark Gable and from Mary Pickford to Greta Garbo and Dorothy Lamour, a radio program called "The Lone Ranger," Will Rogers, Bob Hope, Fred Allen, and a score of other humorists, and Émil Coué saying "Every day in every way I am getting better and better" while thousands of other people said it dutifully after him.

Emotional and practical extremists of all stripes and colors clamored for public acclaim, and seldom a day passed that some orator did not reach the climax of his speech with a sentence beginning "If this great nation does not immediately" and ending with the word "disaster" or "revolution" or "chaos."

During the 1920's, pros and antis argued the Red scare and its accompanying intolerance in florid periods. "My motto for the Red's is SOS—ship or shoot," said Guy Empey, whose hit war book had made him a spokesman of national stature. "I believe we should place them all on a ship of stone, with sails of lead, and that their first stopping place should be hell." "America," mourned Katherine Fullerton Gerould for the liberals, "is no longer a free country."

Lothrop Stoddard contended that dark-skinned persons were a worse threat to civilization than the Germans or the Reds, and Henry Ford blamed everything he considered evil on the Jews. Both were made insignificant by the *Hairdresser*, a magazine of the 1920's, militantly declaring that American womanhood and the best interests of the public were threatened by an even worse menace—"the effort to bring women to barber shops for hair cutting."

There were those who, singlehanded, went from one extreme to another during the era. "Given a chance to go forward with the policies of the last eight years," said Herbert Hoover in 1928, "we shall soon, with the help of God, be in sight of a day when poverty will be banished from this nation." "We are at the end of our string," he declared with equal force in 1933. "There is nothing more we can do."

The times marked new highs for all extremes, especially cynicism. "Here was a generation," said F. Scott Fitzgerald in the 1920's, "grown up to find all Gods dead, all wars fought, all faiths in man shaken."

If that generation had plenty and enough to regard with cynicism, it also had its spokesmen, among them Wilson Mizner, a New York confidence man who had been schooled in his craft in California and the Alaskan gold fields, the poor man's Scott Fitzgerald.

Perhaps more than any other, Mizner put into words the contemporary disillusionment of the common man. Nothing escaped the bite of his wit, not even himself. When his wealthy wife once caught up with him in a hotel lobby after a quarrel over finances and hurled a barrage of greenbacks in his face, he reported that he picked up eight thousand dollars before he realized that he had been insulted.

"Why should I work?" he asked a reporter indignantly. "I've committed no crime. I hate work like the Lord hates St. Louis." For a time in his youth he was a professional boxer, but he always denied

286

it. He got his gnarled hands, he said, "knocking down dames in the Klondike."

Women, dames, or ladies, were targets for some of his most devastating cynicisms. "Treat a whore like a lady and a lady like a whore," he said. He dismissed a stage star who quarreled with him by telling her that she was "a parlayed chambermaid." An Alaskan pal fired on a stranger for insulting the pal's girl, Goldie. "How could you insult Goldie?" Mizner wanted to know.

Some of his social comments, as reported by Alva Johnson in *The New Yorker,* gained historic stature. When told that Coolidge was dead, Mizner was the first to utter the classic "How do they know?" Authorship was one of his pet peeves. "Writing is too damn lonesome," he declared. "If you steal from one author," he said, "it's plagiarism; if you steal from many, it's research."

One of his most burning hates was the law. "Are you trying to show contempt of court?" a judge demanded, inspiring the reply: "No, I'm trying to conceal it." An irate customer haled him into court during the Florida boom. "Did you tell this man he could grow nuts on the land he bought?" Mizner was asked. "I told him he could *go* nuts," Mizner said indignantly.

"He'd steal a hot stove and come back for the smoke" was one of his favorites that is perpetuated in the language, and "You're a mouse trying to be a rat." To a radio star he said, "If you don't get off the air, I'm going to quit breathing it."

Nothing was sacred. He used to raise a stake by having a pal wire Mizner's mother that her son was dead and please send money to save the body from a pauper's grave. "Stop dying," he once wired brother Addison, "I'm trying to write a comedy." A girl quarreled with him and then threw herself from an eleventh story hotel window. Mizner immediately went out to lay a bet on No. 11 in the afternoon races: "You can't tell me that isn't a hunch." Dying himself in 1933, he asked for a priest, a rabbi, and a Protestant minister. "I want to hedge my bets," he explained.

If an American couldn't find anything else to do, he indulged his superlative pioneer exuberance by moving.

Earlier, and even up until 1910, this was difficult. He had to hire a china-packer to pack his china; a furniture-packer to pack his furniture; a hauler to haul his goods to a station. He had to make a separate arrangement for shipping as well as for hauling at both ends of the line.

But soon all moving services were combined under one management. From early beginnings in the 1890's with horse-drawn moving vans, transfer of household goods grew by leaps and bounds during the twentieth century. With the development of auto trucks in the 1920's, moving became a national pastime, first traditionally in October, eventually clear around the calendar.

For a time, only the brave and the victims of necessity moved long distances. By 1941, whole armies of households moved clear across the country. In that year, six of the largest long-distance haulers did a combined business of some twelve million dollars. In 1945, the figure had increased 96 per cent to more than twenty-three million. J. C. Capt, director of the United States Census and one of the most resourceful and imaginative statistical savants of modern times, stated in March, 1945, that "never before in the history of our country has there been so great a shuffling and redistribution of population in so short a time." The combined total of migrants during the war period he estimated conservatively at 27,300,000 persons.

More were reported to come. With war's end, some of the leading long-distance movers began a campaign proving that you can have your furniture packed and sealed at your front door in America and unsealed and unpacked anywhere in the world. One aspect of the drive included postwar pictures showing American household goods being unloaded in Helsingfors, Finland, another being drawn by oxen in Bulgaria, a third hauled by coolies in Tientsin.

". . . Americans are always moving on," observed Stephen Vincent Benét in *Western Star:*

> It's an old Spanish custom gone astray,
> A sort of English fever, I believe,
> Or just a mere desire to take French leave,
> I couldn't say, I couldn't really say. . . .

Elsewhere he said:

> ". . . when you ask about Americans,
> I cannot tell their motives or their plans

Or make a neat design of what they are.
I only see the fortune and the bane,
The fortune of the breakers of the earth,
The doom arisen with the western star."

The design is verily not neat, the motives and plans obscure, the future dark. But is tomorrow's promise baneful and fraught with doom? What of the high, crusading idealism of the people as they followed their star under such leaders as Wilson and Roosevelt? What of the promises of democracy?

[10]

The Heroes of the People

Woodrow Wilson

Wilson adventured for the whole of the human race. Not as a servant, but as a champion. So pure was this motive, so unflecked with anything his worst enemies could find, except the mildest and most excusable, a personal vanity, practically the minimum to be human, that in a sense his adventure is that of humanity itself . . . and one day the world will know it, even the fools. . . . He left, even though defeated, a hope, a promise . . . a symbol . . . a fragment from out of his heart . . . to serve for one who will come after . . .
—WILLIAM BOLITHO, *Twelve Against the Gods*

Any man more right than his neighbors constitutes a majority of one.
—HENRY DAVID THOREAU

It is no use to throw a good thing away merely because the market isn't ripe yet.

—MARK TWAIN

Woodrow Wilson played three roles in his life. He was a Puritan preacher by breeding and training. He was a champion of democracy by choice. Imponderable circumstances made him a mystical crusader for world peace.

Each of these roles he played with romantic, Dickensian intensity, as if a greater One than Dickens had destined him to be the very Spirit of Democracy, past, present and future. Perhaps because of this intensity, plus the idealism that dominated everything he did, his three lives were integrated into a brilliant whole. But because of it, too, and because of the kaleidoscopic way, in times of crisis, he switched from one role to another, it was never difficult for his foes to portray him as insincere. His friends, often and again, were thrown into wordless confusion, or forever lost to him.

The Puritan preacher was a role in which he was cast the day that he was born, December 28, 1856, son of the Presbyterian minister Joseph Ruggles Wilson, and of Jessie Woodrow, daughter of another Calvinist. Both had numerous ministers on their family trees, and the baby's father summed up the parental hopes when he declared the baby "dignified enough to be Moderator of the General [Presbyterian] Assembly."

A churchman's household, it was prayerful, dignified, Bible-reading, to a degree feminine—there were two older sisters—and militant in its intellectual pursuits. There was fulsome moralizing and long evenings during which the elders read aloud to the children; longer discussions among the parents and visiting intellectuals to which the children listened in; careful grooming of the boy's mind.

At first this bore no substantial fruit. Partly owing to the family's being thrown into the turmoil of the Civil War, partly to the child's reluctant interest in school, "Tommy" (Woodrow) Wilson did not learn to read until he was eleven, and was an indifferent grade-school scholar. Once he played hookey to go to a circus, occasion for the only spanking he ever got, from his teacher. But he was not a boy's boy. Thin, nervous, subject to attacks of indigestion, somewhat pompous after the fashion of children too much thrown with serious-minded elders, Tommy was something of a problem chick, and not a too promising one at that.

When he was a year old, the family followed the father to a new pulpit at Augusta, Georgia, where they lived till Tommy was eight. Three of his most vivid memories typify the unusual stresses of his childhood. At four, he recalled later having heard a man shout that Lincoln had been elected—there would be war—and running to his father to discover what it meant. At eight, he saw Jefferson Davis, president of the Confederacy, marched through the streets a prisoner of Union soldiers and, a short time later, stood awestruck and looked up into the benign face of the defeated Robert E. Lee.

While the child, at least in his home, never learned the bitterness of war hatred, he was schooled in the stringencies of defeat. His father never took a strong stand on slavery but stood with the South on its right to secede.

Augusta, though not in the line of Sherman's devastating campaign, suffered from lack of food, clothing, and heat during the last half of the war, and near Tommy's home was a hospital burgeoning the screams of the fevered and wounded. Afterward, at fourteen, he moved to Columbia, South Carolina, which had been a smoking ruins in the wake of Sherman's men. Carpetbaggers ruled it now, and although his father ranked high in the community as a professor in Columbia Theological Seminary, the dregs of defeat were dust on the tongue at almost every meal.

The problem of molding Tommy into a man worthy of the family traditions and ambitions was one with which, from all the evidence, his parents dealt understandingly. Tall, dark, handsome, charming, and a wit and scholar, Joseph Wilson spent long hours with the boy and, either out of sympathy or with remarkable prescience, insisted then and always that Tommy would be a great man.

The mother, educated beyond most women of her times, proud, with a slow Scotch anger, protected the boy to such a degree that as a man he was never able to live without a woman's sympathy. He worshiped her with an ardor matched only by his love for his father. To his wife, years later, Wilson wrote:

"I remember how I clung to her (a laughed-at 'mamma's boy') till I was a great big fellow: but love of the best womanhood came to me . . . through those apron-strings. If I had not lived with such a mother I could not have won . . . such a wife."

Slowly the boy began to show signs of intellectual and spiritual fervor. The campus atmosphere at Columbia helped, and he began to study, mostly what he liked, not what was required of him, but with real interest and, at times, imagination. First recorded intellectual passion was ships and navigation. It reached a climax with his writing make-believe letters from himself, an admiral, to the Navy Department. History fascinated him from the first and he manifested a growing interest in the British parliamentary system. A taste for literature developed and his father was especially pleased when the boy cultivated a natural talent for oratory.

By the time, at fifteen, when he went to college at Presbyterian Davidson, near Charlotte, North Carolina, he had become a member of the church and been indoctrinated with the pride of family, the love for public service, and the uncompromising righteousness which was his heritage from his parents.

He considered "no bad motto" Edmund Burke's saying that "public duty requires that what is right . . . should be made prevalent; that what is evil should . . . be defeated."

As for right and evil, Wilson got the definitions direct and imperative from the Calvinists in chill and uncompromising terms. God and his own conscience were his font of righteousness. Every man, he came to say, is a "distinct moral agent, responsible not to men . . . but . . . through his own conscience to his Lord and Maker." In crisis, guidance must be sought from an "intelligent power" outside oneself.

It was Puritanism at its best—and its most dangerous.

If there was any doubt as to how he would wield it, his attitude toward his unbending ancestors made the matter clear. He was as proud of these "troublesome Scotchmen . . . pugnacious, masterful, singleminded, conscientious, and obstinate," as he was of being one of them—"sometimes a man's rootage means more than his leafage." One of his favorite sayings was that while a Yankee always thinks he is right, a Scotch-Irishman knows it.

His first college venture was not heartening. Davidson, isolated, war-poor, and bleak, taxed his none-too-robust health to the point where fellow students considered him lazy and indifferent. He played center field on the baseball team; in a student body of 107, he was an "average" scholar. By the end of a year he was ready to return home.

He moved with his family to Wilmington, Delaware, and there lived out more than a year of poor health, lonely, reserved, a voracious reader now, but lacking enthusiasms as much as he lacked friends.

And then, almost overnight, he came alive. At seventeen, the family decided that his health was enough restored for him to try at least a semester at Princeton, which had been his father's school. With some misgivings—he had never been North before, had never even heard "The Star-Spangled Banner," and was, besides, deficient in ancient languages and mathematics—he was bundled off to the Presbyterian stronghold.

He returned vividly awakened, his reserve and shyness brightened by a quiet charm, his laziness routed by a vital nervous drive that was seldom to desert him till old age.

But the marks of his youth remained with him. Although he was passing into the phase in which he would become most notable as a champion of democracy, always there would be about him the hint of a gentleman of the old school, a strong family man, prayerful, Bible-reading, with few outside friends and no intimates.

Most men, however close to him, he called by their surnames. The last letter he ever wrote, to as intimate a friend as his biographer, Ray Stannard Baker, began "My dear Baker," and ended, "Pray accept my assurances of my unqualified confidence and affectionate regard." He once told the first Mrs. Wilson that it was impossible for him to give "more than a glimpse of the thoughts and impulses and affections which are part and parcel of myself."

Deeply imbedded in him was intellectual as well as spiritual snobbery. At Princeton, Baker records in *Woodrow Wilson, Life and Letters*, Wilson was "most at home in rather small groups and preferably with men who had intellectual interests."

Those whom he liked, he tended to idealize, as he idealized humanity in general. "When we call a thing human," he once said, "we have a spiritual ideal in mind." Those falling short of the ideal won his righteous wrath.

A Puritan sees blacks and whites only; there are no grays, no colors. In the soul of a Puritan burns a fierce flame, for better or for worse.

Wilson, the champion of democracy, appeared in his early manhood, first offsetting, eventually clashing openly, sometimes bitterly, with the Wilson of Calvinism.

"After all," he said, dismissing rootage, "what makes or distinguishes a man is not that he is derived from any family or any training, but that he has discovered for himself the true role of manhood in his own day."

For Wilson, in the world to which he grew up, this role was to be a champion of democracy, first in educational and literary circles, then in politics, finally in statesmanship.

It was a road almost as circuitous as the one which led him to manhood. "The profession I chose," he said in the simplicity of retrospect, "was politics; the profession I entered was the law. I entered the one because I thought it would lead to the other." Actually it was far from being that direct and simple.

Princeton lured him away from his father's fondest hope, the ministry. He showed increased interest in history and shone at debate and at being stubbornly loyal to his convictions. The legend is that he lost one of the school's highest debating honors by refusing to take a side in which he did not believe. He made a few friends and came to enjoy himself, despite his reserve, immensely. He was graduated in 1879, at twenty-two, without honors.

There followed a period of studying law at the University of Virginia, ended by a recurrence of poor health. Friends of this period reported him still reserved and shy, but also affable and sociable enough to win praise for his "fine courtesy." He had not accumulated enough interest in democracy to visit Monticello—he said he "came around to Jefferson" later—but he had progressed to the point where, despite his southern upbringing, he shocked all and sundry by declaring that Lincoln had been right in preserving the Union. Thenceforth, Lincoln was one of his heroes.

Returning home for eighteen months, he studied enough law between attacks of nerves and indigestion to begin practicing at Atlanta, Georgia, when he was twenty-five, if it can be called practicing when a young lawyer passes the bar but, so far as the record reveals, gets not a single case.

He took refuge in an attitude of intellectual superiority—"here the chief end of man is . . . to make money" and students were considered "mere ornamental furniture"—and in seeking an intellectual sanctuary. This was Johns Hopkins at Baltimore, Maryland, then boasting the most advanced graduate school in the country.

But there was another, more permanent refuge—"one of the deepest, if not the deepest, awakenings of his life," in Baker's estimate. He met Ellen Axson.

The daughter of the Presbyterian minister at Rome, Georgia, four years his junior, and perhaps the only person in his life who could both thoroughly understand and at the same time manage him, she began their relationship by urging him to "seek the highest things he felt in his soul." But there was also gaiety and good humor and passion in their alliance, and the deepest confidences, and love letters of unabated ardor over a period of three decades. It was a romance of high ecstasies which seldom are sustained in a human relationship.

He was adult now—he had dropped the Tommy as well as the Thomas—he was Woodrow Wilson. They married when he was twenty-eight, the year he got his doctor's degree at Johns Hopkins in history. His thesis was an attack upon the slow and bureaucratic methods of the United States Congress.

The couple went to Bryn Mawr College, where the bridegroom was associate professor of history and political economy for three years. Two more in the same capacity at Wesleyan ended when he accepted the appointment as professor of jurisprudence and political economy at his alma mater, Princeton. He was thirty-three and on the threshold of his great academic successes.

Even these successes were slow in maturing, and they lacked the spectacular progress which marked his later career. He early gained local and professional reputations for his oratorical clarity and for frequent essays on politics, many of which appeared in national magazines.

This was the heyday of his happiness. Student and faculty came to regard with deep affection his long-jawed, homely face, stern in repose, vividly alight in conversation. To those whose background and future represented the antithesis of the democracy which he came to preach, his beliefs were considered allowable professorial eccentricities. He won an ardently youthful following. He could hold them all spellbound with his lectures. They loved him for his excellence at billiards, his serious-minded if mediocre game of golf, and the passionate enthusiasm with which he celebrated every football and baseball victory and mourned each defeat.

At home, warmed by the love and understanding of Ellen and the affection and admiration of his three daughters, he reached the nearest peace on earth he was ever to know. A devoted father, he spent long hours at the education of his children, but they were to remember more vividly his playing with them, and the high comedy of his entertainment.

"It has always amazed me to read that father was cold or grim or aloof," wrote Eleanor Wilson McAdoo years later in *The Woodrow Wilsons*. "Warm, close friendships were a necessity to him, a stimulant that he prized, guarded, and requited in full measure."

He used to regale Ellen and the children with impersonations.

"I think the drunken man was the general favorite. We made him do it over and over and the whole household responded with shouts of glee. . . . The heavy Englishman was second best. . . . A Scotch burr and an Irish brogue were in his repertoire, and he told Negro tales to perfection. . . . I remember him in a hat of mother's, a feather boa, and a long velvet curtain trailing behind him as he walked . . . a society woman greeting her friends in a gushing manner and falsetto voice. He was a very good actor and many times expressed a humorous wish that he had chosen acting as a career."

He amused them in other ways. After he became president of Princeton, one year the home-game football crowds wrecked his garden and yard, shortcutting to and from the field. Next year, he fenced the yard and did verbal battle with those who tried to tear the fence down. He succeeded in making his point, but some of the rebuffed alumni made more of it than others did when later he battled for his democratic ideals.

The break which gave him the presidency of the university came when he was turning forty-six. Three years later he began preaching the reforms which changed him from an acceptable and not unsuccessful money-raising university president to a national figure crusading for democracy.

Perhaps the change can be attributed to the Calvinist welling up in him for too carefree enjoyment of his professorship at the best academic country club in the nation. Perhaps it was a hidden disgust with himself for raising money among millionaires for beautiful buildings. Or perhaps it was from too many midnights spent conning the realities of democracy. Whatever it was, he appeared almost full blown, a turgid champion of democracy where yesterday had been a harmless and affable professor with a talent for thrilling oratory and political essays.

It began auspiciously enough, and in the gayest of friendly settings. Speaking before a banquet of alumni at New York's old Waldorf-Astoria, he asked them blandly for more than two million dollars for instituting a preceptor system at the university—having young, educated graduates coach a group of undergraduates—personalize and elevate to enlightened friendship the hitherto dull and undemocratic relationship between student and professor.

The audience at the Waldorf first greeted his two-million-dollar touch with whistles, but he brought them around to applause. Although he did not get all for which he asked, by the fall of 1905 some fifty "companions and coaches" were "consorting" with under-graduates.

Up to this point, he had moved with rare success and skill, getting what he wanted, but keeping the majority of the university behind him in doing so.

Either the ease with which he had gained his point, or the growing urge in him to expand democracy on the campus, inspired him to make his next move with more confidence and less diplomacy. He proposed that the exclusive upper-class clubs on the campus be abolished and that, instead, the school be divided into democratic "quadrangles," where every man was equal to another, professors included. Princeton snobbery was outraged, old grad as well as un-dergrad. Some of the professoriate, led by Dr. Andrew Fleming West, dean of the graduate school, capitalized on the student and graduate reaction and the campus was split into two bitterly warring factions.

Abruptly, the Calvinist in Wilson, who conceivably had been squirming at the crass salesmanship of money-raising as well as the democratic going-on generally—"he was a shy person and dreaded meeting strangers," Eleanor records—Woodrow the Puritan sud-denly reappeared on the scene and turned defeat into disaster.

Despite the pleas of friends, at least one of whom he dismissed as a traitor, and despite the realities of the situation, he stuck to his quadrangle idea, even going so far as to write a favorable report on it without consulting membership of the committee who, ostensibly, were the report's authors. Steadily at work among conservative, en-dowment-giving alumni, his faculty opponents gained ground.

But the crusader for democracy, not the Puritan, claimed the last scene of the drama.

Undoubtedly conscious that his campaign had gained national prominence, and perhaps not unaware that it had political possibili-ties, the crusader made a speech in Pittsburgh in 1910 that marked him as a liberal and raised him undeniably to national stature.

Churches, he said, were serving the classes, not the masses, and had "more regard for pew rents than for men's souls." So also with universities. They must "be reconstructed from the top to the bot-tom."

Then, for no apparent reason—he was still the president of a university, not a politician—he added:

"Political parties are going to pieces. They are busy with their moral regeneration and they want leaders who can help them accomplish it."

If Wilson, the Puritan, cringed from such leadership, there was no indication that Wilson, the crusader for democracy, was unwilling.

He who had attended the University of Virginia without visiting Monticello, had come around spectacularly to Jefferson.

"I challenge you," he said, "to cite me an instance in all the history of the world where liberty was handed down from above. Liberty is always obtained . . . by the great movement of the people."

The intellectual snob was muted. "Genius is no snob," he declared, speaking of Lincoln, another of his heroes. "This is the sacred mystery of democracy, that its richest fruits spring up out of soils which no man has prepared and in circumstances amidst which they are least expected."

The champion of the people was sometimes betrayed by his other, Calvinist self. His Presbyterian face, he once remarked wryly, alarmed enemies and repelled friends. "You cannot imagine," he wrote as a candidate assailed by his constituents, "an invasion by the people of the United States! . . . Not a moment am I left free. . . . I thought last night I should go crazy with the strain and confusion."

But the crusader did not flinch from his duties. Abandoning scholastic cloisters and communion with books, resolutely he faced toward the turmoil of the market place.

He picked a good state and a good time. He could hardly have been more astute in either respect, and to say that he did it with reluctance would be to confound credibility. He knew history; it would be indicting his intelligence to imply that he did not also know what he was doing.

The Democrats in New Jersey at the time could not win, despite a state political machine under Senator James Smith. The Republicans had a better one. Both were notorious for protecting big business and especially corporations, which found Jersey justice eminently to their liking and sought its shelter from widespread points across the nation. But the Republicans were the ins and had a little bit of the edge in the matter of campaign funds. Boss Smith needed a convincing crusader with clean hands and no political commitments. Wilson ideally suited the role. Would he run?

There followed one of the most bizarre political poker games in American history. Smith dealt. Wilson said he did not want to play. Smith cajoled and dealt again. Wilson said all right—and turned his cards face up on the table. He would stand for no controls by the machine. He would speak for reform and he would mean it. If elected, he would refuse to heed Smith's advice on patronage and even refuse the ex-Senator an opportunity to run for re-election two years hence.

Smith looked at the cards, blinked, and, holding his own close to his vest, agreed to play. The best explanation for his decision is that he felt anybody as naïve as Wilson, and with such ability as an orator, should be taken into camp quickly before the Republicans got hold of him. As for Wilson defying the machine after election—Smith owned the machine. And Wilson had defied a bunch of stuffed shirts down at Princeton without much success. The game began with Boss Smith grinning broadly.

He continued happy throughout the campaign. When the Republicans challenged Wilson's sincerity, pointing out Smith's backing, Wilson made a ringing reply that underlined all that he had told Smith privately. The boss and his cronies agreed that it was excellent politicking. Wilson was elected by a plurality of 49,000. Everybody celebrated—and the new governor moved in to do exactly what he had said he was going to do. By the time another election rolled around he was able to tell Boss Smith flatly that Smith could not run for the national Senate.

This was in 1912. Wilson was fifty-six and at the height of his abilities; and national Democrats needed a crusading candidate to head their ticket almost as badly as had the party leaders in New Jersey.

Wilson played politics now, with veteran skill and with little regard for the dour Scotch Calvinist in him, playing it with the democracy of the people always in mind, even if, at times, the people confronting him were politicians.

Hardly had he assumed office in New Jersey than the Democrats called a caucus on one of his reform bills. Over protests from some of the legislators—doubtless Smith men—Wilson attended. Taking the floor, he spent three hours discussing the bill, ending with an oratorical appeal for party unity.

"We all came out of that room," said one state politico afterward, "with one conviction: that we had heard the most wonderful speech of our lives. Even the most hardened of the old-time legislative hacks said that."

It won them over not only to the bill, but to the whole Wilson program—direct primary laws and a corrupt practices act, both aimed at the political bosses; an employers' liability act to aid labor; and the creation of a public utilities commission and a set of seven laws aimed at protecting the public from exploitation by big business.

Nationally, he moved with equal astuteness. Never relinquishing his liberal beliefs, he skillfully allayed alarm among conservatives in the party. In the spring of 1911, for no urgent reasons, he managed to make an eight-thousand-mile tour of the country, speaking scores of times. He was charming both on the platform and in personal contacts. Ellen was invaluable. To Joseph P. Tumulty, New Jersey-Irish liberal who was to become Wilson's White House secretary, she was "the better politician of the two." She forced him to meet people regardless of his mood. Invariably, as his daughter recalled, he surrendered—"and once the ice was broken, enjoyed himself more than anyone else."

Notably, Ellen engineered an informal dinner and invited William Jennings Bryan, whom Wilson had attacked, but who was still the head of the national Democratic party. Skipping politics, the two men regaled each other with stories and left fast friends. Tumulty, hearing of it, credited Ellen with paving the way for Wilson's nomination.

It did not come that easily. Bryan was already committed to Champ Clark of Missouri, who had a clear majority in the early balloting when the convention got under way at Baltimore, but not the two thirds necessary for nomination. On the eleventh ballot, New York, with ninety votes, broke to the Missourian and it looked as if he were the nominee. Indeed, Wilson, watching anxiously from out of town, agreed to release his votes to Clark. Only by a furious phone call did William Gibbs McAdoo, one of the most enthusiastic of the Wilson backers, get the order rescinded before it could do irreparable damage.

The deadlock held for three more ballots, when Wilson moved on Bryan, who had figured earlier in the convention as an opponent of the New York, Wall-Street-controlled vote. If New York had gone over to Clark, how could Bryan justify sticking with him? Bryan couldn't and said so in a dramatic turnabout which stampeded the convention to Wilson.

The campaign that followed, although President William Howard Taft was the regular Republican candidate, became a duel between Wilson and Theodore Roosevelt, leader of the Bull Moose liberals who had broken with the Old Guard machine. This split in the Republican vote gave Wilson a perhaps unbeatable advantage. Nevertheless, he ran strongly against T. R., and that doughty warrior confessed to William Allen White that he thought "the American people are a little tired of me."

Taft, relinquishing the White House, made one of the few sage and pertinent comments of his career.

"I'm glad to be going," he said. "This is the loneliest place in the world."

It was not lonely for Wilson, it was stimulating and inspiring—at first.

The mantle of his accession to the presidency was soon spangled with liberal successes in office. The crusader for democracy was at his best. Reviving a custom which no president had honored since the elder Adams in 1797, he delivered his first message to the Congress in person. The Congress was politically in his hands, but he worked with them amicably to achieve his reforms. Always there was the gentle and understanding Ellen, guiding, tactfully advising, making and holding friends.

The first year of his administration saw passage of the Underwood (lower) Tariff Act, opposed by strong industrial lobbies, which Wilson routed by direct appeals to the public. He revived the income tax. Currency was reformed under the Federal Reserve Act, designed to break the dictatorship of private bankers over the nation's financing.

Body blows to monopolies were scored in the Federal Trade Commission Act and the Clayton Anti-Trust Act, and labor was aided when it was ruled that strikes were not a violation of federal law. Woman suffrage and the eight-hour day became legal.

Wilson's legislative record of reforms was the most sweeping since Jefferson's.

It was stopped in mid-term by World War I and its all-absorbing problems.

Much has been made of the facts that during his first term Wilson stood for strict neutrality, that he was re-elected on the slogan "He kept us out of war!" and that he then declared war on Germany.

All these things are true. But it is also true that in this, the war problem, he took greater care and was more successful in determining and reflecting the thoughts of the American people than in any other one thing he did in his entire career. The confusion and the accusations are perhaps due to the fact that he linked the war problem from the first with the peace problem, concerning which he went both beyond the people and beyond his time. But, concerning war, he followed the people with a precision which, in review, is one of the great masterpieces of democratic leadership.

Consider the war's calendar of events:

Wilson declared for strict neutrality when hostilities began. William Jennings Bryan, Secretary of State and a complete pacifist, resigned when Wilson's language concerning submarine warfare became "too strong," but neutrality continued to prevail. How painstakingly it was observed may be gathered from the reminder that the *Lusitania* was sunk in the spring of 1915, more than two years before we declared war.

Equally shocking was the sinking of the *Sussex*, a year after the *Lusitania*. Again war was avoided following a strong protest from the President and the German promise that subs would not attack without warning or without saving lives.

This was all in the spirit of the American people at the time. As Wilson worded it for them, they were "too proud to fight." They regarded the Continental conflict as something that did not concern them. They wanted as little part of it as possible.

In the fall following the *Sussex* sinking and the German pledges concerning submarine warfare, Wilson ran for re-election on the kept-us-out-of-war slogan. All evidence, every step that he had taken, indicates that he undoubtedly had done just that.

Late in January, 1917, the Germans, in an insolent message, notified the United States that they planned to resume unrestricted submarine warfare. Still Wilson made no move toward conflict, recommending instead that Congress authorize an armed neutrality for our ships. This recommendation Congress turned down. War was in the air. Wilson checked the temper of the people. They felt that the Congress was right. He still delayed, hoping against hope. But the mandate was unmistakable.

Then, and only then—on April 2, 1917—did he ask the Congress for a declaration of war.

Paralleling these actions on the war problem were equally logical moves concerning peace.

The guns had hardly begun to roar in Europe before Wilson offered, on August 5, 1914, to mediate. There was no response from either side. The offer was repeated in the fall, and again after he was re-elected. On this occasion, Germany answered directly with evasions, indirectly with its announcement of a return to unrestricted submarine warfare. The Allies were specific concerning peace—they would talk terms with the Hun on the basis of complete restitution.

To the Germans, after a time, the reply was war.

To the Allies, Wilson replied with his "peace without victory" speech on January 22, 1917, one of a series which led him rapidly to become a lonely, mystical crusader for world peace.

The loneliness was partly owing to the times, partly to his office, partly to the Calvinist welling up in him in righteous and sometimes dictatorial indignation on discovering that there were those who would put their personal dislikes ahead of permanent peace. Even the crusader for democracy contributed to the loneliness, for Wilson linked with his ideas for world peace a presentation of democracy more pure than any leader's since Jefferson. Indeed, to read his major utterances during his presidency is to have a brilliant summary of modern democracy at its most ideal.

From his first inaugural he urged his fellow citizens to new heights of democratic achievement, and before the end he had gone so far beyond them that they faltered and failed to follow.

He did not pioneer the philosophy of democracy, as Thomas Jefferson had done; but more than any other leader since Jefferson, he expounded it, orienting it in the modern world, giving it the wider horizons which that world afforded. He prepared democracy, as it were, for export, and gave to his exposition of it all the vivid talents of every aspect of his character, now preaching Biblically as a Calvinist preacher, again using the crisp, crystalline language of a champion of the people, yet again speaking, sometimes with the brutal practicality, more often with the mystical prophecy, of a crusader for world peace.

This he did with such vision that a summary of his words, some of them uttered even before the first World War, are as fresh today as when he spoke them, casting an eerie and revealing light on tomorrow as well as yesterday:

If I did not believe that the moral judgment would be the last judgment, the final judgment, in the minds of men as well as at the tribunal of God, I could not believe in popular government. The greatest forces in the world and the only permanent forces are the moral forces.

There is a pretty fine analogy between patriotism and Christianity. It is the devotion of the spirit to something greater and nobler than itself. No man who thinks of himself and afterwards of his country can call himself an American. America must be enriched by us. We must not live upon her; she must live by means of us.

There is but one longing and utterance of the human heart, and that is for liberty and justice. We came to America, either ourselves or in the persons of our ancestors, to better the ideals of man.

It does not behoove a nation to walk with its eyes over its shoulder. I hear a great many people at Fourth of July celebrations laud the Declaration of Independence who in between Julys shiver at the plain language of our Bill of Rights. The Declaration cannot mean anything to us unless we append to it a similar specific body of particulars as to what we consider the essential business of our own day.

Do not let us go back to the annals to find out what to do, because we live in another age and the circumstances are absolutely different; but let us free our vision from temporary circumstances and look abroad at the horizon and

305

take into our lungs the great air of freedom which has blown through this country and stolen across the seas and blessed people everywhere; and, looking east and west and north and south, let us remind ourselves that we are the custodians, in some degree, of the principles which have made men free and governments just.

As I think of the life of this great nation, it seems to me that we sometimes look to the wrong places for its sources. We look to the noisy places, instead of trying to attune our ears to that voiceless mass of men who merely go about their daily tasks, try to be honorable, try to serve the people they love, try to live worthy of the communities to which they belong. They are the breath of the nation's nostrils; they are the sinews of its might.

America must have a consciousness different from the consciousness of every other nation in the world. On all sides it touches elbows and touches hearts with all the nations of mankind. This country is constantly drinking strength out of new sources by the voluntary association with it of great bodies of strong men and forward-looking women out of other lands. It is as if humanity had determined to see to it that this great nation, founded for the benefit of humanity, should not lack for the allegiance of the people of the world.

There have been other nations as rich as we, there have been other nations as powerful, there have been other nations as spirited; but I hope we shall never forget that we created this nation, not to serve ourselves, but to serve mankind.

Among the silent, speechless masses of the American people is slowly coming up the sap of moral purpose and love of justice and reverence for humanity which constitutes the only virtue and distinction of the American people.

We were very heedless and in a hurry to be great.

We have squandered a great part of what we might have used, and have not stopped to conserve the exceeding bounty of nature. We have been proud of our industrial achievements, but we have not hitherto stopped thoughtfully enough to count the human cost, the cost of lives snuffed out, of energies overtaxed and broken, the fearful physical and spiritual cost to the men and women and children upon whom the dead weight and burden of it all has fallen pitilessly the years through.

The great government we loved has too often been made use of for private and selfish purposes, and those who used it had forgotten the people.

At last a vision has been vouchsafed us of life as a whole. We see the bad with the good, the debased and decadent with the sound and vital. With this vision we approach new affairs. Our duty is to cleanse, to reconsider, to restore, to purify and humanize every process of our common life without weakening or sentimentalizing it.

Legislation cannot save society. The law that will work is merely the summing up in legislative form of the moral judgment that the community has already reached. Enact a law that is the moral judgment of a very small minority of the community, and it will not work. Most people will not understand it; and if they do understand it, they will resent it; and whether they understand it and resent it or not, they will not obey it. If you try to enact into law what expresses only the spirit of a small coterie of a small minority, you know or at any rate you ought to know beforehand that it is not going to work.

We shall deal with our economic system as it is and as it may be modified, not as it might be if we had a clean sheet of paper to write upon; and step by step we shall make it what it should be.

There can be no settled conditions leading to increased production and a reduction in the cost of living if labor and capital are to be antagonists instead of partners.

The only way to keep men from agitating against grievances is to remove the grievances.

There can be no permanent and lasting settlements between capital and labor which do not recognize the fundamental concepts for which labor has been struggling through the years. The right of labor to live in peace and comfort must be recognized by governments, and America should be the first to lay the foundation stones upon which industrial peace shall be built.

The man who seeks to divide man from man, group from group, interest from interest in this great Union is striking at its very heart.

The firm basis of government is justice, not pity. Society must see to it that it does not itself crush or weaken or damage its own constituent parts.

This is the high enterprise of the new day: To lift everything that concerns our life as a nation to the light that shines from the heartfires of every man's conscience and vision of the right.

America's only reason for existence as a government, was to show men the path of liberty and of mutual serviceability, to lift the common man out of the paths, out of the sloughs of discouragement and even despair; set his feet upon firm ground; tell him, "Here is the high road upon which you are as much entitled to walk as we are, and we will see that there is a free field and no favor, and that as your moral qualities are and your physical powers so will your success be. We will not let any man make you afraid, and we will not let any man do you an injustice."

Those are the ideals of America. We have not always lived up to them. No community has always lived up to them, but we are dignified by the fact that those are the things we live for and sail by; America is great in the world, not as she is a successful government merely, but as she is the successful embodiment of a great ideal of unselfish citizenship. That is what makes the world feel America draw it like a lodestone.

We are in the world to do something more than look after ourselves. America has a great cause which is not confined to the American continent. It is the cause of humanity itself.

The spirit of the United States is an international spirit. It is as if the nations of the world, sampled and united here, were in their new union and new common understanding turning about to serve the world.

We cannot long conceal the fact that we are just as human as any other nation, that we are just as selfish, that there are just as many mean people among us as anywhere else, that there are just as many people here who want to take advantage of other people as you can find in other countries, just as many cruel people, just as many people heartless when it comes to maintaining and promoting their own interests; but you can show that our object is to get these people in harness and see to it that they do not do any damage and are not allowed to indulge the passions which would bring injustice and calamity at last upon a nation whose object is spiritual and not material.

We believe that the day of Little Americanism, with its narrow horizons, when methods of "protection" and industrial nursing were the chief study of our provincial statesmen, is past and gone and that a day of enterprise has at last dawned for the United States whose field is the wide world.

We are Americans for Big America, and rejoice to look forward to the days in which America shall strive to stir the world without irritating it or drawing it on to new antagonisms, when the nations with which we deal shall at last come to see upon what deep foundations of humanity and justice our passion for peace rests, and when all mankind shall look upon our great people with a new sentiment of admiration, friendly rivalry and real affection, as upon a people who, though keen to succeed, seeks always to be at once generous and just and to whom humanity is dearer than profit and selfish power.

The nations of the world must unite in joint guarantees that whatever is done to disturb the whole world's life must first be tested in the court of the whole world's opinion before it is attempted.

We are provincials no longer. There can be no turning back. We are to play a leading part in the world drama whether we wish it or not. What affects mankind is inevitably our affair.

The world must be safe for democracy.

The shadows that now lie dark upon our path will soon be dispelled and we shall walk with the light all about us if we be but true to ourselves—to ourselves as we have wished to be known in the counsels of the world and in the thoughts of all those who love liberty and justice and the right exalted.

The people of the world are awake and the people of the world are in the saddle. Private counsels of statesmen cannot now and cannot hereafter determine the destinies of nations. If this is not the final battle for right, there will be another that will be final. Let these gentlemen not suppose that it is possible for them to accomplish this return to an order of which we are ashamed and that we are ready to forget.

This age is an age which looks forward, not backward; which rejects the standards of national selfishness that once governed the counsel of nations and demands that they shall give way to a new order of things in which the only question will be, "Is it right?" "Is it just?" "Is it in the interest of mankind?"

The principles of public right must henceforth take precedent over the individual interests of nations, and the nations of the world must in some way band themselves together to see that the right prevails as against any sort of selfish aggression.

My dream is that America will come into the full light of the day when all shall know that she puts human rights above all other rights and that her flag is the flag not only of America but of humanity.

Let us pray Almighty God that in His good time liberty and security and peace and the comradeship of a common justice may be vouchsafed all the nations of the earth. . . .

But it could not be, he was too soon, one man against an army of men to whom nationalism was a habit and peace a mirage.

Each step he took, no matter what he did, tragedy haunted him, and failure. He had hardly begun before the worst blow fell. In 1914, his beloved Ellen died. This unquestionably colored everything he did thenceforth and to his disadvantage, for without her gentle urging he saw fewer and fewer people, becoming more and more isolated as the war went on.

His loneliness was aggravated when, in 1915, he married Mrs. Norman Galt, who encouraged his bent toward solitude.

The brilliant man-to-man salesmanship to the Congress which had marked his campaign for domestic reforms was woefully lacking in his campaign for the League of Nations. Much of his major policy they learned by reading the papers; when he spoke to them, it was too often a blunt order; he steadfastly refused compromises of any sort.

Similarly, he sought no help from Allied leaders. Although there were liberal groups in both England and France who agreed with him, and although for four years there were foreign diplomats in Washington whom he could, possibly, have won over, he sought out neither group until it was too late. "He doesn't want to see any of us," the French ambassador summed up bleakly in Washington early in the war.

Wilson's stand on peace was that of the self-righteous Calvinist to whom all opposition, however reasonable, was evil; support was expected as a matter of course. The Allied statesmen must be "forced" to "our way of thinking." When he spoke in person to the British people on his way to the Paris conference, he did not feel it necessary to mention their tremendous losses and sacrifices. He told the French Chamber of Deputies that he had "come to work out for you" a peaceful world.

Forced to compromise on the peace abroad, he came home to face

309

a Senate which, by an excruciatingly ironic turn of events, was controlled by the Republicans with a majority of one. The one—Truman Newberry—was later forced out by the scandal of his campaign expenditures against Henry Ford, but he was a senator long enough to establish the Republican rule and place Henry Cabot Lodge of Massachusetts in charge of Senate foreign affairs.

Lodge, as reactionary, vindictive, embittered, and arrogant a man of property as ever faced a man of the people, cut Wilson's peace plans to ribbons despite the fact that in 1916 he had stood with Wilson on the same platform and endorsed a league of nations. Too shrewd to face the wrath of the people by all-out opposition, Lodge fought the Wilson proposals a point at a time, dodging direct issues, chiseling one stone and then another in the foundation, delaying, sabotaging.

Wilson had no choice but to go down, though he fought till the bitter end.

It came when he suffered a stroke midway in a nation-wide campaign tour on the league in October, 1919. He returned to the White House and served out his term, seeing so few persons save his wife that rumors were he had lost his mind.

He lived on in Washington until his death on February 3, 1924, believing to the end that he had been betrayed by friends and foes alike.

In a speech rededicating Congress Hall in Philadelphia in 1915, some nine years before his death, he said that it seemed to him he saw ghosts crowding, spirits of those "whose influence we still feel as we feel the molding power of history itself."

Just before he died, with sudden animation, he told one of his daughters he thought it best, after all, that America had not joined the league. And then the crowding ghosts spoke from the pale lips:

"Our entrance into the league at the time I returned from Europe might have been only a personal victory. Now, when the American people join the league, it will be because they are convinced it is the right thing to do, and then will be the only right time for them to do it." A pause. "Perhaps God knew better than I did after all."

Thus spoke the ghostly Calvinist Wilson and Wilson the champion of democracy, both doubtless urged by gentle chiding from another knowing ghost that once had borne the mortal name of Ellen Axson Wilson.

But no ghost spoke for the third and greatest Wilson, the peace crusader, for he was not to die.

F. D. R.

The most glorious exploits do not furnish us with the clearest discoveries of virtue or vice in men; sometimes a matter of less moment, an expression or a jest, informs us better of their characters and inclinations than the most famous sieges, the greatest armaments, or the bloodiest battles whatsoever.

—PLUTARCH

Great men hallow a whole people, and lift up all who live in their time.

—SIDNEY SMITH

Nothing is so much to be feared as fear.

—HENRY DAVID THOREAU

Although it is easy now to prove the contrary, from his record, about the most dubious man of the people who ever came to Washington was a thirty-one-year-old New York state senator who, in 1913, had just been appointed Assistant Secretary of the Navy under Josephus Daniels and whose name was Franklin Delano Roosevelt.

Young for the post, his appointment by President Wilson could be credited to his tremendous energy, rapid-fire mind, high social connections, wealth, his campaigning for the President, and luck. To have attributed it to his liberal record up to his arrival in Washington would have been to stretch the truth measurably, for if he was at that time a liberal, he was strictly of the parlor variety—an amateur and not a very sanguine one at that.

He was born lucky on January 30, 1882, at Hyde Park, New York, and had been consistently lucky throughout his youth and young manhood.

He inherited social standing, money, and talent from both sides of the house. James, his father, was a large landholder along the Hudson River valley and an officer in a number of large corporations. Sarah Delano, his mother, came from a clan of well-to-do merchants and shippers. Both parents traced their Dutch ancestry back to the beginnings of New York city and state, and one of the Roosevelts, a distant cousin named Theodore, was to become President almost before Franklin was grown.

F. D. R. was educated at the best schools—Groton, Harvard, Columbia—and at home learned the best sports, including riding to hounds and polo. When he was three he took his first trip abroad, and others followed. He learned to speak German and French fluently. The family summered at Campobello, New Brunswick, where he became an expert at sailing a boat. When he was graduated from Columbia Law School at twenty-five, he began practicing law in New York, but soon—some say at the inspiration of his cousin, Theodore—went into politics. At twenty-three he married Anna Eleanor Roosevelt, a sixth cousin. Cousin Theodore, then President, stole the wedding spotlight from the bride and groom.

If it was he who interested the young man in politics, when Franklin first threw his hat in the ring it was on the side of Theodore's opponents, the Democrats. They nominated the younger man for state senator when he was twenty-eight.

It was not an ideal beginning, since a Democrat had not been elected from that part of the state since 1856. Franklin made a whirlwind campaign by automobile. When all the returns were in, he had won by a close margin. Whatever his political ideas or future, he had done one thing that foreshadowed his career—he had proved that he was a vote-getter.

Going to Albany, he became associated with the Al Smith Democrats, whose liberal reforms were beginning to make political history. Young Roosevelt soon dramatically identified himself with this group by leading the opposition against Tammany Hall's candidate for the United States Senate, William F. Sheehan.

But working liberals in Albany found him less than enthusiastic about real reforms. When a young social worker named Frances Perkins fought through a bill limiting women's labor to fifty-four hours a week, she found more support from Tim Sullivan, the senator from the Bowery, than from Roosevelt. People thought him arrogant, he talked seldom, he lacked charm, he rarely smiled, and he had "an unfortunate habit—so natural that he was unaware of it—of throwing his head up. This, combined with his pince-nez and great height, gave him the appearance of looking down his nose at most people."

He was astute enough politically, though, to get on the Wilson bandwagon early in 1911 and vigorously support the candidate both at Baltimore and in the campaign. The navy post was his reward.

During his eight years as Assistant Secretary of the Navy he again distinguished himself on the liberal side, but always as a follower of the leader, a good soldier in the ranks rather than a militant crusader for the rank-and-file, of whom he knew little, and in whom he showed even less interest.

His liberalism, it might be said, graduated at this point from the parlor to the classroom. He became imbued with Wilson's domestic and foreign hopes for democracy. He and his wife made many friends among Wilson's following. Roosevelt demonstrated a far-sightedness which was to characterize him many a time in later years when, seeing that war was inevitable, he squirreled away supplies so efficiently for the fleet that the army finally had to appeal to the White House to make the young Assistant Secretary divide up. He also became an adept at getting around government bureaucracy.

Roosevelt had many occasions to meet with Wilson. The President liked him, and the Assistant Secretary admired the President. After the war, Roosevelt went to Europe to liquidate naval supplies and, after coming back on the same boat with the President in February, 1919, joined him in his speaking crusade for the league. Roosevelt continued the campaign after it became a lost cause the next year, when, at thirty-eight, he ran for the vice presidency on the losing Democratic ticket. The professor was dying, his crusade dead. The classroom liberal retired to practice law in New York.

It was the last place you would expect a person of Roosevelt's background to train to become a man of the people, which, in turn, was probably the last thing he then had in mind. Despite his tremendous physical energy, he was worn out. He suffered in addition the mental and spiritual exhaustion that comes from going down with a righteous cause. For more than a decade he had neglected his private business, and the family budget was dangerously low. Like many another good parlor-and-classroom liberal, he found ample excuses for retiring from public service and devoting full time to his private affairs.

But shortly, with brutal and dramatic suddenness, he was pulled precipitously down among the people in an experience which made him forever one of them.

313

It began at the summer home, Campobello. Roosevelt was nearly forty—an age when doctors and insurance experts warn that a man should not attempt too-vigorous athletics. One day he rose early and went sailing with some of his children. Starting home cross-country about noon, they stopped off to help fight a forest fire. They got to the house about four o'clock, exhausted, at which point Roosevelt decided that he would feel better if he swam in a near-by lake and topped his swim off with a plunge in the icy waters of the Bay of Fundy. Then he dog-trotted two miles home and sat down in wet clothes to read his mail. The average human being would either have dropped dead from exhaustion or gone down in a losing fight with double pneumonia. Roosevelt was stricken with infantile paralysis.

It was a bitter blow, and painful. An all-night chill was followed by gradual paralysis of the legs, which remained needle-sore to the touch for three weeks and sensitive for six months. By the following February, he was able to stand with braces; gradually, painfully, he walked. By then, too, he had learned the truth—he was to be crippled for life and there was little or nothing that the genius of the medical world could do about it. They had, in their desperate ignorance, done worse than nothing, during the first ten days of the attack heavily massaging his legs and feet with damaging results. He who had defied illness with amused indifference must live with it incessantly for the rest of his life.

He answered the challenge with no word of self-pity; with an intensive personal study of his disease that pioneered therapy in the field and resulted in his eventually writing what experts regard as "one of the famous case reports (on himself) of medical history"; with excruciating exercises, and with heightened defiance.

Months passed without appreciable improvement. He swung from parallel bars arranged at a height where his feet just touched the ground and were lightly exercised. Standing, he insisted on crutches and made himself walk. Any suggestion from the doctors, however painful, he eagerly tried. A year passed, and a second.

It was in 1924 that he heard of a pool at Warm Springs, Georgia, where the water temperature was 89 degrees and its specific gravity unusually high, making the body float like a feather. Infantile paralysis convalescents were reported to have benefited markedly from bathing at the Springs. The Roosevelts eagerly went there in the fall, renting a broken-down cottage.

Using himself as a guinea pig, Roosevelt first timidly exercised his legs in the water, then his whole body. Clinging to the side of the pool, tentatively and then with growing hope, he flexed the damaged muscles. One day he swam, the next he walked upright in the water without braces. The progress was so marked that he began to talk to friends of "the most wonderful pool in the world." An Atlanta newspaperman, after listening to him, wrote a feature story called "Swimming Back to Health."

Thus was born the latter-day character of Franklin D. Roosevelt, President of the United States; for to anyone knowing victims of infantile paralysis who have fought their way back to health, it is a commonplace that their whole personality is markedly different from a person who has not gone through that devastating flame. A polio patient has done the impossible, made something from nothing, fought against overwhelming odds and won. Why shouldn't he be an optimist, dauntless, vigorously confident that the future is bright? Polio courage, unlike Dutch courage, is a thing of the spirit and undying. Roosevelt had acquired it in tremendous abundance.

He mortised three other stones into the structure of his character during those bitter months.

Unable to move about, frequently bedridden, he became a voracious reader.

"You fellows with two legs," he once told Charlie Michelson, the Democratic party press agent who retells it in his book, *The Ghost Talks*, "spend your spare time playing golf, or shooting ducks or such things, while I have had to get all my exercise out of a book."

His favorite subjects were political histories and memoirs, American history generally, farm and agricultural literature, and—the American indispensable—detective stories. He followed the newspapers more closely than was possible for any other contemporary in active political life, and there is evidence in his subsequent public statements that he refreshed his mind by drinking deeply from the classics and from the writing of his favorite Americans, including Lincoln, Whitman, and Thoreau.

The second stone was put into the structure with the untiring aid

315

of Louis McHenry Howe, an ex-newspaperman who had picked Roosevelt as a president when the two worked at the Navy, and the aid of Mrs. Roosevelt.

Howe saw to it that, despite his invalidism, Roosevelt met and talked with the right people politically.

Mrs. Roosevelt, equally untiring and more realistic than her husband about the ground-root personalities of social reform, made it her business for him to meet them. These social workers and labor leaders, telling of their problems and their hopes, took him in endless conversations from the parlor and the classroom down into the slums and the factories, the shanties and the tenements.

The third stone hit him between the eyes. His interview with the Atlanta reporter, widely printed, brought to the shabby cabins and ramshackle hotel at Warm Springs a pathetic army of polio victims from all over the nation, seeking advice, therapy, miracles.

There were no doctors at the resort, no nurses, no adequate facilities of any sort. The Groton-Harvard graduate and Hyde Park aristocrat found the newcomers getting under foot, interfering with his routine, crowding the pool, and in many cases embarrassing him by pleas for funds. But he found them crippled as he was crippled and full of hope as he had become filled with hope. As he was to say himself later, at Warm Springs he discovered the people of the nation and with them shared their problems, their sufferings, and their dreams. He received the human inundation with the happy lilt of friendship and warming grin that was to mark his dealings with people, high and low, thenceforth.

"During that first year," he said later, "I was doctor and physiotherapist rolled into one." He and Mrs. Roosevelt learned the unrewarded exasperations that come from running a broken-down hotel. Risking their depleted funds, they bought the Springs, converted it into a nonprofit foundation, and browbeat friends and acquaintances into contributing. Two thirds of the Roosevelt personal fortune went into the project. Under his administration, it grew into a national institution. A little more than ten years later, it became the Foundation for Infantile Paralysis, devoted as much to finding a preventive for this disease as to developing its therapy.

Its founder was never to complete his own ambition, to walk at ease. In 1924, Al Smith asked him to nominate "the happy warrior" at the Democratic national convention in the old Madison Square Garden, New York. Roosevelt coined the phrase, but it was not his speech that won him his greatest personal ovation. Appearing before a large assembly for the first time since he was stricken, he struggled on crutches to the speaker's platform. The convention waited in sympathetic silence. Reaching the rostrum, Roosevelt laid his crutches aside, stood erect, and smiled.

Here was the complete man, the matured personality. Never again would his sympathy for suffering be synthetic, parlor-grown, or smelling of the lamp. He was now, in fact, not in theory, a man of the people. He had been into a far and somber land, and had returned to become one of them.

The character which thus emerged and, less than a decade later, became the President of the United States, has been subjected to more exaggerations, pro and con, than any other in modern times. Roosevelt has been portrayed as God, Satan, and almost every extreme of human personality imaginable. His enemies pursued him beyond the grave. Typical of the character assassination that continues to this day is an editorial which appeared, less than a month after his death, in the New York *News* bracketing his passing with that of Mussolini—"lynched is the correct word" and Hitler—"his cadaver has not been dug up at this writing." "The chief thought which these deaths have stirred in us," the *News* concluded, "concerns the holes that have been blown by these deaths in the 'indispensable man' theory." Yet he is also unrivaled in American history for the number of common people, at home and abroad, who gave him their unquestioning loyalty while he was alive and mourned him as a father in death.

He himself once summed up his philosophy too simply by saying, "I am a Christian and a Democrat." Another oversimplification is in Charlie Michelson's *The Ghost Talks:* "Perhaps the mystery of Roosevelt's character would evaporate if his fellow citizens ceased regarding him as either a superman or a supermarplot and instead would take him as a highly intelligent person with much governmental experience and, presumably, the normal excellencies and defects of most of us."

Intelligent he undoubtedly was, though never scholarly. His memory was phenomenal. While governor of New York—from 1929 until he went to the White House in 1933—a subordinate once attempted to brief for him lengthy testimony given by Mayor Walker of New York before a committee investigating Walker's administration. Roosevelt interrupted to quote the testimony verbatim. He was constantly astounding people by recalling conversations months or years later. "I always marveled," said Donald Nelson, head of war production and a wizard at figures, "at the President's ability to recite from memory interesting and pertinent facts to fit every occasion. Some of them were strange and rare statistics, and I never knew how he could cram and retain them in a mind so full of information."

It was not an intelligence of memory only. It was a mind persistently eager for new ideas and new policies. Perhaps the most incisive index to the democracy of the man was his self-stated policy of entering the White House with "an open door and an open mind." To keep it open, he was at times accused of pretending to agree with someone's viewpoint only to declare himself later to be on exactly the opposite side of the question. He had simply indulged himself in his favorite pastime of garnering information, or in his equally expansive love for people.

In interviews, as in writing speeches, the most accurate estimate of him is probably Michelson's: "I was never present when a big speech was born that the President did not take the political viands offered and cook them in his own individual way."

Outside Washington, a steadily growing opinion during his career in the White House held that he was an incompetent executive. Inside Washington, government officials generally as steadily disagreed if they were partisan to him during his career. Since his death, more and more of the professional government workers look back on him as an administrative genius.

He surrounded himself with men, often objectionable so far as their personalities were concerned, through whom he constantly checked what was going on everywhere in the government. Informed of bad management or abuses, his action was prompt and often drastic. He made numberless mistakes. Some of his appointments turned out badly, and he was chronically incapable of getting rid of the men in question.

But he also made brilliant choices, untrammeled by personal feelings. To the secretaryship of his favorite bureau, the Navy, he sent Frank Knox, a Republican who had publicly called Roosevelt every name he could lay his tongue to or dared to print. A tremendous battleship program was getting under way, and a driver, a producer, was needed to fill the post. Knox turned out to be ideal.

Roosevelt made some bad errors in policy, and there were frequent failures. But it would be difficult to imagine a more efficient and more honest administration of the turbulent affairs which he managed.

Throughout his presidential career, he was accused of lacking a knowledge of economics. Even so sympathetic a friend as Frances Perkins says that he read little in the field.

It is probably more accurate to say that he knew the economics of the men of property all too well. His economics was that of a man of the people.

"It shall never be said," he declared even before he reached the White House, "that the American people have refused to provide the necessities of life to those who, through no fault of their own, are unable to feed, clothe, and house themselves. The first obligation of government is the protection of the welfare and well-being—the very existence of its citizens."

Also deeply imbedded in his economic philosophy was supreme confidence in the productive powers of the people. He asked pleasantly for 50,000 planes before we entered the war, a request that brought protest from the economic and production experts of the nation.

"Now," said so established a liberal as John T. Flynn in *Country Squire in the White House* (to the delight of all who opposed Roosevelt), "now he wants planes—not some reasonable number that can be produced, but some fantastic number that cannot be produced." "In 1944," Donald Nelson recorded recently by way of rebuttal, "the output of planes had soared to 96,369. . . . Recapitulating, we find that between January 1, 1940 [about the time Flynn's book came out], and August 14, 1945, we produced 303,317 military aircraft. . . . Even these figures do not tell the complete story because of the greater size, speed and firepower of the later planes. . . ."

Politically, to put it mildly, F. D. R. was far more Democrat than Christian, having learned to regard everyone with certain reservations in the rough and tumble of his years as governor of New York and in his campaigns for the nomination and the presidency; to act with brutal decisiveness in a crisis; and to time public pronouncements down to the exact and ideal moment, the perfect phrase, the most subtly appropriate tone.

He came to the White House in better health than anyone in modern times, with the possible exception of Cousin Theodore. He had not only regained his former tremendous vitality; he had learned to protect it. Save for his legs, he was as strong as an ox. Anyone who swam with him in the White House pool learned by getting ducked the tremendous power of his arms and shoulders. Once, sitting on the edge of a bed between sons Elliott and James, both near-heavyweights, he ended an argument by lying back, grabbing them from behind by their belts, and flipping them across the bed to the floor. Again, in 1940, he landed a 235-pound shark after an hour-and-a-half battle.

In informal personal contacts, not involving the nation's business, it seemed virtually impossible for him not to like, and charm, friends and foes alike. "The President always greeted you with a big smile and a hearty handshake," said Donald Nelson in *Arsenal of Democracy*, "and you felt from his manner that you were the one person in the world that he really wanted to see at the moment—that if kings and prime ministers were cluttering the outer office they would have to wait. . . ." "Mr. Roosevelt," drily remarked Merriman Smith, White House correspondent in his book *Thank You, Mr. President*, "knew how to say 'my old friend' in a dozen different languages." With a few exceptions, the President could say with Will Rogers that, differences aside, he never met a man he didn't like.

Sometimes his friendliness reached classic heights. At a Pearl Harbor hospital, greeting a marine who had helped amputate his own leg, F. D. R. flashed his famed smile and said, "Good morning, Doctor, I understand you are quite a surgeon. I happen to be a pretty good othopedist myself—what about a consultation?" "Gee—*the President!*" exclaimed another wounded—"not merely the President of the United States," in the words of Vice Admiral Ross T. McIntire in *White House Physician,* who accompanied him on the innumerable hospital visits upon which Roosevelt always insisted, no matter how taxing his schedule—"not merely the President, but another human being, one struck down as they themselves were stricken." With these, with all humble and stricken folk, he was always radiantly human.

But he could also be tough and he could be formal. "No President was ever feared so much in press conferences," in Merriman Smith's judgment. "He could be as rough and tough as a Third Avenue blackjack artist." Again, reporting on the President's speech before the Teamsters Union in the 1944 campaign: "He set out deliberately to pick a dock-walloping brawl with the Republicans." "He had a smile and a friendly word for everybody in the crew," said a pilot who flew him frequently, "but he never let us forget he was bossman. He could be as cool and formal as a cut-glass punchbowl at an Embassy reception."

In less official surroundings he loved informality. Arriving at a cocktail party of guests awed by his presence, he broke the tension with "Well, get me a drink—that's what I came for!" Fala, the Scotty that became a world-famous mascot after the Teamsters' speech, knew he could scrounge tidbits from his master even when so famous a visitor as Winston Churchill was at the White House.

His personal likes were for the oldest sweater, the most battered hat, the well-worn tweed jacket. His bed was made of cheap iron and the mattress was thin and hard. He ate heartily, but liked simple dishes.

From 1924 until he was first elected President in 1932, his luck rode with him. In 1928, he ran for governor of New York to bolster Al Smith's presidential campaign. It failed—but Roosevelt was elected by 25,000 votes. Louis Howe, aided by a new recruit, Big Jim Farley, for years schooled in New York political promotion, immediately began a quiet campaign for the next Democratic presidential nomination. In 1930, Roosevelt was re-elected to the governorship by an unprecedented plurality of 725,000.

Farley and Howe got him the nomination at Chicago, whence Roosevelt broke all precedents by flying. With Hoover haunted by the necessity of explaining the market crash and the depression, the Democratic candidate's acceptance speech and subsequent campaign was noncommittal.

On repeal of Prohibition, something which Al Smith had also advocated, he was definite. "For the rest," commented Elmer Davis, in the New York *Times*, of Roosevelt's acceptance, "you could not quarrel with a single one of his generalities. But what they mean (if anything) is known only to Franklin D. Roosevelt and his God." So completely did he mask his mind that Walter Lippmann wrote, "Franklin D. Roosevelt . . . is no crusader. He is no tribune of the people . . . no enemy of entrenched privilege. He is a pleasant man who, without any important qualifications for the office, would very much like to be President."

His wish granted, he moved with dramatic and heartening rapidity to restore the nation's confidence and bolster its tottering financial structure. He had, among other things, promised government economy, but when the nation-wide hardship of the people became evident, he advocated liberal spending. Cost regardless, he moved quickly toward "re-establishing the purchasing power of the people," and a balanced economy free from abuses and excesses.

The open door and the open mind worked overtime. Closing banks until each proved itself financially sound, he quickly restored federal credit, at the same time abandoning the gold standard and revaluating the dollar. Against monopolies and financial abuses he moved with the Securities and Exchange Commission, against unemployment with the Civilian Conservation Corps.

The Tennessee Valley Authority was authorized to serve as a pilot plant on utility rates, and others followed. Foreclosures were stopped, a farm relief law passed. Plans for a system of public works and federal employment (W.P.A.) got under way. The National Recovery Act (N.R.A.), with its goal to establish fair business practices and help labor as well as restore production, was on the books by midsummer.

Other laws followed, notably the Gold Reserve Act of January, 1934, revaluating the dollar, and the Social Security Act of 1935, providing for unemployment compensation and old-age insurance.

Most of the early laws were passed without opposition and while the entire nation, including the men of property, watched with approval. They were passed, a great many of them, in haste. The nation was in a state of collapse and bewilderment and needed a strong shot in the arm. Big business had failed and was frightened half out of its wits. Roosevelt, according to such intimate observers as Ernest K. Lindley, "went to work in Washington somewhat under the spell of the pleasant idea that we were all just one great happy family." So long as he was saving their dress shirts for them, the men of property were willing to sit by and wait, if with misgiving, at least without hostility.

The laws having been passed, the New Deal set out to enforce them, and serious opposition arose. First thunderhead was N.R.A., which both business and economic observers agreed, in retrospect, was unwieldy and unenforceable. It presumed too much altruism in the happy family once each man's selfish interests were at stake.

General Hugh S. Johnson, administering the act, was a warrior, not a conciliator. He wore himself out fighting for the codes and then refused to let his frayed nerves be twitched by New Deal associates whom he considered incompetent. Confusion resulted. It would probably have been inevitable, considering the impossible task the act was supposed to perform.

The Supreme Court capped the conflict by declaring N.R.A. illegal and then moved on the New Deal agricultural reforms.

The men of property chorused approval, bitterly salted with invective.

Compared to what came after, early criticisms of Roosevelt and the New Deal were not unreasonable. "Well, he is still wild in many of his methods," summed up one of his most violent haters, Westbrook Pegler, as late as 1937, "and he is not to be trusted with a loose rein for an instant, but in spite of all this he has accomplished some reforms, and, much more important, he has stirred the whole nation for once into an appreciation of the real problems of poverty, unequal distribution, unequal opportunity, dictatorship, and the rights and obligations of the states. Never in our time have people been so conscious of the burden they carry in taxes, of the meanness which a complacent upper class will practice on the help, and of the government's duty to do something real and personal for those who are so far down that they can't help themselves."

By comparison to 1940, the election of 1936 was mild when it comes to invective. The people responded by returning Roosevelt to the White House with a popular majority of eleven million and an electoral vote of 523 to 8.

Flushed with victory, the President turned on the Supreme Court.

323

"I seek to make democracy work," he declared, and began a bitter attack on the "nine old men." As militant as he, the men of property flocked to the court's defense.

Roosevelt threatened to pack it with New Deal partisans or overrule it through the Congress, but before he could carry out any of his threats, the court, as Michelson puts it, "awoke to the necessity of getting into step with the liberal movement and astonished the country by a complete judicial somersault." It recognized labor as a national, rather than a state, problem, and generally got itself in tune with the turbulent times. Roosevelt summed up the outcome by saying he had "lost the battle but won the war."

To a degree he had. But more clearly than ever before he had set himself firmly in opposition to the reactionary elements of big business. Unable to blast his popularity and his administration in a frontal assault, they resorted to the most bitter personal attack ever leveled at a President, bar none, bar not even Jefferson, Jackson, or Lincoln.

Forgotten were his early, brilliant moves to bring the country back from the brink of economic collapse; obscured were his fundamental beliefs in the rights of the people and his faith in democracy. With the campaign of 1940, when he broke one of the oldest national traditions by seeking a third term, he was assailed unmercifully from all sides by the men of property. Bolstered by the support of many sincere and thoroughly democratic people who believed, among other things, that three presidential terms were too many for any man, and heartened by an equally sincere and earnest candidate in Wendell Willkie, big business poured funds and energies into a stop-Roosevelt drive as they had not done in any national campaign in the nation's history.

At heart, they shouted, Roosevelt was a dictator. He would declare war "before the election, if necessary, to assure success of the third term campaign," according to Representative Harold Knutson of Minnesota. Bishop A. W. Leonard of the Washington area of the Methodist Church confirmed this—Roosevelt was paving the way "for a totalitarian state." Labor was warned by the Chicago *Tribune* that it faced "the slavery and low standards of dictatorship," and the same newspaper stated that "the White House has become an imperial palace and Mr. Roosevelt is acting as if he were the absolute ruler of people . . . who could be sold into war as lightly as if they were eighteenth century Hessians."

If not a Communist, he and Mrs. Roosevelt were fellow travelers, and he an economic irresponsible. "There is no village council in this country that hasn't a greater sense of responsibility about money . . . and more horse sense on the subject of spending it than the President of the United States," said Senator Robert A. Taft of Ohio.

He was attacked particularly from the gutter and by inuendo. "The secrets of his foreign policy," declared Congresswoman Jessie Sumner of Illinois, "are locked up in executive closets like the corpses of Bluebeard's wives." Elliott Roosevelt had just been appointed a captain in the Air Forces. "Many Ask Army Jobs Like Elliott's," said a page one Chicago *Tribune* headline, and Republican campaign buttons bore the legends "I Want to Be a Captain" and "I Don't Want Elliott to Be My Captain."

What was said in print was complimentary contrasted with the words-of-mouth hurled against him and his closest associates. Harry Hopkins (the fact was ignored that he had administered W.P.A.'s millions without a single major scandal) was a crackpot and a thief. Mrs. Roosevelt was a "nigger lover." As for the President himself, all you had to do was visit him at the White House and hear his manical laugh to realize that he was completely insane with power.

His only objective, now that he had wrecked the country, was to drag it into war.

"The President's love of military and naval might and display," trumpeted Flynn, "his truculence about the command of the seas, his well-known sympathies both by blood and sentiment with England, his belief in the doctrine of collective security, his dilemma in finding means to spend money and ways of holding popular approval of spending, the rising tide of political antagonism that was generally recognized before the war began—put all these things together and you have the conditions that set his mind off in the direction of military adventure. . . . He is still trying to make people believe that the Germans can invade the United States by airplane—a proposition so preposterous that he cannot get a single military man to support it."

But the accusations were in vain. With a war on the horizon, and on the basis of his record in avoiding it, plus Willkie's inferior talents in both record and experience, Roosevelt was again the victor.

In his foreign policy from the beginning, he did everything possible to avoid making the mistakes which he knew so well Woodrow Wilson had made. Here the circle was complete. He became a newer, more realistic Wilson, an idealist with a hard core of embittered knowledge of what had gone before, and an open mind to the problems raised by what, in this most modern of wars, could happen now.

His foreign policy, after a few preliminary fumbles, was of, by, and for the people, and against American imperialism. His administration was early credited with a victory in helping eliminate the brutal Machado dictatorship from Cuba. United States oil interests were eased peaceably out of Mexico and the Good Neighbor policy extended throughout South America.

Beyond the desire to spread democratic friendship as far as it would go, there was a more realistic objective which was later to be realized—uniting the Americas against the fascist states. Flynn and conservative military advisors to the contrary, the future was to reveal that Germany, if victorious on the Continent, would have been able without major difficulty to mount an attack by air on the Americas.

Despite this somber promise, neutrality was the policy of the Congress for as long as it could stand up against the awful news pouring in from Europe. The attempt was made to eliminate all Wilson's prewar mistakes by law. The Neutrality Act of 1935, with amendments in 1936 and 1937, prohibited armament exports and loans to belligerents, and provided for federal control of United States munitions industries in peace as well as war.

Roosevelt meantime was far ahead of Wilson in asking the potential opponents to attempt settlement of their difficulties in a peace conference. He did it before war started; Wilson did it afterward.

But when his peace pleas were answered with warlike diatribes by Hitler and Mussolini, and one after another continental neutral was trampled under foot, he began to advocate both aid to the Allies and armament at home.

At first, a majority of the people were against it, but as the months wore by and the Nazi conquests extended farther and farther, the tide gradually turned toward war. Samuel Flagg Bemis, in *A Diplomatic History of the United States*, sums up the change:

"Despite and notwithstanding the neutrality acts, the United States drifted into war with Germany at the end of 1941 because it was scared for its own national safety. It resorted to unneutral action to prevent the defeat of Great Britain whilst it armed itself to meet the mounting danger. The people of the New World had seen the scrupulous neutrals of Europe go down one by one under the heel of the conqueror: Denmark, Sweden, the Netherlands, Belgium, Luxembourg, Albania, Yugoslavia and Greece. They had seen Hitler attack Russia in unblushing violation of the treaty of nonaggression that he had concluded with that power on August 23, 1939, a week before he began the war. The United States feared that if Great Britain fell, its turn would come next. In this desperate fear for its own safety it had come to throw its lot in gradually with the British Empire, including Canada."

East and west, we were in the ring sparring with our Axis opponents before, at Pearl Harbor, the Japanese beat us ignobly to the first punch.

Many an American pacifist, sincere or insincere, declared that if we went to war he would have no part of it. Many another pessimist, high and low, believed that we were too soft for combat, our youth too carefree, our industry and labor too interested in their own selfish ends.

When war came, with rare exceptions, the nation—all the nation—united in creating the greatest war production and fighting machine the world has ever known. To the Allies went supplies in such an increasing flood that the Germans and Japanese were at last overwhelmed. To desert and distant jungle island went the youth of the land in combat which outsmarted and eventually outnumbered the enemy.

The agonies of the first months of war, darkened by the defeat at Pearl Harbor, were aggravated by the confusion in production. One man was tried, and then another. His mind still open, and masking his anxiety, the President finally appointed Donald Nelson. Behind him, industry and labor, many of its individuals hating the ground that Roosevelt trod, fought their way to the greatest production efficiency and volume in history.

Roosevelt, always partial to the Navy, was to see it become the greatest of marine fighting units. The Air Forces, dominated by conservatives almost to the moment fighting began, came from behind, also to achieve world leadership. Training problems (the enemy were schooled veterans); supply problems (the war machines had to be designed, the factories retooled); distribution problems (the fronts were distant and the needs multitudinous owing to Allied shortages) —all were met and solved.

Wearied by two terms, the President hurled himself into the fray with all-out abandon. Admiral McIntire reports these were the most difficult days of his work: "The President felt a deep personal responsibility for every American sent abroad, and looked on any sparing of himself as little short of betrayal. Our daily schedule [of exercises and examinations] went by the board, and my protests were brushed aside." (*White House Physician.*)

He worked late into the night. He refused to take adequate vacations. Gone were his favorite relaxation—trips to sea. They were canceled because of the submarine menace, but it is doubtful that he would have taken the time had they been possible. When he traveled, it was to check up on training, on production, to forward the war or the future of peace, to visit the sick and wounded.

McIntire worried, but always his worry changed to marveling. Thinner, subject at times to attacks of influenza and chronically bothered by sinus trouble, Roosevelt kept going at concert pitch and seemed to thrive on it. America had hardly entered the war when he celebrated his sixtieth birthday anniversary, vigorous and alert.

As if to challenge his physique as he once had, only to go down with polio, he added to his war work an intensive campaign for permanent peace. Almost a year before our entry, he had declared for his four freedoms—of speech and worship, from want and aggression —and he pressed for implementing them from that day.

Lip-service by some leaders to his ideas on world peace did not daunt him, nor the eventual opposition of empire-building Winston Churchill and the peasant cynicism of Stalin. Here appeared Roosevelt-the-realist at his most biting, in contrast to Wilson-the-pure-idealist.

"Churchill," he said, as recorded in Elliott Roosevelt's *As He Saw It*, after the two had become intimates, "told me that he was not His Majesty's prime minister for the purpose of presiding over the dissolution of the British Empire. I think I speak as America's President when I say that America won't help England in this war simply so that she will be able to continue to ride roughshod over colonial peoples."

"When we've won this war," he said again, "I will work with all my might and main to see to it that the United States is not wheedled into the position of accepting any plan that will further France's imperialistic ambitions, or that will aid or abet the British Empire in its imperial ambitions."

He was equally realistic about the dangers of losing a neutral position in our relationships with Russia and England.

"The biggest thing," he said after the second Cairo conference, "was in making clear to Stalin that the United States and Great Britain were not allies in one common bloc against the Soviet Union. I think we got rid of that idea, once and for all. I hope so. . . . Our big job [is] making sure that we continue to act as referee, as intermediary between Russia and England."

He did not make Wilson's mistake of lecturing other leaders. He traveled far and worked hard to persuade them into unity during the war and into a permanent, United Nations unity once peace came. That, in the end, even before victory was realized, was his absorbing dream.

"War isn't the real force to unity," he said, in full accord with Wilson's belief that "great democracies are not belligerent." "Peace is the real force. After the war—then is when I'm going to be able to make sure the United Nations are really the United Nations."

He became very tired.

"Medical experts to the contrary," says Merriman Smith, who saw the President with great frequency during his years in office, "Mr. Roosevelt did not want to run for a fourth term. Age was beginning to tell on him. He had lost much of his vitality. The specter of illness was increasingly visible. But . . . his love of political warfare, his vanity and his firm belief that the country needed him got the best of his judgment. His attitude toward Governor Thomas E. Dewey, the 1944 Republican candidate, was one of unvarnished contempt. He shuddered at the thought of Dewey in the White House." (*Thank You, Mr. President.*)

And so he ran, this time drawing attacks from the opposition so bitter that they were picked up and broadcast to American and allied troops by the Axis forces with whom we were at war. Two favorite Axis reprints:

"The people who support the New Deal ticket this fall are supporting the Communists and building them up for the day when they plan to bring the red terror sweeping down upon America. A New Deal vote is an invitation to murder." (Chicago *Tribune*.)

A vote for Roosevelt would buy "a monarch" and "sell out democracy." "That is what Mr. Roosevelt is asking us to do; that is what he is running for." (New York *News*.)

Winning, the President had gone through the campaign, thought his doctors, as well as could be expected for his age. It was perhaps an ominous way of putting it—he was now sixty-three. A rest was recommended. With the war practically won, he should take it easier.

He took the rest at Warm Springs, where once before he had won his way back to life. But this time it was not to be, it simply could not be. A weariness beyond the reach of man swept over him.

It had been a long and sometimes bitterly heartbreaking road he had traveled since first he entered the White House, dramatically to stem the tide of the nation's worst depression. Along the road had been N.R.A. and A.A.A. and C.C.C. There had been the fights for social security, and against the utilities and the stock exchange and the Supreme Court; and there had been three campaigns, each more bitter than the last.

And Pearl Harbor, and war.

There had been the terrifying knowledge that must be kept from all but the necessary few that we were in grave jeopardy of attack, ill-prepared for victory, needful of time that had slipped through the fingers of a people who could not believe that the dictators were as predatory as they said they were.

330

And the slow building of the war machine. And the dead and the wounded.

There was the dramatic meeting in mid-ocean with Winston Churchill, followed by Casablanca, Cairo, Teheran, Cairo again, and Yalta.

And the weary hours of travel. And the wearying conferences.

And along with all these superhuman duties, the overwhelming hunger of the man that drove him beyond endurance to see the people and visit the soldiers of democracy, to look this one and that in the eye and shake his hand and hear him speak of his problems or his wounds—to joke with him or laugh him out of his worries.

A longer road than any man had ever traveled and survived. Too long, too bitter, too utterly taxing.

But not without hope—never without hope. Just before the end, writing for the San Francisco meeting of the United Nations, he said:

"The only limit to our realization of tomorrow will be our doubts of today. Let us move forward with strong and active faith."

He died April 12, 1945, as the United Nations meeting got under way.

[11]

There Is the Republic . .

When the blow hit him (the Republican party) . . . he said, "It wasn't my fault." And it wasn't his fault. It was everybody's fault. It was your fault—it was my fault—it was the Lord's fault. He just stepped in and said—"Wait a minute. How long has this thing been going on here—this living on dog-eat-dog principle? We'll stop this thing right here now, and give the folks a chance to reorganize and redeem yourselves." That's what the Lord told him. . . . He had his third and last stroke last Tuesday. He went to his Maker a physical wreck but fundamentally sound. And on his tombstone . . . it says: "Here lies a rugged individual, but he wasn't rugged enough to compete with the Democrats."

Now we come to that grave question . . . reincarnation. Does the soul return in another body? I believe it does. . . . I don't know what animal he'll come back in. It won't be as big as an elephant. . . . It will have faith. Its whole soul will be consecrated to service. Will this animal be needed? It certainly will be, for the Democrats by that time will have passed out through too much power. The Democrats could never stand power as long as the Republicans could, because they never was used to it. They're getting cocky already, and they've only been in there overnight.

So the Republicans, being the first to die, they'll be the first to come back. So let's say a good word for the deceased and tell him to be ready to move over in his grave—the Democrats will be crawling in there with him pretty soon.

—WILL ROGERS after the 1932 elections
(from P. J. O'Brien, *Will Rogers*)

The people choose and the people's choice more often than not is one more
  wash-out.
Yet the strong man, the priceless one who wants nothing for himself and has
  his roots among his people,
Comes often enough for the people to know him and to win through into
  gains beyond later losing,
Comes often enough so the people can look back and say, "We have come far
  and will go farther yet."

. . . And across the bitter years and the howling winters the deathless dream
    will be the stronger,
    the dream of equity will win.
                                    —CARL SANDBURG, *The People, Yes*

Some folks say the republic is a place where certain parties have great privileges and possess little character, and most other parties have great character and few privileges.

The republic is a place where every man holds stubbornly to the conviction that he can do a better job of running the country than anybody alive.

It's a place where anybody who achieves any prominence of any sort is encouraged to sound off on any and everything and usually does, especially on politics.

It's full of people who are sentimentally hardboiled about earning money and sentimentally softboiled about giving it away.

It's full of people who'll shoot the works at the drop of a hat.

It's full of people who can't stand prosperity. If they have a small income they live beyond it, and if they have a large income it's disgraceful the way they spread-eagle.

Or don't kid yourself, the republic is the women, the girl friends expecting boy friends to get ahead in the world, and the apron-string moms and the fat dowagers holding all the blue chips.

It's a place of extremes—it's a lousy place—it's the best place in the world.

Some folks say the republic is Alexander Hamilton. Hamilton had the pay-off, why shouldn't the people who own the land and the mines and the factories that make the country the success it is—why shouldn't they own the country, too?

The republic is George Washington, fighting through hell and high water and winding up a millionaire. It is Thomas Jefferson, swearing eternal hostility against every form of tyranny over the mind of man; or don't kid yourself again, it's none of those fancy guys, the republic is guys like Priddy Meeks busting his way west into the unknown and singing while he did it. It's down-to-earth guys like Andy Jackson and Abe Lincoln and Walt Whitman. It's trick guys—Harry Reichenbach, Wilson Mizner, Huey Long—it's fireballs like Nat Bacon—it's the pious churchers all the way from

333

Roger Williams and the Mathers to Henry Ward Beecher and Neshan the Terrible, and you name one down there in the parsonage
on the corner.

It's Franklin D. Roosevelt following up for Woodrow Wilson,
and it's hundreds of thousands of schoolteachers, there wouldn't be
a republic right now if it wasn't for the soldier boys and the sailor
boys—it's the workingmen, it's the capitalists—it's resources, where
would you be without resources?—it's power, it's ideals.

Some folks say . . .

The republic is all the people.

Upon all the people, regardless of the society or the time in which
they are fated to live and die, depends the success or failure of that
society and its leaders.

The most subtle lesson that humanity has to teach, and the most
important, is that deep in the people lies an idealism and a strength
that no man or group of men in all time have been able to destroy or
even to subdue.

The people have been misled, during long, awful moments of history, from the same lack of knowledge and sophistication which
makes them the prey of patent-medicine salesmen and political charlatans. But beneath this surface there is deep within them a rich wisdom that flowers slowly in the toil and tears and barren living that is
too often their heritage. It is a wisdom singularly lacking in materialism—what have they got to lose?—and a wisdom too profound for
the understanding of any man or clique of men, however wise, however clever.

For the people is not a mob, a mob is something else again, this is
a vast collection of persons, some identifying themselves with one
group or another, but mostly a multitude of individuals—each a
novel, an endless library of personalities—individuals inwardly independent of the group, none relating himself to the great river of
which he is a part, each (or by twos or threes) inwardly apart from
the massed humanity at his elbow. Together they are the republic,
builders of empire, rulers of empire, people of democracy, each individual a potent drop in the whelming, forward-moving, exuberant,
unhurried, incredibly gigantic and sentient river of humanity flow-

ing on and on, endlessly flowing, ever forward-moving—toward the breaking day—toward the morning sun!

Oppose the wisdom of the people, and inevitably you will be destroyed; nor will a blind clinging to the things material—the mansions and the museums, the guns and the power—postpone the destruction longer than the tick of history's clock; and postponement will make the reckoning more devastating when it comes.

Nor will an attempt to destroy the wisdom of the people, in order that you may continue to delude and dominate, postpone the destruction longer than the tick of the clock; and postponement will make the reckoning more devastating when it comes.

Always these things apply.

They are the sum and substance of history, and their import is as inexorable as death.

Bibliography

The author enjoyed the numberless favors which are given, eagerly and efficiently, to anyone seeking aid from the much (but never too much) praised staffs of the New York Public Library and the Library of Congress.

Few periodicals are listed here. Those used in the text are there credited; all that were consulted would make too long and irrelevant a list.

This bibliography was compiled to give credit where credit is due, and therefore omits books which were tried and found wanting because the authors, as Louis Adamic has pointed out somewhere, habitually inhaled a "fallacious cultural atmosphere—and exhale it back again." The list, like the book itself, does not pretend to be complete. Indeed, both hardly scratch the surface in a field which, despite the academicians and the American legendeers, is an unlimited source of vital and exciting material.

Adamic, Louis. *My America*. Harper and Brothers, 1938.

Adamic, Louis. *Dinner at the White House*. Harper and Brothers, 1946.

Adamic, Louis. *A Nation of Nations*. Harper and Brothers, 1945.

Adams, Henry. *History of the United States*. (9 vols.) Charles Scribner's Sons, 1917.

Adams, Jane. *Twenty Years at Hull House*. The Macmillan Company, 1910.

Allen, Frederick Lewis. *Only Yesterday*. Harper and Brothers, 1931.

Allen, Frederick Lewis. *Since Yesterday*. Harper and Brothers, 1940.

Andrews, Charles M. (Editor). *Narratives of the Insurrections*. Charles Scribner's Sons, 1915.

Asbury, Herbert. *The Gangs of New York*. Alfred A. Knopf, Inc., 1928.

Asbury, Herbert. *The Barbary Coast*. Alfred A. Knopf, Inc., 1933.

Asbury, Herbert. *Carrie Nation*. Alfred A. Knopf, Inc., 1929.

Asbury, Herbert. *Gem of the Prairie*. Alfred A. Knopf, Inc., 1940.

Baker, Ray Stannard. *Woodrow Wilson, Life and Letters*. (Potomac Edition, 8 vols.) Doubleday and Company, Inc., 1946.

Bancroft, Frederic. *Slave-Trading in the Old South*. J. H. Furst Company, 1931.

Barnes, Albert. *The Church and Slavery*. Philadelphia, 1857.

Barnum, P. T. *Dollars and Sense; or How to Get On*. New York, 1890.

Barnum, P. T. *The Humbugs of the World.* New York, 1866.

Barnum, P. T. *The Life of P. T. Barnum, Written by Himself.* Redfield Brothers, New York, 1855.

Beer, Thomas. *The Mauve Decade.* Alfred A. Knopf, Inc., 1926.

Bell, J. C. *Opening a Highway to the Pacific, 1838-46.* New York, Columbia University Press, 1921.

Bemis, Samuel Flagg. *A Diplomatic History of the United States.* Henry Holt and Company, Inc., 1942.

Benét, Stephen Vincent. *We Stand United.* Rinehart and Company, Inc., 1945.

Benét, Stephen Vincent. *Western Star.* Rinehart and Company, Inc., 1943.

Berkeley, Sir William. *A Discourse and View of Virginia.* London, 1663.

Berkeley, Sir William. *The Lost Lady: A Tragy Comedy.* London, 1639.

Birdoff, Harry. *The World's Greatest Hit.* S. F. Vanni Publications, New York, 1947.

Birney, James Gillespie. *The American Churches, the Bulwarks of American Slavery.* Newburyport, 1842.

Bloch, Jean Libman. "Walter Hunt." An article in *The New Yorker*, Oct. 19, 1946.

Bolitho, William. *Twelve Against the Gods.* Simon and Schuster, Inc., 1929.

Bolton, Charles K. *The Private Soldier Under Washington.* Charles Scribner's Sons, 1902.

Booth, William. *In Darkest England and the Way Out.* Funk and Wagnalls Company, 1890.

Booth-Tucker, Frederick de Latour. *The Life Of Catherine Booth.* (2 vols.) Fleming H. Revell Company, 1892.

Bowers, Claude G. *Jefferson and Hamilton.* Houghton Mifflin Company, 1928.

Bowers, Claude G. *Jefferson in Power.* Houghton Mifflin Company, 1930.

Bowers, Claude G. *The Tragic Era.* Houghton Mifflin Company, 1929.

Bowers, Claude G. *The Young Jefferson.* Houghton Mifflin Company, 1945.

Bradley, Hugh. *Such Was Saratoga.* Doubleday and Company, Inc., 1940.

Branch, E. Douglas. *Westward.* D. Appleton-Century Company, Inc., 1930.

Brodie, Fawn M. *No Man Knows My History: The Life of Joseph Smith, the Mormon Prophet.* Alfred A. Knopf, Inc., 1945.

Brooks, Van Wyck. *The Flowering of New England.* E. P. Dutton and Company, 1941.

Brooks, Van Wyck. *The Life of Emerson.* E. P. Dutton and Company, 1932.

Brooks, Van Wyck. *New England: Indian Summer.* E. P. Dutton and Company, 1940.

Brooks, Van Wyck. *The World of Washington Irving.* E. P. Dutton and Company, 1946.

Broun, Heywood. Columns in the New York *World*, 1927.

Calhoun, Arthur W. *A Social History of the American Family.* (3 vols.) Arthur H. Clark Company, 1917 (reprinted 1945).

Carpenter, Edmund J. *Roger Williams.* Grafton Press, 1909.

Castiglioni, Arturo. *A History of Medicine.* Translated and edited by E. B. Krumbhaar. Alfred A. Knopf, Inc., 1941.

Chambers, J. S. *The Conquest of Cholera, America's Greatest Scourge*. The Macmillan Company, 1938.

Colton, Calvin. *A Voice from America to England*. London, 1839.

Colver, Anne. *Mr. Lincoln's Wife*. Rinehart and Company, Inc., 1943.

Commons, J. R. and Associates. *History of Labor in the United States*. The Macmillan Company, 1918.

Commons, J. R. *Races and Immigrants in America*. The Macmillan Company, 1920.

Crocker, Uriel H. *The Cause of Hard Times*. Little, Brown and Company, 1886.

Daniels, Jonathan. *Frontier on the Potomac*. The Macmillan Company, 1946.

Depew, Chauncey M. *One Hundred Years of American Commerce*. D. O. Haynes and Company, 1895.

DeVoto, Bernard. *The Year of Decision: 1846*. Little, Brown and Company, 1943.

Dibble, R. F. *John L. Sullivan*. Little, Brown and Company, 1925.

Dictionary of American History, The. Charles Scribner's Sons, 1940.

Dutton, C. E. (Captain, U. S. Army) *Geology of the High Plateaus of Utah*. U. S. Gov't Printing Office, 1880.

Eberlein, Harold Donaldson. *The Practical Book of American Antiques*. Garden City Publishing Company, 1916.

Edholm, Charlton. *Traffic in Girls and the Florence Crittenden Missions*. Woman's Temperance Publishing Association, 1893.

Ehrmann, Herbert B. *The Untried Case (The Sacco-Vanzetti Case)*. Vanguard Press, Inc., 1933.

Emerson, R. W. *Collected Works*. Houghton Mifflin Company, 1921.

Ernst, James. *Roger Williams, New England Firebrand*. The Macmillan Company, 1932.

Ervine, St. John. *God's Soldier: General William Booth*. The Macmillan Company, 1935.

Fast, Howard. *The Selected Works of Tom Paine*. Duell, Sloane and Pearce, Inc., 1945.

Flynn, John T. *Country Squire in the White House*. Doubleday and Company, Inc., 1940.

Forbes, Esther. *Paul Revere and the World He Lived In*. Houghton Mifflin Company, 1943.

Frankfurter, Felix. *The Case of Sacco and Vanzetti*. Little, Brown and Company, 1927.

Fuller, George W. *History of the Pacific Northwest*. Alfred A. Knopf, Inc., 1931.

Fülöp-Miller, René. *Triumph over Pain*. Translated by Eden and Cedar Paul. Blue Ribbon Books, 1938.

Greenwood, Isaac. *The Circus; Its Origin and Growth Prior to 1835*. The Dunlap Society, 1898.

Hatch, L. C. *The Administration of the American Revolutionary Army*. Longmans, Green and Company, 1904.

Hibben, Paxton. *Henry Ward Beecher: an American Portrait*. Doubleday and Company, Inc., 1927.

Holbrook, Stewart H. *Lost Men of American History*. The Macmillan Company, 1946.

Hughes, Rupert. *George Washington*. (3 vols.) William Morrow and Company, 1926.

Hulbert, A. B. *The Call of the Columbia*. The Stewart Commission of Colorado College and The Denver Public Library, 1934.

Hulbert, A. B. *Forty-Niners*. Little, Brown and Company, 1931.

James, Marquis. *The Life of Andrew Jackson*. Bobbs-Merrill Company, 1940.

Jameson, J. Franklin (Editor). *Johnson's Wonder-Working Providence (1628-1651)*. Charles Scribner's Sons, 1910.

Johnson, Alva. *Legend of a Sport (Wilson Mizner)*. Four articles in *The New Yorker*, Oct. 10, 17, 24, 31, 1942.

Johnson, Hugh S. *The Blue Eagle from Egg to Earth*. Doubleday and Company, Inc., 1935.

Josephson, Matthew. *The Politicos*. Harcourt, Brace and Company, Inc., 1938.

Josephson, Matthew. *The Robber Barons*. Harcourt, Brace and Company, Inc., 1934.

Kane, Harnett T. *Louisiana Hayride*. William Morrow and Company, 1941.

Knyveton, John. *The Diary of a Surgeon in the Year 1751-1752*. Edited by Ernest Gray. D. Appleton-Century Company, Inc., 1937.

Laut, Agnes C. *The Overland Trail*. Frederick A. Stokes Company, 1929.

Lee, James Melvin. *History of American Journalism*. Houghton Mifflin Company, 1917.

Levinson, Edward. *I Break Strikes! (The Technique of Pearl L. Bergoff)*. Robert M. McBride and Company, 1935.

Loud, Grover C. *Evangelized America*. Dial Press, 1928.

Lincoln, Abraham. *Complete Works*. Edited John G. Nicolay and John Hay. D. Appleton-Century Company, Inc., 1894.

Lindley, Ernest K. *Halfway with Roosevelt*. The Viking Press, Inc., 1936.

Lindley, Ernest K. *The Roosevelt Revolution*. The Viking Press, Inc., 1933.

Lindsay, Vachel. *Collected Poems*. The Macmillan Company, 1945.

Lundberg, Ferdinand. *America's 60 Families*. Vanguard Press, Inc., 1937.

Marcy, Rudolf. *The Prairie Traveler, a Handbook for Overland Expeditions*. Harper and Brothers, 1859.

Mason, Louis B. *The Life and Times of Major John Mason of Connecticut, 1600-1672*. G. P. Putnam's Sons, 1935.

Mather, Cotton. *The Diary of Cotton Mather*. Part I 1681-1708. Part II, 1709-1724. Massachusetts Historical Society, 1911-1912.

McAdoo, Eleanor Wilson (in collaboration with Margaret Y. Gaffey). *The Woodrow Wilsons*. The Macmillan Company, 1937.

McIntire, Ross T. *White House Physician*. G. P. Putnam's Sons, 1946.

Meeks, Priddy. *Journal of Priddy Meeks*. Utah Historical Quarterly Vol. 10, Nos. 1, 2, 3, 4. Salt Lake City, 1942.

Michelson, Charles. *The Ghost Talks*. G. P. Putnam's Sons, 1944.

339

Murdock, Kenneth B. *Increase Mather*. Harvard University Press, 1925.

Nelson, Donald M. *Arsenal of Democracy*. Harcourt, Brace and Company, Inc., 1946.

O'Brien, P. J. *Will Rogers*. John C. Winston Company, 1935.

One Hundred Years of Temperance. New York, 1886.

Oregon Trail, The. Compiled and Written by the Federal Writers' Project of the Works Progress Administration. Hastings House, New York, 1939.

Padover, Saul K. (Editor). *The Complete Jefferson*. Duell, Sloan and Pearce, Inc., 1943.

Padover, Saul K. *Democracy by Thomas Jefferson*. D. Appleton-Century Company, Inc., 1939.

Padover, Saul K. *Jefferson*. Harcourt, Brace and Company, Inc., 1942.

Parkman, Francis, *The Oregon Trail*. Little, Brown and Company, 1872.

Perkins, Frances. *The Roosevelt I Knew*. The Viking Press, Inc., 1946.

Phillips, Ulrich Bonnell. *American Negro Slavery*. D. Appleton-Century Company, Inc., 1918.

Phillips, Ulrich Bonnell. *The Economic Cost of Slave-Holding in the Cotton Belt*. Ginn and Company, 1905.

Pickard, M. E. and Buley, R. C. *The Midwest Pioneer, His Ills, Cures and Doctors*. R. E. Bauta, Crawfordsville, Ind., 1945.

Pusey, W. A. *The Wilderness Road to Kentucky*. Doubleday and Company, Inc., 1921.

Reichenbach, Harry (as told to David Freeman). *Anatomy of Ballyhoo: Phantom Fame*. Simon and Shuster, Inc., 1931.

Representation to Congress by the Morton Testimonial Association, A. Washington, D. C., 1864.

Riegel, Robert E. *America Moves West*. Henry Holt and Company, Inc., 1930.

Riis, Jacob A. *How the Other Half Lives*. Charles Scribner's Sons, 1890.

Root, F. A. and Connelley, W. E. *The Overland Stage to California*. Crane and Company, Topeka, Kansas, 1901.

Roosevelt, Elliott. *As He Saw It*. Duell, Sloan and Pearce, Inc., 1946.

Salmon, Lucy Maynard. *Domestic Service*. The Macmillan Company, 1901.

Sandburg, Carl. *Abraham Lincoln: The Prairie Years*. (2 vols.) Harcourt, Brace and Company, Inc., 1926.

Sandburg, Carl. *Abraham Lincoln: The War Years*. (4 vols.) Harcourt, Brace and Company, Inc., 1939.

Sandburg, Carl. *The People, Yes*. Harcourt, Brace and Company, Inc., 1936.

Schlesinger, Arthur M., Jr. *The Age of Jackson*. Little, Brown and Company, 1945.

Schriftgiesser, Karl. *The Gentleman from Massachusetts: Henry Cabot Lodge*. Little, Brown and Company, 1944.

Shephard, Esther. *Walt Whitman's Pose*. Harcourt, Brace and Company, Inc., 1938.

Smith, Merriman. *Thank You, Mr. President*. Harper and Brothers, 1946.

Spears, John R. *The American Slave Trade*. Charles Scribner's Sons, 1907.

Stead, William T. *If Christ Came to Chicago*. Albert Whitman and Company, 1894.

Sullivan, Mark. *Our Times: America Finding Herself*. Charles Scribner's Sons, 1927.

Sullivan, Mark. *Our Times: Pre-War America*. Charles Scribner's Sons, 1930.

Sweet, William Warren. *Religion on the American Frontier*. Henry Holt and Company, Inc., 1931.

Sweet, William Warren. *The Story of Religions in America*. Harper and Brothers, 1930.

Tebbel, John. *An American Dynasty*. Garden City Publishing Company, 1947.

Tourtellot, Arthur Bernon. *Woodrow Wilson, Selections for Today*. Duell, Sloan and Pearce, Inc., 1945.

Tumulty, Joseph P. *Woodrow Wilson as I Know Him*. Doubleday and Company, Inc., 1921.

Twain, Mark. *A Connecticut Yankee in King Arthur's Court*. Harper and Brothers.

Twain, Mark. *Huckleberry Finn*. Harper and Brothers.

United States Census Reports.

Van Doren, Carl. *Benjamin Franklin*. The Viking Press, Inc., 1941.

War Cry, The. *The Official Periodical of the U. S. Salvation Army*.

Washington, George. *The Writings of George Washington, from the Original Manuscript Sources*. Edited by John C. Fitzpatrick. U. S. Government Printing Office, Washington, D. C., 1944.

Wendell, Barrett. *Cotton Mather*. Dodd, Mead and Company, Mass., 1926.

White, William Allen, The Autobiography of. The Macmillan Company, 1946.

Whitman, Walt. *New York Dissected*. Introduction and notes by Emory Holloway and Ralph Adimari. Primavera Press, Inc., 1936.

Whitman, Walt. *Leaves of Grass*. All available editions contemporaneous to Whitman. New York, Boston, 1855-1891.

Williams, Roger. *The Bloudy Tenant of Persecution*. London, 1644.

Williams, Roger. *Christenings Make Not Christians*. London, 1645.

Willich, A. F. M. *The Domestic Encyclopaedia*. (5 vols.) Philadelphia, 1804.

Willison, George F. *Saints and Strangers*. Rexnal and Hitchcock, Inc., 1945.

Winwar, Frances. *American Giant: Walt Whitman and His Times*. Harper and Brothers, 1941.

Woodward, W. E. *George Washington: The Image and the Man*. New York, Liveright Publishing Corporation, 1926.

Worthington, Elizabeth S. *The Biddy Club*. A. C. McChurg and Company, Chicago, 1888.

Wright, Carroll D. *Comparative Wages, Prices, and Cost of Living*. Wright and Potter Printing Company, Boston, 1889.

Wright, Richardson. *Hawkers and Walkers in Early America*. J. B. Lippincott, Company, 1927.

Index

NOTE: Italic page numbers, where used, refer to the main discussion of an item.

Dean, Priscilla, 261
Debs, Eugene V., 201, 265
Declaration of Independence, 88, 89-91, 95, 305
De Lancy, governor, 19
Delano, Sarah. *See* Roosevelt, Sarah Delano.
Delaware River, crossing of, 78
Democracy, 53-54, 332-35; Jeffersonian, 91-93, 103-04; and Huey Long, 264, 271-72; Puritan attitude toward, 21-22; Whitman's credo of, 245-50; and Woodrow Wilson, 304-09
Democrat Party, 196, 299-300, 301, 312, 321, 332
Depew, Chauncey M., cited, 338
Depressions, economic, 187-88, 274
Derby, Conn., 127
Detroit, Mich., 215, 282
De Voto, Bernard, quoted, 109; cited, 338
Dewey, Thomas E., 330
Dibble, R. F., cited, 338
Dickenson, Levi, 127
Dickinson, Charles, 150
Dinwiddie, Robert, 70, 74
Diplomatic History of the United States, A (Bemis), 327
Divorce, colonial, 9
Donner Party, 113
Dorchester, Daniel, 57
Douglas, Stephen A., 165-66, 172, 173, 178
Doyle, Peter, 242
Drinking. *See* Liquor.
Drum-Taps (Whitman), 244
Duke, Sir Edward, 35
Duke, Elizabeth. *See* Bacon, Elizabeth.
Duke, Ivy, 263
Duluth, Minn., 215
Dutch colonists, 6, 7, 16, 28, 37, 38
Dutlih, Eugene, 219
Dutton, C. E., quoted, 107; cited, 338

East Portland, Ore., 214-15
Eastman, Monk, 191
Eberlein, Harold D., cited, 338
Edholm, Charlton, cited, 338
Edison, Thomas A., 130
Edmonson, Thomas, 130
Edmundson, W., 31-32
Edwards, Jonathan, 254
Education, 6, 37, 47, 61
Ehrmann, Herbert B., cited, 338
Eliot, Charles W., 280
Eliot, Joseph, 15

Elizabethtown, Ky., 164
Emancipation Proclamation, 180
Emerson, Ralph Waldo, 168, 229, 230, 234, 235-38, 243; cited, 338
Empey, Guy, 286
England, 18, 19, 44, 45, 100-01, 105, 139, 153-54, 169, 256, 262, 263, 309; and the American Revolution, 47-48, 49, 69, 76-80, 88-89. *See also* Great Britain.
Entertainment. *See* Recreation.
Epic of America, The (Adams), 196
Epidemics, 11, 33, 135, 190
Erasmus, quoted, 252
Ernst, James, cited, 338
Ervine, St. John, cited, 338
Euclid Avenue Baptist Church, Cleveland, 196-97
Evans, Oliver, 128
Everett, Edward, 168, 231

Fairbanks, Douglas, Sr., 262
Fairfax, George William, quoted, 66
Fairfax, Sally, 73
Fala, 321
Farley, "Big Jim," 277, 278
Farley, James, 321
Farnham, Eliza, 116-17
Fashions, 285
Fast, Howard, cited, 338
Fauquier, Francis, 87
Federal Bureau of Investigation, 274
Federal Reserve Act, 302-03
Federal Trade Commission Act, 303
Federation of Organized Trade and Labor Unions, 194
Fenno, John, 98
Ferdinand IV, king of Naples, 93
Fessenden, William P., 171
Finnegan, "Jack," 207
Finnicke, Mrs. Mary, 4
Fires, 16-17
Fisk, "Jim," 64, 133
Fitzgerald, F. Scott, 286
Florida, colonial, 4
Flowering of New England, The (Brooks), 230
Flynn, John T., 319, 325, 326; cited, 338
Folk-tales, 13-14
Forbes, general, 75
Forbes, Esther, quoted, 7, 10, 15-16; cited, 338
Ford, Edsel, 284
Ford, Henry, 283, 286, 310

White, William Allen, 302
White House Physician (McIntire), 320
White Plains, battle of, 76
Whitman, George, 226, 239, 250
Whitman, Jeff, 226
Whitman, Louisa Van Velsor (Mrs. Walter, Sr.), 226-27, 239
Whitman, Walt, 202, 226-51, 277, 333; quoted, 34, 106, 164; cited, 341
Whitney, Eli, 128
Whittier, John Greenleaf, 231, 234
Wilkes-Barre, Penn., 223
Wilkinson, Hannah, 128
Wilkinson, James, 151
Willard, Frances E., 62
William and Mary College, 87
Williams, Roger, 19, 24-32, 34, 334; cited, 341
Williamsburg, Va., 42, 87, 88
Willich, A. F. M., cited, 341
Willison, George F., quoted, 2, 17-18, 21; cited, 341
Willkie, Wendell, 324, 326
Wilmington, Dela., 293
Wilson, Eleanor. *See* McAdoo, Eleanor Wilson.
Wilson, Ellen (Mrs. Woodrow), 295-96, 301, 302, 309, 311
Wilson, Jessie Woodrow, 291, 292
Wilson, John, 21
Wilson, Joseph Ruggles, 291, 292
Wilson, Woodrow, 266, 273, 289, 290-311, 312-13, 326, 329, 334; quoted, 164

Winchell, Walter, 258
Winn Parish, La., 265, 266
Winslow, Edward, 8
Winters, Keyes, 279
Winthrop, John, 9, 21, 25, 28, 31
Winwar, Frances, 243; cited, 341
Wisconsin, 121
Witchcraft, 13, 23-24, 33
"Witch-hunts," 274, 280
Women, 7-12, 59-61, 131-32, 191-92, 303
Woodrow Wilson, Life and Letters (Baker), 294
Woodrow Wilsons, The (McAdoo), 296
Woodward, Stanley, 223
Woodward, W. E., cited, 341
World War I, 263-64, 303-04
World War II, 326-31
Worthington, Elizabeth S., cited, 341
Wright, Carroll D., cited, 341
Wright, Fanny, 160
Wright, Richardson, cited, 341
Wythe, George, 87

Year of Decision: 1846 (De Voto), 109
Yorktown, battle of, 80
Young, Arthur, 282
Young, Brigham, 110, 111
Young, Clara Kimball, 262

Zenger, John Peter, 18
Zong, the, 142